PEOPLE OF THE WHEAT

PEOPLE OF THE WHEAT

Culture and Cultivation in North Texas

REBECCA SHARPLESS

University of Texas Press
AUSTIN

Publication of this work was made possible in part by support from the J. E. Smothers, Sr., Memorial Foundation and the National Endowment for the Humanities.

Printed in the United States of America
First edition, 2026

♾ The paper used in this book meets the minimum requirements of ANSI/NISO Z39.48-1992 (R1997) (Permanence of Paper).

Library of Congress Cataloging-in-Publication Data

Names: Sharpless, Rebecca author
Title: People of the wheat : culture and cultivation in North Texas / Rebecca Sharpless.
Description: First edition. | Austin : University of Texas Press, 2026. | Includes bibliographical references and index.
Identifiers: LCCN 2025029045 (print) | LCCN 2025029046 (ebook)
ISBN 978-1-4773-3332-7 hardcover
ISBN 978-1-4773-3333-4 pdf
ISBN 978-1-4773-3334-1 epub
Subjects: LCSH: Wheat trade–Texas–History–19th century | Wheat trade–Texas–History–20th century | Wheat–Texas–History–19th century | Wheat–Texas–History–20th century | Wheat–Economic aspects–Texas–History–19th century | Wheat–Economic aspects–Texas–History–20th century | Wheat–Social life and customs–19th century | Wheat–Social life and customs–20th century | Wheat–Harvesting–Texas–History–19th century | Wheat–Harvesting–Texas–History–20th century | Farm mechanization–Texas–History–19th century | Farm mechanization–Texas–History–20th century | Flour industry–Texas–History–19th century | Flour industry–Texas–History–20th century | Baked products industry–Texas–History–19th century | Baked products industry–Texas–History–20th century | Food habits–Texas–History | Women cooks–Texas–Social conditions–History–19th century | Women cooks–Texas–Social conditions–History–20th century | Charities–Texas–History–20th century | Art patronage–Texas–History–20th century | Philanthropists–Texas–Biography
Classification: LCC F391 .S528 2026 (print) | LCC F391 (ebook)
LC record available at https://lccn.loc.gov/2025029045
LC ebook record available at https://lccn.loc.gov/2025029046

doi:10.7560/333327

The University of Texas Press gratefully acknowledges the Jack and Doris Smothers Endowment in Texas History, Life, and Culture for its support of this publication.

In grateful memory of
Robert A. Calvert
and
Jack Temple Kirby
Exemplary historians and mentors

CONTENTS

ILLUSTRATIONS

FIGURES

MAP

TABLE

PEOPLE OF THE WHEAT

FIGURE 0.01. *Velma Fuller Kimbell at the opening reception for the Kimbell Art Museum, October 1972. Kimbell Art Museum, Fort Worth, Texas, constructed 1969–1972, Louis I. Kahn (1901–1974), architect. (© 2024 Kimbell Art Museum, Fort Worth)*

PROLOGUE: "DEFINITIVE EXCELLENCE"

THE ART CRITICS RAVED. HILTON KRAMER OF THE *NEW York Times* declared, "It's one of the greatest buildings of its kind in the world." Rosamond Bernier, founder of the Parisian art periodical *L'Oeil*, commented, "This is absolutely a marvelous museum." And most pointedly, Charles Cowles, publisher of New York's *Artforum* magazine, observed, "Only a half-dozen museums can afford such a facility. And only three or four can afford the funds needed to acquire such collections. This is phenomenal."[1]

It was October 1972, and the museum that the critics found so compelling was the Kimbell Art Museum in Fort Worth, Texas, which was celebrating the new home for its collection from around the world. The building was indeed extraordinary, designed by American architect Louis Kahn and constructed as a series of curved vaults made of reinforced concrete and travertine marble with narrow plexiglass skylights that allowed natural daylight into the galleries.[2]

The artwork in the exquisite structure belonged to Kay and Velma Kimbell, who began collecting European art in the 1930s and created the Kimbell Art Foundation in 1936. Kay Kimbell died in 1964, leaving his entire estate to the foundation, and Velma contributed her share of the community property the following week. In a vision statement in June 1966, the museum board announced its intention to acquire and retain works of "'definitive excellence'—works that may be said to define an artist or type regardless of medium, period, or school of origin."[3] In other words, the Kimbell would have only the best of the best.

As guests in gowns and black tie entered the museum's north garden court, they were greeted with the bronze statue *L'Air* by twentieth-century French sculptor Aristide Maillol. The strains of Ran Wilde's orchestra filled the galleries.[4] An imaginative guest, however, might have discerned another sound behind the music: the soft whisper of wind blowing through a field of tawny grain, ready for harvest. For the Kimbell fortune began not with cattle, not with cotton, nor with oil, but with wheat—a grain usually associated with other parts of the United States, not with Texas.

But Texans the Kimbells were, and to Fort Worth they brought their global art collection. They, and the Texas-grown wheat they milled, had a profound impact on their home, the area generally known as North Texas.

As William Cronon points out in *Nature's Metropolis*, his masterful study of Chicago and its "hinterlands," the economy and culture of a region are forged not by just one thing—a crop, a people, or a commodity—but by a multitude of factors.[5] And so in this book we will look at the role that wheat played in shaping North Texas. Not all farmers grew wheat, but a significant number of them did, and it was the second-largest crop in this highly productive agricultural area. Milling wheat provided income for mill workers, sometimes fortunes for mill owners, and fresh, locally made flour for almost everyone in the region. Virtually all people in North Texas ate the products of the wheat farmers and millers, baked into the region's beloved biscuits, birthday cakes, and tortillas.

For more than a century, the passage of time in North Texas—six counties south of the Red River today known as the Dallas–Fort Worth Metroplex, and in 2025 home to more than eight million people—was marked by the rhythms of growing and milling wheat. Wheat was turned into flour, and the money that it generated built homes and churches, acquired art, and endowed charitable institutions. Flour became bread for sustenance and pastries and cakes for celebrations.

Wheat provides a lens that brings into focus what makes North Texas distinctive. More than anywhere else in Texas or the American South, the flourishing economy of this area just below the Red River included growing and processing wheat.[6] For a century, wheat made North Texas different from the open cattle ranges to the west, the sprawling fields of cotton to the south, and the dense pine forests to the east. Six counties—Cooke, Grayson, Denton, Collin, Tarrant, and Dallas—comprised the area that persistently grew wheat from the 1840s to the 1970s and that observers called the "North Texas wheat belt." Thus, North Texas became the southernmost area of concentrated wheat agriculture in the United States. Wheat provided a contrast in cultivation and in culture, both symbolic and real, to bordering fields of cotton. Americans perceived wheat and cotton as a "duality": the grain was a symbol of free labor and the fiber an emblem of slavery.[7]

Wheat also provides a look at how agriculture and industry changed, particularly in the late nineteenth and early twentieth centuries. Processes

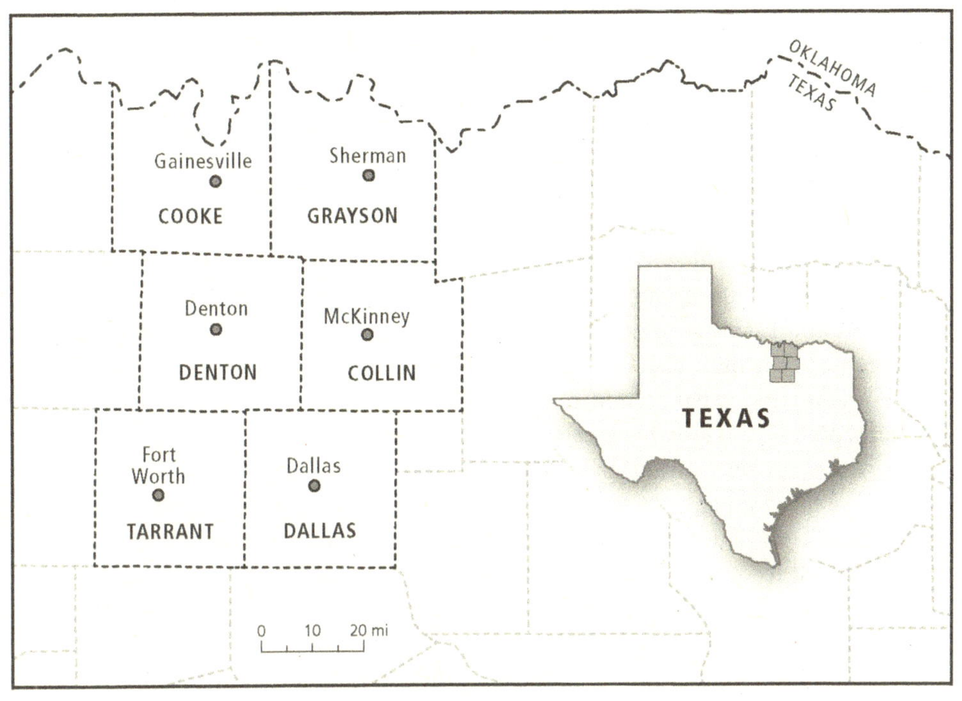

MAP 0.01. *The six counties of the "North Texas wheat belt." (Cartography by Erin Greb)*

that had been done by hand for millennia—reaping, milling, and baking—became mechanized, a change that some writers refer to as a revolution. At the beginning of the period examined in this study, North Texas was a grassland. In the nineteenth century, colonizers divided it into privately owned farms that grew corn, cotton, and wheat. Cotton farming remained a matter of hand labor well into the twentieth century. But wheat farming underwent mechanization, and North Texas growers were part of that international trend, moving from harvesting by hand with sickles and cradles to employing large machines that cut and bundled the grain automatically. Likewise, milling evolved from an ancient process with two grindstones crushing the wheat to vast mechanized operations with dozens of steps. And baking went from cooking on a fireplace hearth to, again, an automated activity in which machines performed the myriad steps in producing a loaf of bread. As each of these activities became more mechanized, more capital was needed to acquire the equipment, hence shutting out would-be investors with fewer resources. Growing, milling, and commercial baking all went from being somewhat accessible to being tightly constrained.

Wheat growing and milling also shaped the culture of the region. The farming of winter wheat sculpted the rhythms of rural life, with planting in the fall and harvest in the late spring; this schedule dovetailed neatly with the demands of the cotton crop, usually planted in April and harvested between August and November. Flour mills provided income—sometimes seasonal, sometimes year-round—for workers in towns and the growing cities. Mill buildings in towns and cities marked the landscape of the area. Flour marketing gave rise to the musical style known as western swing and to one of the most notorious politicians in Texas history, W. Lee O'Daniel. And millers and bakers donated to charities and to the arts, their generosity and preferences creating local institutions.

Now, in the second quarter of the twenty-first century, the Kimbell Museum is among the most visible reminders of the legacy of wheat in North Texas, but it is far from being the only one. Grain elevators and huge silos still tower over the landscape. Built to be indestructible, they dominate parts of every North Texas city, concrete artifacts of a mostly forgotten industry.

This book is the story of how wheat influenced the lives of people in one particular region of the United States. But in the beginning, before the people, was the land. To the grasslands and the rivers we go first.

INTRODUCTION: SOIL AND PEOPLE

TO UNDERSTAND HOW WHEAT SHAPED NORTH TEXAS, we must understand the region itself—its land, water, and climate. To an unappreciative eye, craving mountains or ocean waves, the landscape lacks drama. The terrain is almost flat in many areas. All the trees either grow along waterways or have been planted by humans. The impression is largely one of sky spanning the wide horizon—a hard blue bowl on hot days, a vast scrim of clouds on stormy ones—and of sameness.

To a more attuned observer, the landscape has nuance. Some places lift into hills. In other spots, creeks and rivers cut channels of varying width and depth, and small trees find welcome along their circuits. Heavily forested fingers of sandy land, known as the Cross Timbers, divide the prairies in spots. But overall, this region, a ninety-mile stretch along and south of the Red River, is as it has been for millennia: smooth and mostly flat.

The rolling prairieland began as part of a vast Cretaceous-period sea, and the fossils of marine creatures still appear in the limestone that formed as the water receded. An underground aquifer, later named the Trinity, developed in the limestone, watering the landscape from below. Over time, soil overlaid the limestone: some red, iron-laden sand, but most of it thick black alkaline clay, sticky when moist, hard as stone when dry, and almost unbelievably fertile.[1] Two shallow rivers that eventually cut through the surface flow from northwest to southeast, meandering to the Gulf of Mexico several hundred miles away. The one to the north was named Río Rojo by the Spanish because of its red color. The second ambles through the landscape in four forks, joining in three places until it becomes a single course that Spanish explorers called Río Trinidad—today known as the Trinity River. Numerous streams, some nourished by springs, feed the rivers, which remain shallow, slow, and sluggish except after heavy rains.[2]

The climate that developed on this rolling land is warm and somewhat dry. The growing season extends from March to November, and rainfall is about thirty-five inches a year—more in the more humid east and less to the drier west. Summers are "repressively hot," with the sun nearly vertical at the summer solstice. Lack of rainfall is a persistent worry. Data from post–oak tree rings indicate that at least three major droughts occurred in the seventy years before American colonists arrived in North Texas. As drought "appears to follow no simple pattern in time or space," there are few ways to prepare for it.[3]

The plants that adapted to the region were mostly grass, part of a vast swath that stretched more than 1,500 miles, from what we now call South Texas to Manitoba. Deep roots allowed the prairie grasses to maximize precious moisture. Sometimes growing more than six feet tall, and buttressed against heat, cold, flood, and drought, these grasses include big and little bluestem, Indian grass, switchgrass, and side oats grama. Occasionally, fire swept the landscape, killing any small trees that tried to establish themselves amid the grasses. After a fire, the grasses returned, lush from the pruning. Trees—oaks, hackberries, pecans, bois d'arcs, cottonwoods—survived only along the shallow creeks and the rivers.

People appeared gradually in this panorama of grass and sky. Native Americans first arrived in North Texas perhaps ten thousand years ago. They lived along the waterways and in the trees, venturing into the grass to hunt and to gather. A limestone outcropping later called the Balcones escarpment provided a natural highway for north-south travelers. The Native Americans grew corn for much of their sustenance, and they gathered seeds and nuts to bake into bread. Over the centuries, the Native American population of the region shifted and adapted fluidly. By the end of the eighteenth century, the Wichita ranged throughout North Texas. The Shawnee came to North Texas in the early nineteenth century, and Delawares occupied the region as well.[4]

In the sixteenth century, the Spanish claimed all of Texas, but they found nothing to like on the prairies. There was no gold or silver, and their resources were already stretched thin. So they stayed away: the closest Spanish settlements were in San Antonio, almost three hundred miles south, and Nacogdoches, two hundred miles to the southeast. Life went on for the Native Americans irrespective of the edicts of the Spanish government—and after 1821, the Mexican government.

But Americans were different. In 1819, the Adams-Onís Treaty set the international border between the United States and Spain at the Red River. The United States began forcibly relocating groups of Native American people to the region north of the river, in the area they dubbed "Indian

Territory." After one armed revolution in 1821, Texas became part of the Republic of Mexico and, after a second one in 1836, seceded from Mexico to form the Republic of Texas.

North Texas, far from the war zone and the bustling Texian towns on the Gulf Coast, was a remote component of the fledgling nation. Eager to populate their new country, the Texas government passed laws giving land to any "free white . . . head of a family" who would reside on it and pay for its survey. In 1838, the so-called headright law provided 640 acres for the head of a family and 320 acres for a single man.[5] Distant though North Texas was, the officials of the Republic included it in their planning, believing that it served a strategic purpose. Vice President David B. Burnet in 1840 labeled the region "the inland frontier" and called for a "colony of brave and active yeomanry" to protect "our borders from the Indian tomahawk."[6] Native Americans reacted to the colonizers with unsurprising irritation, and violent clashes continued until 1839. Throughout the 1830s the Chickasaw and the Choctaw relocated their nations immediately north of the Red River. Native Americans and Texians eyed each other warily, the shallow orange waters of the river separating distinctive cultures.

Burnet's desire to shelter Anglo colonizers from Native Americans became largely unnecessary in only a few years. Texas President Mirabeau B. Lamar expelled the Shawnee and Delaware from the region in 1839, forcing them to move north into Indian Territory. Remnants of these and other native groups gathered loosely along Village Creek, in what is now eastern Tarrant County. Texas military forces began harassing the natives in the summer of 1840, and in 1841 troops led by General Edward Tarrant destroyed the village and the natives' corn crops. Tarrant ordered the construction of a fort nearby and named it for its commander, Jonathan Bird. When Sam Houston became president of Texas for a second time in 1842, he negotiated a treaty, called the Bird's Fort Treaty, with several groups of Native Americans scattered across North Texas, including the Shawnee and the Delaware remainders. The groups and the Republic of Texas vowed not to make war again. Although natives and colonizers continued sparring for another thirty years, for all practical purposes, Native Americans no longer lived in North Texas by the time Texas joined the United States in 1845.

With the removal of the Native Americans, North Texas became available for colonization, mostly from the United States. The chapters that follow look at how Americans viewed the agricultural paradise of North Texas, which would give rise to cities, large and small. Wheat was the first substantial economic part of this paradise, joined later by cotton.

At its heart, however, this book is not really about wheat but about people: the people who planted wheat, harvested it, milled it, baked it, and

FIGURE 0.02. *The North Texas prairie in winter, Hunt County. (Photography by Matt White)*

ate it. It's about how people used wheat, wheat flour, and items made from wheat as organizing principles of their lives that determined how they spent their time and their money and how they prepared their food. North Texans shared their stories in letters, diaries, local histories, and interviews. I have tried to use their words to explain how wheat shaped their lives, from figuring out how to buy huge farm machines to taking the first sweet bite of shared wedding cake. Brides and grooms in North Texas who were negotiating that public ceremony almost surely were not thinking about the wheat they were consuming, but they were participating in a culture made by wheat nonetheless.

The book is arranged chronologically, from the 1840s, when Anglo colonizers arrived, to the 1970s, with the dedication of the Kimbell Art Museum. We will see how North Texans made their region unique for 130 years and beyond.

1 / "OUR PRAIRIE FLOUR": COLONIZATION, 1840–1861

OXEN PULLING HEAVILY LADEN WAGONS BROUGHT American colonizers to North Texas. Robert Horn, who came to Texas from Tennessee with his parents and siblings in 1857, vividly described the ox teams: two to eight yokes, or teams of two, "placed one in front of another and hitched to a long heavy chain fastened to the wagon axle or some other part of the wagon." Each pair of oxen was joined with a yoke "made of strong wood, usually hickory," and each pair had a distinctive purpose, Horn wrote: "The team next to the wagon was called the 'wheel team,' the one in front, the 'lead team,' and the ones between were known as 'swing teams.'"[1] The wooden spindles of the wagons, "'greased' with tar," made a "screaking" sound that "could be heard for a mile or more." Every wagon had a driver, known as a teamster, a highly skilled worker who knew intimately the abilities and temperament of each of his oxen. The teamster wielded a whip braided from four to eight strands of rawhide. Horn recalled, "'Crack your whip' was the signal for all teamsters to start on the move."[2]

And so to the prairie the colonists came, women, men, and children from north and east, all their belongings packed on wagons that "screaked" as they tracked across the grassland. These families had big dreams for life on the North Texas prairie. The culture they created was distinctive and laid the groundwork for a region that would stand apart from all others.

With generous land grants and the forced departure of the Native Americans, Anglo colonization efforts in North Texas began in earnest in the 1840s. Officials from the Republic of Texas realized that the Native American path up the Balcones escarpment would make an excellent road from the capital in Austin to the Red River, and surveyors started their work on it in 1840.[3] In November 1841, Tennessee native John Neely Bryan arrived to establish a trading post, and he built a shelter on the east bank of the Trinity River, close to the proposed road. When the government abandoned Bird's

Fort in early 1842, several families moved east to join Bryan in the settlement he named Dallas. On the Red River, the community of Preston Bend grew up on the north end of the Balcones, with trading posts and a ferry across the river to Indian Territory. But these hamlets remained small.

Also in 1841, for reasons that remain completely unknown, twenty men from Louisville, Kentucky, applied to the Republic of Texas for a colonial grant. Under the terms of the grant, they were to settle six hundred families in North Texas. Led by English-born William C. Peters, the colonists came overland, crossing the Red River on the so-called Preston Road, which had only recently been a Native American pathway.[4]

By 1845, the Peters Colony had almost nine hundred families. More than 80 percent of them were farmers, but there were also professionals and skilled craftsmen among them: physicians, schoolteachers, preachers, merchants, millwrights, blacksmiths, carpenters. Fifty-six percent of them migrated from Missouri, Illinois, or Tennessee, with another 25 percent coming from Arkansas, Kentucky, or Indiana. Almost all were from the Upper South or the Ohio Valley; a mere 3 percent came from the Lower South. The families in the Peters Colony accounted for more than three-quarters of the North Texas population in 1850.[5]

Some of the migrants came involuntarily: 106 enslaved people were brought to North Texas by their enslavers. Thirty-one white families—about 3 percent of the original settlers—held human property. The enslaved people left behind all that was familiar and loved as they made the long trek overland with their owners. At first, most of them lived in small groups, isolated among their white enslavers.[6] Besides their noisy wagons, the Peters colonists dragged along with them the conflict roiling the United States.

Even as they established farms across the grant, the Peters colonists also began creating small towns that provided the usual array of services needed by an agrarian society. The reciprocal relationships between the towns and the countryside started early. Historian Elizabeth York Enstam observed, "From the time of earliest settlement, Dallas and Dallas County grew together. Dallas and its surrounding countryside were interdependent, linked in a close, almost symbiotic process of development. Merchants, craftspeople, and professionals in the village depended for their livelihood upon the agricultural trade; in turn, farmers needed the services, manufactured goods, and markets available in the village shops and stores."[7] Dallas required farmers, and farmers required Dallas. The State of Texas soon organized the area into counties: Collin, Dallas, Denton, and Grayson in 1846 and Cooke and Tarrant in 1849. The Peters Colony contracts expired in 1848, under a cloud of controversy, and other colonizers began moving into the region.

Thirty miles southwest of Dallas—about a day's ride on horseback—at the confluence of the Clear Fork and the West Fork of the Trinity River, the US Army made a foray into North Texas in 1849. After the end of the US–Mexican War, the American government began establishing forts to create barriers between Native Americans and colonizers. The fort they built on the Trinity was the farthest north in a string of eight that stretched to the Mexican border. After much consideration, Major Ripley Arnold chose a site on a bluff overlooking the river, with broad vistas to the north. Forty-seven men, members of Company F of the Second Dragoons, many of whom were veterans of the US–Mexican War, arrived in May 1849. At least seventeen of them had immigrated from Germany, and eight had come from Ireland. Seven others hailed from other parts of Europe. Thus, two-thirds of the original inhabitants of Fort Worth were born outside the United States. A woman and children were present from the beginning. Catherine Bryant Arnold, known as Kate, joined the commander at the fort in late 1849, along with their four children. The Arnolds also had "four or five servants" and entertained often in their two-room dogtrot house—so often, in fact, that Fort Worth was designated a "double rations post."[8]

The government closed Fort Worth in 1853 and relocated the troops a hundred miles west to Fort Belknap in Young County. By that time, a hundred or so people had settled around the fort, and they moved into the abandoned buildings. The establishment of a small town, bearing the name of the former fort, was underway, but by 1860 it had a mere 350 souls.

Adding to the diversity in the region, two groups of settlers came to North Texas from France. In 1848, a group of French utopian socialists who called themselves "Icarians" migrated from Le Havre to settle at the conjunction of Denton and Oliver Creeks. Their land grant was considerably smaller than the million acres they thought they were receiving, and it didn't adjoin the Red River, as they had been led to believe. The settlement endured only a few months, and many of the colonists returned to France.[9] A second socialist group from France, eventually numbering about 350 people, moved onto the south bank of the Trinity River in western Dallas County in 1855 and named their colony La Réunion. Among other crops, they tried growing wheat, which they milled at the establishment of Green Coombes, a Peters Colony arrival, but the colony lasted less than two years. Some of the former colonists stayed in Dallas County, giving a distinctly French air to the region.

Between 1850 and 1860, the total population of North Texas rose fivefold, to more than 50,000 people. The number of enslaved people increased by a factor of ten—from 451 individuals to 4,376, representing almost 11 percent of the total population. Texas was a slave country, and the enslavers who came there brought slaves with them, both because they could and because they believed that doing so would be economically advantageous.[10]

In the 1840s, North Texas gained population faster than other areas of the state. Drier, cooler, and with many fewer trees to fell than in East Texas, the prairies seemed boundless in their potential for producing bountiful crops.[11] As early Dallas historian John Cochran observed about his father, North Carolinian William Cochran, and his peers, "The people were exceedingly anxious to bring it [the land] under the influence of the plow and see what it would produce."[12] The settlers would tame the wild prairie for their use.

Throughout the 1840s, most people in North Texas ate mainly corn. The wondrous grain grew easily, was simple to harvest, and, if stored properly, stayed good almost indefinitely. But the white settlers of the region wanted wheat, accustomed as they were to its luxurious softness and unparalleled ability to make high-quality bread, pie crusts, and rudimentary cakes. Coming from the Upper South, they knew how to grow and mill wheat. And in North Texas, they found land and climate well suited for it.

Many people associate wheat with "amber waves of grain" and think of it as a quintessentially American crop. It is not, however. Wheat cultivation arose in western Asia about 8500 BCE, then steadily spread to areas with moderate, dry climates across the Eastern Hemisphere. Europeans came to love flour made from wheat. It milled more finely and accepted leavening more easily than any other grain. Heavy grains like barley, rye, and millet might sustain life, but they would never rise as gloriously light as wheat flour did. And so, as Europeans began moving to the Americas, they brought wheat with them. The Spanish delighted in excellent wheat crops in Peru and the Mexican highlands.

When the English colonized North America, beginning in 1607, they too cultivated wheat. By the early eighteenth century, Virginians grew enough wheat to export surpluses to England. As colonists spread across the Appalachian Mountains, they took wheat with them. In the mid-nineteenth century, farmers in the Kentucky Bluegrass region, northern Missouri, eastern Tennessee, and especially the Shenandoah Valley raised substantial amounts of wheat.[13] The Americans relocating from these areas to new lands in Texas were experienced in growing wheat and producing bread from it, and they were intent on making these native lands bear the crops from the Old World.

Migrating from Maury County, Tennessee, a place with an established wheat culture, Peters Colony member William Cochran sowed wheat on his tract northwest of Dallas in the fall of 1845. The next spring he "and all his neighbors were overjoyed at its astonishing yield." Likely mostly by luck, they had come to a land that was just cool enough and dry enough that wheat would thrive.

Continuing to experiment, Cochran then planted cotton, which also produced abundantly. The settlers were ecstatic: they could grow side by side "the cereals of the north and principle [*sic*] staple of the south . . . on the same farm to perfection, the same year."[14] The prairies could produce year-round, yielding two highly desirable staple crops, and the colonizers could eat the wheat and sell the cotton. North Texas promised to be a farmer's utopia.

At first, feeding his family remained the farmer's priority. Because they were so isolated, colonists had to grow their own wheat if they wanted wheat flour. The region had no navigable streams to bring goods by water, and the nearest port was at Jefferson, 170 miles away on the Red River. Bringing flour overland was impractical and expensive. Even the US government faced problems. Most of the provisions for the soldiers in North Texas came from the United States through the Gulf of Mexico through Houston, up the Trinity River as far as it was navigable, then overland. Between November 1850 and June 1851, the Fort Worth army post received more than fifty tons of supplies from Houston. Rations included beef or pork, flour or "hard bread" (similar to hardtack), beans, coffee, sugar, and salt. Quartermaster Samuel Starr reported that, while they could buy beef locally, flour was almost unobtainable.[15] The army post needed wheat and flour grown in the area.

Making North Texas suitable for cultivation, however, was no easy task. The thick, deep-rooted grasses, part of an ecosystem that stretched from Mexico to Canada, yielded grudgingly, even painfully, to cultivation. When Anglo settlers first arrived in the grasslands, the big bluestem, little bluestem, and side oats grama grew "belly deep to a saddle horse." Only "prairie plows" hitched to oxen were sufficient for the task. When Jacob Routh began breaking land in 1851, he discovered that the horses he brought with him from Tennessee were too light, and he had to trade 120 acres of land with his neighbor, John Beverly, for a yoke of oxen. The grasses also tested the abilities of plows. The earliest plows were made of cast iron, which rusted, dulled easily, and broke often. The thick soil clung to the plow blade, requiring frequent cleaning. In the 1850s, John Deere perfected a steel moldboard plow, which was stronger and more flexible than iron, turned the sod as it broke it, and was affordable for ordinary farmers because it could be mass-produced.[16] Merchants in Galveston, the nearest seaport (still 290 miles away), began offering steel plows in addition to those made of cast or wrought iron.[17] North Texas farmers with money at last had the tools they needed to uproot the prairie and start widespread cultivation.

Robert Horn recalled in great detail breaking the land. Oxen—stout, strong, and intelligent, with enormous stamina—were the stars of the show. "The prairie was then broken by oxen, four to ten of them, hitched to a large plow with a cutter in front to crack the surface. Some plows had an axle and a wheel on the land slide; others were held in place by handles. The soil was turned bottom side up as smooth as if it had been laid that way by hand."[18] The grasses, so perfectly adapted over thousands of years, had met their match and were buried beneath the clay.

Once the prairie sod had been broken, it was ready for sowing. North Texas farmers usually planted the winter variety of wheat, sowing it in the fall and harvesting it in the late spring. Winter wheat suited the climate, as it easily tolerated Texas winters, while spring wheat (planted in the spring and harvested in the fall) could not withstand the hot summers. And winter wheat meshed well with the rhythm of cotton, which was planted in April and harvested in late summer and early autumn. While the two crops could not quite occupy the same land, as boosters had hoped, their requirements fit together neatly throughout the year. The only time of substantial overlap might have been the harvesting of the wheat with the chopping, or thinning, of young cotton plants in early summer.

Because wheat requires intensive labor only at harvest, many families in the nineteenth century did most of the field work themselves, not only in the great wheat-growing regions in the North but also in North Texas. Yet enslavement played a significant role in wheat farming in the latter region, just as it did in the Virginia Piedmont, which was by far the most prolific wheat-growing region in the South in the antebellum period.[19]

In 1860, sixty North Texas farmers in the region each grew more than a thousand bushels of wheat and presumably sold it on the commercial market rather than using it for family consumption. Thirty-two of these farmers, or 53.3 percent, enslaved people. Producing at least 7 percent of the wheat in the region, they most likely deployed those enslaved people in the wheat fields. The three who held twenty or more humans could have been classified as planters, among the largest enslavers in the state. Eight of the enslavers who grew more than one thousand bushels of wheat held between ten and twenty people each. One-third of the enslavers held as many as eight people, while half held fewer than five. Thus, enslavers made up a much larger sector of large wheat farmers in North Texas than in the South as a whole, where they comprised less than 25 percent of the population. We have no direct evidence of enslaved people working with wheat in North Texas, but census records show that this group of enslavers did not farm cotton, which would have required a lot of labor. It stands to reason that the enslavers used slaves for wheat cultivation.[20]

While these enslaved people were only a small number of the total in North Texas—278 enslaved people out of 4,376, or 6 percent—they still complicate the picture of southern slavery. Most wheat farmers in the United States did not use slave labor, and most enslaved people in the United States did not work with wheat. But enough of them did to show that enslaved people grew crops other than cotton and that they created wealth for their enslavers who chose to grow wheat. Thus, wheat became implicated in enslavement in Texas and its spread westward. As historians have observed about Virginia, North Texas was not the plantation South. But it also was not the free North. North Texas was distinctive.[21]

In the early years, North Texas farmers planted only enough wheat for their own families' consumption, in plots of ten acres or fewer. That situation changed quickly, however, between 1850 and 1860. The amount of North Texas prairie broken for agriculture accelerated rapidly and with it the size of the wheat crops, particularly in Dallas and Collin Counties. Farmers could feed their families and also have some wheat left for sale.

The yield in Dallas County in particular approached that of the established wheat-growing areas of Virginia. Even without figures from Tarrant County, North Texas produced one-third of the Texas wheat crop in 1860. The rich black clay could yield astonishing abundance. In the late 1850s, one farmer in Grayson County grew forty-three bushels of wheat per acre, which then sold at 50 to 75 cents a bushel.[22] Despite transportation issues, boosters predicted that production would soon extend beyond

TABLE 1.1. WHEAT PRODUCTION IN NORTH TEXAS, 1850–1860

	Bushels of Wheat	
County	*1850*	*1860*
Collin	2,433	137,528
Cooke	0	12,446
Dallas	2,983	194,264
Denton	176	31,373
Grayson	1,485	80,862
Tarrant	384	No report
Six-county total	7,461	456,473
State totals	41,729	1,478,345
Percentage of Texas total	17.8%	32.38%

Source: US Census of Agriculture, 1850 and 1860.

subsistence farming and that wheat farmers would grow enough to sell in the market as well as for home use. Clearly, North Texans had reason to be optimistic about the potential of wheat.

Whether enslaved or free, the people of North Texas began their wheat-growing season by planting. The first identified variety of wheat in North Texas was Red May, which had been brought to North Texas before 1850 by settlers from Missouri.[23] Red May, a soft wheat that was low in protein and gluten, made baked goods that were tender rather than tough. Red May also tolerated cold and had "extraordinary" drought tolerance—always a benefit in North Texas.[24] Clifton Scott, whose father built an early mill in Dallas, recalled that Red May yielded sixty pounds of wheat per bushel of seed.[25]

Most North Texans planted their wheat in October.[26] Before the Civil War, the majority still used the ancient method of sowing their wheat "broadcast"—tossing the seeds by hand onto the ground. The next step was covering the seeds with a light layer of soil, usually with a mule- or horse-drawn plow, then going over them with a harrow, a set of teeth or tines set in a frame that broke up clods and smoothed the soil. The ill-prepared settlers of La Réunion made harrows by roping together wooden logs.[27] By the late 1850s, a few up-to-date farmers were planting with seed drills, mule-drawn machines that opened the soil, dropped seeds into several rows at once, and covered them. With a drill, a single worker and one or two horses could plant eight acres a day.[28] Although the *Dallas Daily Herald* mentioned seed drills occasionally, they did not appear in newspaper ads until 1860, when a Galveston merchant offered "Willoughby's premium" brand.[29] Most Texans continued to scatter their seed by hand.

The wheat sprouted before the first freeze, which usually occurred in November, and then it grew throughout the winter. It required virtually no cultivation or attention, leaving farmers free for other pursuits. Some farmers grazed cows on the rich wheat grass as it developed during the cold months. By early spring, the grass began to send up seed heads that ripened and turned golden in the warming sun. Harvest often began in late May. If a farmer was growing cotton, that crop would be well along by the time of the frenzied wheat harvest.

The head of each stalk of wheat bears numerous berries, and each berry is surrounded by a husk. The harvesting processes of cutting the stalks, gathering them, and then removing the husk from the individual berries have challenged humans for at least ten thousand years. Until the nineteenth century, wheat was harvested with hand labor. In some North Texas communities, hand labor continued into the early twentieth century.

The oldest harvesting tools were sickles and scythes, curved blades attached to short or long handles, respectively. The harvester simply grabbed a handful of grain stalks, swung the blade by the handle, and cut the stalks, which then fell in every direction. The grain cradle—a straight scythe with long perpendicular arms that caught the grain as it was cut and then laid it in neat rows—appeared in the 1760s and was a dramatic improvement over older methods. A deft worker using a cradle—almost always a male—could harvest up to two acres a day, more than twice the amount possible with a scythe.[30] Although grain cradles were sold in Texas by 1848, in 1850 Joseph Brown Rogers made his own cradle to cut his eight acres of wheat in Denton County. North Texans knew about the grain cradle technology, even if they couldn't get their hands on it, but continued to use scythes, which were smaller and more compact than cradles.[31]

After the grain was cut, it had to be gathered and bundled, a tedious and time-consuming task. The early colonists collected armfuls of stalks and used strands of wheat straw to tie, or bind, them into bundles called sheaves.[32] Sometimes women and children helped with the wearying but essential work of collecting the stalks.[33] Harvesters then gathered several sheaves and leaned them upright against each other to form shocks. The shocks had to be assembled carefully so they would not sag or fall. They dried outdoors for at least several days, and then they could be moved from the fields and stored indefinitely.

The first step in making the wheat berries edible was threshing, or, as some North Texans said, thrashing—removing the husk from the berry. The most primitive means of threshing wheat was simply whacking the wheat head with a stick. One step up was to use a flail, a stick from which a second stick, known as a swipple, dangled. The flailer swung the stick and struck the grain with the swipple. Flailing was slow and exhausting, and North Texans substituted "tramping" by oxen and horses as quickly as they could. Burman D. Burch, who came to Cooke County in the 1850s, explained: "When we thrashed, we cleaned off a place on the ground. We set the wheat with its heads up on the clean ground. We took eight or ten horses and run them over it till it was tramped out."[34] Tramping remained inefficient, but it used horse power rather than human power, and it was better than sticks.

Once the husks were separated, the next step was removing the straw and the chaff from the kernels. Early North Texas farmers used wooden pitchforks to rake the straw from the wheat. They then winnowed, or removed the chaff (separated husks) from, the kernels by tossing the grain into the air and letting the wind blow the chaff away as they caught the kernels in a basket.[35] Charlie Davis from Cooke County recalled his father, Thomas Davis, describing the harvest process as "threshing the wheat and tromping it out with oxen. Then they raked that straw off. They would get up in a tree with the wheat and pour it out on the ground and let the wind blow that chaff out."[36] Oxen and wind separated grain from straw and husk.

Texas grain farmers began at a propitious time when hand agriculture was declining in Europe and the United States and mechanization was taking over. North Texas was remote, however, and getting bulky machines to the region was not easy. They were brought by water to Galveston or Jefferson, then overland by oxcart—a slow, expensive process. Yet some determined farmers bought machines and managed to bring them to the prairies.

Developed in Maryland and Virginia in the 1830s, mechanical reapers—which cut the stalks of wheat and laid them neatly into piles—spread slowly into North Texas through the 1850s. These early two-wheeled machines, drawn by a horse with a rider, were fairly simple. A reel grabbed the grain, and a cutting blade attached to a gear sliced the stalk. Dallas County historian John Cochran described the work of the mechanical reaper: "These reapers cut the grain and caught it on a platform behind and on which a man with a wooden pitchfork rode and raked it off into bundles. It took five good binders to bind or tie the grain as fast as it was cut and piled."[37] The reaper cut the grain, but everything else still had to be done by hand.

Threshing machines, patented in the United States in 1837, eased the process of removing the wheat berry from the chaff. The farmer tossed the wheat—kernel, stalks, and all—into the machine. A set of rotating blades snapped the wheat heads from the straw, then beat the heads to remove the kernels.[38] The kernels exited the machine from a hopper, while the stalks and chaff poured out through another port. Powered by teams of horses or oxen walking in a circle, the machines reduced the amount of human labor by 75 percent.[39] A thresher with two horses and eight or ten humans might clean 150 to 300 bushels of wheat a day. Dallas inventors Kilbourn and Company on Ten Mile Creek in southern Dallas County claimed that their machine could clean 500 to 600 bushels using eight horses.[40]

Some North Texans created their own harvesting machines. In 1859, the Kilbourns were manufacturing "square draft reapers" that could cut a swath six and a half feet wide, and the Wilson brothers, also in Dallas, were perfecting their model on the eve of the Civil War.[41] Most harvesters, however, came from other parts of the United States. Companies such as Miller, Wingate & Company from Louisville, Kentucky, advertised directly to North Texans and shipped their goods to Jefferson, where the purchaser became responsible for transporting the machine to the prairies.[42] Texas middlemen also imported machines into the state. In 1859, Grant and Compton of Galveston handled a wide array of agricultural tools, from scythes and cradles to "Manny's Celebrated Combined Reapers and Mowers" from Rockford, Illinois, and Emery Brothers' "Threshing Machines and Separators" from Albany, New York. They advertised heavily in Dallas but did not indicate how the machines would be transported from the Gulf Coast.[43]

North Texans also acted as agents for specific manufacturers. T. C. Hawpe, who ran a flour mill at Pleasant Run in Dallas County, became the agent for "Wheeler's Improved Patent Combined Thresher and Wind-rower" from Albany, New York. His 1858 ad stated that the threshers were "on hand in Houston" but did not say how they would reach North Texas.[44] Apparently the most ambitious agent in the area was North Carolina–born Jeremiah Sherwood of Millwood, Collin County. In the early 1850s, he became an agent for McCormick's reapers from Chicago.[45] In 1859, he acted on behalf of Miller, Wingate of Louisville for that company's "Combined Reaper and Mower, Patented Nov. 23, 1856, and June 30, 1857." The machine cost $150 plus shipping to Jefferson. Sherwood indicated that the machines could also be in Millwood by May 1, presumably at an additional cost. The trip from Jefferson, probably in a wagon pulled by oxen, would take a month.[46] Sherwood also handled threshers made by D. H. Hoover and Son in Ohio. Although he advertised them as "the best and cheapest Thresher and Cleaner ever brought to Texas," their cost was substantial: $260 plus freight for a machine to be powered by four horses and $300 plus freight for an eight-horse model.[47]

After the grain and chaff were separated, by whatever method available, the grain could be stored until it was milled. Storage had its own problems, of course, particularly in the form of weevils, rats, mice, and other would-be thieves, and dampened grain could rot or sprout. Texans built granaries, or storage buildings, to protect their grain and keep it as dry as possible. Although we know little about these early structures, they were probably wooden and raised off the ground. Real estate ads listed granaries—sometimes multiple ones in a single location—as amenities to a property.[48] Good wheat storage was an asset.

Right off the stalk, wheat kernels are not really edible. To make them into food, they must first be ground and then they need to be cooked. The dilemma of grinding and cooking wheat has challenged humans from the beginning of wheat agriculture more than twenty thousand years ago. Over the millennia, people in various locations invented crude methods for grinding wheat into flour, such as hand mills called querns. The technology took a giant step forward in the last century BCE, when people developed the process of grinding wheat between two parallel stones. They also learned to use animal power to turn the stones. With grindstones, animal power, and a steady supply of grain, increasing numbers of people had access to wheat flour over the centuries.[49]

As Anglo colonizers arrived in North Texas, a few stalwarts tried to grind their own grain, because there simply were no mills. In 1846, the second year after William and Elizabeth McCullough Sachse arrived in Collin County with the Peters Colony, William raised "a little wheat" and ground enough of it in a coffee mill for Elizabeth to make "brown biscuits."[50] When George Jackson's family came to Dallas County in 1848, they could not immediately acquire land. A neighbor allowed John Jackson, George's father, to grow three acres of wheat on his land. At harvest, they threshed the wheat with a flail and ground it in a hand mill. George Jackson recalled, "That was the sweetest bread I ever remember eating."[51] Perhaps wheat bread brought memories of home, where things might have seemed a little simpler. The satisfying taste of yeast-leavened bread and the softness of the texture in one's mouth would have contrasted with the grit of cornbread. A slice of wheat bread was more than just bread.

Often, people used hand-cranked steel mills to grind grain, usually corn but occasionally wheat. Beverly Leonidas Rogers, the oldest son in his family, remembered walking three and a half miles from his family's new home in Denton County to a steel mill in about 1850: "Together with negro Al, [he] shouldered a bushel of wheat and walked three and a half miles to a steel mill (something similar to our coffee mills), bolted on an elm tree. The hopper held nearly a peck of wheat. We took turn about turning, and by late dinner time we were on our way home again."[52] These mills, which required muscle strength to turn, were often jokingly referred to as "Armstrong mills."[53] One wonders if Al got to enjoy any of the wheat flour he had toted over the miles.

Given the difficulty of hand milling and the expanding fields of wheat, North Texans quickly began building mills. Every new mill had multiple impacts on its environment. In constructing a mill, an entrepreneur did several things that altered the physical environment, such as changing the course of streams and maybe importing loud steam engines. In providing a service that people desperately wanted in their efforts to obtain good food for their families, a miller provided for his own family with the profit he made from grinding wheat for others. He created a community center, where people (mostly men) congregated, swapping news and entertaining themselves while they waited for their flour to be ground. Commercial centers and villages developed around mills.

Building a mill took accuracy and care, and millwrights, the men who constructed them, were highly skilled. Millwrights traveled long distances to ply their trade. In 1850, the US census taker counted William Laytham, a seventy-year-old native of England, with the family of W. A. Ferris in Dallas

County. Presumably Laytham was living with the Ferrises while he supervised the construction of their mill on White Rock Creek.[54]

With no banks in place in North Texas, all financing for mills was private. In 1858, Robert Fitzhugh of Collin County bought his brother's and father's interest in a "steam saw and grist mill" on his land on Wilson's Creek. He paid his brother, William Fitzhugh, $987 cash, and he financed $1,500 with his father, John Fitzhugh, to be paid in annual sums of $200. While the Fitzhughs carefully registered their arrangements with the county, the transactions were nonetheless personal: people who knew each other—in this case, family—dealing directly with one another.[55]

After funding was secured, the next task in building a mill was deciding on a power source: animal, water, or steam. That choice guided the selection of a site, preferably near one of the dirt roads in the region. If the mill was to be powered by water, it would have to be on a creek or river, few of which in North Texas had a reliably strong flow year-round. The creek or riverbank had to be sturdy enough to support the weight of the mill machinery or the whole apparatus might crumble into the water. If the mill were to be powered by animal treadmill, it could be placed anywhere. The constant care of the animals complicated maintenance, however. Steam mills were the most powerful and flexible, but they were also costly and dangerous. A mill builder had much to consider in making his decision.

The next task would be to acquire material for the structure. All building materials were scarce in North Texas. Although sawmills were increasing in number across the region, large timbers were rare on the prairie. The Cross Timbers—heavily forested fingers of sandy land that extended north-south throughout North Texas and Oklahoma—were populated with relatively small trees, particularly post oaks and blackjack oaks, which had limited use for construction.[56] Lumber often had to be bought and hauled from the forests of East Texas—again, a trip by oxcart of several weeks. Despite the inconvenience, most early mill buildings were made of wood. When they could, mill builders used locally sourced wood both for the structures and for the mill equipment. The mill built in 1852 by the Witt brothers, Wade and Preston—who had come to Texas as part of the Peters Colony—was made mainly of rock, almost surely local limestone. The timbers, from "the woods" (probably the Trinity River bottoms), were cut from oak trees and measured a stout one foot square.[57]

Charles B. Moore and Henry S. Moore, millwrights and brothers, moved to Collin County from Tennessee in 1856 and 1858, respectively.[58] They fashioned the main shaft for a mill in neighboring Fannin County from local bois d'arc, which was tough, sturdy, and difficult to work with.[59] In their correspondence, the Moore brothers discussed the shortages of wood. Henry complained to Charles in 1860, "There is none of the lumber hauled yet from the mill and can't be for a couple of weeks. The Big round posts and press timbers are to get yet and will be hard to find."[60]

At the heart of a wheat mill were the millstones (also referred to as buhr-stones or burr stones), two flat circular stones of equal size. The stones in the first mill at Pilot Point, for example, were forty inches in diameter.[61] The bottom stone, the bedstone, was fixed in place parallel to the ground. The top stone, or runner stone, was suspended above the bedstone, just high enough so that when it turned the two stones would grind the grain between them but not touch and strike sparks. The stones were "dressed" with grooves cut into them that scissored the grain kernels into particles. The best ones came from France and Germany (known as Cologne stones), and in Dallas in 1859 a pair sold for anywhere between $100 and $510—a sizable investment.[62] In 1856, the Witts advertised that their business was "got up on the principle of the Northern flouring mills, with Large French burr rocks."[63] Despite the growing national tensions, the Witts freely acknowledged the influences of the North on wheat culture in the westernmost part of the South. Most North Texas mills also had a separate set of stones for cornmeal, as wheat required a distinctive grinding motion. Corn could be pounded, but pounding a wheat kernel simply made it bounce.[64]

The metal parts of the mill, usually iron but sometimes steel, had to be purchased out of state. The Witts bought the machinery for their 1853 steam mill in St. Louis. It came down the Mississippi River to the Red River in Louisiana and thence into the port at Jefferson. From Jefferson, the machinery arrived in Carrollton in ox-drawn wagons.[65] The Moore brothers bought iron cogwheels and shafts from several northern vendors. The enterprising Preston Witt purchased a sixteen-foot-long boiler from a ship wrecked in the lower Trinity River. It was a fine piece of equipment, "fabricated in England by hand."[66] Thrifty builders also salvaged equipment from other mills. When the Foote mill in Millwood burned in the summer of 1860, resourceful neighbors removed the boiler and engine and hauled them about fifteen miles to the Robert Fitzhugh mill southeast of McKinney. The parts were too dear to waste.[67]

Before the iron parts were set in place, they had to be thoroughly seasoned, which was the practice of putting a layer of heated oil on the metal surface to lessen friction and reduce the likelihood of rust. Henry Moore queried his brother: "The cogs are to be delivered here next Saturday green [untreated][.] [W]hat do you think of seasoning by boiling in tallow[?] [H]ow soon can it be done[?]" Boiling iron equipment in beef fat might seem innovative, but many rural Texans used animal fat to grease machinery. Henry frequently fussed about the lack of care taken by mill owners: "They grease every thing with impure Hogs fat . . . [if] they grease at all[.]" One wonders what Henry meant by "impure." Any bits of flesh in the hog fat could easily jam the gears, and one can imagine the smell of a mill lubricated with beef and hog fat on a hot day.[68] But seasoning and greasing were crucial to a mill's success, since these practices kept the equipment in working order.

The goal of milling was to produce pure, silky white flour made mostly from the endosperm of the wheat kernel, with as little of the exterior covering (called bran) and chaff remaining as possible. To that end, ambitious mill owners invested in equipment to clean the wheat both before and after milling. In 1858, Green Coombes advertised that, in addition to a steam engine and two runs, or pairs, of stones, he had "a first rate smut mill" and "superior bolting clothes."[69] Smut mills, invented in the late eighteenth century, used brushes and air to remove dirt from the wheat before it was ground. Bolting machines consisted of cloth-covered reels that were turned, sometimes with a hand crank, to remove the leftover bran from the flour. The finest bolting cloth was made of silk, but bolting cloths could also be fashioned from wool, linen, or horsehair.[70] As they did for agricultural machinery, merchants outside North Texas took orders for milling equipment. In 1859, A. Z. Rumsey of Houston offered "Reapers, Threshers, Engine, Smut-Mills, Bolt and Bolting Cloths."[71] The advertisement of L. J. Webster of New Orleans for "Anchor Brand Bolting Cloth" from New York did not indicate how the goods would reach Dallas.[72] By whatever means, Coombes and his competitors obtained the best equipment available to them.

The work of mill building took its toll on the people involved. Charles Moore dreaded one assignment because of the heat and the biting insects that infested areas near water: "The Linnin job will have to be done right in hot weather and I think it will be the very devil down there among the moscketoes." He also suffered from the symptoms of silicosis: "My health is good as [ever?] except hoarseness from breathing the mill stone dust."[73] Lanson Clark, a Peters Colony settler in Collin County, was "a large, fine looking sandy-haired man of some 250 pounds. He was so strong that he could take an anvil by the horn and lift it off the block or take a 40 gallon barrel, roll it up his knees, and drink out of the bunghole." Nonetheless, he died of pneumonia in 1850 "after working in water all day starting a gristmill in Denton." He was thirty-eight years old and left a widow and six children.[74]

The most common type of mill in North Texas in the early days was the treadmill, powered by oxen or, less often, horses. Treadmills were easy to construct and could be sited anywhere. A frame held the treadmill, which functioned in the same way as the ones found at gyms today: the constant motion of the animals' feet moved a belt, which in turn powered the spindles, shafts, and gears that turned the runner stone. The more animals there were moving the belt, the more power the tread generated to turn the millstones. By some standards, the animal-powered mills were "primitive," but they "answered the purpose and [were] greatly appreciated by the early settlers."[75]

Martin Luther Foote, born in 1852, described well the original oxen treadmill built by his father, John Wesley Foote, and his partners in Millwood in Collin County: "This mill was run with a large wheel thirty or forty feet in diameter. They placed several oxen on one side of this inclined wheel, for it took about eight heavy oxen on the wheel to give it power. The oxen were fastened on to the wheel so they could not back off. When the brake was thrown off the wheel began to move and the oxen began to walk. They would walk all day and not gain a foot on their travel." North Texans used as many as twelve oxen at a time to power their grain mills.[76]

Horses were lighter in weight and had less stamina than oxen, so North Texans employed them in mills more rarely. Cobb Hart's mill in Weston, Collin County, was "crude," but John Cochran remembered the horse mill owned by Peters Colony settler and Disciples of Christ minister Amon McCommas east of Dallas as "much superior to any previously built."[77]

In Europe and the eastern United States, running water from rivers and creeks powered many mills, often depicted in a picturesque and romantic manner in illustrations. The flowing water rotated a wooden wheel that turned the gears that turned the millstones. Author Clare Leighton remembered hearing a water mill: "the stumbling, growling sound of the turning of the wheel."[78] On the Texas prairies, water could be an uncertain source of energy, but people built these types of mills nonetheless.

As mentioned earlier, the first step in building a water-powered mill was to find a creek or river with enough water to turn a mill. Mill builders had to appraise the situation carefully. Writing from Fannin County, Henry Moore commented to his brother Charles, "Plenty of water here[.] [F]rogs can swim up to the stack half round it[.] [H]ogs can most swim in mud N [north] of the mill."[79] In Dallas County, James Horton built a water-powered mill on the West Fork of the Trinity at a shallow spot his father had named Eagle Ford. In 1858, during a severe drought, Horton assured potential customers, "We have water plenty at all seasons, and persons may rely on no detention."[80]

The next steps would be damming the water course and building a channel, called a mill race, to funnel the water into the wheel that powered the millstones. Dams popped up all over North Texas in the 1850s, with at least two on the Elm Fork of the Trinity River in Dallas County.[81] Dams and millraces could have negative effects on the people downstream, diminishing their water flow. No disputes made the North Texas news, however.

Yet, despite the boasts of developers, in drought-prone North Texas low water could put an end to milling "a large portion of the year."[82] During the drought in 1858, for example, the mills on White Rock Creek in Dallas County were idled by lack of water.[83] In July 1860, Henry Moore commented that the owners "expect to have water enough to run the Excelsior Mill a week more." After that, anyone wanting flour would have to wait for the next rain.[84]

The most sophisticated and strongest form of mill power before the Civil War was the steam engine. Steam engines used pressure to power the pistons that provided the energy to turn the millstones—ironically measured as "horsepower." The engines had advantages over animal power, requiring no food or rest, and over water, since they could be located anywhere and could run all year regardless of weather. They were not foolproof, however. Steam engines were expensive and dangerous, they tended to explode, and they required large stocks of wood for fuel, posing, again, no small problem on the prairies. They also weighed more than a treadmill and could create foundation problems for a mill.[85] Steam mills, furthermore, introduced noise and pollutants to the countryside in ways that animal and water power did not. A visitor to the Gold and Donaldson Mill in Dallas in 1858 commented that he found its steam engine "puffing, blowing up clouds of steam and smoke to some purpose, grinding 250 bushels per day."[86]

Despite the challenges, North Texans welcomed steam engines as positive innovations. In Cooke County, for example, locals referred to the one owned by Lattimer and Richie as simply "the steam mill"; not just any mill, it was one that their neighbors would recognize immediately.[87] More powerful than the mightiest oxen, a steam engine could easily drive two or three "runs," or pairs, of stones. Numerous owners of treadmills quickly sold their old-fashioned mills and built steam mills. The Wetsel family, for example, built a mill powered by twelve oxen shortly after their arrival in McKinney as part of the Peters Colony in 1848. The family sold that mill and in 1852 built a steam mill.[88] In 1853, the Witt brothers left their first mill and moved several miles west to construct a two-story-rock steam mill on Farmers Creek.[89] Others converted their existing water- or animal-powered mills to steam.[90] Some newer mills had steam engines from the beginning. In the Dallas County community of Cedar Springs, the Dallas Steam Mills commenced grinding wheat and selling flour in 1856. With two runs of stones powered by a fifty-horsepower steam engine, the mill churned out eight thousand pounds, or forty barrels, of flour a day.[91] Advocates believed that the progress was worth the cost, danger, noise, and smoke.

But the old ways also had their defenders. Dallas newspaper editor J. W. Latimer, writing for the *Texas Almanac,* championed water- and horse-powered mills, observing that their products were just as good as those made by steam mills. The water mills "during dry seasons, are inoperative a large portion of the year, but do an excellent business when there is a sufficiency of water."[92] And some people preferred the taste of water-ground grain. Clare Leighton noted that steam-ground grain had "the burnt taste of the heat." Steam-powered stones turned faster and generated greater friction, heating the grain as it split.[93] But for most consumers, greater quantity outweighed this perceived decline in quality.

By 1860, mills had spread across North Texas. The US Census of Manufactures for that year listed thirty-seven flour mills in five counties: thirteen in Collin County, ten in Grayson, seven in Dallas, four in Denton, and three in Cooke. Tarrant County had several more that were not counted. A multitude of other sources show that at least seventy-eight existed between the 1840s and 1860. The mills supported families and contributed significantly to the local economy. Thirty-six men appeared in the census as millers (those in charge of a mill)—twenty in Dallas County and sixteen in Grayson. Census takers counted another eighty-two men who worked in the mills: twenty-five in Collin County, twenty-four in Dallas, nineteen in Grayson, eight in Denton, and six in Cooke. Most mills employed two people, and none had more than four. These mills brought much-needed wages into Texas households, averaging between $20 and $35 per man per year.[94]

Milling work mattered to individual families as well as communities. West of Dallas, Green Coombes tried to sell his mill in 1859, observing that it was "doing good business and is constantly employed." But 1860 found him still milling, supporting his wife, Mary Coombes, and their three small children, and also boarding Joseph Roye, a French-born miller, and Gustavus Hetten, a Belgian-born clerk, likely from the defunct Réunion colony. Thomas A. Campbell, a Kentucky-born miller, his wife, Margaret Campbell, and their three small children lived in the next household.[95] Millers tended to be men with families who were seeking stable situations on the developing prairie. All those enumerated were white.

It is likely that enslaved people worked in North Texas mills. The owners of at least fifteen mills—about 19 percent of the total—enslaved people. Most enslavers possessed two or three people, often a woman and children. George Washington Record and Joseph W. Ellett, partners in the mill at Record's Crossing on the Elm Fork of the Trinity in Dallas County, had the most, enslaving seventeen and sixteen people, respectively. Next were Trevezant Hawpe at Pleasant Run, Dallas County, and William Forman, in Plano, Collin County, who enslaved eight people each. Third-generation miller Zachariah Thomas Motley brought significant wealth with him from Bowling Green, Kentucky, in 1856, including a large cache of gold—some in a chest that Zachariah used as a wagon seat and some "tucked into the undergarments" of his wife, Mary Permelia "Polly" Lynn Motley, according to family stories. In 1850, he enslaved six people and brought his human possessions to Texas with him; by 1860, their number had grown to ten, and Motley had engrossed more than six thousand acres of land in eastern Dallas County.[96] While they most likely worked in the fields, enslaved people almost surely formed part of the workforce at some of the mills.

Even as the owners sought prosperity, the milling business proved unpredictable, and they frequently bought and sold properties. But the mills could also be profitable. Demand for flour was always high. The Excelsior Mills in Fannin County ground three days a week, using poor-quality wood to fire the boiler, and in 1860 the mill sold every bit of the flour its workers managed to grind. "Never can keep any on hand," Henry Moore reported to Charles.[97] Clifton Scott of Dallas remembered that his father "sold the flour as fast as he could grind the wheat, at $4 to $4.50 per 100 pounds at the mill."[98]

Some mill owners amassed significant wealth. Although they probably had money when they arrived in Texas, their dealings in the new place also prospered. James Horton of Dallas and Samuel Keller of Lancaster, for example, reported real estate and personal wealth of almost $20,000 each in 1860. Keller enslaved at least three people. William Augustus Gold, who combined his mill at Cedar Springs with a distillery and a store in downtown Dallas, had wealth of more than $30,000, including two enslaved people. Madison Moultrie Miller was another enterprising sort who owned a huge retail store with more than $100,000 worth of inventory and a mill in the hamlet of Pleasant Run in Dallas County. In 1848, Miller built "the biggest house in Dallas County." The construction of the fifteen-room house—which featured cedar floors, copper gutters, and two brick chimneys—took more than a year. The forty-foot dining room "had a table as long as the room." The house served as both a home and a hotel, and workers at the mill lived there as well as Miller, his wife, Mary Parks Rawlins Miller, and their three children. Many wealthy families were linked personally and financially. For example, Samuel Keller and Madison Miller were married to sisters and lived close to each other in southwestern Dallas County. Miller owned a third of Keller's mill. Samuel and Lucinda Ann Rawlings Keller reared the Millers' son after his father died in 1860.[99]

Mills created communities by fostering local businesses that drew customers from far and wide. They were items of wonder. Charles Moore concluded one letter by saying, "I must quit now for yonder comes about 40 women to look at the mill."[100] They also served as community centers, almost exclusively for men. The Witt mill in Dallas County had a racetrack where "a visitor . . . could get action if he thought he had a fast horse." The Witt mill was also a trading center for game hunters: "Hanging from a limb of a big pecan tree in the mill yard could often be seen the butchered carcasses of deer and buffalo and bear." The writer concluded, "The abundance of game, the good water, and the fact that there was available a well-drained camping ground all served to make the Witt Mill a popular rendezvous and frequently there was such a rush of business that it was necessary to wait a week or more for service, but these weeks were never dull."[101]

Mills sometimes had stores connected with them so that a farmer could buy other supplies while he waited for his flour. The Witt mill, which quickly became known as the Trinity Mills, also had a sawmill and a general store furnishing flour, lumber, and other supplies to colonists in the region. The Mill Store had more than 250 names on its list of customers in 1860–1861. Of those names, sixteen could be identified as female—about 6 percent. The stores, like the mills, were predominantly male spaces.[102]

Mills also became gathering places for legal and extralegal events. The mill owned by Archibald Leonard, who was part of the Peters Colony in northeast Tarrant County, was the site of a large oak tree where two white horse thieves and "several Negroes" were hanged.[103] At least two mills, Leonard's and one owned by Henry Cockrum in Gainesville, functioned as polling places in 1860.[104]

From small beginnings, wheat cultivation and milling soon became important parts of the North Texas economy. At the most basic level, wheat served as a token of barter, as grocers and other merchants accepted it in place of cash. In 1859, W. W. Peak and Brother, Wholesale and Retail Druggists and Apothecaries, in Dallas, offered "rugs, cigars, tobacco, jewelry," and even dental surgery in exchange for wheat taken "at the highest market prices." The next year they sold everything from hatchets to silks, satins, and laces on the same terms.[105] George Washington Record, a Peters Colony settler who operated a blacksmith shop as well as the Osceola flour mill near Dallas, accepted wheat and corn "for all shop work."[106] Presumably the merchants who received the wheat had understandings with mills to buy the wheat from them. Accumulations of wheat appeared in the wills of prosperous North Texans, included as assets along with horses and featherbeds.[107]

There were two kinds of flour mills: custom and merchant. Custom mills ground for individuals, who often took home flour made from their own wheat. A farmer brought his wheat to the mill himself and paid the miller with a portion of the flour that he ground, known as a toll. Merchant mills bought wheat from various farmers, mixed it, and sold the flour in large lots to grocers and other customers, including the US Army.

Most of the earliest mills in North Texas were custom mills that served the immediate area. In the 1840s and 1850s, trips from farm to mill could be long, often as far as thirty miles, and numerous people mentioned treks of a hundred miles.[108] Burman Burch, who came with his parents to Cooke County in 1857, recalled, "We had to go 30 miles to [the] mill and sometimes the roads was so bad we could not get there."[109] The Woody family in Wise County, west of Denton, took turns with their neighbors to make repeated 140-mile round trips to Dallas for flour. Sam Woody recalled, "Once or twice a year load up a wagon to which five or six steers [oxen] were hitched, and after a week's trip to Dallas you would have enough flour to give bread to your family and some of the neighbors for a number of weeks, until it would be the turn of someone else to make the trip."[110] Sharing the responsibility enabled a few people in Wise County to have a steady supply of flour.

Once a farmer arrived at the mill, the waiting crowds could be daunting. At the horse mill owned by Aaron Overton in Dallas, an observer counted twenty-seven wagons waiting with loads to be ground.[111] James P. Bates remembered having to be firm with the mill personnel to be serviced fairly: "The sacks were all numbered and ground according to numbers if you remained and insisted on your rights. To wait our turn then was the common lot of us all."[112] Sometimes customers got involved in the process to speed it along. Seventeen-year-old Beverly Rogers, whose family came to Denton County in 1850, went "fourteen miles on the head of Honey Creek to Squire Hart's one-horse mill." Young Beverly bolted, or screened, the flour while the miller kept grinding.[113]

As mentioned earlier, the miller exacted tolls—taking a fraction of the finished flour—as payment for grinding. In the 1840s and 1850s, the tolls often reached 13 to 17 percent.[114] Throughout history, customers had often suspected millers of unfair dealings—by overcharging, undersupplying, or selling shoddy goods—and North Texans were susceptible to the long-standing tensions between miller and customer. The high tolls were a particular point of contention. "Uncle Jack" Durrett remembered the early Feild mill in Fort Worth as the place where Seaborne Gilmore, the first county judge of Tarrant County, "licked the miller who was charged with over-tolling."[115] Durrett did not indicate if the unnamed greedy miller learned his lesson.

Consumers had to trust millers in other ways. While customers like Bates and Rogers took home flour made from their own wheat, others accepted flour made from others' wheat in the same amount as their own.[116] Custom mills also sold finished flour to consumers who did not grow grain and would not have known the source of the wheat. Millers assured buyers of their fairness. Green Coombes promised "as good flour as can be found any where in this section."[117] The Cedar Springs Mill asserted that it had "attained the reputation of making the best Flour in the State, and the present proprietors intend to keep up that reputation."[118]

Merchant mills, larger than custom mills, did less work for individual farmers and more for sale to retail outlets and people who did not raise their own wheat. In 1843, Peters Colony grantee John Cole bought land on the Cedar Springs branch of the Trinity River, about two miles north of the eventual Dallas town site. Cole opened a general store, and soon a community sprang up. In 1856, the Dallas Steam Mills commenced operation there, grinding wheat and selling flour.[119] The proprietors, Massachusetts-born William Augustus Gold and Kentucky native Richard C. "Dick" Donaldson, also had a distillery and operated a store in Dallas. They traded flour for wheat and did custom grinding for individual farmers, but only on Saturdays. The rest of the milling time was reserved for their wholesale business. Their "sole agent" was Ellis Merrill Stackpole, also a native of Massachusetts, who was married to Eliza Crozier, the sister of Donaldson's wife, Mary Susan Crozier. Stackpole settled in Dallas by 1858, "having determined to make Dallas his permanent home." He bought the store of C. W. Adams, and there he carried all sorts of goods, including school supplies, for which he would take cash, credit, wheat, corn, or oats in payment.[120] Local millers proudly advertised in the newspapers. As early as 1855, the Witt brothers and Gold and Donaldson had competing ads in the *Dallas Herald*, using identical graphic art featuring a plow and a steamship. The Witts offered "at all times on hand a supply of flour," while Gold and Donaldson promised to supply flour "on short notice."[121] People with money who wanted flour could have it.

The largest mill in North Texas before the Civil War was owned by Julian Feild and Ralph Man in Tarrant County. Feild, a native of Virginia, moved to Fort Worth in 1854 and opened a store with the financial support of William Gold and Richard Donaldson. Feild and Man built the first flour mill in Tarrant County in 1856 on land that Feild owned on the Clear Fork of the Trinity, just west of its confluence with the West Fork and the original town site of Fort Worth. The mill was constructed of cottonwood and painted white.[122]

In the *Dallas Herald*, Feild and Man bragged about their three runs of stones, which were "put up under the superintendence of a most experienced mill-wright—one of the proprietors." Their superfine flour, they declared, was "as good as any manufactured in the country."[123] A credit reporter observed in 1855 that the firm was "doing a large business[;] attentive to business and being located upon a frontier that is rapidly populating must do well."[124] Unfortunately, in the late 1850s North Texas saw its worst drought in hundreds of years, and Man and Feild soon had to get out of the business. They sold their interest in the mill to David Mauck.

Man and Feild then went twenty miles south to another Tarrant County tract owned by Feild, on Walnut Creek. On the ruins of a mill erected by Charles Turner, they built a mill from local wood, powered first by water and then with a horse tread. Then they constructed, with brickmaker S. W. A. Hook, a three-story mill powered by a steam engine. That mill gave rise to the community known as Mansfield. In 1863, the two became family when Ralph Man married Julia Alice Boisseau, the sister of Henrietta Boisseau, who was Julian Feild's wife.[125]

Most North Texas customers were local, but some made their way to the region to buy flour and haul it back to their home communities. Most notable were "caravans of Mexicans from San Antonio and Mexico," who came in oxcarts to purchase flour, for which they always paid cash.[126] In 1859, the *Dallas Daily Herald* noted, "Large quantities of flour have been purchased at the numerous mills in this county and conveyed to distant parts of the State by Mexicans. The presence of their singular carts, and the novel mode of working their oxen, attracted great attention from our citizens. Many of the carts and their drivers were from the city of San Antonio."[127] Notably, San Antonio was in the United States, although almost 300 miles away. The Mexican border was an additional 150 miles beyond San Antonio. These customers, regardless of nationality, had a long trek.

In other parts of the state, Texans were eating flour from wheat grown in the Midwest and brought downriver, through the Gulf of Mexico, and across land.[128] In the flourishing community of Marshall, near the Louisiana border, merchants advertised "St. Louis flour."[129] By the time this flour reached consumers, it had traveled thousands of miles by water and land and had been ground for months. Why, observers demanded, were these Texans not eating Texas flour?

Advocates in Austin, Houston, and elsewhere called for Texas flour. A Galveston writer griped in 1853, "We are paying about eight dollars per barrel for flour brought nearly two thousand miles while we have better wheat land within a distance of two hundred miles."[130] A visitor to Dallas in 1858 sadly commented, "The barns are teaming [*sic*] with wheat and the mills with flour, and yet we are constantly importing thousands of barrels of flour from other States, and cannot make use of our own, thus impoverishing ourselves and enriching others."[131] By 1859, a writer in Houston saw brighter days ahead. He estimated that 60 percent of the flour sold in the state was imported from outside, but that the Texas share was rising quickly.[132]

North Texans, itching to meet that demand, pointed to messages from other parts of the state. Merchants in Crockett, more than 150 miles southeast, were expecting Dallas flour. A Dallas writer bragged, "Even in Jefferson, where navigation would be supposed to keep them well supplied with flour from the Mississippi, our prairie flour is held in high repute. The *Jefferson Gazette* says that much of the flour now sold in that city was raised in this neighborhood and carried there by wagons."[133] A would-be supplier did the math, pointing out that "we can haul cheaper from Dallas one hundred miles than from Houston the same distance, and our flour is much preferred; in some places am assured that they will give fifty cents more for it per hundred for the reason that they do not get fresh flour from the latter place until fall, and then they are liable to be deceived." North Texas flour would be fresher and more reliable, if not cheaper. Texans were hungry for it.[134]

A few North Texans tried to meet the in-state demand by hauling flour by oxcart to other cities. In 1856, the *Dallas Daily Herald* reprinted a notice from the *Austin Times,* two hundred miles to the south, proclaiming the availability of several hundred barrels of "Texas flour, from Dallas and the surrounding counties." The notice declared that the flour had been tried and was "excellent and beautiful" and sold "readily."[135] The sons of the Creager family of Grayson County took flour to San Antonio, three hundred miles to the south, and had to "peddle it out" themselves because there were no wholesale or commission houses to facilitate the sale.[136] As an enterprising teenager, future cattle baron C. C. Slaughter spent three months in 1854 going between East Texas, Dallas, and Collin County, trading flour for lumber and making a profit of $520.[137]

A few motivated millers sent their goods out into the larger world by hauling them to Jefferson. From Jefferson, flour could go down the Red River to the Mississippi River and out through the vast shipping networks of New Orleans. Individuals such as John A. Hust of Tarrant County took ox teams loaded with wheat or flour on the four-week round trip to Marion County, bringing back essentials such as salt, sugar, coffee, tea, rice, cloth, and lumber.[138] Once an entrepreneur arrived back in North Texas, he might save the imported goods for his own family's use or sell them for a profit.[139] But it was slow going: Dallas County resident John Franklin Stark drove ox teams to East Texas several times and estimated the average pace at eighteen miles a day.[140]

Some boosters nonetheless had even higher aspirations. A Houston writer opined that if Texas had flouring mills to compete with St. Louis, the state could supply the West Indies and the southern United States and "still have a million or so barrels to ship to New York and Liverpool."[141] To prove the point, in 1859 the Houston merchants and cotton Factors Ennis and Co. shipped a thousand bushels of Texas wheat to Liverpool "as a new adventure." Presumably they tucked the wheat in alongside one of their regular England-bound shipments of cotton bales.[142] Dallas merchants R. R. Fletcher and Company in 1860 sent wheat (likely by oxcart) to the Texas and Central Railroad terminus in Millican, Brazos County, then to Houston by rail and then by ship to New York. It could be done, but it wasn't easy.[143]

Large-scale mills such as Man-Feild, Trinity, and Dallas found a good customer in the US government, which needed to supply its military posts to the west and the residents of reservations to the north. Requiring thousands of pounds of flour and bread, the government often had to import from locations as far away as New York. Those supplies came through ports on the Gulf Coast and then went by oxcart to the forts. Small wonder that military officials welcomed more local sources of flour that had not survived hard trips at sea and transport over hundreds of miles overland.[144]

In 1856, before the Native Americans were removed to Indian Territory, Preston and Wade Hampton Witt of Dallas County won the contract to supply the two reservations on the upper Brazos River with flour. Their total commitment was for 227,000 pounds, to be delivered in monthly increments.[145] After the relocation of the natives north of the Red River, the Witts' government contracts shifted to supplying the US Army forts. (The native groups relocated from the southeastern United States grew wheat in subsistence amounts for their families, not in quantities large enough to have a surplus.[146]) In February 1859, the Witts dispatched eight wagons, each pulled by twelve oxen, with forty thousand pounds of flour bound for Fort Chadbourne, more than two hundred miles to the west.[147] Through 1859 and 1860, the US government requested proposals to supply the troops at nine military installations across Texas with "merchantable superfine (or extra) Texas Flour, of good and wholesome quality," delivered in "strong durable sacks of twilled cotton, one hundred pounds each." For Fort Cobb, in the Caddo Nation, the flour would total eighteen thousand pounds a year, "of the best merchantable quality, and to be furnished monthly in sacks of 100 pounds each."[148] North Texans did their best to take advantage of the opportunity. Alice West Floyd recalled the work of her father, Robert Jentry West, in the 1850s: "The flour, meat and such other supplies as we produced on our farm were added to the loads and freighted West to supply the government forts with food for soldiers and horses. Father had the contract for supplying Fort Cooper, Belknap, Graham, Phantom and others. Mr. Tom

Chenoweth was employed to be in charge of the supply train on the trips to the forts."[149] Fort Cooper was the farthest away, about 170 miles from the Floyds' farm near Carrollton. But all the forts took many days to reach with slow-moving oxen. At each location, cooks and bakers of varying skill turned the flour into bread of equally fluctuating quality.

For everyone, whether miller, merchant, or buyer, infrastructure remained the problem. Oxcarts were painfully slow, and the Trinity remained unnavigable. Champions of North Texas grain cried out for railroads. If Texans could just get their wheat and flour to New Orleans and then into the Gulf and the Atlantic, North Texas would become a grain "empire."[150] But until the railroad finally arrived in North Texas in 1872, oxcarts would have to suffice.

Texans were sure that their flour could compete with that brought from elsewhere. In 1859 Dallas newspaper editor J. W. Latimer waxed enthusiastic over the prospects in the region. North Texas wheat, he declared, was sweeter, livelier, more flavorful, and "decidedly superior to that brought from the North." Warm spring temperatures ensured "sure and rapid" ripening.[151] Texans aggressively pitted themselves against outside producers. "Dick" wrote in 1858 that North Texans "lack only means of transport to compete with that raised in the famed valley of the Mississippi and this even in their own markets." The flour made by Gold and Donaldson of Dallas, he continued, was "of the very best description equal if not superior to the extra branded St. Louis."[152] An unnamed writer from Houston proclaimed that Texas flour "has also amazingly improved in quality, and we now frequently see bread made of Texas flour quite as white and twice as sweet as the best Plants' Extra, or any other double extra brand that is brought to the State."[153] Texans believed their own press. The *Dallas Daily Herald* trumpeted, "'Dallas Flour' is beginning to be known and appreciated in every section of our State, and wherever used, has invariably, we believe, been preferred to the best Western flour. Our mills can make as good if not better flour than can be had any where in the States."[154]

At last, North Texas millers were given a way to prove the quality of their products. In 1859, the Dallas Agricultural and Mechanical Society began a fair that included competitions for agricultural produce. The Coombes mill took the prize in 1859 for "an excellent article of flour." The following year, Hawpe and Ellis at Pleasant Run won the contest. For that victory, the Dallas newspaper credited not the mill owners but the miller, "one of the most experienced millers in the country. Mr. Spencer has shown that he is thoroughly qualified for the duties of his profession."[155] Coombes and Spencer obviously had what milling historians John Storck and Walter Dorwin Teague described as characteristics of expert millers: "a sensitive thumb and ear and eye" as well as "a canny awareness of the special needs of his mill," a creature "of personality, mood, and temperament."[156] North Texans were producing great flour. All they needed was a means of getting it to the eagerly waiting world.

The ultimate purpose of all this flour, of course, was to bake it. Raw flour is inedible, and people have labored diligently to turn it into something that will sustain life and, incidentally, taste good. For most of human history—and in North Texas during the 1850s—flour has provided sustenance in the form of bread, and sweets have been rare.

Virtually every household in North Texas before the Civil War did its own baking. While San Antonio, Houston, and Austin all boasted numerous professional bakers, North Texas had few. The historical record mentions only three in the region before 1861, two in Dallas and one in McKinney, and we know little more than their names. William Traughber from Kentucky, who owned a saloon in Dallas before his death in 1850, might have offered baked goods to go with the liquor. In 1860, Charles Mastrand, a native of Prussia, was living alone in central Dallas. In McKinney, William Perdew, age fifty-seven, listed his profession as a baker and confectioner (someone who made candy and other sweets).[157]

So baking at home it would be. Most home bakers were women—wives, mothers, daughters. Some enslaved women cooked for their enslavers, and those who had families probably baked for them as well. Alice West Floyd remembered that "Aunt Jane," an enslaved woman, cooked for the Wests in a kitchen separated from their house in Dallas County. Jane or "her helper" carried the food to the house.[158] Across the region, women baked corn and wheat for families, whether their own or someone else's.

As they moved from the East, families may have cooked on open fires, but that practice ceased once they built houses. Virtually all the first houses had fireplaces made of rock, probably native limestone. A good example of early North Texas housing still stands 170 years later in southwest Dallas County. In 1846, twenty-year-old Everard Sharrock Jr. immigrated from Illinois with his parents and siblings as part of the Peters Colony. As an unmarried man, he received 320 acres of land in the hills overlooking Mountain Creek. In 1846 or 1847, Sharrock and eighteen-year-old Sarah Elizabeth Robbins, also a native of Illinois, married. As the headright law allowed, they then received an additional 320 acres. Almost surely with the help of Sharrock family members, Everard and Sarah built a one-room cabin of cedar and winged elm logs, a mere fifteen feet long and fourteen feet wide. They constructed the fireplace and chimney from cream-colored limestone, likely taken from a nearby outcropping. The stone blocks were two to five inches thick, with larger blocks placed at the corners, and the blocks were probably daubed with mud. A hand-hewn mantel stretched across the opening. The

FIGURE 1.1. *Fireplace, Sharrock farmstead.*
("Everard Sharrock Jr. Farmstead," US Department of the Interior)

opening for the fire was four feet wide. Sarah and Everard Sharrock had three children while living in the tiny house. They sold the land and house to Thomas Young in 1853 and moved to California, seeking a new fortune in the gold fields.[159]

Sarah Robbins Sharrock and other colonists baked on the hearths of their fireplaces. Using wood for fuel, they carefully built fires, which presented significant challenges. They and their children had to gather fuel constantly—a difficult task on the grassy prairies—and once laid, the fire had to be carefully tended to continue burning. An experienced cook knew how to "bank" the fire to keep it smoldering through the night, ready to flare come morning. Early Collin County residents recalled borrowing fire from neighbors when they neglected their own and let it go out.[160] Women baked simple cornbreads on the hearth. Many also used the rimmed pot known as a Dutch oven, piling hot coals on the lid to surround the bread with heated air.[161] Made of iron, Dutch ovens were heavy to transport and prone to rust, requiring diligent care, but they were invaluable tools.

The stoves that were becoming common in the East gradually made their way across the prairie. A few stalwarts may have brought their stoves with them from their former homes. Other colonists bought them new. Gold and Donaldson, of Dallas Steam Mills fame, advertised cooking stoves in

1855.[162] By 1856, the Waddell family in McKinney had a "cooking stove," which they also used for heat.[163] With the dissolution of the Réunion colony, disappointed immigrant Michel Delasseaux offered a "very large French patent cooking stove" for sale in 1860.[164] The stove probably came from the communal kitchen of the Fourierist experiment. Baking in a stove oven still required fire, and a cook had to be inventive to estimate the temperature of their oven. By and large, however, oven baking was easier and allowed more refinement than hearth cooking.

In addition to home-grown flour and cornmeal, people could create some of their own baking ingredients from animals they brought with them to Texas or acquired once they arrived. They kept chickens, which were easy to care for, although eggs had to be gathered daily and supplies varied with the season. Hogs, which provided lard, were also simple to house and feed but challenging to slaughter and butcher. Some people in cities as well as rural areas kept cows, which ate a lot and required constant care. Their milk supply, being dependent on their reproductive cycle, was uneven. But from the cream women made butter, usually with dasher churns. At the 1859 Dallas Fair, Mrs. Ben Hunter received the premium of $2 for "10 pounds butter, packed," as well as $1 for "5 pounds butter, fresh."[165] Packed butter, preserved in brine, was said to stay good for a year.[166] By 1860, Dallas merchants sought to buy ingredients from farm people, asking for flour, butter, eggs, and pecans "taken in exchange for goods, at cash prices."[167]

For leavening, bakers almost surely used homemade yeast caught wild from the air or made from potatoes, and some used starters they had brought with them when they moved to Texas. Mariah Young Buchanan carried her starter from Virginia to Farmers Branch, Texas, in 1857. According to family history, Buchanan "had prepared a large stone jar with the sour dough starter and after each 'cooking' it was replenished with corn meal, flour, hops and water. The crock was set so the sun's heat could ferment the dough as they drove along."[168] Buchanan knew her starter well enough to keep it alive across a thousand miles.

Colonizers also turned to the bounty around them to provide ingredients for baking. The skill of an enslaved man, Levi, brought honey into the lives of the West family in Dallas County. The Wests came from Tennessee in 1845, bringing "their slaves" with them. Alice West Floyd recalled, "Wild bees gave us a start of bee hives. The negro man my father owned, Levi, put out syrup to bait the bees, then followed them to their hives. Enough bees were taken to make a good start besides giving us plenty of honey." Levi had the knowledge of bees required to find a hive, relocate it, and make it thrive as well as the courage to engage wild bees.[169] The people who enslaved him benefited hugely from his intelligence and determination.

The Wests and the people who worked in their fields planted sorghum cane in addition to wheat, corn, barley, oats, and millet.[170] Sorghum cane (unrelated to grain sorghum) quickly became one of the most popular sweeteners in Texas and across the South in the 1850s. Syrup making became a ritual each fall, with the squeezing of the cane and the cooking of the syrup.

Humans in North Texas have long enjoyed wild blackberries and their smaller cousins, dewberries, braving their thorns to pick the ripe fruit. Soon after their arrival, Texas colonizers began making cobblers, or deep-dish pies, from them. Colonizers brought with them peach and plum trees, whose fruit could be eaten out of hand, cooked while fresh, or dried for future use.[171]

Imported supplies for baking were limited; for instance, the only spices advertised even in big-city Dallas were ginger and nutmeg. By 1858 merchants W. W. Peak and Brother announced the availability of sugar, molasses, crackers, almonds, peanuts, and English walnuts.[172] Dallas miller-turned-grocer George Baird bragged about his "Whybrow's celebrated pie fruits" imported from England: pineapple, peaches, quinces, cherries, plums, "et cetera": "These fruits put up in air tight cans, hermetically sealed, and are as fresh as when first taken from the trees."[173] Canned pie fruits brought sweetness and a taste of the tropics to those Dallasites who could afford them. And surely North Texans made pies from local peaches, blackberries, and dewberries.

The Réunion settlers, accustomed to nice things, brought baking supplies with them from New Orleans. One shopping list from 1855 included twenty barrels of biscuit (probably the tough, long-lasting bread sometimes known as hardtack), some sweet and some unsweetened; 100 pounds of lard; 100 pounds of salt; 68 pounds of white sugar; and 137 pounds of brown sugar, all hauled overland from Houston. Presumably the colonists planned to buy wheat flour locally.[174] Their hopes for good food were dashed as much as their hopes for prosperity in North Texas.

For most early Anglo Texans, anything made from wheat was a luxury. Josiah Pancoast, a farmer in the Peters Colony, wrote to his sister in New Jersey in 1847: "Nor have I tasted a piece of wheat bread since I left home." He was optimistic, however: "Next year we shall have plenty of wheat."[175]

The most common use for wheat flour was in making biscuits, small round cakes served hot in individual portions. Biscuits might have several ingredients, but the most common were flour, lard, and some kind of chemical leavening, most likely baking soda (sodium bicarbonate) at this time. Whether rolled and cut or dropped from a spoon, biscuits were the wheat bread that North Texans ate most often. As we have seen, the Sachse family ground their wheat in a coffee mill and enjoyed "brown biscuits" laden with bran.[176] Beverly Leonidas Rogers took his family's wheat crop to the mill fourteen miles away and made it home with freshly ground flour in time for supper. In celebration, his mother violated her "long-kept custom of biscuit for Sunday breakfast only."[177] The Rogers family normally ate cornbread at every meal except the morning of the Sabbath, but on that particular weekday Nancy Brooks Rogers honored the new supply of flour with biscuits.

Making bread leavened with yeast was tricky, particularly before standardized commercial products became available. While many bakers most likely made rolls, in individual portions, others made yeasted loaf bread, which required several hours to rise, took lots of fuel to bake, and became stale quickly once cut. By 1860, the writers of the *Dallas Herald* were crowing about the bread displayed at the Dallas Fair. Wheat was abundant, and the writer extolled the "luxury" of "rich white bread."[178] In 1860, the second year of the fair, Mrs. H. Hunter took home the premium for "light bread," while Mary Elizabeth Hawpe—an unmarried twenty-four-year-old native of Tennessee who lived with the family of her brother, the wealthy miller at Pleasant Run—received a certificate for hers.[179]

Among the scarce treats in the early days of colonization was pound cake, a simple mix of flour, sugar, eggs, and butter. William H. "Billie" Beeman, who came to the Dallas area in 1842, remembered, "For the first few years, before we began to raise wheat, flour was a luxury but few could afford. Judge John Thomas, the first judge Dallas County had, was about the only man in the county who could afford to have flour and sugar. I went to a wedding at his house once and they had pound-cake." John Thomas, with his wife Elizabeth Massengill Thomas, hosted the wedding guests overnight in their home north of Dallas. Several people were disappointed when "old man Wilburn" gobbled up all the leftover cake the next morning.[180]

By 1860, the food situation had eased a bit for town people, but sweets remained scarce. At the Dallas Fair in 1860, pound cake was the only dessert in the baking competition, and Mrs. H. Hunter, already honored for her bread, also took the prize for that.[181]

Over a twenty-year span, colonists and enslaved people from the United States and France figured out how to make lives on the western edge of the United States: how to break the prairie sod, how to make wheat flourish, how to build mills and travel to them, and how to create food from limited supplies of flour and other ingredients. But as they spread American ways in North Texas the nation was breaking apart, and North Texans would find themselves on opposing sides of the conflict. After Texas seceded from the Union, wheat and flour would play an important part in the coming conflagration.

2 / "THE GRANARY OF THE CONFEDERATE STATES": CIVIL WAR, 1861–1865

NORTH TEXAS WAS A BLOODY AND VIOLENT PLACE before and during the Civil War, largely because the colonists came from both the Upper South and the Lower South and held sharply diverging attitudes toward enslavement and secession. The counties in North Texas split in their enthusiasm for secession, with Dallas, Denton, and Tarrant firmly supporting the Confederacy and Collin, Cooke, and Grayson voting to remain in the Union.[1] Neighbor truly was pitted against neighbor as the nation divided.

Crop selection both reflected and helped to create the split in the population. While they also raised cotton and ran cattle, the residents of this region grew more wheat than anyone else in the rest of Texas. And wheat required significant labor only at harvest, unlike the crops of the Lower South and Texas—cotton, tobacco, sugar, and rice—which needed tending all through the growing season. Not surprisingly then, the free residents of the Red River counties enslaved fewer than five thousand people in 1860. While this number was not insignificant, and the percentages had certainly increased in the 1850s, it was only a fraction of the number of enslaved people in the plantation country to the south. Hence, although few North Texans publicly supported the abolition of slavery, they had much less reason to fight to maintain it than did people enmeshed in the cotton economy.[2] Furthermore, as historian Dale Baum argues, the US government provided lucrative markets for North Texas wheat farmers, who supplied the military forts to the west and the reservations in Indian Territory to the north. Many wheat-growing North Texans wanted to maintain their status in the Union and keep up the flow of flour to American facilities. Many also felt uneasy about the Native Americans, and they feared the consequences if the Union abandoned their defenses to the west.[3]

Tensions ran high. In the brutally hot summer of 1860, fires erupted across the region during the so-called Texas Troubles. Half the buildings in downtown Dallas and most of downtown Denton disappeared in flames. Although objective evidence pointed to the heat and flammable materials as the causes, southern sympathizers blamed the fires on Unionists and abolitionists, and they hanged more than thirty people, black and white, and possibly as many as a hundred. Whatever their political leanings, farmers, millers, and sellers of wheat all suffered from the fires. Crill Miller, whose farm was in south Dallas County, lost his "wheat stacks and cribs." One can easily imagine the dry grain going up in flames under the hot, parched, windy conditions.[4]

Two flour mills burned that miserable July, one in Tarrant County and one in Collin County. Missourian Archibald F. Leonard had dammed the West Fork of the Trinity River east of Fort Worth in 1856 and built a three-story mill, powered by a water turbine. In 1860, the mill served as a public polling place. When it burned in 1860, locals claimed, without evidence, that abolitionists had torched it.[5]

In Millwood, on the East Fork of the Trinity River in southeastern Collin County, the Foote Mill had a fine steam engine and was valued at $10,000. It also burned in July 1860, and locals again assumed it was arson on the part of local abolitionists.[6] Martin Luther Foote, son of mill owner John Wesley Foote, later put forth a more plausible explanation: a local citizen named Walter Cooley had started but not finished building a windmill, and "he and another man, by the name of Hull, burned the mill, as they left the country." As mentioned above, enterprising folks salvaged the boiler and the engine, moving them to a mill southeast of McKinney.[7]

Mills continued to serve as community centers, and partisans on both sides of the divide claimed their spaces. An alleged meeting of Unionists was held at "Lattimer's and Richie's steam mill" in Gainesville during the trials that resulted in the lynching of forty-one American sympathizers in October 1862.[8] The Gainesville violence touched the milling community. Henry Cockrum, a thirty-one-year-old miller born in Missouri, was hanged for his Union loyalties.[9] His important role as a miller did not save Cockrum.

The prospect of war emboldened some millers. Even after Texas seceded from the United States in February 1861, North Texans enthusiastically continued investing in mills. In southern Dallas County, a new steam mill at Pleasant Run opened in early 1861, "prepared to grind wheat and corn in any quantity and at short notice." Madison Moultrie Miller, a wealthy merchant and founder of the community of Pleasant Run, bought the powerful mill equipment at Waterton, New York. Trevezant Hawpe, one of the wealthiest men in Dallas County, and D. Y. Ellis purchased the business after Miller died. The mill could process four hundred bushels of wheat in twenty-four hours, and the proprietors promised to grind promptly for customers from distances far away while they waited.[10] The miller, the Mr. Spencer whose prize-winning abilities we discussed previously, was "one of the most experienced millers in the country."[11] In 1862, John E. Wheeler sold his mill in Gainesville to James O. A. Whaley for $2,500—whether in Confederate or US dollars is unclear. Wheeler had broken his hip and most likely could no longer continue the physical work of milling.[12] But the business of his mill went on, and it grew into the largest milling business in Cooke County under the Whaley family's ownership.

Marketing flour to the domestic market continued too, at least for a while, and never at the volumes East Texans wanted. Three weeks after war broke out in South Carolina, Houston merchants were anticipating the arrival of the first flour of the new crop from Dallas County.[13] With the onset of the harvest in late May, Dallas merchants eagerly offered "new spring and summer goods" in return for wheat.[14] The Union navy began blockading the Gulf Coast in July 1861, and savvy Texans realized that there would be money to be made as a result. H. D. Taylor from Houston wrote in July 1861 that "the demand for flour in the lower country will no doubt be large," and a correspondent from San Felipe in Austin County commented that "large amounts of Northern Texas Flour may be sold in [this] section, if the farmers and millers of this region will send it there." The farmers of the lower Brazos and Colorado "raise no wheat and cannot get barreled flour in consequence of the blockade." A Dallas respondent concluded, "We are confident that we will have to furnish all Southern Texas with breadstuffs for some time to come."[15]

Gradually, however, the realities of war began to creep into North Texas as 1861 rolled by. The Confederate military needed flour to feed its troops. Farmers, knowing that they could soon be absent fighting for the Confederacy—or, for some, the Union—planted large crops of wheat in October while they could still "stay at home and make bread for the soldiers."[16] They also increased their plantings of oats and corn, and they cut back on the size of their cotton crops.

Several thousand North Texas men served in the Confederate army, perhaps 15 percent of the total free male population, and many of them battled in cavalry units in the western theater. Mill owner Trezevant Hawpe raised the 31st Texas Cavalry Regiment in 1862. He served only briefly, but the regiment fought throughout the war without him.[17]

Some general accounts say that during the war women did more of the physical work than in peacetime, participating in tilling as well as shocking

FIGURE 2.1. *Catherine Bunting Coit. (Courtesy of Angela Fabry)*

the ripe grain.[18] At least some of the more elite women of the region stepped into roles typically considered male. Catherine Bunting Coit's husband, John Coit, left her with their three young children and seven enslaved people on their farm north of Dallas to serve in the Confederate army. Although Catherine Coit never worked in the fields, she took over the sales of wheat and corn produced by the enslaved people. In August 1864, she wrote to her husband, "You hate to think of my having anything to do with such matters, but—but—but I think—I think—you ought to be a little proud that your wife can attend to your affairs in your absence. Every lady has to do the same now whose husband is in the army, at least a great majority do." Catherine Coit, who had been valedictorian of Harmony Female College in North Carolina, felt good about her management skills.[19] Other women, however, may not have reacted positively to their increased responsibilities.

The number of enslaved people in the region doubled during the war, as the people who enslaved them had forced them to come to Texas to prevent their liberation.[20] Local farmers hired them as farm laborers, either in return for food and clothing or by paying their wages to their enslavers. A Captain Waller reported in the spring of 1863 that those enslavers "having negroes to hire can get good wages for them in the wheat region."[21] With the extra labor, farms increased their yields of wheat, corn, and oats.[22] Working in the wheat fields must have seemed strange to the enslaved people from the east, since they were used to growing cotton and sugar cane. And one wonders if they knew that their work was feeding the army fighting to keep them enslaved. It is unlikely that they tasted much of the fruits of their labors, if any at all. Across the South, enslaved people got flour only when their enslavers gave it to them as a gift.[23] It remained the food of the privileged.

With hungry soldiers and civilians alike needing food, the Confederate government considered mills essential for the war effort. Rather than expecting or allowing women to run the mills, the Confederacy excused men from combat duty to do so. In Collin County, Walter Yeary was operating a treadmill. When the war began, he closed it and enlisted in the Confederate army, "but he was soon sent back home to re-open the mill."[24] His work was judged so important that his military service record noted that he was "detailed as a miller."[25] Similarly, Fort Worth miller David Mauck "entered the service as a cavalryman but was soon detailed to run the mill to make flour for the people and the soldiers," according to his widow's pension application.[26] In 1863, the Confederate Conscript Service offered to furlough draftees to work as teamsters to haul flour from "the mills" (at unspecified locations) to Dallas for storage.[27] The Confederacy allowed soldiers and "conscrips" to work in the mills throughout the war and in November 1864 demanded an accounting from all mill owners of the men in their employ.[28] Making flour was an important part of making war, and the Confederate government looked to North Texas to help.

The Confederate government was a needy, if soon impoverished, buyer for wheat. The 1861 crop, harvested in the earliest months of the war, was abundant, and in November, Jones C. Easton of McKinney queried the Confederate government about selling or donating "the vast amount of flour, grain, &c, that is now in the hands of our planters." The Confederate secretary of the treasury, Christopher G. Memminger, replied affirmatively, explaining that farmers could take "corn, wheat, flour, etc., near as convenient to army depots."[29]

Boosters were well aware of the importance of North Texas to the war effort. In October 1861, a writer to the *Dallas Herald* suggested that the

Confederacy create a military depot in Dallas, noting that "Dallas county is furnishing flour, under heavy contracts, to the contractors and subcontractors, at San Antonio, for the use of the army."[30] The Confederacy established the headquarters of the quartermaster-general of the Trans-Mississippi Army of the Confederacy in Dallas to collect food and supplies for the soldiers.[31] Julien Feild, owner of the largest mill in Tarrant County, was commissioned into the quartermaster's department and "instructed to stay at his mill, grind wheat, load his freighters with flour, and keep them moving to Shreveport and Jefferson."[32] Merchants from San Antonio sent agents to buy flour that they in turn sold to Confederate installations on the Texas seacoast and its southwestern forts.[33]

Because flour was so precious, it had to be guarded. An 1861 Dallas writer demanded army presence for the "safety and protection of our grain growing section," as "the wheat region is the granary not of Texas only, but of other portions of the C.S. [Confederate States]."[34] That work became some men's wartime service. On the order of a "Col. Magruder," John Benedict Yeary, the son of miller Walter Raleigh Yeary, spent two years of the war protecting his family's mill at Farmersville in Collin County rather than deploying into the Confederate army.[35] Mills were always prone to fire, and what might have been ordinary conflagrations once again came under suspicion of being sinister activities. In March 1863, when the large mill at Cedar Springs burned, $25,000 worth of wheat and flour that belonged to the Confederate government as well as to individuals was lost.[36] Four months later, the new Hawpe and Miller mill at Honey Springs also burned, and the *Dallas Herald* opined that "there is hardly a doubt but the fire was the work of an incendiary." The paper observed, "This is the second case of mill burning in this county during the present season, and the mills burnt were both of them superior mills, and capable of doing a large business. Is it not a warning to our citizens to be on the look out for suspicious persons, and particularly ought the mill owners to have constant and watchful guards at all hours of the night around their mills."[37] Even with guards, mills might not always have been safe.

Difficulties notwithstanding, milling continued at a healthy pace throughout the war. Archibald Leonard rebuilt his burned mill east of Fort Worth in 1862, and it operated throughout the war.[38] John S. Ballard built the Terry Mills, or City Mills, in Dallas sometime after 1860 and sold it to Methodist minister and former Dallas mayor Thomas Emory Sherwood in 1863. Local millers charged rates for their flour somewhat above peacetime prices. Despite the owner being a minister, in January 1863, "Sherwood & Co." advertised that they would "grind Wheat for the sixth bushel and Corn for the fifth"—an expensive 16 percent toll.[39] Similarly, in April 1863 (three months before it burned), the Hawpe and Miller's Mill, which bragged that it was "now in first rate running order and capable of grinding six hundred bushels of wheat in 24 hours," also charged a 16 percent toll.[40]

In April 1863, a "bread riot" broke out in the Confederate capital of Richmond, Virginia, with desperate women assailing grocers for flour and meal. At the same time, North Texans advertised having plenty: "We now have on hand a large amount of flour for sale and will purchase Wheat at the market price, delivered at our mill, at all times," boasted Hawpe and Miller of Dallas County.[41] Catherine Bunting Coit wrote to her husband in August 1863 that their wheat promised to yield between five and six hundred bushels. The family also had corn, barley, "12 acres of good cotton," sweet potatoes, and peas. "So you see there is no danger whatever of our suffering," she assured him.[42] Coit, of course, had enslaved people to grow her crops, and we do not know if that abundance was extended to the enslaved. Labor shortages curtailed the flour supplies of other families. Kate Jones James, whose family lived in north Dallas County, remembered, "In the absence of men, there was no one left to sow wheat, and for some time we had to live on corn bread." Even at that time, however, wheat bread was not completely unknown. James recalled, "Most every family hoarded some flour to use in case of sickness, and generally enough to make biscuits every Sunday for breakfast." So even North Texans who didn't enslave others still had some flour.[43]

At the same time, flour was dear in other parts of Texas. Houston businessmen in particular, unable to import flour from the Midwest, tried to get North Texans to part with their wheat and flour. In September 1863, Thomas M. Bagby visited Dallas, looking for wheat or flour to purchase for use in Houston and Galveston. He represented a "supply association" established "to supply, first, the families of soldiers, then the poor, and lastly the members of the Association with bread stuffs at a reasonable price." Surely, faced with such noble aims, Dallasites would relent.[44] Throughout 1863 and 1864, Houston buyers continued to beg for flour even as rumors spread of speculators.[45] North Texans were not particularly sympathetic. An anonymous Dallas writer in August 1863 observed that the *Houston Telegraph* was complaining "lustily of the scarcity and high price of flour in that market" and wondering "whether there is any wheat in Northern Texas to spare." The writer commented snidely, "Well, we are not sure as to the exact quantity, but think there is plenty; at least we hear no complaint here."[46] The residents of the Red River counties would feed themselves and the Confederate soldiers before they would supply the unfortunate Texans of the Gulf Coast.

From the beginning of the war, the wheat and flour market was intertwined with the Confederate government. On the one hand, millers at first welcomed the Confederate economy. The Dallas Steam Mills noted in November 1861 that they would accept Confederate bonds and treasury notes in payment for flour.[47] By the middle of the war, however, grain was proving more stable than Confederate money. In Dallas in 1863, physicians began tying their fees to the price of wheat, demanding grain or its equivalent in money for their services.[48] The golden sheaves had more tangible value than shaky Confederate dollars.

With wheat in such high demand, both the state and national governments tried to regulate the market. The Confederate government moved quickly to counter price gouging on wheat and flour. In June 1861, wheat was 60 cents a bushel. By the summer of 1862, prices had risen dramatically. On August 2, John G. Good, the Confederate provost marshal, issued a general order setting the price of wheat at $2 per bushel and flour at $6.50 per 100 pounds.[49] In September 1863, presumably to avoid speculation, the State of Texas set the prices for grain and flour: "Wheat, prime, white or red," and flour graded good or superfine.[50] Even in abundant North Texas, values rose, though not as much as in other regions of the South. Catherine Coit wrote to her husband in April 1864 that wheat had gone from $5 to $18 a bushel and that flour in Collin County, likely from local farms, was selling for an outrageous $2 a pound. The increases might have been due to the devaluation of the Confederate dollar, but there might have been shortages as well.[51]

Deprivation in other parts of Texas finally touched North Texans. John Henry Skiles of Dallas was appointed to the Confederate quartermaster's office "to run a train of ox wagons to haul provisions for the Confederate Government to Arkansas posts," according to his son, Eugene Rumsey Skiles. The younger Skiles recalled that the trains consisted of eight to ten wagons, each pulled by sixteen yoke of oxen, with "Negro drivers." As we have seen, driving oxen took skill, and these drivers, likely enslaved, had the talent to manage the heavy wagons and enormous teams of oxen. Skiles recounted that "somewhere between Calvert and Dallas"—possibly Waco, and probably in September 1864—"he was attacked by forty women armed with guns demanding him to turn over to them one wagon load of flour and meal. It seemed that they were the wives of Confederate soldiers in the war. They thought it was time the Government was turning over something to them. My father said he made them a polite speech, telling them he had nothing to fight with but ox whips. So he just cut loose the team from one wagon except the wheel oxen and pulled to the nearest house and unloaded the same." Needy women had taken up arms to provide for their families, and Skiles did not resist.[52] The Central Texas confrontation is less well known than others in Richmond, Mobile, and elsewhere, but those women held the Confederate government responsible for their well-being just as much as their eastern sisters did.

Wheat and flour continued to be a source of concern in the waning days of the war and its immediate aftermath, both locally and nationally. Four days after the South's surrender, the *Dallas Herald* published a statement from Confederate President Jefferson Davis decrying the sale of flour for $700 a barrel and proposing a credit structure for the government.[53] Local citizens feared the chaos that ensued at war's end. In May 1865, a month after the surrender, Catherine Coit wrote that she needed to send wheat to the mill for grinding, but "no one is venturing out on the roads now on account of the robbing and murdering by returning soldiers and officers." Coit probably was not exaggerating. Confederate physician J. H. P. Baker described the situation around Dallas as "wholesale robbery" as he witnessed the large-scale theft of flour and wheat as well as sugar, corn, bacon, and salt by marauding former troops.[54] But Texans also feared the government. Coit had a wagon of wheat "ready to start" to the mill at Cedar Springs but heard a rumor that the Confederate government was pressing wagons into service so that "the government" could get flour and grain to Dallas "before the army arrives."[55] There was no government, and no army came, but the people of North Texas did not know that six weeks after the surrender in Virginia.

Amid local violence and national turmoil, wheat and flour remained a constant for North Texans throughout the Civil War. Millers built new facilities and repaired damaged ones.[56] Ox wagons laden with flour continued their laborious journeys.[57] By the end of the war, wheat and flour were still available, even at prices inflated by flimsy Confederate currency.[58]

The response to the end of the war was muted in North Texas. Surely some residents felt joy as they anticipated the return of their soldiers. African Americans celebrated their freedom even as they wondered what that meant for them and their loved ones. What did those nine thousand people left in North Texas think, now that they were free but only barely?

North Texas, spared the physical damage of war, was primed for a boom. And boom it did.

3 / FROM PRAIRIE TO PRODUCTION: GROWING, 1865–1900

IN AUGUST 1872, COLLIN COUNTY FARMER ROBERT Horn borrowed oxen from a neighbor. He recalled, "I began to break prairie with three yokes, but soon had to stop on account of the heat. The new ground was heavy and the roots were so thick and close-matted that it was hard pulling."[1] A year and a half later, he "broke prairie all day." After fixing a problem with his plow, he wrote, "I could then feel the gang take hold and sink deeper into the ground, snapping the grass roots with a popping musical noise."[2]

In North Texas after the Civil War, many people agreed with Horn that the expanses of prairie grass should become arable fields, and the people set about making them so. The North Texas prairies enticed settlers more than ever. With the thick clay Blackland Prairie in the east and sandier soils in the west, the flat savannahs and undulating hills of the region proved an alluring landscape for determined types who could scarcely wait to turn grassland into farmland. And those farms, they believed, should include wheat.

Boosters extolled the agricultural benefits of North Texas. The Texas Bureau of Immigration, a short-lived state agency, declared in 1875, "Should the immigrant . . . wish to raise cotton, wheat, corn and stock, let him settle in *upper* Central Texas."[3] They were eager to let would-be Texans know that the staple crops of the South and Midwest both thrived in North Texas. One agronomist advertised the fertility of the soil: "On much of the waxy lime lands of Texas . . . direct fertilization of wheat is unnecessary," especially if farmers rotated their crops.[4] And those new farms would be mechanized. Methodist minister/promoter Homer Thrall observed in 1879, "The entire prairie east of the upper cross timber is a beautiful and very gently rolling country, scarcely broken by rocks, stumps, gullies, or anything else which could impede or interfere with the progress of gang-plows, reapers and mowers, or any other agricultural labor-saving machinery, whether propelled by steam or other power. Indeed, the cultivation of wheat has for years been done by the use of such implements, propelled by horse or ox-power."[5] Clearly North Texas was suited for growing wheat.

People took these promoters at their words and moved to North Texas. Between 1860 and 1900, the population of the six counties grew more than sevenfold, from about 41,000 people to 305,000. Dallas County alone went from 8,600 people to 83,000 in those four decades.

More people wanted land than could buy it, and by 1900 in the counties to the east—Grayson, Collin, and Dallas—the number of tenant farmers and sharecroppers outnumbered the landowners by a ratio of about three-to-two. They almost surely farmed cotton. The system upon which sharecropping rested—dividing the cotton and corn crops into "shares"—mitigated against raising wheat. A large majority of North Texas farmers were white. African American farmers in the six counties before 1900 could be counted in the hundreds, not the thousands, and the number of those who owned land—and therefore would have been free to raise wheat—never reached more than a hundred in any one county.

Most of the African Americans who migrated to the region lived in the towns and cities. By 1900, two-thirds of the African Americans in Dallas County lived in the city of Dallas, and 72 percent of those in Tarrant County lived in Fort Worth. In Grayson County, 56 percent of the African Americans lived in either Sherman, the county seat, or Denison, a new railroad town. In Collin, Cooke, and Denton Counties, African Americans were less than 7 percent of the total population. The presence of approximately two thousand African Americans in each county was hardly insignificant, but they were greatly outnumbered by their white neighbors.[6]

Despite the relatively small African American population of North Texas, the racial violence endemic to the Reconstruction South erupted there in its full ugliness. Rural circumstances affected attitudes and aggression. In June 1898, tempers flared because of damage to the wheat crop. A Dallas reporter wrote, "Excessive rain has about ruined the biggest wheat crop that Texas has known for ten years. For two weeks past every day and night the clouds have poured down their water upon the entire yield as it stood shocked in the field. It is now dwelling and sprouting, which, of course, renders it worthless for milling purposes, but possibly it may do to feed hogs."[7] As a result of the rain, "30 or 40 strange negroes . . . congregated" in Plano, "compelled to loaf around town, owing to so much rain lately that they could not obtain work in the country." In response to the presence of these unknown African Americans, racial terrorists known as "whitecappers . . . visited nearly every [African American] cabin in town, giving the inmates from four to ten days to leave." Jake and Laura Cebron lived on Main Street in Plano, and when the whitecappers knocked at their door, Jake met them with a rifle in his hand. The whitecappers fired numerous shots into the house, killing Laura and her unborn baby.[8] Although two men were charged with murder, the terrorism continued across the region through the summer of 1898. The Brenham newspaper reported, "Negroes are leaving Pilot Point in response to warnings issued by white-cap organizations in Denton County."[9] As we have seen, North Texas had been the scene of racial violence in the past. Continued immigration from the east would not ease those tensions.

Between 1865 and 1880, the majority of white immigrants to North Texas were still from the Upper South, with almost half of them originating in Missouri, Tennessee, or Arkansas.[10] Land agent Isaac R. Worrall wrote in 1867 of immigrants "pouring in by every thoroughfare and every crossing on Red river." He praised the new arrivals as "a good class of people, sturdy farmers from Missouri, Tennessee, and Kentucky" who brought "muscle, intelligence, enterprise, energy, and agricultural skill."[11] The Wells brothers, William Henry and James, for example, came in 1874 from Virginia, crossing Indian Territory as they made their way to Collin County, where they bought 120 acres of rich Blackland Prairie in the Plano area for $8 an acre.[12]

Other newcomers migrated from other parts of Texas. The *Dallas Weekly Herald* observed in December 1866, "Continually—hourly—we see trains of emigrants coming into our town, some bound further west, some who have Dallas for their destination, some looking for a location for a new home. They come from all the older Southern and Northwestern states, but some of them we notice are from the cotton portions of our own state, seeking the fertile prairies where they can get wheat lands. Those from eastern Texas generally settle in this vicinity."[13] The *Weekly Herald* writers believed that immigrants found wheat growing more desirable than cotton and were moving to where the grain would flourish. The ability to mechanize appealed to new arrivals too. District Judge R. L. Waddill of McKinney wrote to a friend shortly after the Civil War, "Many citizens in Southern Texas are selling out and coming to Collin to educate their children and raise wheat with machinery applied to husbandry."[14]

Immigrants from Germany and their children, many of whom had been born in the midwestern United States, moved to Cooke and Denton Counties in the late nineteenth century. The settlers of Blue Mound, who began arriving in 1876, were Methodists from Saxony.[15] In Round Grove, newcomers in the 1890s came from Prussia and belonged to a religious group known as the German Evangelical Synod. The entrepreneurial Flusche brothers, Joseph, August, and Emil, established the towns of Lindsay and Muenster in Cooke County and then moved south to Pilot Point to build a Catholic church and bring German residents to that thriving area.[16] As they created their communities anew or joined established neighbors, the Germans brought expertise in wheat farming, both from Europe and from states to the north.

No matter where it originated, the trip to North Texas remained difficult for travelers. Robert Jamison recalled the stories that his grandmother, Martha Ray Lowery, told about the family's move from Alabama to Cooke County in the late 1870s. Her husband, Jeremiah Lowery, received a land grant from Texas Governor Richard B. Hubbard. Lowery told her grandchildren that "they would come to lots of places where there wasn't even a trail, much less a road. They had to ford the rivers. They would take the wagon to the river and drive the oxen across the water. They would take long ropes, tie them to the wagons and the men would get on horses and hold the ropes to keep the wagons from washing down the river. The oxen would pull them across from the other side. It took them about two to three months to come from Alabama to Texas."[17] Hermann Barthold, one of the founders of Blue Mound, immigrated from Saxony to Illinois. He ventured alone to Texas, then returned to Illinois to bring his wife, Maria Sippel Barthold, and their six children. The young family stayed in Dallas for a year, then set off across the prairie in 1878. They cut their way "through briar and underbrush to reach Hickory Creek," taking five days to make the fifty-mile trip to their 280 acres just northwest of Denton. They lived in a tent for two years until they could bring wood from Sherman, fifty miles away, to build a house.[18]

But the new Texans came despite the arduous travel, and across North Texas, prairie became wheatlands. So closely identified with the golden shocks were North Texans that the citizens of Sprowls' Corner in Dallas County changed the community's name to Wheatland in 1885.[19]

After the Civil War, all the land in North Texas was held in private hands, with no public land remaining. Nonetheless, people with money could acquire large tracts. In 1867, a writer for the *Texas Almanac* commented that "land is cheap, and can be obtained in quantities to suit almost any means. The farms are usually made upon tracts of from 640 to 1280 acres, from 50 to 100 acres of which are under cultivation, the rest lying idle, or serving as public pasture."[20] Sometimes buyers engrossed large areas of land, then sold it in smaller parcels. In the 1870s, attorney and rancher Jonathan "Jot" Gunter held vast amounts of land in Cooke and Grayson Counties, which he sold to individuals. In anticipation of the arrival of the Missouri-Kansas-Texas Railroad, Gunter's partner, William Benjamin Munson, bought much of the property that became the community of Denison. In the Sivells Bend area of Cooke County, four miles south of the Red River, brothers William and Addison Yancey bought about seven thousand acres in 1869 for the express purpose of wheat agriculture.[21]

Even though the tough grass that covered the prairie still challenged new landowners, the native prairies across North Texas fell before the plows pulled by oxen. The number of farms grew, and the number of acres that had been "improved," or prepared for agriculture, rose dramatically: from 51,728 to 377,591 in Collin County, for example, between 1870 and 1900.

Farmers chose whether they would plant wheat or cotton on their acreage. Cotton dominated in many areas, but wheat maintained a strong showing. Farmers continued to delight in the fact that they could raise wheat over the winter and follow it with a crop of corn or cotton in adjacent fields.[22] The gold of ripening wheat and the new green of young cotton and corn made a striking patchwork on the prairie landscape. In a recruiting pamphlet from 1891, German entrepreneur Emil Flusche trumpeted the benefits of Denton County: "Among the special advantages which this northeastern part of Texas has to offer can be mentioned its favorable location which makes it possible the advantageous cultivation of the products of the North as well as those of the South. . . . Another advantage is that two crops can be reaped from the same field in the same year. Thus, for example, after wheat or oats, still cotton, millet, potatoes, etc."[23] Ben Bowman from Collin County bragged to a friend in Tennessee: "Here we can raise as fine a wheat as is raised in the USA. . . . Here we can raise one bail [*sic*] of cotton per acre."[24] Charles Moore grew cotton and wheat on his Collin County property for more than twenty years. In 1873 he wrote, "My sister[']s boys work with me on my farm. They get the cotton and I get the wheat."[25] In September 1890, he commented that his helper, John Drury, planted wheat in the morning and picked cotton in the afternoon.[26] Occasionally, the needs of the crops conflicted. Robert Horn, who raised only grain on his Collin County farm, observed: "One time a neighbor of mine, a large cotton planter, was in the weeds, but could get no help, as wheat harvest was on in full swing."[27] Weeding and thinning the cotton would just have to wait.

By the end of the Civil War, farmers were growing a variety of winter wheat—some soft, suitable for tender treats such as cake, and some hard, with more protein, better for baking sturdy bread. Varieties included Early May, California, and old standby Red May. A writer for the *Texas Almanac* "believed" that Early May, which ripened early, was the favorite. The writer also thought that "many farmers" sowed two or three varieties of wheat to stagger ripening, but some, he sighed, planted the same kind year after year, showing little regard for innovation.[28] When the very popular Mediterranean strain made its way into Texas in the 1870s, it became one of the most widely planted varieties.[29]

Adventurous seed salespeople began importing multiple varieties, often without specifying the strain but noting only its origins in the North.[30] The Holloway Seed Company in Dallas, for example, offered Fultz, Improved Little May, and Beardless Nicaragua in 1899. A soft red winter wheat, Fultz came from Pennsylvania after the Civil War.[31] Wheat from cooler climates did not always thrive in North Texas, but botanists were willing to give the new strains a try.

Because the quality of North Texas wheat mattered, farmers continued to search for the best varieties. In 1877, a group of millers and grain dealers combined to offer substantial prizes for superior wheat. At the Agricultural Fair of North Texas, held in Dallas in October, the prizes included $40 and $20 for the first- and second-place "red wheat" and identical amounts for "white wheat."[32] (The color distinctions referred to the bran, but the varieties also had different characteristics. Red wheat has more protein and a nuttier taste than white owing to the greater presence of tannins.) In 1899, Collin County farmer Francis Emerson "secured some new wheat from Illinois with the view of testing a very important matter to the wheat raisers of north Texas."[33]

North Texas wheat caught the attention of early agricultural scientists. The State of Texas created the Texas Agricultural Experiment Service in 1887, and in 1893 the service established a temporary station at McKinney.[34] Scientists sought to discover varieties of wheat that would thrive on the Blackland Prairie and fertilizers that would improve yields. They planted 215 varieties of wheat and found 57 that did better than the widely used Mediterranean, most notably Missouri Blue Stem and Scott. They did not, however, discover any fertilizer that helped.[35] The soil was sufficiently fruitful by itself.

As North Texans tried different varieties of wheat, merchants across the region advertised seed wheat from the Ohio Valley, and in September 1890 Denton County farmer Charles B. Moore traveled by wagon to McKinney, where he paid $1.25 a bushel for thirty-two bushels of seed wheat.[36]

To many observers, wheat farmers' preparation of the soil was appallingly casual. In the fields that had been used for corn, farmers simply felled the cornstalks and then spread the seeds around the debris. Charles Moore used a team of mules to drag a chain over the spent cornstalks to break them, while his helper, John Drury, pulled a log. More fastidious farmers raked and burned the cornstalks. Robert Horn waxed lyrical about the process in 1876: "October was wheat sowing month with me. . . . I would work all day at raking cornstalks and then burn them at night. It was a beautiful sight to see a great pile of dry cornstalks on fire on a dark night, while you stood within the circle of light and felt the cheerful warmth of the flames; then when the pile burned low, and the sparks quit flying, to take a long stalk with a large shuck on it and set it afire in the blaze and make a run to the next pile and set it. I always enjoyed burning stalks."[37] If the fields had been planted in cotton, farmers frequently simply ignored those stalks and planted around them.[38]

As in the first days of colonization, many North Texans broadcast their seeds by hand, tossing handfuls of the light tan, oval grains as they walked. By 1866, S. P. Samuel in Dallas was selling various sizes of "mechanical broadcast seed sowers," which scattered the seed mechanically with an interior wheel—similar to today's small-scale fertilizer spreaders.[39] Broadcast sowing had the advantage of being fast and easy. Because wheat didn't need to be grown in rows, it was well suited for this method. But broadcast sowing wasted a lot of seed.

By the late 1860s, however, machines known as seed or grain drills became increasingly common in North Texas. Pulled by a horse or mule, a grain drill planted in rows, piercing the soil at a predefined depth and sending each seed into the ground at a uniform distance from the next. An ad in the *Dallas Herald* for "Bickford & Huffman's world renowned premium grain drill" outlined the benefits of "sending an even, continuous stream through each tube." Their product wouldn't clog, and it would perform "equally up hill or down, side hill or level." Bickford & Huffman guaranteed "no bunching of grain!"[40] The rich prairie soil proved difficult, however, for grain drills. In 1877, the C. S. Mitchell Hardware Company of Dallas offered the "Kentucky Grain Drill"; manufactured in Louisville, it was "the only drill that we are assured works satisfactorily on our sticky black land."[41] The use of drills spread rapidly after 1880.[42] Some farmers offset the expense of a drill by sharing or borrowing. Charles Moore wrote in 1890, "John finished drilling wheat (21 ½ acres) and took Bryan[']s drill home before noon."[43]

Another type of planter, which farmers also shared, was a pulverizer, which crumbled the soil and then inserted the wheat. Charles Moore borrowed a pulverizer from his neighbor, Windsor Chambers, in October 1886. His helper, Sam Cole, planted eighteen acres of wheat in three days with Chambers's machine, which, Moore observed, "beats the drill in trashy ground."[44] In 1895, John Drury planted wheat among the "standing stalks" with a mule-drawn pulverizer belonging to Moore's neighbor, Francis Bounds.[45] The Moores apparently spent little time preparing their land and sowed their wheat amid the debris of other crops.

After the seed was in the ground, the farmer plowed to cover it. Plows were big business in North Texas. Starting in the 1870s, after the arrival of the railroad, national firms set up agencies in Dallas. Companies such as the Weir Plow Company, based in Monmouth, Illinois, built imposing buildings in downtown Dallas for their imported wares, which they sold locally, through Indian Territory, New Mexico, and across the international border into Mexico.[46] Plows varied in size. One observer made the careful distinction that some farmers used "a single turning plow," which turned one row at a time, but they more often employed a "gang plow," which turned two or more rows at a time. Using a gang plow, this author believed, saved half the time needed for planting.[47]

After plowing, farmers smoothed the soil with a harrow, a frame set with teeth and pulled by horses or mules, that raked the soil, breaking up clods and aerating. After harrowing, farmers leveled the top with a brush, sometimes made of tough tree branches. Charles Moore commented on November 28, 1881, "I sowed 4 1/2 acres of wheat and Willy Vaughter[a young hired helper,] OBannon[,] and Sylvanus [Gains, a hired helper] plowed and brushed it in and now I'm done putting in wheat 68 acres. Last year I finished putting in 33 acres on the 16th of Dec. I have sowed about 75 bushels on 68 acres."[48] Moore was well pleased with the increased speed.

As in the past, once planted, the wheat required almost no care, and farmers continued to graze their cows on the growing crops between December and March. A writer for the *Texas Almanac* pointed out that experts debated the practice, but he defended it, arguing that cows that grazed on wheat produced superior butter, of "a rich golden color," that "keeps much longer than that made from the ordinary prairie grass."[49] In 1874, J. M. Day moved to Denton County to establish a "large wheat farm and thoroughbred stock ranch," possibly to take advantage of a mutually beneficial situation in which both grain and livestock could thrive.[50]

Because of the relatively dry climate, funguses such as rust and smut were much less present in North Texas than in the eastern United States.[51] Pests could be worrisome, however. A grasshopper invasion in October 1867 brought clouds of insects. Several inches deep on the ground, they came into houses, devouring sacks of cornmeal and flour. North Texas farmers delayed sowing their wheat until the weather cooled, but even then, the insects ate the young wheat into late November.[52] Less dramatic but more disgusting were worms, which in 1885 overran the Lazyneck community in Collin County. Britt Simmons reported to the *McKinney Democrat* that "a little brown worm is working on the wheat, and is causing a good deal of alarm."[53] Weevils made occasional appearances as well.[54] Larger critters caused problems too. Charles Moore complained repeatedly about "wheat birds." In 1879 he reported that his helpers killed rabbits and hung them in the wheat to attract hawks and buzzards, which would frighten the wheat birds.[55] Before the arrival of barbed wire in the mid-1870s, keeping cattle out of the wheat fields also proved a challenge. In 1872, Moore had "more trouble than an old woman," losing "a good deal of sleep" over his efforts to bar the stock from his wheat field.[56]

Like all farmers, North Texans suffered from too much rain or not enough. The years 1880 and 1887–1888 were exceptionally dry.[57] Challenged by weather and pests, North Texas farmers and the business community vigorously tracked their yields per acre. A bad year could bring fewer than ten bushels of grain per acre, while an excellent year might produce more than thirty. In 1872, Charles Moore delighted in the yield of "37 ¼ bushels" on his best acre, with an overall average of thirty-three bushels. Six years later, however, he wrote disappointedly, "Finished thrashing by noon. Made 359 1/2 bushels off 45 acres [an average of eight bushels per acre]; 114 of it good and dry, the rest some of it light and some funky damp and sprouted."[58] Like farmers everywhere, North Texans were subject to all manner of perils that could destroy their family's livelihood.

North Texas wheat usually became ripe in the second half of May, as much as six weeks sooner than wheat grown to the north.[59] The harvest brought a dramatic period of intense activity as farmers worked to bring in their grain. At the close of the Civil War, almost all this work was done by hand. By 1900, almost all of it was done by machines. As this change made wheat farming ever more capital-intensive and expensive, it became the province of those who had the money to buy equipment or access to loans to finance it.

The first step was still cutting the wheat, which some farmers continued to do by hand. Robert Horn cradled his own wheat in June 1875. He recalled, "Since it was rather slow work and I had other duties to perform, I did not finish for several days."[60] As noted earlier, mechanical reapers were in use in Texas before 1860 but were uncommon. The *Texas Almanac* reported that, in 1867, "the favorite" reapers in use were the Kentucky and Buckeye Harvesters, along with Maury's and McCormick's Reapers. Drawn by four horses, the machines could cut twenty to twenty-five acres a day.[61] John Wesley Culwell, who was born in 1858 and lived in the Weston community in Collin County, eloquently described the need for skill on the part of the driver: "Pa hired a man by the name of Hall to run this reaper. He was then, or had been, a stage driver. Four horses were hitched to the reaper, two near the wheel, and two in front of these, and not every person could drive four horses strung out that way. Plenty could drive two or even three or four yoke of oxen thus strung out with one yoke in front of the other, but to drive horses this was another thing. None of us boys had ever had two spans of horses, but all could drive oxen."[62]

While early threshers were run by animals, by the 1870s some farmers had begun using steam power. In June 1875, the *McKinney Enquirer* noted that many people went to see the steam thresher "running in the field of Mrs. Tucker." The newspaper writer noted approvingly, "It did the work in a thorough manner and quite rapidly."[63] But people feared the volatile boilers and possible explosions. The little town of Plano played it safe. In 1893, they prohibited the use of steam threshers and other steam-powered equipment within town limits. An observer noted, however, that this ordinance was "not strictly adhered to."[64] Some daring sorts preferred to risk the danger of steam engines rather than tolerate less powerful sources of energy.

Reapers were a big improvement over cradles, but they were just a first step into mechanization. Binding the wheat into sheaves still required a lot of work. A good reaping crew needed ten men: "one to drive and manage the machine, one to rake, and eight men to bind and shock."[65] John Wesley Culwell described vividly the meticulous hand work in Collin County:

> The grain, as it was cut, would be raked off the apron of this reaper on to the ground and would lie in a long row on the ground. The men would follow after and would pick up a small hand full of the cut grain in the straw which was from 2 feet to 30 inches long and wrap it around more straw, and tie it there, like a string would be tied around any kind of package, and this was called "binding" the wheat or oats—as the case might be. It was quite an art in those days to bind wheat or oats, and many never did learn how to do this successfully, that is, tie it so it would stay till the bundles were hauled to the stack and there stacked to wait to be thrashed. As the grain was bound into these bundles, it was put into small shocks, with heads of the straw pressed together with the butt-end of the bundles on the ground, with about 12 to 20 bundles in a shock, depending on size of bundles as well as size of shock. This was done to keep the grain from rotting, after it was wet with rain. If the bundles were left lying on the ground, the grains would sometimes begin to sprout, and thus ruin the grain. After it was thus shocked, it would be hauled to a place near the lot or home and stacked to wait on the thrasher.[66]

Charles Moore commented in May 1879 that bundlers Jeff and Clarence "kept up with the harvester but they got into better wheat this evening and it ran them hard." Heavier yields per acre required faster work for humans to keep pace with the machine. Charles's brother Henry followed the bundlers, gathering the bundles into shocks.[67] If the sheaves were to be left in the fields for a while, they might be "capped": spreading a sheaf over the top of the shock to protect it from sun, rain, and frost. Darrell Myers recalled, "Three to four bundles would be laid on sides on top of shock to 'cap' the shock or to shed water off the side."[68] In July 1885, Mac Smith of Farmersville testified to the effectiveness of capping, telling the local newspaper that where the wheat had been capped, "but little [had been] injured" by bad weather.[69]

The mechanical binder, invented in the early 1870s, alleviated the difficult binding process. The implement cut the grain, gathered it into a sheaf, and tied a strand of wire around it. Wire proved problematic, however, as it could get caught in the mechanism, was hard to dispose of, and could cause great hazards in the milling process. In 1880, the Deering Harvester Company of Chicago eliminated that problem by inventing a binder that used twine rather than wire. (Company owner William Deering further enlarged his fortune by establishing a twine factory.)[70] Workers followed the binders, collecting sheaves into shocks. Darrell Myers remembered the carefully orchestrated movement of machine and humans: "Usually the shockers would start after five rounds of the binder which would discharge the bundles in a fairly straight row." The shockers gathered the bundles and leaned them upright together, making a shock six or seven feet in diameter.[71]

Once gathered, the wheat stood in the fields, awaiting storage or processing and still a long way from being edible. Threshing remained the next step. After the Civil War, some people still threshed in the old ways; a few farmers even used flails. Most, however, adopted threshing machines as soon as they could. In 1867, writers for the *Texas Almanac* called for more threshers: "Last summer a large amount of wheat was destroyed by rain, because of the scarcity of threshers in the country. And even after the new machines arrived, and were put to work, the crop was not all threshed out until after September. There never has been until last year a sufficient number of either reapers or threshers in the country."[72] Gradually, if slowly, reapers and threshers spread across the region.[73]

Threshers functioned on a couple of systems of scale. Smaller units were operated by individual farmers, who harvested for their neighbors in return for a toll—every twelfth bushel, perhaps—or for cash.[74] Larger units, including the "combine," which cut and threshed simultaneously, arrived in the 1880s. Powered by heavy steam engines, the combines had to be pulled from place to place with teams of horses or mules, then set up for their work. Sizable itinerant crews of men began moving through the countryside, cutting first one farmer's grain and then that of his neighbors. The machine owner received a part of the harvest in payment. Cash payments to the members of the crew sometimes supplemented the income from their own crops. Marion Sylvester Chambers from Grayson County, for example, "made extra money by being the separator man for Mr. Taylor's threshing crew."[75]

Harvesting was very demanding work for the laborers. Henry Coit, born in 1862, recalled the work schedule in the late nineteenth century. The "hands," he said, awoke at 3:30 a.m. and breakfasted at 4:00 to be in the fields by daylight. They worked until sundown; in May, that made for an average of fifteen hours a day. They received $1.50 a day, plus room and board, which "much of the time" meant sleeping in stacks of wheat straw, according to Coit. He observed, "Of course, with a crew of fifteen young men this wasn't enough to tire them, so they were able to kick up a bit of rough house and hi jinks far into the night."[76]

The women of the families whose wheat was being threshed were often responsible for feeding the traveling crews. Teams of strong young men, working long hours, had tremendous appetites. Charles Moore commented on the burden on his wife and daughter in 1897: "Ten or twelve hands dined here. The wagon hands dined at Webbs and came through the field to load[;] got here with wheat and threshing began at 1 PM. Threshed nearly 340 bushels 12 or 15 supped with us and 8 or 10 of them sleeping with us. . . . Mary and Linnet had no help and got to bed tired at 11." The next day, he remarked, "Half the hands moved up to Youngs on Johns place and set the machines. Half the hands stayed here for dinner," referring to the midday meal. Moore concluded, "Linnet and Mary had a hard time and are tired."[77] Feeding a dozen or more ravenous workers three times a day wore out North Texas women.

Some of the more established threshing crews eventually adopted portable "cookshacks," with a cook who traveled with the workers to feed them. Cookshacks eliminated the expectation that local women would feed the crews and provided reliable, controllable nourishment for the crews. The Coit family bought a shack that was nine feet wide and fifteen feet long, built on a large wagon chassis. Henry Coit described it in detail:

> The walls consisted of two sections, the upper section being about five feet high by fifteen feet long and hinged at the top. When in use this wall section constituted an awning when raised to keep off the sun or rain. The men stood under this awning to eat food that was placed on the lower section, which was a board fourteen inches wide, by the length of the shack. It was hinged at the bottom edge and when lowered to position served as the table, being held in that position by straps at either end. Both sections of wall folded into the body of the shack for travel. Inside

FIGURE 3.1. *Cookshack with an unidentified man. (Collin County Farm Museum 2011.03.065)*

> at the back of the shack was the wood or coal burning cookstove with its pipe extending out through the roof. As soon as the last meal at a location was consumed, the sides would be folded up, the mules hitched to it and away it went to the next farm. The grub was rather plain but considered tops with the men.[78]

Charles Moore recorded both the possibilities and difficulties of using threshing crews. He worried about letting down his fences to let the thresher in but also noted the satisfaction of a quick harvest: "Thresher started early and got done and left here by 10 AM. We got made right at 400 bushels 17 bushels per acre of wheat good grain good dry all in the bin all but the toll," meaning the portion that he owed the owner of the thresher.[79] With the Moore harvest accomplished, the threshing crew was off to the next farm. At the end of the season, their work was done for another year. The machines were idled, and the workers returned to their regular lives.

North Texas farmers acquired agricultural equipment from numerous sources. Some local machine shops offered the homegrown variety. In 1867, the *Texas Almanac* bragged of machine shops at Dallas, Cedar Hill, and Lancaster, "where reapers and thrashers, and all other agricultural implements, are manufactured as cheap as anywhere in the North, and of a better quality."[80] In 1876, the Dallas Plow and Agricultural Implement Manufacturing Company boasted about two plows, invented by company owner Joseph Payne, that were specially designed for the region's sticky clay soil.[81] The following year, the company "encourage[d] home manufacture and keep[ing] the money among us."

With the coming of the railroad (discussed later), increasing amounts of heavy machinery arrived from outside Texas to be sold by North Texas dealers. In the 1870s, numerous implement dealers, particularly in Dallas, were agents for companies from the Midwest. As such, they brought virtually no capital into the business, but they did make imported goods available to North Texas buyers.[82] In the 1870s, dealers were concentrated in Dallas and Grayson Counties. Gradually Dallas came to dominate the market. In 1889, the *Dallas Morning News* crowed that Dallas's "business in this line runs way up into the millions." The writer continued, "Nearly all of the northern and eastern manufacturers are represented here and Dallas is the chief distributing point for this class of goods in the southwest." As in the past, Texans freely acknowledged the ties of wheat culture to the North. One dealer reported selling a hundred sulky, or riding, plows in a season with "harvesters" and "thrashing machines" in "corresponding figures."[83] In 1892, Cecil A. Keating, president of the Keating Implement Manufacturing Company in Dallas, declared his town to be the "second largest farm implement depot in the world."[84]

Although Dallas was the epicenter of the implements market, the action extended past the big city. In June 1898, the *McKinney Democrat* reported that the local firm Parlin & Orendorff had sold fifteen "new binders" and "five new complete threshing outfits," as well as 43,000 pounds of twine.[85] In 1899, William Killgore, the Gainesville agent for the Harvester King cutter and binder made in Harvey, Illinois, proudly advertised the names of five local men who had bought that machine from him that year.[86] Still, like everything else related to agriculture, the implement business had its risks. Credit assessors for R. G. Dun & Company of New York City commented about Ellis and Huffman, a Fort Worth company, in 1878: "Still think they are doing too much business on a credit basis and bad crops might seriously affect them the coming summer[.] [I]t is a question."[87] Of course, that was true of all agricultural enterprises. Everything depended on the quality of the harvest.

Companies from the North moved into the region with the railroad. In 1875, the D. M. Osborne Company of Auburn, New York, established a branch office in Dallas. By 1885, its office occupied a four-story stone building at the corner of Main and Broadway. The manager, J. B. Hatch, oversaw sales in Texas, Indian Territory, Mexico, and New Mexico. The company touted various machines, including the "No. 11 Osborne Self-Binding Harvester," citing its simplicity, durability, reliability, speed, and strength. All the "wearing parts" were made of steel and were "case hardened," with a hard coating on the exterior.[88]

These marvels had to be paid for, of course, and farmers often needed credit. The banking system in North Texas developed slowly. All lending was done by sellers or private bankers until 1873, when state-chartered banks were established in Sherman and Dallas.[89] An easier alternative was for the manufacturers to extend credit. In 1867, a writer for the *Texas Almanac* hoped that the merchants would work with the farmers in making implements available for purchase: "There have been agencies established in several towns for their sale, and it seems to be the determination of the agents to afford every facility for enabling every farmer to supply himself on reasonable terms."[90] At Lancaster, a foundry sold castings (items made of molten metal poured into a mold) "to repair mills, reapers, and threshers . . . promptly and on reasonable terms."[91] In 1866, A. G. and J. R. Cummins of Grapevine offered threshers and "other agricultural machinery" from Wheeler, Melick and Co. of Albany, New York, including transportation. They required half payment in cash up front and the balance in three months. They did not mention interest rates.[92] In 1885, persons seeking "terms and prices" from the Weir Plow Company, an Illinois manufacturer with an agent in Dallas, had to write to the company but could expect "prompt answers."[93] The new Texas constitution of 1876 forbade interest rates of more than 10 percent, though that statute might have been ignored or twisted. But whether through banks or manufacturers, prosperous North Texans found ways to buy machinery.

The size of the machines proved to be a limiting factor. The "Harvester King," advertised in Gainesville in 1899, cut and bound a "twelve-foot swath," doing "the work of two six-feet machines with one man and six horses in place of four men and ten horses." The manufacturers swore that it would cut fifty acres of grain a day. The agent, William Killgore, observed that "the biggest wheat farmers are all buying the Harvester King."[94] But therein lay the problem: only large-scale farmers, with relatively flat land, could use these gigantic machines. The end of small wheat farming was already in sight by 1900.[95]

Although most farmers wanted to turn their wheat into food or cash as soon as possible, the grain kept well under the right circumstances. Small farmers stored their wheat at home. A writer for the *Texas Almanac* in 1867 cheerily observed, "After threshing, the wheat is exposed to the sun for a day or two, and then put away in granaries, where, if kept from the light, it will keep sound for years, undisturbed by the weevil."[96] Although the writer didn't mention the possibility of rats, raccoons, and other would-be thieves, presumably a high-quality granary would protect against furry pests as well as insects. In 1871, Charles Moore bragged, "Henry and I finished weather boarding wheat house all but 2 plank. I've got the best wheat house or granery [*sic*] in the county. It has 4 separate bins and they hold nearly 200 bushels each."[97] Even small granaries posed the danger of grain entrapment, in which a person could literally drown, unable to pull themselves out of the grain and asphyxiating. In Grayson County in 1892, a Mr. H. Phillips was measuring wheat in his granary when a large box of seed wheat fell on him. His young daughter, too small to lift the box off him, "kept the wheat away so that he would not smother" and successfully called for help.[98]

After it was threshed, wheat might take several paths. For small farmers, turning wheat into food for their families—producing flour, bartering it for other foods, or selling it for cash with which to buy groceries—was their first commitment. In 1876, Charles Moore paid eight bushels of wheat to a neighbor for a "five months old boar pig."[99]

In the years immediately after the Civil War, farmers could also barter for goods and services. In 1866, Saunders, Claypool, and Co. of Dallas offered "staple and fancy dry goods, groceries, &c," in return for wheat or for cash. Wheat, the merchants proclaimed, was as good as American "green-backs."[100] Mary Jane Johnson announced in the *Dallas Herald* that she would accept wheat as payment for dresses, capes, bonnets, and hats in her shop on Main Street, including those she had personally bought in New Orleans.[101] When the White Rock Male and Female School, eight miles north of Dallas, opened in September 1866, it received payment for tuition and board in the form of "wheat delivered at the Mills in the neighborhood, taken at the market price."[102] In 1866, in a slight twist, four wealthy Fort Worth citizens contributed the money to buy a load of flour, which they sent to East Texas to trade for lumber. The lumber served to fit up a room in the Masonic lodge for use as a school.[103] This is an early example of how money from wheat could help good causes. All these exchanges were personal, between the farmer and the merchant, and they diminished as the North Texas economy became more sophisticated.

Some farmers sold their wheat locally for cash. In 1885, the J. F. Caldwell grocery company assured customers that "farmers bringing grain of any kind to the city will always find a ready market and the highest cash price at this establishment."[104] Charles Moore and his neighbors received immediate payment for the wheat that they hauled to the local mill. In 1883, Moore wrote that the mill "gave me a check for my 300 bushels of wheat for $262.50."[105]

Other growers traded their wheat for ground flour. As in the past, they might get flour made from their own wheat or receive an equivalent amount from other people's grain. The Farmer family's general store in Farmersville, Collin County, had a lively trade in wheat and flour and kept careful accounts of the amounts they bought and sold. For example, they purchased ten bushels of wheat at $1.50 per bushel from H. D. Markham in February 1869 and then a month later sold him a barrel of flour for $6.00.[106] In October 1871, Charles Moore wrote, "Henry and I got home from Sherman last night with 894 ½ pounds of flower [*sic*] made out of 24 bushels of wheat after 1/6 [17 percent] toll was taken out." Prices varied with demand. In 1881, Moore took ten bushels of wheat to Weston and received 240 pounds of flour—only two-thirds of what he had gotten ten years earlier.[107]

Wagons loaded with wheat still moved slowly toward the ports or railheads behind teams of oxen.[108] National and international markets beckoned, but without railroad connections, North Texas remained a backwater wannabe. North Texans chafed at the flour from the Midwest for sale in their local markets.[109] They calculated the quality of their wheat and flour, and they were sure that their early harvest gave them a competitive edge. They yearned for a railroad.[110]

Finally, the day came that so many had anticipated for so long. The Houston and Texas Central (H&TC), from the Gulf Coast, reached Dallas in 1872 and the Red River in 1873. The Missouri-Kansas-Texas (familiarly known as the Katy) arrived at Denison from the north on December 24, 1872. When the H&TC crossed with the Katy at Denison the next year, the Texas railroad system was at last connected to a national network. In 1873, the Texas and Pacific Railway (T&P) finished a line from Texarkana to Dallas and then, after being delayed by financial panic, finally pushed west to Fort Worth in 1876. After the railroads arrived, the commodity market in North Texas expanded quickly. At the same time, Texas produced enough wheat for export for the first time in 1875. The stage was set for a bonanza.[111]

As the railroads laid down their steel tracks, commission merchants—businesspeople who took wheat on consignment from farmers and sold it in the national market—moved their headquarters to the region. Notably, they did not buy the wheat outright from the farmers but merely sold it on their behalf and then paid them after the sale. In 1875 Denison, itself a creation of the railroad, A. R. Collins was a "general commission merchant" for flour and grain.[112] Merchants in the tiny German Catholic town of Lindsay, Cooke County, received "grain and hay in carload lots . . . at any time."[113] By 1890, Pilot Point, in Denton County, was "handling" 250,000 bushels of wheat per year.[114]

Dallas soon became the headquarters for numerous commission merchants of various sizes. In 1882, Carnegie and Wood advertised as "commission merchants and dealers in provisions, grain, and western produce."[115]

Henry Loeb, "grocer and commission merchant," offered "liberal advances" for grain and cotton, plus a convenient location "opposite T&P [Texas and Pacific] Depot."[116] Because commission merchants took the very sources of the livelihoods of farmers and small dealers, they had to establish trust by the people who turned their crops over to them. F. T. Jones, new to Dallas in 1885, "succeeded the well known firm of A. Oppenheimer & Co." He promised "liberal advancements . . . judgment and discretion" and gave references through two Dallas banks.[117] In other words, farmers could receive advances on the grain that they consigned, even before the commission merchant sold it. Adolph Metzler, a "commission merchant and wholesale dealer in grain and produce," promised that he had no conflict of interest (apparently unlike his competitors). His references included bankers and wholesale grocers.[118]

As the grain market grew, businessmen believed that they needed stronger mechanisms to ensure fair prices for themselves and the farmers, protecting the market from being flooded with grain at harvest time and strapped at other times of the year. In the early 1880s, North Texas businessmen thus developed exchanges, modeled on older entities in Chicago and St. Louis, to handle the buying and selling of commodities, including wheat. Throughout the year, they bought and sold "futures" on grain that had yet to be harvested, keeping the prices uniform. Exchanges tried to maintain discipline over the market by setting rules and times of trade.[119] A writer for the *Dallas Herald* explained in April 1882, "Dealing in futures is now a recognized business in which nearly every business man, planter or farmer engages to a greater or less extent."[120] A group of Dallas businessmen formed the "Grain and Produce Exchange," choosing "grain and commission merchant" August Oppenheimer as its first president.[121] Representatives of the 125 members met every day: "At noon the house is rapped to order and a regular list called, such as wheat, corn, oats, cotton, rye, barley, bran, flour and twenty minor articles, and when each article is announced[,] trades are made in it." According to an observer, the process was efficient and dependable: "Buyer and seller transact in fifteen or twenty minutes business which, by the old methods, would require hard work and four or five hours. . . . The rules of the Exchange are as perfect a system of equity between buyer and seller as could well be devised, and are largely based upon the rules governing similar exchanges in the great cities of the United States."[122]

For a time, farmers sought to enter the grain business themselves, working cooperatively to obtain favorable prices. The Farmers' Alliance, the largest and strongest of the cooperative movements, discussed in 1887 the formation of its own cotton and small grain exchange.[123] But private business mostly prevailed. Businessmen in Fort Worth formed a grain exchange, along with a cattle exchange, in 1894. A spokesman for the Fort Worth Chamber of Commerce reported that the headquarters would be in the chamber building and would "have daily reports by wire from all the great grain and cattle markets of the United States."[124] They kept their eye on the world market too. A writer for the *Dallas Herald* in 1899 commented that "war in the Philippines and Transvaal insure[s] a good price for food products."[125] Through the sale of commodities, North Texas linked itself to the world.

Regional boosters recognized the need to tell the world about the wonders of North Texas agriculture. To advertise its abundance, Fort Worth businessmen decided to host an agricultural exhibition—a "Karporama," they dubbed it. In holding such an event, they were following the lead of cities throughout the United States. A writer for the *Fort Worth Daily Gazette* observed in February 1889: "New Orleans [has] her sugar cane palace, Sioux City her corn palace, and why not Fort Worth her Spring Palace?"[126]

Calling the exhibition the "Texas Spring Palace," planners hired Fort Worth architect Arthur Albert Messer to design an elaborate building constructed completely from Texas materials and decorated with Texas agricultural products. It was to be, they declared, "a wheat palace, a corn palace, a cotton palace."[127] The structure featured a colossal center dome and eight turrets; these exotic nods to Moorish and Victorian architecture were typical of other exhibition halls of the period. The fanciful building, made entirely of Texas wood, came together in only thirty-one days.[128]

The decoration of the building, however, took three hundred men and women six weeks to complete. The type of decor, known as crop art, appeared prominently at the 1876 Centennial Exposition in Philadelphia.[129] The Fort Worth promoters hired E. A. Allen, who had decorated three of the Sioux City Corn Palaces. The decorations required sixteen carloads of wheat, seven cars of millet, and ten acres of cornstalks as well as alfalfa, Johnson grass, cedar, cotton, wool, moss, broomcorn, rye, and sorghum.[130]

The 1889 Spring Palace, which ran from May to June, was a smash hit, with visitors from forty-two states and seven countries.[131] In 1890, the exhibition returned bigger and even better, and wheat again played a prominent part in the decor. The main dome featured the wheat sheaf as "the central idea," with the golden grain shown in at least five different ways. A "representation of the Goddess Ceres" held in one hand a "sickle and in the other a sheaf of wheat."[132]

The Spring Palace came to a horrifying end, however. On the night of May 30, 1890, a flash fire destroyed the main building, which was filled with dry grains and grasses, in a matter of minutes. More than five thousand people were in the building at the time, but miraculously, only one person,

Fort Worth engineer Al Hayne, died as he was helping others escape. The exhibition was never revived. But in its short life, the Spring Palace brought North Texas agriculture—including wheat—to the attention of the nation.

After the Civil War, people flocked to the prairies of North Texas, where they chose to make their living either as farmers or as town people. Those who decided to farm weighed the choice between cotton and wheat. If they chose wheat, they had to gauge their finances carefully as expensive machinery became available. And they lived their days around the needs of the wheat crop, from dropping seeds to feeding hungry harvesters. Each summer the farmers released the wheat from their hands into the mills and the markets. The millers are the next people in the story.

4 / OXEN TO ELECTRICITY: MILLING, 1865–1900

ACROSS TEXAS AND THE UNITED STATES AFTER THE Civil War, people wanted flour and were willing to spend good money for it, and the entrepreneurs of North Texas intended to supply their needs. In the late nineteenth century, mill owners built facilities of ever-increasing size, and the technology that they used altered dramatically. The millers in North Texas had to roll with these changes or be left behind.

As the North Texas economy adjusted after the Civil War, flour milling continued, both on a local scale and, increasingly, as part of regional trade. Old mills continued operating or came back to life, while entrepreneurs built new facilities that were larger and more sophisticated. Millwrights must have been extraordinarily busy, as mill owners loudly advertised the repairs that they had made. Only months after the war ended, numerous Dallas businessmen were moving ahead. City Mills owner William Sherwood in September 1865 declared that "the mill is now in excellent order and successful operation, capable of grinding 500 bushels of grain in 24 hours." Though he promised to make "as good flour . . . as any mill in Northern Texas," his customers would pay handsomely for it—an exorbitant toll of one-fifth, or 20 percent, of their harvest. (In the 1850s the toll had been 17 percent or less.)[1] In the southern part of Dallas County, the King family reported that they had bought "and thoroughly repaired" the Lancaster Mill. Not only that, but they had procured "the services of an experienced Miller and an experienced and practical Engineer," and they were ready to grind both wheat and corn.[2] The Osceola Mills, on the road to Birdville, were for sale in the summer of 1866, "in perfect repair and fine running order, having been thoroughly overhauled and repaired since Christmas."[3] The owner of the old Excelsior Mills, on Rowlett's Creek, had a steam engine and was looking for a "good practical miller."[4] The new owners of the Trinity Mills were planning to run their "thoroughly repaired" mills on September 20, 1866.[5] Mill owners were looking to make good in the new Texas economy.

Employment in Reconstruction-era Texas could be fluid, and some men with training in other areas invested in mills. James E. Scott, for example, president of the City Mills in Dallas, was a "Methodist preacher." He was listed in the 1870 census as a miller, and his tombstone in Montgomery County, Texas, reads: "Rev. James E. Scott."[6] While "Dr. Johnson," the mayor of Jefferson, Texas, did fine as an investor in the C. M. Terry Mills in Dallas, the credit histories of other men cast shadows on their community standing. Two physicians especially came in for scathing critique. Dr. Roy Beverly Scott, born in Virginia in 1823, owned a mill and more than five hundred acres of land in northeast Dallas County. He served as an alderman for the City of Dallas. Credit assessors, however, reported in 1874 that his debts outweighed his assets and sneered, "He has no capacity for management is . . . sort of a good for nothing fellow that wears kids gloves and has others to do the work."[7] Dr. Michael Lambkin Woods, a Tennessean who arrived in North Texas before 1851, owned a steam mill in northwest Tarrant County in a community called Fair Oaks. Immediately after the Civil War, his finances were good, but by January 1870 his indebtedness had caught up with him. The assessor wrote that he was "quite embarrassed by law suits that will most likely break him up. . . . Physician dishonest and wholly unreliable. Claims a good quantity of real estate has not a perfect title to any land in this county." In June 1872, the assessor wrote, "L. M. [*sic*] Woods is totally unreliable in financial transactions."[8] Woods may have been an esteemed physician, but the credit reporter thought otherwise of him as a mill owner.

At least one mill builder overextended publicly and disastrously. William S. Parker's day in the sun, though bright, was fleeting. In 1876–1877, he built a mill in Dallas at a cost of $20,000, mostly with borrowed money, and was in trouble from the outset. The Dallas press eagerly followed the development of the mill, noting in July 1876 that the building's footprint at the end of Main Street was "beginning to present an imposing appearance."[9] In December, the *Dallas Herald* proclaimed that Dallas would become "the flour center of Texas" and that Parker would be recognized as a key factor in that development.[10] Credit reports, however, painted a different story. Parker was struggling under a mountain of debt. In September 1876, a credit reporter noted that Parker "has so far paid his workmen," so at least he was able to meet payroll. A month later, the *Dallas Herald* breathlessly observed that the mill was a "mammoth and showy building" that when completed would need a workforce of fifteen to twenty men.[11] But in January 1877, the credit bureau reported, "All this gentleman has in the world is mortgaged up to the handle, even his stock of fuel and wheat on hand. The mill is unquestionably one of the finest in the state but he has been unable to run it for want of capital. He values the mill at $40,000." In 1878, Parker sold the mill to local bankers William H. Gaston and W. H. Thomas and left town.[12]

Maybe because it required physical strength, used machinery, and occurred in public, the commercial milling business was dominated by men. So intensely gendered was the space that few women ever entered a mill building. But there were at least three notable exceptions in Dallas County: widows Persis Olive Mallory Newton, Mary Elizabeth Morton King Horton, and Sarah Horton Cockrell operated mills in their own right in the 1870s and 1880s. James Horton had built the Eagle Ford mill six miles west of Dallas in 1857. As a partnership between Horton and millwright Ezra Williams Newton, the mill thrived for thirteen years. A credit reporter wrote in 1870, "Newton manages the mill in which there is about $10,000 invested. Horton is the monied man and a farmer." Newton died in January 1871 at the age of forty-eight, leaving his widow and three children, two of them under the age of ten. The credit reporter commented, "Newton dead, Horton going on without change. . . . He is a fine businessman and an elegant gentleman." Apparently Ezra Newton left his share of the mill to his wife, Persis, who was forty-three at the time, and James Horton ran the business for five years. He died, however, in April 1876 at the age of fifty-nine and left his part of the mill to his second wife, Mary Elizabeth Morton King Horton. In June 1876, the credit reporter noted approvingly, "Mill now run by Horton and Newton, two widow ladies. . . . The Horton Estate is worth over $50,000. The ladies are good for all they will contract." Molly Horton, as she was known, was only thirty-five at the time of her husband's death and fabulously wealthy. She and her stepson, James's son by his first wife, were settling the estate in December 1876. But in early 1879, she and Persis Newton still owned the mill. William M. Luck, a miller born in North Carolina in 1830, had bought half of Molly Horton's interest and was paying her on time. Regarding Persis Newton, the evaluator noted, "Mrs. Newton owns a good farm in this valley[,] some stock and team. Would consider her in easy circumstances." The pair of widows controlled their wealth and retained their husbands' mill, apparently undaunted by the gender conventions of the day.[13]

Even more impressively, James Horton's younger sister, Sarah Horton Cockrell, was a significant force in the building of Dallas. After her husband's murder in 1858, she built and owned several hotels, established a bridge company, and invested heavily and successfully in Dallas real estate, eventually owning one-quarter of downtown Dallas. She always ran her affairs from her home rather than an office.[14] In 1874, perhaps under the

FIGURE 4.1. *Sarah Horton Cockrell as a young woman. (Courtesy of the DeGolyer Library, Southern Methodist University)*

influence of her brother, she entered the milling business. With her son-in-law Mitchell Gray and a millwright named H. S. Kimball, she established the Todd Mills, named for the company in St. Louis that sold the equipment. Styling herself as S. H. Cockrell, she erected a frame building four stories high with five runs of buhrstones, capable of producing 250 barrels of flour a day. The Dallas newspaper boasted, "The machinery is new and of the best character that could be purchased in the northern cities."[15] In 1875, Cockrell became sole owner of the mill.[16] She sold it to the Farmers' Alliance for $56,000 in June 1888. When the Alliance's financers foreclosed a year later, she took the mill back and installed a five-hundred-horsepower engine. In mid-April 1891, the mill burned, and city water pressure was insufficient to extinguish the fire. The insurance on the mill, from twenty-five companies, totaled $32,000. Only three weeks later, the Stanard Company of St. Louis bought "the entire Todd mills plant and good will, together with the real estate on which the property is located, for $76,000."[17] Sarah Cockrell, Molly Horton, and Persis Newton all demonstrated that women had the perseverance and acumen to run a mill successfully.

Mills both created communities and changed established ones that they entered. In 1874, Collin County boosters bragged of having twelve "towns and villages," including Rhea's Mill and Wysong's Mill, both clustered around grinding facilities.[18] Rhea's Mill had a post office—an indication of solidity—from 1876 until 1907.

In an existing city, the construction of a flour mill could alter the area around it for better or worse. Marion Day Mullins remembered living near the Bewley Mills in Fort Worth in the 1890s:

> Because Bewley Mills, the largest flour mill in this part of north Texas, was located on Cherry and North Streets, and because a brewery was adjacent to the railroad tracks on South Lamar and flanked by a lumber yard, it was decided to lay one block of pavement on 13th Street from Lamar to Taylor, with brick. Now the brick was laid on a bed of sand and not morticed in. So when the heavy wagons that serviced the mill, the lumber yard and the brewery passed over the loose brick they stirred up the sand so it too blew through our living room windows. The sound of the horses iron shod feet, accompanied by the steady rumble of the heavily laden iron bound wheels of the wagons are among those I'll never forget.[19]

The Bewley mill created dust and noise for area residents. And as we have noted, steam engines made noise, released smoke, and posed a fire danger. But communities welcomed mills despite the unpleasantness.

As their fortunes grew, mill owners shaped communities with their financial resources. Not only did Ralph Man work with Julian Feild to create the settlement that became known as Mansfield, but he had an impact on the material environment of southeastern Tarrant County. Man donated the land for a section of the Mansfield Cemetery in 1876, part of his deep involvement with the Cumberland Presbyterian Church.[20] In 1865, he built a one-room log cabin for his home on West Broad Street, and in 1867 he added a brick parlor and dining room on the east side, with a breezeway between the old and new sections. About 1870, Man enclosed the breezeway and built a second story with three bedrooms. The house featured oak floors and a walnut handrail and newel post on the staircase.[21] The Man home stands as a museum in 2025, a reminder of the prosperity that wheat once brought.

Confederate veteran, large landowner, and successful wheat farmer John Ramsey "Jack" Sullivan immigrated to Denton County from Missouri. He "helped organize" the Sanger Mill and Elevator Company as well as two banks. In 1879, he and his wife, Nancy Jones Sullivan, had an elaborate house built on their farm by "a Mr. McGuire from Jefferson" for their family, which included eight children. The house featured double front doors, "beautifully carved in a Chinese design with serpents and leaves entwined." They brought wallpaper from Jefferson, the first in the Sanger area. Only eight years later, the family built a similar house in Sanger.[22] The Sullivans used their wheat wealth to create fine homes.

Ever hopeful, millers and investors continued to erect small businesses at rural crossroads, such as Dexter, in Cooke County, and Collinsville, in Grayson County.[23] The correspondence between mill builders Henry Moore and his brother Charles Moore speaks of the opportunities and difficulties in building mills. Based in Denton County, the brothers traveled throughout North Texas, constructing and repairing mills. Henry wrote from Titus County in February 1870 of overhauling a boiler and furnace in an existing mill that was to be moved a mile and a half to a new location. He fretted about getting timber hauled for new construction a mile and a half away. He wrote often regarding the food that the crew endured in their travels: pork, "salad," flour, coffee, sugar, molasses. Henry himself occasionally had to turn his hand to cooking, with dire results. Still, he observed, the money was good: "I could if dismissed tomorrow and paid off go home and return and do the same thing over and over make about 750 a year, and full work a year (not to be expected) would amount to 1460."[24] Two weeks later, he was still working on the boiler, made in 1858 of "first rate iron . . . 20 feet long 46 in diam. double flued[.] [W]e will make it nearly as good as new." He sent his brother detailed specifications of the boiler and its capacity. Henry praised the owner of the mill and projected a successful future.[25] Charles wrote back to Henry, negotiating for parts for the mill, giving detailed specifications and costs of many possible purchases. None of them were cheap. An "engine 10 × 20 boiler 22 ft 42 in Boiler irons and chimney" would cost $1,700. The vendor could also supply such goods as bolting cloths, buhrstones, "portable underrunners," or hullers, and smut mills.[26] Later in the year, Charles was in Cass County, writing to his brother in similar detail about shafts and drum shafts and count wheels. Getting skilled workers and obtaining materials in a timely way kept Charles anxious.[27]

Like harvest time, mill building taxed the women of the millers' families, as feeding the building crews often proved difficult. In March 1898, the Jernigan family was having a flour mill constructed near their home in Sedalia, Collin County. The women of the family had about had enough. The mother, Laura Jernigan, wrote to the Moore family, "We ought to have written to you before now but Claud [daughter Claudia, age fifteen] and I have had to cook cook cook all the time since I was at your house three big meals every day sometimes for seven men[.]" Eleven-year-old Laura Belle added to the letter, writing, "We have got seven men to cook for[.] Ellic Turner is here helping to put up the mill house[.] [H]e eats as much as to are [two or] three men[.] [I]t keeps Claud and I busy waiting on him[.] [H]e is another eater from eaters-ville."[28] "Cook cook cooking" for "eaters from eatersville" wore the Jernigan women out, perhaps even more than the men who did the building.

Accommodating the dominant forms of agriculture in the region, some enterprising North Texans built cotton gins and wheat mills at the same locations. Frank Jackson came to Renner, Collin County, in 1873 and built the first gin, the first flour mill, and the first grain elevator "in the area."[29] The mill in Blue Ridge, Collin County, had "two gins with mill attachments" in 1880.[30] John Kirkpatrick constructed his cotton gin in Lebanon, Collin County, then added a flour mill in 1884.[31] Most of the combination mills and gins had separate buildings, and the mills were small affairs, though in Whitesboro, Grayson County, the Kenchen and Hudgens flour mill and cotton gin had a small wheat mill, a small corn mill, and a cotton gin all in the same building.[32] As with the growing season, the harvest seasons were separated by at least two months—often more—and occupying the same sites made fiscal sense.

Small mills still held local significance. Charles Moore could leave his house early in the morning with his wheat, go to the mill, and be home by "dinner," as they called the midday meal. By 1880, if Collin County residents couldn't or didn't want to go to McKinney, the county seat, they could take their grain to Copeville, Melissa, Farmersville, Blue Ridge, Rhea's Mill, or Plano. The mills were small, but they served their neighborhood purpose.

Well into the nineteenth century, small mills still used animal power, particularly oxen. John Wesley Culwell observed that "not every ox could be used" on a treadmill, and "a yoke of oxen that would tread the wheel was very valuable."[33] Sometimes the treadmills were continuations of older businesses. Thomas C. Roberts settled near Whitesboro in the late 1840s and for decades continued to "run an old fashioned tread wheel ox mill—the only mill in western Grayson [County] . . . for many years."[34] Other millers built new treadmills in the postwar years. In 1867, Richard Corn, a prosperous farmer in Marysville, Cooke County, hired William DeWees, who had built a mill in Millwood in the 1850s, to erect an ox mill. David Harrison Sapp remembered that the building was probably three thousand square feet. The tread wheel was forty feet in diameter and required six to ten oxen to power it. Sapp, whose father assisted in the construction, recalled, "People came from Montague County, Clay County and the Indian Territory to get their wheat and corn ground."[35] The first flour mill in Denton County, near Bolivar, started out in the 1860s as an ox-powered gristmill. The mill equipment was sold several times before finding its home on Duck Creek.[36] But change was afoot. In Little Elm, Henry Hill bought a steam-powered cotton gin in 1868 and ran a wheat mill with the same boiler. People "for miles around" came to use it.[37]

In the county seats, mill owners followed national trends, ramping up the scale of their enterprises with steam power and enlarged capacities, intending to supply flour for the wholesale trade, not to village stores or individuals.[38] Forward-looking millers were poised to enter the industry just as industrial, high-capital milling began to conquer it. North Texans joined the wave of industrialization that transformed the milling industry, following the lead of huge milling businesses in the Midwest. The change would be staggering.

European inventors, more concerned with the quality of flour than the quantity, began experimenting with cylindrical rollers in the 1830s. Designers across eastern Europe tinkered with the process, and Swiss engineer Jakob Sulzberger made important modifications. By 1870, variations of the Sulzberger mills appeared in the United Kingdom. Horizontal rollers, made of steel, worked in pairs to crush the grain. Multiple sets of rollers reduced the wheat further with each subsequent rolling. Rollers made more flour from a given amount of wheat, eliminated the "high costs" of stone dressing, and could be operated at a much larger scale than buhrstones.[39]

The Washburn Company in Minneapolis, the forerunner of Pillsbury, imported the roller mill into the United States in 1880.[40] By enabling midwestern mills to grind spring wheat into palatable flour, the roller mills, along with a machine called a middlings purifier, set up Minneapolis to become the colossus in the field of milling.[41] In North Texas, the Todd Mills quickly followed Washburn's lead, advertising in September 1883 "the only full and complete ROLLER MILL in the State of Texas."[42]

Millers had to make the difficult decision to change from the revered grinding stones to rollers. As rollers quickly spread across Texas, some mills kept their buhrstones even after they installed the new technology. In 1883, Murray Percival Bewley built a new mill in Fort Worth with three sets of stones and three sets of rollers, at a cost of $20,000.[43] In Sherman in 1885, the Sherman Milling Company had three runs of stones but added a double set of rollers, while crosstown competitor Eagle Mills had two runs of stones and eight sets of rollers. Nor were these improvements limited to the county seats. In 1884, John Kirkpatrick in Lebanon, Collin County, added a flour and corn mill to his existing cotton gin business. He built a new, four-story building and bought all new machinery, including eleven sets of rollers, powered by a forty-horsepower engine. The Plano newspaper reported that the mill was "one of the features of Lebanon."[44]

A reporter for the *Fort Worth Gazette* carefully explained the process of the rollers used in the Cameron and Tatum Mill, built in Fort Worth in 1888. It was at the time the largest mill in Texas, capable of producing 700 barrels of flour and 250 barrels of cornmeal in 24 hours.[45] The mill had seventeen sets of double rollers, each set eighteen feet long and five feet in diameter, powered by a 250-horsepower Corliss engine fueled with three steam boilers. The first five sets of rollers had corrugated surfaces, with smaller and smaller ridges on each successive set. The first roller broke the kernel to remove the germ, the oily center that turned rancid quickly. The next four rollers fractured the kernels into large particles with the bran—the tough outer covering—intact. The separated bran was sent to a bin to be made into animal feed. After each break, the wheat went into aspirators and purifiers to remove anything that wasn't kernel. The sixth through seventeenth sets of the rollers were smooth, designed to reduce the "purified particles" into grades of flour with increasing levels of refinement.[46]

As the Cameron mill showed, the rollers were the heart of a modern milling operation but were by no means the only equipment in these mills. The larger the mill, the greater the number of accessories it housed. A battery of new machines purified the wheat before it was ground and the flour after it was made. First the wheat had to be cleaned of dirt, dust, and other foreign elements, from rocks to the fungus known as smut. For these tasks there were scalpers, scourers, brushes, aspirators, smutters, and magnetic machines, which checked for bits of metal that might be present—for example, binding wire. Then, as the grain went through the various rounds of reduction between the rollers, it was repeatedly sieved and cleaned. With the grain kernels growing progressively smaller, the bits of bran that clung to them were removed, often with a device called a purifier, which used currents of air to blow away the chaff.[47] The most common cleaning apparatus in North Texas remained the bolting chest. As we have noted, bolting cloth, made of silk, had been used to screen flour for centuries. By the 1880s, bolting chests consisted of reels with three grades of silk of differing coarseness. The flour that sieved through the finest silk was "super fine flour," the middle grade was "shorts," and the coarsest grade of flour still had bran. When the flour was finally finished, it was packed into barrels or cloth bags for shipping.[48]

Large mills had multiples of every kind of machine, but even small mills had their share. For example, the Kenchen and Hudgens flour mill and cotton gin in Whitesboro, with only two runs of stones, had a purifier, a centrifugal reel, which spun the wheat to clean it, a brush machine, and a smutter. Millers bought machinery from all over the midwestern United States—Ohio, Michigan, Illinois, St. Louis, Indianapolis, Minneapolis, Chicago—and especially around Buffalo, New York. Like vendors for farm implements, sellers of mill machinery had outposts in North Texas. In Dallas, Sinker, Davis & Co. was a branch of an Indianapolis company that sold all the goods necessary for a flour mill.[49] Mills had never been strictly local affairs, but now the small crossroads mills were giving way to nationally connected behemoths, funded with large amounts of capital.

Large mills required large workforces, while smaller enterprises scraped by with a few seasonal workers. At its busiest, in 1886, the Empire Mill in Dallas had a president, vice president, secretary, and treasurer; a superintendent, grain buyer, and bookkeeper; a millwright, elevator foreman, and chief engineer; first, second, and third millers; and eleven "workers," all white.[50] In the Census of Manufacturing for 1870 and 1880, all mill employees were males over the age of sixteen. There were no women. The work was generally seasonal. Only about 10 percent of the mills ran twelve months a year, so most mill workers had to find other work for a varying number of months. Even the largest employer, Burrus in McKinney, ran full-time only ten months a year, and Empire, mentioned earlier, ran only six months. Wages varied as well. The most poorly paid "ordinary laborer," as the census called them, earned a mere 40 cents a day, while those earning the most received $3.50 a day. Wages were highest in Dallas, where laborers commonly received $1.50 a day. "Skilled mechanics" were paid anywhere from $1 to $4 a day in Tarrant County. The most common wage for skilled work across North Texas was about $2 a day, the equivalent of perhaps $1,200 a

FIGURE 4.2. *Workers from the Anchor Roller Mills in Fort Worth, late nineteenth century. (Courtesy of the Fort Worth History Center, Fort Worth Public Library)*

month in 2024 wages.[51] Despite its importance, mill work was not particularly lucrative for workers.

Milling could bring good returns for owners and investors, but success was not guaranteed. Small mill owners came and went, frequently selling their businesses or quitting.[52] The business demanded start-up capital for facilities and then money to meet continuing expenses for wheat, wood or coal to fuel the boilers, labor, and maintenance. For example, the owners of the McKinney Creager and Bro. Mill in Van Alstyne—presumably Daniel McKinney Creager and one of his many brothers—were "good men," according to credit reporters, but had mortgaged their farms to buy the mill and then taken a lien on it "to secure payment for machinery etc. etc." They also owed "heavily for labor[,] wheat and wood etc. etc." By November 1876, they had "failed"; unable to overcome their start-up debts, they lost not only their mill but most likely their farmland as well.[53] Similarly, in June 1875, J. W. Jones and his brother in Cooke County were said to be "industrious but have managed badly and [are] largely in debt." In May 1877, they were described as "hopelessly in debt," having mortgaged everything they owned. By May 1878, they had "gone into involuntary bankruptcy."[54] In every county, the records told similar stories of debt and closures. In Dallas, William F. Bachman's mill was "running but mortgaged for all it is worth" in November 1874. The following July, the record starkly noted: "Gone."[55]

Funding for mills came from a variety of sources, including banks, whether private, state, or national. A few male millers used money belonging to their wives for their investments. Under Texas law, property acquired by either spouse before marriage remained separate, in keeping with Spanish precedent.[56] Credit assessors noted that Tom Carroll of Dallas "controls property belonging to his wife . . . individually he is worth little or nothing." About C. Miller, who stood higher in the assessor's estimation, the report noted that he "had the use of $10,000 [about $300,000 in 2025] belonging to his wife."[57] His peers believed him to be "honest et cetera, not a particularly good businessman." In 1875, his brother-in-law, Ewing, joined the business, and in 1876, they were "burned out."[58] One wonders if Mrs. Miller ever saw her money again. In any case, both Carroll and Miller used their wives' money to finance their less-than-spectacular ventures.

As we see with the Miller family and others, fire constantly endangered flour mills, their air filled with volatile grain dust. Companies, especially the larger, more sophisticated ones, took extra care to protect their investments from fire. Beginning in 1869, the Sanborn Fire Insurance Company kept thorough records. The Sanborn maps provide exacting details about countless businesses in the United States, including mills. Mostly illuminated with oil lamps—electricity was just coming into the bigger cities—and powered by steam boilers fired with wood or, in more developed establishments, coal, the mills were explosions waiting to happen. Possible defenses against fire varied with the size of the mill. The most advanced had standpipes, or internal fire hydrants, built into the structures as well as human watchmen on duty overnight. More modest establishments kept barrels of water with buckets or hoses on each floor of the mill. Many invested in hand grenades filled with carbon tetrachloride, to be thrown at the base of the fire. Despite these precautions, at least five North Texas mills burned between the Civil War and 1900, including the Todd Mills in Dallas, which had all the precautions and burned anyway.[59]

Destruction of property by fire obviously caused financial difficulties, and a mill business might or might not recover. J. W. Jones of Cooke County attempted to rebuild after his mill burned, as did Tom Carroll of Dallas County, using his wife's money. Both ended up failing in business. With the right financing, however, investors could turn disaster into opportunity. Two fires in Gainesville showed the flexibility of entrepreneurs and the availability of financing. In January 1888, a small fire broke out at the Brady Brothers Mill in Gainesville. The workers thought it was extinguished, and the night watchman even fell asleep, only to be awakened by flames. The building, with its contents—twenty-four thousand pounds of flour, five hundred bushels of corn, "considerable wheat," $500 worth of bags, and all the machinery—was a total loss, amounting to $15,000. The Bradys had insurance, but it covered only one-third of the damages. Nonetheless, in a couple of days the Bradys were planning a new building on the same lot, and the Missouri Pacific Railroad was promising to build a spur to the new structure. Only a week after the fire, S. Hoffman of Milwaukee, representing the machinery manufacturer Edward P. Allen and Co., was in Gainesville to work with the Bradys in selecting their replacement equipment.[60]

By 1891, the Bradys' local competitor, the Whaley Mill, established in 1869, had grown into a large enterprise powered by steam. The Whaley Mill exploded on July 7, 1891, and the building was completely destroyed. The insurance company cleverly covered fire but not explosion, so the company had to borrow money from the local bank to rebuild. The opening of the new mill in 1892 revealed that the Whaleys had installed a new roller mill, with a capacity of 150 barrels a day. The Whaley company bought out the Bradys in 1896. By 1899, they were milling five hundred barrels of flour a day.[61] The Whaleys had risen like phoenixes from the ashes.

As mills grew in size and complexity, the machinery in them became increasingly capable of causing severe injury to workers or even killing them. The New Era Mill in Fort Worth was the site of two deadly incidents in five years. In 1889, a conveyor belt crushed the leg of one of the mill owners, F. J. Tatum, and he died minutes later. In 1894, when S. Harvey Largent, the chief engineer, was caught on a wheel, his head was dashed against the stone floor with every revolution of the wheel.[62] When John Randol died in an accident at the family's Tarrant County mill in 1894, his brother, Robert Randol, deeded an acre of land near the mill for the cemetery where John Randol and other family members are buried.[63] Mills brought wealth, but they also took life. At this point in the United States and in Texas, companies had no obligations to pay for workers' injuries or deaths.

Financial downturns could crumble even established mills. In 1878, Matthew W. Deavenport started a mill, near downtown Denton, that made a flour known as Silver Lake. The mill thrived throughout the 1880s but ceased operation about 1890. The building stood vacant until it burned in 1896.[64] The highly regarded J. W. Moore Mill at Melissa impressed all observers. Regarded as the "largest and finest" in Texas through the 1870s, the business eventually "broke the owners."[65]

The most spectacular failure might have been that of Julian Feild, who built his first mill in Fort Worth in 1857 and then with Ralph Man established a fine mill in the community that came to bear their names. Despite—or perhaps because of—his contracts to furnish the Confederate army, the end of the Civil War found Feild in debt, with all his real estate mortgaged. In the 1860s, the mill resumed its trade with the US government, sending flour to the revitalized military outposts to the west, but the venture did not go well. In April 1871, a credit assessor wrote, "Field [*sic*] has been engaged in furnishing flour to troops on Texas frontier and has been much disappointed in not realizing his money. Through this has been embarrassed." During the same time, Mansfield wheelwright and carpenter Peter Guilford built five wagons that were subsequently loaded with flour from Feild's mill and bound for Fort Sill in Indian Territory. In May 1871, a month after the credit report, a group of Kiowa attacked the wagon train in Young County, killing the wagonmaster, Henry Warren, and six teamsters. Three teamsters escaped and alerted the US Army. US General William T. Sherman, who happened to be near the attack site, ordered the capture rather than the killing of the Native American leaders, marking a significant chapter in the so-called Red River Wars between the United States and Native Americans.[66] Feild, of course, lost all his flour. In July 1876, a credit reporter wrote that Feild was "hopelessly broke." Sometime after 1890, after more than three decades in Tarrant County, Feild moved to San Diego, California, and died there in 1897.

While individuals like Julian Feild continued to own mills, by the 1880s national mill companies had entered North Texas and consolidation of the milling business had begun in earnest. The E. O. Stanard Milling Company of St. Louis, which billed itself as the largest miller of winter wheat in the United States, bought two large mills in Dallas, Todd and Empire, from the Cockrell family.[67] Local businessmen reportedly were excited about the amount of capital that Stanard brought, calling the purchases "a long step toward making this city the great grain center of Texas." Dallas realtors were sure that the purchase by Stanard would develop the city into "the Minneapolis of the South."[68] Some Dallas businesspeople might have feared the loss of local autonomy, but the public stance toward Stanard was one of welcome.

During this period, some people were less than delighted by the increasing scale and complexity of businesses across the United States. Texas farmers reacted to the industrialization and expansion of corporate capitalism by creating organizations that endeavored to enhance farmers' position in the marketplace. The Farmers' Alliance, established in Lampasas, Texas, in 1877, tried various types of business enterprises, particularly cotton gins and stores. They established "cooperative" flour mills in McKinney, Dallas (operating as the Alliance Milling and Manufacturing Company of Dallas County), Denton, Gainesville, Marysville (Cooke County), Sherman (grinding both corn and wheat), Collinsville (Grayson County), and Denison, as well as in other locations outside North Texas.[69] Cooperative mills were owned by the farmers who used them—in this case, the members of the Farmers'

Alliance. The Alliance mill in Dallas was organized in 1885 with a capacity of two hundred barrels a day, and in 1893 it expanded its capacity to five hundred barrels per day.[70] The Denton mill, established in 1886, was by far the largest and best known, with seven hundred stockholders. The owners purchased their equipment from the John T. Noy Company of Buffalo, New York. Noy employee Alfred Grant came to test the new equipment. He decided to stay in Denton and remained as head miller for more than thirty years.[71] By 1894, the Denton mill was selling its award-winning wares as far away as Mexico.[72]

Members of the Farmers' Alliance had difficulty keeping their mills in business, but the Alliance provided a firm foundation for other companies. In 1890, after William C. Burrus and his son, J. Perry Burrus, bought the Farmers' Alliance mill in McKinney and reorganized it as the Collin County Mill and Elevator Company, they quickly enlarged its capacity to 750 barrels per day.[73] In 1892, the mill, newly lighted with electricity, ran twenty-four hours a day through the summer months. The local newspaper happily reported, "Very recently the management have placed a dynamo machine in the large building with 40 candle lighting capacity. We visited the mill last Saturday night and found the mill beautifully illumined with electric lights and the night force as busy as bees in the different departments."[74] The newspaper failed to record how the employees felt about working through the night. Richard A. Chapman, a native of Tennessee who moved to Grayson County as a child, bought the Farmers' Alliance mill in Sherman in 1897 and renamed it for himself. The next year Chapman greatly upgraded the equipment, catching the attention of the milling publication *The Roller Mill*, published in Buffalo, New York. The reporter for the journal breathlessly listed all the company's new equipment, purchased from the Edward P. Allis Company of Milwaukee. Capable of grinding 260 barrels of flour in twenty-four hours, in its first six months the mill ran "day and night to fill orders."[75]

As mills were shifting from stone to rollers and growing in size and sophistication, they needed increasing amounts of grain. Storage systems called elevators began to dot the North Texas landscape. Although grain elevators had been invented in the 1790s, they did not appear in North Texas until after the Civil War. Grain elevators are complex mechanisms that use a combination of power and gravity to move grain. When grain arrives at the elevator—whether by wagon, ship, or train—the equipment scoops it, raises it to the high point in the building, and dumps it. Gravity then moves the grain to a storage site, most often a bin.[76] Because of the need to elevate the grain, even the earliest elevator buildings were at least three stories high, and often they were the tallest structures in an area.[77]

Adjacent to the elevators—and often almost as tall—were storage bins, which in the nineteenth century were made of wood or steel. Like mills, wooden elevators, filled with grain dust, were highly combustible. Working in an elevator could be unpleasant, as the dust irritated the noses and lungs of workers and created skin rashes. Perhaps most terrifying, grain could literally drown a person, as it "piles and flows like water." In elevators large or small, a person slipping into a bin of grain could be pulled under and, just as in water or quicksand, quickly asphyxiated.[78]

Despite the dangers, elevators became necessary as large mills needed to store sizable quantities of grain. In 1875, news was buzzing among the businessmen of Dallas that a new grain elevator was becoming "a fixed fact." It would have a capacity of 100,000 bushels and would make Dallas "the central grain shipping point for the interior of Texas."[79] That elevator burned in 1883 and was rebuilt the same year. By 1885, the "Central Elevator," as it was called, was run by a thirty-horsepower steam engine. It rose sixty-two feet and had a capacity of one hundred thousand bushels. The Central Elevator was similar, local boosters said, to those in Chicago, St. Louis, and "other great grain centers."[80] Its nearest competitor, at the Todd Mills, was less than half its size.

The huge Cameron New Era Mill in Fort Worth, built in 1888, also had a giant elevator, holding two hundred thousand bushels of wheat. The elevator was 106 feet tall—more than ten stories—and had thirty-four bins. The first story was built of brick, and the floors above were wood with iron cladding. Wheat came by railroad and was weighed, then lifted to the top of the elevator and distributed into the bins according to quality. When needed for processing, the wheat went from the bins to the mill via a conveyor belt, then was lifted to the fourth floor of the mill to begin the refining process.[81] The Cameron elevator was soon eclipsed, however, by the 102-foot tall, ironclad structure of the Dallas Elevator Company, with a capacity of eight hundred thousand bushels, and the Arbuckle Brothers Elevator on the Katy railroad in Dallas, with a million bushels in its 114 ironclad bins.[82]

Even small elevators benefited millers, as they could "buy when [wheat was] at its lowest, and store it away to be ground when wanted."[83] By the end of the nineteenth century, towns like Valley View in Cooke County, Van Alstyne in Grayson County, and Sanger in Denton County had elevators.[84] Farmers could sell their grain at the elevator and receive payment on the spot, or they could consign it, waiting to be paid until the elevator operator sold their grain to millers or other buyers.[85]

North Texas millers were always defensive about the quality of their product. They started out trying to catch up with St. Louis. Then, after the Civil War, Minneapolis began its astonishing rise to preeminence.

Many North Texan consumers thought that imported goods were superior to local ones, and millers had to disabuse them of that error. As Dallasite Frank Cockrell wrote, "The public thought you could not make good flour out of Texas wheat."[86] Even boosters spoke cautiously, taking pains to point out both the quality of local wheat and the skill of the men who milled it. A Gainesville writer declared the Whaley product to be proof that Texas could produce excellent flour: "A very superior grade of flour can be manufactured at home. It is true that much care is used in the selection of wheat but given a No. 1 grain and with the assistance of the head miller the local plant continues to turn out as fine a product as any mill in Texas." The company sold its flour across North Texas and into "Indian Territory and Oklahoma Territory."[87] In 1896, the Burruses joined the chorus of voices publicizing the superiority of North Texas wheat: "We buy direct from our Home Producers in Competition with the world's market and sell direct to home consumers, against all comers. . . . Simply because our Texas Wheat is Unequaled."[88]

Saying that your flour was great was all well and good, but mills needed to prove their claims. Agricultural fairs gave them the opportunity to demonstrate their quality. As early as 1875, the J. W. Moore Mill near Melissa, Collin County, "took the premium of [the] Houston state fair with their flour over St. Louis mills" and thus were said to be "making the best flour in the state."[89] Competing successfully against flour from the Midwest surely showed the quality of Texas products. The Farmers' Alliance mill in Denton won the most awards of all. In 1886, it started its run of winning prizes at the Texas State Fair. The prizes, observers said, proved the worthiness of Texas flour, confounding skeptics who were "turning up their noses at flour made in the state, and declar[ing] none of it fit to use." The Alliance miller was "as good a head miller as the country can afford."[90] In 1895, the Alliance mill captured a "first premium" at the "great St. Louis exposition" in the "mill center of the United States." The *Denton County News* congratulated "management and miller."[91] The mill took two blue ribbons at an 1898 fair in St. Louis—one for soft wheat flour and one sweepstakes prize. In addition to crediting its millers, the Alliance mill also recognized the farmers: "The wheat from which the premium flour was made was grown by J. W. Underwood on his farm five miles west of Denton."[92]

Searching to find their niche in a hypercompetitive market, wholesale mills began marketing their products heavily in the decades after the Civil War. Mills depended on brand recognition to sell their wares to consumers. In North Texas, mills started introducing names, often fanciful, for the various grades of flour in the 1870s. By 1889, the Empire Mills sold eight grades, each a slightly different quality: from the finest, silkiest Empress through Queen, Princess, Duchess, Monarch, Sultan, and Khedive, down to the coarse Chief, full of bran.[93] The descent from snowy white Empress to dark Chief might well reflect racial attitudes embodied strongly in colonialism at the time. Other mills offered between four and six grades. The Alliance mill in Denton in 1890 offered four grades, from first patent or "extra fancy patent" Peace Maker, the most highly refined, to "low grade" Daisy, the coarsest, with bits of bran.[94] Mills tutored consumers to ask for flour by its trade name.

Even as they competed against each other, millers anxiously watched for opportunities to act together to manipulate the market. In the late nineteenth century, American business owners experimented with different forms of organization to forestall competition and maximize their own profits. From the beginning, mill owners worked in concert to control the marketplace. Legitimately, they sought to minimize costs. For instance, the "Millers' association of Dallas county" met in June 1875 to talk about "securing more moderate and equitable railroad freight charges."[95] In 1886, Mark Evans of Fort Worth's Novelty Mills invited fifteen Texas millers to meet in the "great opera-house" with no press in attendance. They reportedly discussed grain supplies, amid shortages, and insurance rates, and they officially formed the Texas Millers' Association.[96] The grain dealers, who sold grain rather than milling it, organized in 1891, then merged with the millers to become the Grain Dealers' and Millers' Association of Texas. In keeping with the times, when monopolies were coming under national scrutiny, they tried to avoid the appearance of collusion, declaring: "This association shall in no manner regulate the prices or values of grain, each member having the right at all times to buy or sell at his own option where and when he may."[97] As we will see, however, their efforts to look innocent fell short in the coming decades.

The people of North Texas developed the milling industry to levels of increasing sophistication in the late nineteenth century as they built big buildings and bought expensive machinery to make fine, silky flour. Some also died in mill accidents. The money they made continued having an impact on North Texas society as they fed their families and built homes. The next chapter focuses on how North Texans brought flour into their kitchens.

5 / FROM BISCUITS TO ANGEL FOOD CAKE: BAKING, 1865–1900

IN THE LATE NINETEENTH CENTURY, AMERICAN BAKing came to resemble what we know today, and people eagerly embraced the new ways. Industrially produced flour became increasingly cheap and uniform in quality. New leavenings, such as commercially made yeast and reliable baking powder, brought new loftiness and tenderness to baked goods. Cookstoves with ovens replaced open hearths. Formerly enslaved African American women moved into the towns, seeking employment and often finding it as cooks in private households, usually those of white people. North Texans adopted these changes as enthusiastically as anyone else in the United States.

For many Texans, however, particularly in rural areas, cornbread remained the staple, with biscuits made from wheat flour enjoyed only as treats. Bread baking—particularly yeast bread—remained complicated and intimidating for novices, and a lot of people simply did not have the money to buy flour. Corn remained easier to grow and mill, and cornmeal stayed cheaper than wheat flour. But most people wanted wheat flour despite its preciousness.

Almost all urban Texans bought their flour in stores. As we have seen, local mills produced numerous brands and multiple grades of flour, but competitors from outside Texas also stocked neighborhood store shelves. Rivalry from "northern flour" was in full swing by 1873, when Dallas merchants Simmons and Lake offered "the best brands of St. Louis Family Flour" to its clientele.[1] In 1885, father and son Thomas F. and Joseph M. McEnnis, natives of St. Louis, carried at least seven brands of flour from Missouri mills, as well as sugar and molasses "direct from plantations," in their store on Commerce Street in Dallas.[2] In McKinney in 1899, local merchants Goostree and Houston offered "highest grade northern flour and good flour from home mills." To label local flour as merely "good" clearly deemed it inferior to the imported product.[3] North Texas cooks had to decide which product to purchase.

Regardless of where their flour came from, North Texas cooks made quick breads, particularly biscuits.[4] W. T. Land from Collin County recalled that in the 1870s biscuits were still a treat, a special offering reserved for Sundays.[5] As wheat flour became more available, many women, both black and white, made biscuits by the dozen almost every morning.

In the late nineteenth century, bread leavened with yeast remained something exceptional, but that would change with the spread of commercially made yeast that proved more reliable than most homemade yeast.[6] Dallas businesses manufactured yeast cakes while competitors imported them from St. Louis or offered national-brand Fleischmann's from Cincinnati.[7] Most North Texans made their yeasted bread at home, where either the housewife or a female domestic worker put in the hours of labor to produce a loaf or rolls. Across the former Confederacy, when formerly enslaved women moved to urban areas and took jobs as domestic workers, cooking was often part of their new job, whether or not they had any previous training or skill. In 1866, Catherine Bunting Coit wrote to her niece, "I cannot keep a cook." Either Coit or her employee would find fault with the situation, and she would fire the employee or the employee would leave. At one point Coit discharged a cook whom she could "not trust . . . to make up bread."[8] The cook may not have had prior knowledge of the intricacies of yeast bread, and the skill was important enough to Coit—a matter of "trust"—that she considered it grounds for dismissal.

The cash prizes awarded at the State Fair of Texas for both quick and yeast breads show the variety that a home cook might produce. In the 1890s, the fair segregated its awards by race. African American and white women competed only against women from their own race, and the breads they submitted were not the same. Each group of women vied for the best yeast-rising white bread and, curiously, the best salt-rising bread, a peculiar variety from Appalachia leavened with a strong-smelling starter that had become a national fad.[9] Only white women competed for the fashionable brown and graham breads made with dark flour and thought to be healthful. Only African American women could win prizes for cornbread and for labor-intensive beaten biscuits, another oddity. The dough of this type of biscuit was leavened with many repeated whacks of a heavy object. Beaten biscuits, which had largely disappeared after the Civil War, were widely associated with white people's nostalgia for the days of enslavement.[10] Perhaps the contest designers thought that cornbread was beneath white women, that brown bread was too desirable for African Americans, and that maybe if they incentivized beaten biscuits they would become popular again. Whatever the reasons, women entered the contests and took home their money and prizes. Superintendent N. C. Harllee of the "colored department" of the fair reported in the *Dallas Morning News* in 1894, "Saturday, Oct. 27 will be 'cake day' at the fair with the colored people and there will be more varieties of cake, salt-rising bread, biscuit, hoecake, johnny cake, cornbread, pone bread and all other kinds of bread than has ever been exhibited at the state fair. We have many fine cooks in the ranks of the colored women, the very best in the land, and this year they are going to show what they can do."[11] And presumably they did.

With the increased availability of leavenings, sugar, and spices, sweets became more common. Baking powder, a miraculous new leaven that made possible cakes of great height, came from local suppliers and national companies. The Dallas Steam Coffee and Spice Mills made its own baking powder, and Hughes Brothers & Co. manufactured "Grape"-brand baking powder and flavoring extracts. Founder John V. Hughes was a retired physician with an interest in chemistry. On the other hand, Dallas grocers Wells and Chambers offered four different brands of baking powder, including the leading national brand, Royal, based in New York City.[12] Whatever its source, reliable baking powder created a new day for bakers everywhere.

Transportation networks—global, national, and local—made possible all sorts of new foods in North Texas. Bakers had different flavors and ingredients at their fingertips if they had the money to purchase them. Spices—most typically cinnamon, allspice, ginger, and cloves—became more readily available. Dried fruit abounded, from figs and several kinds of raisins to currants and multiple varieties of dates. Sweeteners included imports from the tropics—several grades of sugar and molasses—and maple syrup from the North as well as sorghum syrup from Texas and other southern sources. Consumers in town could buy butter, lard, and artificial fats such as Cottolene, made from cotton seed oil. Chocolate—both regular and sweet German—came from Massachusetts.[13] Fresh tropical ingredients such as pineapples, bananas, and coconuts began appearing more often on North Texas tables. Mary Moore wrote to her daughter Linnet in 1899 that she "got a large coconut so Father could make a dipper out of the hull and grated it on my grater that I got from Mrs. [Hester Patterson?] Harpool and it was just like fringe so nice on cake."[14]

Using baking powder and all manner of ingredients, home cooks created cakes of ever-increasing sophistication. Fruitcake, which was a staple in respectable nineteenth-century American homes, occupied much of the energy of home bakers every autumn, and Dallas grocers advertised a lengthy list of ingredients available to big-city shoppers: two kinds of almonds, five types of raisins, two varieties of Turkish layer figs (which meant they were packed in layers), Persian dates, Malaga grapes, currants, and spices (including cinnamon, allspice, ginger, and cloves), as well as "Finest Corsican Glace Citrone [*sic*]; candied orange peel; candied lemon peel; crystallized lemon peel; [and] crystallized cherries."[15] With those ingredients and a lot of time, patience, and labor, Dallas cooks could produce fruitcakes that equaled those anywhere else.

Prize lists from regional fairs show the increasing variety of cakes, driven by the growing availability of ingredients to North Texas bakers and perhaps by how much easier it had become to bake in a stove oven than in a fireplace. In 1877, fairs in North Texas offered prizes only for "fruit and jelly cake," pound cake, fruitcake, sponge cake, marble cake, and crackers.[16] Twenty years later, women competed with multiple types of cakes. The possibilities included cakes leavened with many eggs (always tricky to make), including sponge cake and angel food cake. Jelly cakes were probably rolled sponge cakes with jelly filling. Now mixed into the dark parts of marble cakes were spices or, increasingly, chocolate. Silver cakes and white mountain cakes were vanilla cakes made with egg whites, while chocolate cake might be a light cake with chocolate filling and/or icing, or a cake with chocolate in the actual batter. Gold cake was made with egg yolks. Coconut cakes were usually white mountain cakes with coconut in the frosting, filling, or cake batter, or some combination of all three. Ornamental cakes were heavily decorated with frosting. At the State Fair of Texas, African American women and white women competed in the same categories, but only against other women of their race.[17]

Home cooks did not commonly bake cookies, or at least they rarely mentioned them. When they did, the most popular variety was the tea cake, a simple cookie that was rolled and cut. Smart Dallas matrons served cookies such as "curled wafers" at their social affairs.[18]

Pies received only passing mention, but we know that they might have been made, using homely ingredients such as sweet potatoes. Mary Moore told Linnet that their dinner in 1898 included chicken, "light bread and butter," and sweet potato custard.[19] Starting about 1892, Texans could purchase mincemeat in jars, but it appears that few if any households made their own.[20] And canned "pie fruits" continued to be popular at North Texas grocery stores.

Even though home baking had become easier and more varied, women in North Texas, particularly in the towns, would soon be able to buy rather than make their baked goods.

After the Civil War, the commercial baking industry in North Texas got a slow start. The 1870 census shows a handful of Europeans baking in North Texas—German Henry Bohny in Dallas, Swiss immigrant Andrew Krause

FIGURES 5.1a and 5.1b. *Barbara Schmidt Eberling and Herman Eberling. (Courtesy of Garnette Marlow)*

in McKinney, and French émigré Eugene De Levellette in Denton—as well as a Virginian, James Dorchester, in Sherman. The first commercial bakers in Fort Worth were German natives Barbara Schmidt Eberling and Herman Eberling, who arrived in Fort Worth on the first passenger train from Dallas in 1876. Intent on opening a bakery, they molded and cured the bricks for the ovens themselves.[21]

By 1880, the number of bakers and bakeries in North Texas had grown dramatically. Dallas had eighteen bakers, and Grayson County boasted thirteen. Most Grayson County bakers were in Denison and Sherman, but even tiny Whitesboro enjoyed the services of German immigrant William Bertram. Almost half of the bakers in North Texas came from Europe, with Germany providing the greatest number. Many American bakers immigrated from cooler climes. In Dallas, four migrated from New York. All of them were white.[22]

Opening a bakery took determination. First, the baker had to know his craft, for consistently turning out a high-quality product took skill and experience. Commercial bread baking required physical strength to knead and lift heavy doughs as well as the perseverance to work with fire in hot environments. It also demanded patience during the long cycles of rising yeast. Money was required to meet the capital expenses involved in setting up a bakery, even if it was not huge. A baker needed pans, perhaps a good work table, tools for mixing, and, most important, a reliable oven. Some commercial ovens were made of brick and built into the site, and some were portable metal models. In 1889, Henry Bohny moved from Dallas to Gainesville and advertised having "the best oven in the state."[23] Bakers also had their share of financial obligations. In Fort Worth, each bakery owner paid an "occupation tax" of $10 per year; that was more than the tax levied on a "clairvoyant or mesmerist," who paid $2.50, but less than a physician's tax of $25.[24]

Bakers needed cash or credit to buy the ingredients that went into their baked goods. Good flour and dependable yeast established the quality of the finished product. Gutgeselle's Bakery in McKinney linked the quality of the ingredients and the final outcome: "Best grades of flour. Best bread."[25] And Fort Worth's Turner & Dingee guaranteed that "we are using better Flour in our bakery than any other baker here."[26]

The business was not for everyone. Bakers frequently shifted their location, perhaps seeking lower rents and better foot traffic. They bought and sold their enterprises frequently, and many lasted only a short time.[27] Sometimes they feuded with one another. Edward Krohn of the City Bakery in Fort Worth, "Dealer in Confectioneries, Groceries, Cigars and Tobacco," had a particularly pugnacious personality. He opened his Fort Worth business in 1877, having been through bankruptcy in another location. In 1878, his bakery burned, and he had no insurance. In 1879, he was "in failing condition."[28] He somehow stayed in business, but in March 1883 the City of Fort Worth seized his stock of flour as repayment for a four-year-old debt. The following July, Krohn got into a fistfight in his bakery, and his opponent cut him on the wrist with a saw. Krohn tangled with competitors Ferdinand Perkiewicz and Albert Petsch in 1885. The *Fort Worth Daily Gazette* carried a notice of Krohn's second relocation in a year and noted that "Mr. Krohn takes occasion to say that he has no connection with the 'Star Bakery' whatever."[29] In July 1885, the horse for his delivery wagon ran off and then collided with a buggy.[30] Despite his woes, Krohn remained in business for more than a decade.

Besides Edward Krohn, other bakers had problems as well. Robert Boehle, suffering from illness and a failed business, deliberately poisoned himself in 1887. A German immigrant, Boehle left "an estimable wife" whose family was all in Germany.[31] In February 1890, baker Walter J. Doherty and a vendor, A. J. Mostello, were "having some words over an account." Doherty employee John White tried to "act as a peace maker." Mostello left the scene, returned with his gun, and "shot through the window at White, who was behind the counter waiting on a customer," killing the innocent man.

In April, Mostello pleaded guilty to second-degree murder and received a five-year sentence.[32]

Bakeries often required multiple workers to supply their customers. Bakers usually worked through the night to have fresh bread at dawn, and they not infrequently lived at the bakery where they worked. Ads for bakers went two ways. Some were placed by men wanting a position and advertising their availability. "B.F." from Decatur, Texas, expressed a desire "to finish learning his trade in some first class bakery in any good size city," while an anonymous experienced baker noted that he "understands bread and cakes thoroughly."[33] Conversely, bakeries publicized their need for workers, sometimes in detail. The Early Breakfast Bakery in Dallas was specifically looking for "a German boy to learn the bakery trade."[34] Other employers sought applicants with the different skill sets to bake both bread and cake.[35] Employers wanted their bakers to be "sober" and "steady," although it's unclear whether "sober" referred to their drinking habits, their personalities, or both. Virtually all employers promised "good wages" without saying what they were.[36]

But workers mistrusted the employers, and unions arose in Dallas and Fort Worth. Bakers—mostly in the Northeast and particularly European immigrants whose native countries had histories of labor activism—had unionized across the United States, beginning in the 1860s. When the movement arrived in North Texas in the 1890s, Dallas and Fort Worth bakers became almost the only union members in the South. In 1897, Bakers' Union No. 90 in Dallas declared the Queen City Bakery a union shop, meaning that all employees were union members.[37] In the Fort Worth Labor Day parade of 1899, the candymakers, bakers, and confectioners marched "in uniform, with a handsomely decorated float."[38] In the new century, unions would become important in the lives and work of bakers.

One reason for workers' unhappiness was the deskilling of their labor. As we have seen with milling in the late nineteenth century, when machines began taking over processes long done by hand, mechanization came to commercial baking. In the 1880s, bakery owners began mechanizing the ancient art of bread making by spending large sums of money on equipment that would do the work that bakers had done by hand for millennia. An article from the *New York Star*, reprinted in the *Fort Worth Daily Gazette* in 1888, bragged, "Machines are now used to knead bread, and big bakers who formerly employed five or six men for this work save 20 percent on the cost of labor."[39] The Kleber family, owners of the Queen City Bakery, brought the technology to Dallas in 1899, only two years after the shop went union: "In keeping abreast with the rapid strides of progress we have equipped our Bakery with a modern electric dough mixer and roller. This system is the cleanest and most improved method now used in the manufacture of bread in the eastern cities. . . . You will find it is the most perfect loaf ever manufactured in Dallas."[40] The Klebers also innovated with steam baking, introducing steam into the oven during baking to create bread with a crisp crust and an even crumb.[41] Bakery owners like the Klebers apparently gave little thought to the impact of deskilling an important type of baking, indeed, they may have automated to rid themselves of troublesome unionized employees.

Like many kinds of technology, bread-making machines could prove dangerous. In 1895, P. J. Breen was working at the Edwards Steam Bakery in Fort Worth and caught his hand in a dough roller. He sued, alleging that owner "[John] Edwards put him to rolling dough by machinery, a process that is dangerous to one who is unskilled in the work. Breen was put at this work without being cautioned that it was dangerous, and by reasons of his inexperience his right hand was caught and run through the machinery. The injury disabled him for some time, hence the suit for damages."[42] The case came to trial in June 1897, but no verdict was published.[43] Breen's painful injury cost him time and money as well as discomfort.

Fire continued to be one of the greatest dangers in the baking industry. Wood-burning ovens could catch fire or spark stockpiles of flammable flour, and fires from other sources often spread rapidly. An account from Denison in 1878 gives a good snapshot of the danger. "Mr. Richards, the baker" at the Sherman Cracker Factory, began working on bread shortly after midnight. At 2:45 a.m., he heard a loud noise or explosion in the office. By the time the fire crew extinguished the blaze, the factory owners had lost "nearly a car load of flour," the steam engine, and all the machinery.[44]

Fort Worth had several bakery fires in the late nineteenth century, often complicated by lack of access to water to fight them. In 1884, the Georgia Bakery and the Wright Brothers grocery store burned in the middle of the night. Although they had no insurance, the proprietors of the bakery, Carson and Lochridge, were again producing bread within a week, presumably at a different location.[45] In March 1886, a small fire at the Star Bakery resulted in merriment for the onlookers, if not for the victims. A fire broke out about 10:00 a.m. on the second story, "directly over the baking department, the plank walls catching directly from the stovepipe." The rooms above were "occupied by a number of employe[e]s as sleeping quarters." Leo Lieb, a baker who had probably been up all night producing the morning's bread, awoke and jumped fifteen feet from the window to the street, devoid of all his clothing "except a single garment of a superlatively Seymour [perhaps 'see more'?] cut." Lieb dashed through the crowd and into a house, "the feminine element" screaming "as he passed swiftly by." The bakery owners put the fire out quickly and lost only 250 uninsured empty flour sacks. Leo Lieb risked his life and lost his dignity.[46]

The Star Bakery caught fire again only nineteen months later, with far more dire consequences. The blaze originated "in some unknown way" at 2:45 a.m. and burned six frame buildings as well as a three-story brick building and Germania Hall, a gathering place for European immigrants. The Fort Worth fire department had few tools, as the waterworks had "not been in operation for four days, and the engine [was] out of repair," so they formed a bucket brigade to bring water from a cistern to fight the fire. Helen Bultmeyer and her brother Herman, asleep on the second floor of the bakery, barely escaped the flames. The losses to the bakery, a saloon, a second-hand store, and a livery stable totaled at least $30,000.[47]

In 1890, a fire started in Buer's bakery, which shared the first floor of the Masonic Temple with a confectionery. The bakers had finished their work an hour before the fire was discovered, and while they swore that they had extinguished all the ovens, the fire began in that area. The Fort Worth firefighters had no access to water for at least fifteen minutes. The total loss was $20,000, including the gutted brick-and-stone Masonic Temple.[48]

Dallas firefighters fared better in 1891, when the roof of the North Dallas Bakery on McKinney Avenue caught fire, probably from the oven. The Dallas water supply saved the day. There were two fire hydrants nearby, and the "fire boys" had "two good streams . . . playing upon the burning building in a very few moments." The baker, A. J. Stuart, lost only loaves of bread.[49] Modern firefighting equipment saved the day.

By the end of the nineteenth century, urban shoppers could buy a variety of breads: white bread (probably baked in a pan with straight sides, with a soft crust); crisp-crusted French bread (most likely "cast," or baked free-form on a baking sheet); and Vienna bread, introduced to the United States at the 1876 Philadelphia Centennial Exposition and made with milk rather than water. North Texas bakers also joined the healthy eating craze that was sweeping the United States, producing whole-wheat "Ralston" and graham breads.[50]

The crunchy flat squares known as crackers became common in the nineteenth century. Because they preserved well and transported easily, they were often made in distant locations and shipped to Texas. But by 1873, Dozier and Weyl had opened a factory in Dallas to produce "the finest and best made" crackers.[51] In 1875, the Odell brothers expanded their bread and cake business to go "extensively into the manufacture of crackers as a specialty." A writer for the Dallas newspaper pronounced them "equal if not superior to any we ever tasted."[52] That same year, in Sherman, G. Y. Gray built a two-story fireproof brick building, forty-two by one hundred feet, in which two hundred barrels of "steam-baked crackers," in twenty-six varieties, were produced each day.[53] Crackers were the basis of many quick, cheap meals. Charles Moore wrote in 1897 that the women in his family were so busy putting down new carpets that "they did not stop to get any dinner but eat crackers salmon and butter and we were all real tired last night."[54]

Commercial bakers eventually moved into making sweets as well as bread and crackers.[55] Cakes, pies, and cookies all began appearing in bakers' cases.[56] As with home bakers, the invention of baking powder revolutionized professional cake baking, and bakeries began providing elaborate layer cakes for North Texas tables. Households marked the finest occasions, including weddings, birthdays, holidays, and other celebrations, with bakery cakes.[57] W. T. Wells of Dallas advertised "Layer Cakes (assorted flavors), Gold Cake, Wine Cake . . . Angel Food."[58] North Texas bakeries also produced fruitcake, saving home cooks the labor of much chopping and mixing and the long baking times. The Model Bakery in Dallas promised "the finest ingredients necessary," while competitor Stacey's Bakery offered "over 350 testimonials from leading ladies of Dallas and Texas" about the superiority of its fruitcake. Fruitcakes, dense and sturdy, shipped well, and the Model Bakery sent its cakes to "twenty-nine different towns."[59]

Bakers worked hard to put their best face before the public. Local parades often included entries from bakeries, usually featuring the distribution of some sort of baked goods. In Denison's 1886 Mardi Gras parade, the Denison City Bakery float was "surmounted by an old French baker, who dealt out cookies and ginger cakes."[60] Fort Worth's 1893 Mai Fest procession included three bakeries touting their wares.[61]

Bakers advertised frequently in the newspapers, including the African American press.[62] By 1879, the Star Bakery in Denison was advertising the freshness of its bread and rolls, "delivered twice a day to any part of the city."[63] The freshness theme, tied to local delivery, continued into the 1880s. In 1888, the Ross Avenue Bakery in Dallas declared, "War! War! On and after this date, April 24, 1888, no more Stale Bread! But fresh from the oven to the consumer, and justice for all."[64] The W. T. Wells bakery, also in Dallas, announced that it would have fresh bread "every morning." The bakers for Wells worked throughout the night to have hot bread when customers arose in the morning.[65]

Another source of pride was purity, a harbinger of the reforms around the corner, as Robinson's Lone Star Bakery in Denison advertised "good, light, flakey, white bread that is warranted free from foreign ingredients."[66] Price mattered too. The Model Bakery in Dallas declared its value: "The Model Bakery sells the bread just as cheap by the single loaf as by the dollar's worth."[67] And then there was the appeal to comfort. In April 1896, the

Palace of Sweets Bakery in Fort Worth reminded consumers that "the hot weather has come" and customers could get homemade bread "too cheap to worry over the fire baking."[68] The bakery did not point out to readers the very real dangers to its workers from the heat.

Local citizens often called on bakeries to donate their valued goods, and bakers responded charitably. In 1885, the Fort Worth post of the Grand Army of the Republic thanked bakery owners Perkiewicz and Petsch for their donations to the post's "camp-fire supper."[69] (On the other hand, individual McKinney citizens donated flour to finance a reunion of Confederate soldiers in 1883.)[70] The Denison City Bakery in 1886 "offered to furnish bread to any poor family, with the right credentials," apparently coordinated through "charity associations."[71] In Fort Worth, Sofie Krautter Reich, whose husband Bruno Reich owned a bakery, became beloved for her kindness. Reich, an immigrant from Germany who was still in her twenties and the mother of a young son, made sure that the children of Fort Worth felt cared for. The Benevolent Home of Fort Worth, an orphanage founded in 1887, received bread from the bakery. Mrs. Reich herself often included "some delicacy for the little ones, with a loving word whispered to our boys as she fills their basket. These little messages are carried to the matron and repeated to the children, when their happy voices ring forth a 'God bless Mrs. Reich.'" At Thanksgiving, the Reichs joined other contributors to the orphanage, but Mrs. Reich, the newspaper observed, "remembers the home bountifully every day in the week."[72]

During the late nineteenth century, the relationship between the people of North Texas and wheat changed from earlier days. Growing and milling became increasingly mechanized, and farmers and millers had to decide how much they would adopt the new expensive trends. The railroad brought goods to the region and made exporting possible. Many North Texans saw their diets shift to include more wheat flour and more sweets. In the twentieth century, these changes would only accelerate as people made their choices about how to adapt. The next chapter examines shifts for North Texas wheat farmers in the first decades of the twentieth century.

6 / WHEAT IN THE SPRING AND COTTON IN THE FALL: GROWING, 1900–1940

BETWEEN 1900 AND WORLD WAR II, WHEAT CONTINUED to expand in importance in the lives of North Texans. Farmers grew their biggest crops to date. The number of large milling companies expanded, and the owners of those companies used their wealth to alter the culture of the region through music, architecture, and the visual arts. Increasing numbers of North Texans bought their baked goods from commercial companies, even as home baking became more sophisticated. Throughout all these changes, wheat remained an integral part of the regional economy and way of life.

Urbanization dramatically changed North Texas. The number of farms in the region peaked in 1910 and had declined slightly by 1940. The towns and cities grew steadily, particularly Dallas, with a 1940 population of almost 300,000, and Fort Worth, with 178,000. Grayson County's urban population in Sherman and Denison that year totaled 33,000.[1] But farming, including wheat farming, persisted as an occupation.

In 1900, wheat still comprised a substantial portion of the agricultural products of North Texas, even as cotton cultivation continued to spread throughout the region. In Denton and Tarrant Counties, wheat covered more acres than did cotton; Denton County had an impressive 92,800 acres in wheat. In Cooke County, the ratios of cotton and wheat were fairly close, while in Dallas and Grayson Counties, to the east, cotton was planted in more than double the amount of acreage as wheat. In Collin County, the ratio of wheat to cotton was about three-to-four. Cotton dominated in the eastern part of the county, while wheat held sway in the west, adjacent to Denton County, especially in the "flats" west of McKinney.[2] By 1919, the number of acres in wheat had increased slightly in Cooke, Denton, and Grayson Counties, while acres in wheat fell in Collin, Dallas, and Tarrant Counties. At the same time, the number of acres in cotton rose substantially in all counties. Farmers continued to raise both cotton and wheat on the same farms, if not on the same ground, in North Texas in the early twentieth century.[3] Zelda Davis White, born in Grayson County in 1912, recalled the demands of the two-crop system: "Farming was a never-ending job and all the children participated. . . . The girls often worked in the fields chopping cotton, shocking grain and picking cotton."[4] Combining cotton and wheat kept everyone busy.

Some North Texans looked with disdain at the cotton acreage that was overtaking the region. In 1914, flour mill owner Perry Burrus, who had been forced to import wheat from New York to get enough to grind, urged Collin County farmers to "get away from growing cotton." He preferred to have an ample supply from local growers and believed that North Texas farmers should increase their grain production.[5] Perhaps farmers heard his message, but it seems not to have had a huge impact.

North Texas farmers took their farming seriously and availed themselves of opportunities to learn new methods of growing. In 1903, the Collin County Farmers Institute met to discuss "The Condition and Prospects of the Wheat Crop in Collin County," including such topics as how much to pasture animals on the wheat.[6] With professional guidance, North Texas farmers became more conscious of the quality of their seed.[7] At the Cooke County fair in 1917, entrants competed for the best pecks of winter wheat and "any other variety," with the winner of each category receiving a prize of a dollar.[8]

In 1908, A. M. Ferguson, trained as a horticulturalist at Texas A&M University, left his faculty post at the University of Texas and established a company in Sherman to produce and sell high-quality "field seeds"—corn, cotton, wheat, and other varieties. Ferguson Seed's 1912 catalog offered four varieties of wheat: Sibley's New Golden, which it touted as the best-yielding variety in its tests; acclimated Mediterranean wheat; Rudy wheat from Pennsylvania; and Fultz, an old standard wheat with a "large, roundish, plump berry."[9] Agricultural scientists were making inroads into the North Texas market.

In 1910, the US Department of Agriculture believed that the region was important enough that it established an agricultural experiment station in Denton County, near the community of Krum, to study the problems and crop yields of "the small-grain region of North Texas." Government scientists in North Texas devoted most of their efforts to improving wheat yields. Examining more than two thousand strains of wheat, they isolated a variety that they named, appropriately, "Denton."[10] Denton wheat, a soft winter wheat, was a "typical Mediterranean wheat" that grew tall and ripened midseason. Its stiff straw kept it erect even in the stormy winds of

North Texas.[11] It made particularly good bread flour, producing loaves of heavy weight.[12] Thus, the name "Denton" was enshrined on the list of productive wheat.

Through the early part of the twentieth century, wheat continued to play an important role in the agricultural life of North Texas, and residents paid attention to the prices of both grain and flour through daily newspaper reports.[13] As always, farmers fretted about rain or the lack thereof; smut and rust; and pests, such as the aphid, or plant louse, known as the "green bug" that devastated the wheat crop from Dallas to the Red River in 1906 and 1907. The Texas legislature appropriated $5,000 to studying control methods.[14] Destruction by birds ebbed and flowed. In 1912, A. M. Ferguson observed that farmers had stopped growing "smooth head wheat"—the types lacking bristly awns, or spikes, protruding from the heads—because of bird damage. "With the disappearance of the birds," farmers began using smooth head wheat again.[15]

But change was coming. Wheat cultivation began moving to the Panhandle of Texas around 1900, when farmers started digging wells into the Ogallala Aquifer and installing windmills to pull out the groundwater for irrigation. The drier air in West Texas discouraged disease, and observers also noted the benefits of the flat terrain: "The levelness of the ground facilitates ploughing, sowing, and reaping, and allows the use of large labor saving machinery."[16] Whereas the largest wheat farms in North Texas reached only two or three hundred acres, in the Panhandle a single farmer with machines might cultivate three thousand acres.[17] Economies of scale began to take over.

In 1904, Wilbarger County, in the southeast corner of the Panhandle, joined Denton County as "the banner wheat growing counties of the State."[18] In 1919, Denton County retained its position as one of the top three wheat-growing counties in Texas, with a yield of more than one million bushels. But it was joined by Carson and Gray, two counties just east of Amarillo.[19] Seeing new opportunities, North Texas companies like Ferguson Seed expanded their operations to West Texas.[20]

Yet wheat persisted in North Texas. As they had done for the previous half-century, farmers continued to plant their wheat crops each fall. Some still broadcast the seed, while others used drills to place the seed in the soil. Some drills pressed soft soil over the seed.[21] North Texas farmers still grazed livestock on the growing wheat, and they cultivated, though minimally, in the early spring with "spike-tooth harrow[s] or weeder[s]."[22]

Wheat was still harvested in North Texas much as it had been done in the past, still beginning about the middle of June with farmers cutting their crops with reapers and binders.[23] For many years, farmers continued to employ horse-drawn binders that cut the wheat and tied it in bundles, which then dropped to the ground. Workers—often the wife and children of the farmer—shocked the grain, "setting the bundles on end, with heads to the top, so the sun could dry out the heads."[24] The shocked wheat might stand for several weeks before threshing.[25] Once the dried wheat was ready to thresh, workers loaded it onto a "bundle wagon" and brought the shocks to the threshing machine. In 1925, fourteen-year-old John Wells made $2.50 a day "running" a bundle wagon for Bob Fortner's thresher. Half of the money was his to keep, and half of it paid for the mule that pulled the wagon. Teenage boys coveted such positions.[26]

After the bundled wheat dried sufficiently, it was time to thresh the grain from the chaff. Threshing machines remained large capital investments. Roy Clyde Sanders, who farmed in the Ethel community in Grayson County, operated the separator, or thresher, for George Hurley before buying his own thresher.[27] Sometimes family members or neighbors pooled their resources to buy the equipment. For example, near Lindsay, the Bezner brothers—Joe, John, and Jake—bought a thresher together in 1914.[28]

On some North Texas farms, the use of mules and horses in wheat farming persisted until the late 1920s.[29] By 1900, however, many threshers ran with steam engines.[30] Tom Jackson bought the first steam-powered thresher in the Van Alstyne area. The Case-brand thresher came from Dallas, and the engine was fired with coal or wood.[31] Near Lindsay, Cooke County, Hugo Bezner recalled with great specificity the machinery that his father and uncles bought: "The engine was a Buffalo-Pitts Steamer purchased from Nick Dieter. The separator was a 28-inch cylinder Aultman-Taylor. The big engine [that they bought] about 1920 was a 30–60 Aultman-Taylor tractor and a Rumley 36-inch cylinder separator." The equipment impressed Hugo Bezner enough that he was able to remember it in detail decades later.

Steam engines needed fuel, and so threshing teams included wagons that were filled with wood or, later, coal and carried water to supply the engine.[32] Darrell Myers observed that "each farm[er] was supposed to have enough coal on location to thresh his crop and supply enough to take the equipment to the next client."[33]

Threshing crews still traveled from farm to farm in the region, with crews of workers moving along with the machinery. These crews might consist of twenty to twenty-five men, who usually lived in the area. Janie Hartman commented, "It was necessary for five or six neighboring families to join together to make a crew."[34] Families sometimes traded labor, although the machinery still had its costs. Most thresher owners paid their crews in cash.[35] Richard Daniel proudly recalled that when he married Thelma

Lynch in 1926, "I worked at a thresher and had $40 when Thelma and me got married." The twenty-two-year-old bridegroom thought he had a fortune.[36]

Other crews trekked longer distances. Vivian Stark McCullum remembered that around Frisco in the late 1920s, her family referred to the harvesting crew as "gypsies": "one particular group that camped out in barns, sheds or tents each year."[37] Sometimes crews slept on the ground.[38] Darrell Myers remembered, "Each man would carry his own bedding with him. . . . At night the crew would bed-down on location. Bundles of grain could be used for a mattress or bedding spread on the ground."[39] Locals regarded strangers with suspicion but as a necessity, while they treated neighbors kindly. Nonetheless, the owners of the equipment took positions of responsibility on the crews. F. M. Good owned a thresher in Dallas County, and his sons had the "smart jobs" on the crew: scheduling the routes, running the separator, and troubleshooting the equipment.[40]

The threshing process began with the setup of the separator. Hugo Bezner recalled that it had to be positioned with the wind blowing from the front of the separator to the rear. If the wind direction changed, the crew had to shift the separator accordingly. The crew dug a hole for each wheel, then placed the wheels in the holes. The machine operator ensured that the machine was level. Bezner recalled precisely that Pete Block always took responsibility for that task. Block also ensured the accuracy of the scale on the separator.[41]

Once the separator was in place, the task of threshing began with transferring the bundles or shocks of wheat from the fields to the thresher. Hugo Bezner remembered the process specifically. His family's large operation had fourteen bundle wagons, pulled by horses or mules. Seven "pitchers" worked in the field, each responsible for loading bundles of wheat into two wagons. A field boss helped the pitchers keep the pace. Bezner recalled that "the field boss for many years was Uncle Louie [Louis Frederick Bezner]." Once the wagon was full, the driver took the load to the thresher. In the growing heat of the early summer, children carried water to the workers in the field. Ray Wilde from Cooke County remembered, "My job was to deliver drinking water to the hands working in the field. . . . I rode in either a two-wheel cart or on horseback to deliver the water from jugs with gunney [burlap] sack material around it to help keep it somewhat cool."[42]

At the thresher, men known as "spike pitchers" unloaded the bundles: "Four men threw the bundles into the elevator of the thresher, always head first," said Hugo Bezner. "The spike pitchers at our thresher were mostly Jake [Jacob Robert Bezner] and John [Frank] Bezner, Perk Laux, and a hired man Uncle Jake [Jacob Friedrich Bezner] kept each summer by the

FIGURE 6.1. *Farmers around a thresher just outside Argyle, Texas, late nineteenth century. (University of North Texas Libraries Special Collections)*

name of Fred Banfield."[43] Bundle haulers were not above pulling pranks to "get a little rest." They could deliberately overstuff the separator and "choke it down." Darrell Myers recalled that "they would catch heck from Marion and Clarence [Good, the machine owner's sons] who had to go inside it and pull the straw out by hand." Once the crew had transported all the bundles, they left for the next work site, according to Myers: "When all the grain in a field had been loaded on the bundle wagon these crews would start to the next location to have a supply of bundles ready when the thresher arrived."[44] Not a minute was to be wasted. But occasionally crews asserted themselves over their bosses. Myers said, "I recall one year when the crew wanted off on July 4th for the big celebration that always occurred on that day. The year had been wet and Rex [Good, the machine owner's son] was behind schedule and would not shut down. The crew pulled a strike and went to town anyway. There was nothing he could do but shut down until the next day."[45]

The "separator man" had responsibility for ensuring the smooth operation of the equipment—"mothering" the thresher, as Janie Hartman put it: "He carried out his duties from on top of the machine. This specialist was constantly greasing, oiling, testing belt tension, checking cleanness of the grain and always cocking a sensitive ear toward strange sounds that could mean trouble." The separator had a sound all its own, said Hartman: "the hiss of steam, the whir of gears and the whine of the belts."[46] After the threshers separated the grain from the straw, the grain went into a wagon and the straw was stacked to be stored as feed for livestock.[47]

At the end of a long, hot, dusty day, workers craved being able to rinse off. Oma Lee Scoggin of the Ethel community in Grayson County recalled, "After supper, the hands would pile into an empty wagon and go to a near by [*sic*] stock tank for a bath. They might not have come away with much less dirt, but, at least, the chaff from the grain was washed off."[48] According to Darrell Myers, "The bath tub . . . could be a cattle tank, a creek, or maybe only a water hole in a dry creek. Each man took his own bathing suit with him (the one furnished him by his Maker)[.] Anything wet was a bath tub."[49]

Life on the threshing crews had light moments. Ray Wilde said that the "older men" played tricks on one another and on "the youngsters," especially the "town kids that came out to work." While Wilde did not describe the tricks, he did mention that rattlesnakes "show[ed] up" on more than a few occasions.[50] Workers on the Stark farm sang each night.[51] Roy Clyde Sanders brought ice cream from Ashburn's in Sherman to his crews every Saturday.[52] At the conclusion of threshing, Howard Houston Cunningham gave a party with beer, crackers, and cheese for the workers.[53] And of course, there was always an occasion for young love. William Valentine Graham, from Pilot Point, came with a threshing crew to the farm of James Burnett in Grayson County. He and Mary Ella Burnett met and were married in October 1907.[54]

Feeding threshing crews is a popular part of wheat culture lore. As in the past, women cooked as many as three heavy meals a day for the crews, with "heaps of meat, potatoes, gravy, homemade bread, vegetables and desserts." Lillie Gray Patterson from Dallas County remembered "cooking brown beans with slabs of ham in a five-gallon pot and making five batches of biscuit dough to feed all the crew." She won particular praise for her peach cobbler.[55] Sallie Stark of Collin County fed "hot, tired and hungry men" with salmon croquettes, biscuits, macaroni and cheese, pinto beans, banana pudding, and "many other dishes," all cooked on her wood-burning stove.[56] As always, the hours stretched long. Janie Hartman observed, "Some cooks were up at 3 a.m. to serve breakfast before dawn and hardly ever made it to bed before 10 or 11 p.m. . . . Threshing held little romance for the womenfolk."[57]

As in the past, some threshing crews brought their own cookshacks and cooks with them. The small structures on wheels usually had wood stoves on one end and sometimes had benches attached for the crews to sit on while they ate off tin plates.[58] When Loretta Marie Eberhart and J. B. Wilde married in 1921, they moved into the Wilde family cookshack rather than live with J.B.'s mother.[59] The owners of threshers sometimes hired cooks to staff the shacks. George Elzie Harding of Grayson employed an African American man, most likely a tenant farmer or sharecropper, who lived on the Harding farm and was an "excellent cook."[60] Mathilda "Tillie" Spaeth Schoech, who was born in 1913 and grew up near Lindsay, recalled, "I remember one summer working in George Zimmerer's cookshack. Three large meals and two lunches a day were served. We would get up at three o'clock in the morning and work till ten o'clock at night. After three weeks, I felt dead and I mean dead. For this I got paid $3.00 [about $120 in 2025, less than $1.00 per hour] a week."[61] The crews were not the only people working hard at harvest.

Combine harvesters, which cut, threshed, and winnowed the grain with a single machine, dropped the number of workers on a crew down to five or six. Combines appeared after 1910, became more widespread because of labor shortages during World War I, and grew common in the 1920s. The combines in North Texas were smaller than those used on the plains in West Texas, cutting a swath of six to eight feet rather than twenty to twenty-four feet.[62] But they sometimes worked in multiples. In Tarrant County in 1940, Harry White employed four to six combines to harvest four hundred acres of wheat.[63]

As the grain came out of the separators or combines, farmers had choices. One consideration was a matter of scale. If they were growing only for their families, they could take the wheat directly to the mill to be traded for flour or ground for their own use. It could be stored in a granary for future use, put in bags, or simply "bulked," or left loose. Bulking wheat saved on the cost of bags, but it often left grain vulnerable to deterioration.[64] If the farmer was growing the wheat for wholesale use, he might consign it to a dealer at a local elevator (as discussed later in the chapter) or sell it outright. The wheat market was becoming more complex, and the farmers had to stay abreast of the changes.

Even as wheat became a smaller proportion of the North Texas economy, it remained important in the imagery of the region. In 1936, Texas celebrated the centennial of its independence from Mexico, with observances across the state, but official activities centered on a five-month-long exposition at the state fairgrounds in southeast Dallas.

Wheat served as an important motif for the fair. The Hall of State, the central structure of the exposition, featured images of wheat in many guises, including a central medallion on the bronze screens over the plateglass front doors.[65] The magnificent structure had a room for each of four Texas regions. The North Texas room showcased a fresco by Arthur Starr Niendorff depicting the region. Niendorff, a native of Marshall, Texas, studied

FIGURE 6.2. *North Texas mural by Arthur Starr Niendorff in the Hall of State, Dallas. (From the collections of the Dallas Historical Society)*

"extensively" under famed Mexican muralist Diego Rivera. The cartoon figure "Old Man Texas" embraces a blond, fair-skinned family as well as the skylines of Fort Worth and Dallas. "Cascades of wheat and corn" rest on Old Man Texas and the buildings. A cotton bale also shows agriculture, while trains, a dynamo, and a bank vault demonstrate modernity. Niendorff said that he depicted bundles of wheat flowing "like a kind of waterfall" next to the vault because they "end in a rain of golden dollars, forming a transition between the farm and the city, and indicating again the dependence of the city on the farm."[66] The central "Great Hall" had two huge murals, the work of Yale professor Eugene Savage. One, *Texas of Today,* features a dark-haired goddess figure on a raised platform, with wheat spilling from the right side of the platform. The main entrance to the Hall of Agriculture (in 2025 known as the Food and Fiber Building) includes a mural, *Wheat Harvesters,* designed by Carlo Ciampaglia and painted by Hector Serbaroli. Men attired in togas wield scythes, while a young woman in a classical gown holds a sheaf of wheat. A second mural and bas-relief plaques in the building also depict wheat.

Designers for the fair largely bypassed members of the Dallas art scene, favoring out-of-town talent such as Savage. Among several unsuccessful proposals by local artists, Jerry Bywaters planned a mural that would have included wheat growing in Texas. Builders rejected it in favor of Ciampaglia's classical designs.[67] In 1941, however, Bywaters received the commission for a mural, *Soil Conservation in Collin County,* for the post office in Farmersville, Collin County. In his depiction of a beautifully terraced Blackland Prairie, Bywaters foregrounded a man in overalls and a straw hat, working among sheaves of wheat. Bywaters, who grew up in Dallas and pursued his career there, clearly understood the importance of wheat to the region.

As the world drew near to a second great war, wheat farmers in North Texas continued their annual rounds, from planting to harvest. They faced competition from cotton farmers and from new farms on the West Texas plains, but the discontinuities in agriculture paled before those in milling. Millers had new challenges but also great new opportunities in the new century.

7 / MECHANIZATION, MARKETING, AND MUSIC: MILLING, 1900–1940

THE MILLING INDUSTRY IN NORTH TEXAS, AS ELSEwhere, underwent significant change in the first third of the twentieth century. In 1900, small crossroads mills, equipped with grinding stones, still served families who wanted flour for their own needs. Gradually, however, those mills disappeared, replaced by large urban facilities, particularly in Sherman and Fort Worth. At the same time, grain storage and animal-feed production became big businesses that mixed other grains with the wheat of the Red River counties. To some small-time millers, the changes must have been incomprehensible.

Before cars and trucks became common, local farmers brought their wheat to the mills in wagons pulled by horses or mules, each vehicle carrying about fifty bushels, or three thousand pounds. Even in the twentieth century, "many times the men could not get the wagons unloaded and make the trip home in a day, so they would have to stay overnight and sleep in their wagons."[1] Victor Tinsley, born in western Tarrant County in 1897, recalled his father hauling wheat and corn twenty-five miles for grinding: "I remember my dad taking wheat and corn to Randol's Mill east of Fort Worth on the Trinity River to have it ground into flour and corn meal. He would leave early in the morning and get home late the next night. Of course, he drove a wagon and team and since none of the roads were paved at that time, quite often after a rainy spell, he would get stuck in the mud and have to leave the buggy or wagon until the weather dried up some."[2] Observers recalled "wagons parked side by side in the street for a distance of half a mile" from the local mills.[3] Two or three men at each mill held the mules and horses and dumped the wheat from the wagons.

For some people, the mills were idyllic spots. Katherine O'Riley Hester, born in 1892 in the Tarrant County community of Handley, fondly remembered the Randol Mill, which was maybe five miles north of her home: "It was one of the prettiest spots you can imagine, sitting right on the river bank. . . . It was powered by a very large water wheel moved by the force of the water and had huge stones that ground up the meal. It was a wonderful sight for us little country children to see that big wheel turned by water. There was beautiful shade trees that was almost like a park."[4] We don't know Hester's reason for being at the mill, but it remained a pleasant memory.

Some people didn't wait around for their wheat to be ground and instead traded it for flour that was already ground. Charles Moore observed in 1900 that the farmhand named Willy had taken corn and wheat in the wagon. Willy "got in before night with meal and a sack of new McKinney mill flower [*sic*] $1.00."[5] Mills bought the grain for resale, or they sold it to "independent buyers for shipment all over the world."[6]

In Grayson County, the Hestand family traveled from their rural home to Sherman, the county seat, to get supplies. Glyn Hestand recalled that Saturday morning errands included picking up flour: "Then it was on to Smith Flour Mill to get a forty-eight pound sack of flour." The Hestands took advantage of the mill's storage capacity. Hestand remembered, "Daddy took his wheat there in the summer after harvest; then in the winter, he would pick up flour as we needed it."[7] Worth Milling advertised in 1917 that it would "store your year's supply of wheat and corn, guaranteeing weight and grade from thresher. Delivering product when called for."[8]

Even as the production of grain shifted elsewhere, small mills continued to start up in North Texas. In Krum, Denton County, wheat growing thrived, and in 1901 a group of investors created a new flour mill "where your wheat is grown." Local resident Edward Francis Lamm held 50 percent of the stock, and other area farmers and businessmen bought the other half. The company bought a "giant steam mill" in Wynnewood, Indian Territory, dismantled it, and moved it to Krum. They hired a Canadian, William H. Hobbs, as "chief miller."[9] The mill began shipping ten carloads a week of "Rainbow," "Red Ribbon," and "Lily" brand flours "as far away as San Angelo," a distance of 270 miles. The mill did well enough to remain open for more than a decade, but when it burned in 1915, it did not reopen.[10] Similarly, Chester Good and Don Good launched a mill in Carrollton sometime after 1916. The mill lasted four years, and a local historian observed, "Better flour was flooding the market and customers were no longer satisfied with the coarse flour which their equipment was producing. The old equipment was not made to compete with larger mills."[11]

As cotton spread in acreage, some particularly enterprising businesspeople built both flour mills and cotton gins to accommodate the two crops. Krum, with two flour mills, also had four cotton gins by 1920.[12] Stephen Roach operated a mill and cotton gin near the Cold Springs community in

Grayson County, and Robert Coleman Fisher did the same in Frisco, Collin County.[13] In the young town of Celina, the McKinney newspaper reported in 1903, work was underway on a flour mill and J. H. L. C. English was about to move his gin from the Roseland community.[14] The St. Louis-San Francisco Railway had bypassed Roseland in favor of Celina, and people and businesses followed. The milling and ginning seasons met but usually did not collide, making brisk work for at least six months a year.

Milling, of course, was always a questionable prospect for small operators, and numerous mills closed in the first decades of the twentieth century. The mill in Myra, Cooke County, for example, operated independently for a decade before the larger Whaley Milling Company bought it—and closed it.[15] The revered Randol Mill in Tarrant County ceased operation in 1922, fifty-six years after its establishment on the banks of the West Fork of the Trinity River. One wonders what became of the old stones and the equipment so carefully assembled and tended to over the decades.

A mill in Cedar Hill, fifteen miles southwest of Dallas, demonstrates the difficulties of succeeding as a small operator. Dallas resident Elijah F. Ballard built the flour mill on the right-of-way of the Gulf, Colorado and Santa Fe Railway. By 1919, both the building and all its machinery were mortgaged and the mill's finances were entangled with at least two local banks and numerous individuals. Ballard declared bankruptcy on the Cedar Hill property as well as another mill in nearby Lancaster. The Lancaster mill sold for $11,000, and perhaps the Cedar Hill facility sold as well, for only three years later H. S. Snyder of Fort Worth was trying to unload a mill in Cedar Hill.[16] Snyder reported that the mill and its equipment—including a Fairbanks Morse "Midget Marvel" flour mill—had originally cost $18,000 and he was willing to "sacrifice" them for $3,500 cash—a substantial and almost surely painful loss.[17] The Farmers and Merchants Milling Company in Grapevine, established in 1902, was converted from a flour mill to one making feed in 1936. The feed industry grew as wheat milling shrank in North Texas.[18]

The animal feed industry became established in the United States in the 1890s, and clever millers realized that by-products from milling would make good animal feed. Consequently, millers began building animal feed plants alongside their mills. The plants combined a variety of products, including the bran and chaff from wheat milling, to produce fodder for domesticated animals—poultry, dairy and beef cattle, horses, mules, swine, and dogs.[19] In 1918, the St. Louis–based giant Ralston Purina Company established a Texas division in Fort Worth.[20] By 1920, virtually all the large mills in North Texas had some interest in the feed business.[21] A writer in Sherman observed in 1925 that people buying feed to fatten hogs and cattle were "among the steady and largest customers of the mill men."[22] In at least one instance, feed preceded wheat. In 1922, Gaylord Stone bought an old grain elevator in the Riverside area of Fort Worth and built a five-story mill to make feed. Seven years later, the company, known as Universal Mills, began producing wheat flour.[23]

By the 1930s, large mills often had a combined operation of flour mill, feed mill, and grain elevator.[24] When the Burrus Mill moved north of Fort Worth in the 1930s, it expanded its "Texo Feeds" operation. Animal science was becoming established, and Texo feed was "proven by scientific research, laboratory tests and actual feeding conditions." In addition to grain, the Burrus Mill made feed with cod liver oil, ground meat, bone content, charcoal, minerals, fats, salt, dried milk, ground limestone, and iodine.[25]

Feed mills could be as volatile as grain mills. In 1910, the feed mill adjacent to the Medlin Mill in Fort Worth burned when a piece of metal in a bale of alfalfa struck the steel saws that chopped the alfalfa into bits and sparked a fire. The buildings that burned, the newspaper reported, were all filled to overflowing with corn and "all sorts of feed products." Although the stable burned, all the horses were saved. The fire department was able to keep the flames from the flour mill.[26]

The first two decades of the twentieth century marked significant changes in the construction of large flouring mills, departures that left behind small operators with little capital. The big got bigger, and the small were mostly forced to quit.

The scale and technological sophistication of the new mills dwarfed their predecessors. The four-story Burrus Mill, built in McKinney in 1902, had twenty-four sets of rollers and steam engines powered by coal and crude oil. Electricity illuminated the mill, and water came from the municipal supply. According to local lore, the first time the lights in the mill came on at night, McKinney citizens thought it was on fire: "Here come the little 'pumper' (the pride of the fire department) and everyone running towards the mill."[27] Eight iron tanks stored grain.[28] The Stanard-Tilton Milling Company suffered the devastating loss of its four-story mill in a flood of the Trinity River in 1908. The company built a fine new facility in 1913, half a mile from the river, including a six-story brick-and-concrete mill, a warehouse, and an elevator soaring one hundred feet, at a total cost of $221,000. The plant had direct access to the Gulf, Colorado and Santa Fe Railway as well as the Texas and Pacific Railway. Intended to be fireproof, the mill featured weighted fire doors made of wood panels covered with seamed sheet metal imported from Massachusetts and New Orleans. The doors protected all stairwells, elevator openings, and passages between sections.[29]

FIGURE 7.1. *Pilot Point roller mill, about 1900. (Courtesy of Steve Irick)*

In 1914, the Burrus company constructed a new facility just east of the Union train depot in McKinney. The mill building had fireproof brick walls and a reinforced concrete roof and floor. The company also added the feature that continues to mark grain enterprises into the twenty-first century: reinforced concrete silos. Eight silos, eighty-four feet high, towered above the iron tanks.[30]

An unnamed writer for the McKinney newspaper who toured the facility crowed over the safety features: fireproof doors that divided the mill and an automatic sprinkler system. Employees benefited from the new facility, which had sanitary restrooms and steel lockers for their clothing. Half of the milling machines ground soft, low-protein wheat for "ordinary domestic use," and half ground hard, high-protein wheat for "the use of the bakers"—meaning commercial bread bakers, who needed the extra gluten to make sturdy doughs. To ensure uniform texture and quality, there was "machinery for tempering wheat if it is too hard; to harden it, if it is too soft; to dampen it if it is too dry; and drying it if it is too damp." If a customer demanded "extra white" flour, the mill would use "electric gas" to bleach it, but ordinarily they left the flour in its unbleached state.[31] This level of sophistication would come to characterize wheat mills in years to come.

Like Burrus, other mills evolved quickly. At the turn of the twentieth century, the Whaley Mill in Gainesville had fourteen sets of rollers and six iron grain tanks, each forty feet high and thirty feet in diameter. In 1918, the Whaleys built a new mill, a seven-story structure of reinforced concrete, at a cost of $80,000. Nordyke and Marmon, engineers from Indianapolis, built the mill, which housed twenty-six sets of rolls. By 1940, the company employed sixty people at peak season.[32]

Every time a mill built a new plant, it was larger and more automated than the last. The G. B. R. Smith Milling Company in Sherman constructed a new mill in 1918 at a cost of $500,000.[33] The trade publication *Operative Miller* gushed about the new facility. The building was a "fine reinforced concrete structure with panels and trimming of a light shade wire-cut brick with heavy receding joints. It is a daylight mill and entirely fireproof. . . . The interior of the 'A' mill is finished in white enamel."[34] The new plant more than doubled the capacity of the mill, and natural light and reflective paint made the interior shiny bright.[35]

In 1924, the Kimbell Milling Company moved from Sherman to Fort Worth and built a mammoth flour mill and elevator complex, capable of grinding a thousand barrels a day, on the city's south side. Not everyone in Fort Worth was thrilled with the new behemoth. Fifty-one residents of the South Main area in Fort Worth filed suit against Kimbell, alleging that "dust, chaff and other substances are thrown into the air and circulated upon their homes." Possibly the suit was settled, because it made no further appearance in the news.[36] Other mills shaped the lives of the people around them. The sounds of the mill structured the days of the people of McKinney. H. D. Mouzon recalled "the whistle at the flour mill that told us when to get up, when to go to dinner and when to quit work for the day."[37]

All these new mills featured state-of-the-art equipment. Agents for northeastern manufacturers had offices in Fort Worth and Dallas.[38] The Smith Company in Sherman bought all its equipment from the Wolf Company of Chambersburg, Pennsylvania. It included "16 9×30 Wolf 'Super Type' Ball Bearing Double Roller Mills" as well as Wolf-brand purifiers, bran dusters, shorts dusters, centrifugal reels, wheat washers and driers, "Wolfsifters," and so on.[39] In 1936, the Burrus Mill left its longtime home in downtown Fort Worth for a giant plant, beyond the northern city limits, on the "paved" Decatur Highway. The building housing the mill, which could turn out four thousand barrels of flour a day, was seven stories high with a basement.[40] Two 1,650-horsepower Nordberg diesel engines, from Milwaukee, Wisconsin, powered the mill.[41] For the plant dedication, various vendors advertised in the *Fort Worth Star-Telegram*. They included paint companies, manufacturers of belts and pulleys, concrete contractors, cloth companies, and equipment dealers. The construction project spread the riches in numerous directions.[42]

The Bewley Mills in Fort Worth continued to expand and improve its plant over the decades. In 1907 the company completely overhauled its mill with new machinery and a new "flower [*sic*] purifying system."[43] By 1913, it had converted its plant from steam power to electricity. Sixty men worked at the plant in shifts around the clock, and the annual payroll totaled $50,000.[44] In 1916 the company added new machinery.[45] Jack Gordon, a writer for the *Fort Worth Star-Telegram*, described the milling process at the Bewley Mills in 1923: "After a brief storage, the grain is taken from the bins, treated for insects, and scrubbed and washed numerous times before it finds its way to the initial grinder. There are 26 of these grinders, and the grain must pass thru all of them. The finest flour is extracted first; and as the wheat passes on down the line each regrinding brings forth a lower grade of flour. Air blows the bran out." Gordon observed that spontaneous combustion had been practically eliminated: "Every machine thru which the grain progresses is inclosed [*sic*] and protected from the outside atmosphere. All air inside the grinders is forced there by big fans, after being thoroly [*sic*] washed and cooled by many spouts of water, or, if atmospheric conditions demand it, warmed by steam. Besides this precaution, patent dust collectors, functioning on a vacuum principle, provide additional protection." The flour was sifted on the top floor. The sifters were "huge boxes, looming up like half a freight car, which are vigorously shaken by machinery. . . . They are not permitted to shake in unison and in the same direction."[46] Powerful machinery required powerful protections against accidents.

North Texas mills ground locally grown wheat whenever possible, and they used all that farmers could produce. The 1904 *Texas Almanac* observed that almost all wheat grown in Texas was consumed in Texas: "Being a soft wheat, of fine quality, the millers want it, and exporters can not secure it unless a surplus above the milling demand be produced."[47] The Alliance Mill in Denton, situated next to the lush fields where wheat was still grown in Denton County, used homegrown wheat exclusively in its flour.[48] In 1914, Perry Burrus, son of W. C. Burrus, offered to buy all of the high-quality wheat in Collin County for a dollar a bushel. An unnamed writer for the McKinney newspaper observed that Burrus, "a home product," was offering the latest prices to the farmers.[49]

Increasingly, however, the wheat milled in North Texas came from West Texas.[50] Occasionally, when supplies of wheat grew dire, millers increased their purchases from Great Plains states, particularly Oklahoma.[51] The quality of out-of-state grain did not always meet Texas standards. In 1909, shippers from Kansas City sent six carloads of hard and soft wheat mixed together, which the Texas state dairy and food commissioner declared adulterated and unmillable. The "northern grain men" had deemed the grain acceptable, but Fort Worth classers rejected it as 40 percent hard wheat, implying that they had higher standards than their counterparts elsewhere.[52] In 1920, the desperate Fort Worth Elevator Company even bought wheat from Argentina.[53]

In 1925, a writer from Sherman extolled the popularity of local wheat, observing, "Grayson County produces a high grade wheat, and seldom does any come to the Sherman market that does not test out well enough to get the top of the market. Sherman retail stores handle Sherman made flour, and Sherman people give the home made brands preference because of the high quality of the product." He then told the story of a Sherman grocer who sold all two thousand pounds of the flour he had bought "from his miller." The grocer offered a local housewife a sack of flour "made by a foreign mill a traveling man had left for him to look at and try out" (indicating that he wasn't actually selling the "foreign" flour but just happened to have it on hand). She replied that she would wait until more local flour appeared in the afternoon: "I will wait, my old man can eat cornbread for dinner, and I will give him some hot biscuits for supper."[54]

Local flours faced stiff competition, however, from northern competitors. Individual grocers apparently stocked either local flours or imported ones but not both. In Fort Worth, Turner and Dingee, which served an upscale clientele, sold "Colorado Quail" flour, touting it as "Finest Northern," while in McKinney, P. R. West offered only Pillsbury products—flour, meal, bran, pancake flour, buckwheat flour, and wheat cereal—from Minneapolis. Consumer costs are hard to track because prices were rarely displayed in newspaper ads before the 1930s, and even then it was mostly the national chains like Safeway and A&P that did so. But at least one head-to-head competition emerged: In 1920, flour from the Bewley and Burrus Mills was selling at $1.77 for twenty-four pounds, while imported Colorado Quail flour was going for $1.80 for a similar amount.[55] The local flour had little price advantage. For the most part, local flour mills advertised on their own, not through grocery stores, and they almost never showed prices. They apparently depended on the loyalty of their customers rather than on price. They refused to acknowledge that the big mills in the North could produce flour and ship it to Texas at a lower cost than millers in Texas could charge.

Starting in the 1920s, mills used Texas-grown wheat as a marketing tool, tying it to scientific evidence. W. Lee O'Daniel came from Kansas to Fort Worth in 1925 as sales manager for Burrus and was surprised to learn that Texas commercial bakers were buying flour from Kansas and Oklahoma mills, as they believed that Texas flour was inferior. O'Daniel remembered,

"I knew better. I knew the wheat grown in Texas, because I had operated Kansas mills which ground it. . . . Texas wheat . . . has a high protein content and makes better baker's flour for that reason." O'Daniel brought George Foltz, his miller from Kansas, to Burrus as assistant to the superintendent. O'Daniel recalled, "We installed a laboratory and experimental bakery, which was, I think, among the first of its kind at any Texas mill. Today every flour mill worthy of the name has a laboratory. By constant tests and analyses the quality of the flour is kept constant."[56] Burrus began to use Texas-grown wheat and then to market that practice as part of its appeal. Competitor Bewley also used local pride in its advertising; in 1933 it promoted its flour as "Bewley's Best the Official Flour: Made in Texas from Texas Wheat by Texas Labor."[57] Home economist Irene Nevill Aby, employed by Bewley, wrote in 1935, "Master flour-makers—men who know every phase of flour production from wheat field to your kitchen—carefully watch every ounce of Bewley's Best."[58]

Testing wheat and flour in laboratories began in the 1880s in Minneapolis and spread throughout the upper Great Plains in the early twentieth century. Laboratories assessed how the characteristics of different wheats affected flour, and they looked at how various flours altered baked products.[59] Texas was late to the game, having allowed other regions to pioneer scientific methods and then followed their lead. Millers promised much but delivered little in their efforts in Dallas, as we will see later in the chapter. In 1939, the Whaley Mill in Gainesville installed a cereal laboratory for the purpose of maintaining an absolute uniformity of quality by testing all flour. This scientific precision allowed the company to expand into the production of high-protein "bakery flours" in addition to all-purpose flours for home cooks.[60]

One factor that mills could measure without a laboratory was output. They constantly weighed their production and boasted about it. For example, in August 1903, the Burrus Mill produced 64,716 sacks of flour, each weighing 48 pounds, "the largest month's business in the mill's history."[61] In 1925, Sherman proudly announced its place as the tenth-largest flour producer in the United States. Never mind that the little town produced 4,200 barrels of flour a day while front-runner Minneapolis made 96,000 barrels each day. As far as the people of Grayson County were concerned, Sherman was right up there with Buffalo, Kansas City, and St. Louis.[62] In the late 1930s, Sherman bragged that its three mills made "more flour than any other city in the state"; the town of fifteen thousand people was producing 1 percent of the total production of the United States.[63]

North Texas mills expanded their inventories as new products were produced. Minneapolis milling giant General Mills introduced "Bisquick," a biscuit mix, in 1931. The mix contained flour, leavening, dried milk, and some sort of fat—in the case of Bisquick, sesame oil—and all the cook had to do was add water or milk. In less than a year, at least two North Texas mills had developed mixes of their own. Morten Milling in Dallas made a particular splash with its innovation: hiring domestic maven Lenore Standifer to show consumers how to use its mix.[64] Morten marketed the mixes heavily, appealing to regional sentiment by advertising them as "Southern Biscuits at Their Best" and publicizing its "La France" brand as "a Southern flour ready mixed the Southern way for Old Fashioned Goodness."[65] Morten also touted speed, telling consumers that the mix took "two minutes from carton to oven."[66] In December 1932, the Collin County Mill in McKinney announced its "Marechal Neil Ready-Mixed Biscuit Flour"; apparently named for a popular variety of rose (named in turn for a French general), the mix was sold in 2.5-pound cartons for 30 cents. The package featured recipes for using the mix in "pancakes, chocolate cookies, light rolls, biscuits, drop biscuit and cheese biscuit." Mill president Gibson Caldwell stated that he believed that "the divorce rate will be cut down in Celina and Collin county if housewives use this flour."[67] Presumably inferior biscuits were fomenting marital strife in North Texas.

Several large mills in North Texas underwent corporate change and consolidation, resulting in ties to national companies and local closures. In Sherman in 1909, the G. B. R. Smith Milling Company, owned by rancher and grain dealer George B. R. Smith, who also operated a flour mill in Celina, took over the Eagle Mills, which had been insolvent for two years. The Smith company completely overhauled the mill, buying new machinery and building two warehouses.[68] In 1910, the company bought the Citizens Mill and Elevator in Justin, Denton County, and later acquired "branches" in Howe, nearby in Grayson County, and Greenville in Hunt County.[69] Demonstrating the volatility of the Texas milling business, the Smith company was then sold four times in a fifteen-year period, first to the North Texas companies Burrus in 1926 and Kimbell in 1929. Commander-Larabee of Minneapolis purchased the Smith mill in 1932, enlarging it significantly, and then sold it to the Quaker Oats Company of Chicago in 1941.[70] In the 1920s, communities had taken pride in the fact that the mills and elevators were "all owned by home people," and the sale to out-of-state investors must have been a blow to local egos.[71]

The Fant-Gladney Mill, also in Sherman, had originated in 1899 as a corn mill. In 1904, the company became Brackett-Wallace Mill and Grain Company, and it built a flour mill and a fifty-thousand-bushel steel storage tank. In 1908, the company reorganized as the Sherman Mill and Grain Company; it operated the flour mill until 1913, when Perry Burrus bought the company, placed Sam Gladney "in charge," and changed the name to Gladney Milling Company. In 1921, a stock company headed by E. T. Fant bought the Gladney company and changed its name to the Fant Milling Company.

The large milling company owned by the Kimbell family grew organically through purchases. In 1899, Oakwood store owner Benjamin B. Kimbell bought the small Beatrice Mills in Whitewright, Grayson County. His son, Kay Kimbell, who was thirteen at the time, began doing manual labor at the plant while also going to school. After attending two years of business school, Kay Kimbell became manager of the plant and soon doubled it in size.[72] In 1905, the Beatrice Mill had a forty-five-foot elevator, steel grain tanks, and seven sets of double rollers.[73] In 1917, the Kimbells bought a mill in Wolfe City, Hunt County, named it Kimbell Milling, and moved their headquarters there. In 1921, they purchased the Phoenix elevators at Sherman and relocated their offices to Sherman. In 1924, they built a large milling facility in Fort Worth and shifted their offices there.[74] Also in 1924, Kimbell acquired a half-interest in the Diamond Mill in Sherman and attained sole ownership in 1932, when they renamed it the Kimbell–Diamond Mill and increased its capacity. The original Whitewright mill burned in 1926. Kimbell Milling purchased two other companies in Sherman—Chapman Milling in 1927 and G. B. R. Smith Milling in 1929—as well as Taylor Milling in Denton and three mills outside North Texas. Some of the new acquisitions didn't stay in the Kimbell portfolio for long: Wolfe City burned in 1931 and, as noted earlier, Kimbell sold the Smith mill to Commander-Larabee in 1932.[75]

The Chapman family in Sherman bought their mill in 1897. The three-story building had twelve sets of rolls, and the ironclad elevator soared eighty feet high. After the Chapmans idled the mill in 1927, Kay Kimbell bought it and converted it to an oatmeal plant. The building burned in 1933, and Kimbell did not reopen it.[76] In 1933, Kimbell bought two grain elevators and two warehouses in Melissa, Collin County.[77] Over the course of thirty years, Kimbell had extended its facilities across the region.

Tex-O-Kan, another large group of mills and elevators, resulted from a merger of six Texas and Oklahoma mills in June 1929—Fant of Sherman; Burrus of Fort Worth; Morten of Dallas; Collin County of McKinney; and Burrus Elevators, in Dallas and Lubbock—as well as the Liberty Mills of San Antonio and "probably the Bob White Mills, Kingfisher, Okla." The enterprising leaders incorporated the company in Delaware, most likely because of its favorable tax conditions. Headed by J. Perry Burrus of Dallas, the new corporation had a combined production of nine thousand barrels of flour daily and an elevator storage capacity of three and a half million bushels.[78] The Burrus family and other investors also owned flour mills and textile mills across Texas and in Mexico.[79] In 1938, the Fant family bought back its interest in its Sherman mill from Tex-O-Kan.[80] Tex-O-Kan and Kimbell would dominate the North Texas landscape visually, as their elevators rose over the region, and financially through their dominant share of the market.

In the twentieth century, a new type of grain-related business arose with the need for storage. Humans had known since antiquity that grain can stay good indefinitely if sheltered from weather and vermin. The scale of these operations increased dramatically with technological and legal changes. North Texas dealers bought grain from other parts of the United States, particularly the Midwest, for milling or to store. The Fort Worth and Denver Railway, for example, carried wheat from Colorado and Utah.[81] The first grain elevator in Fort Worth, owned by C. F. Orthwein of Kansas City, was built in North Fort Worth about 1903.[82] Other companies based outside of Texas, such as the J. Rosenbaum Grain Company of Chicago, also constructed facilities in Fort Worth. A local writer noted in 1918 that the Rosenbaum facility was well equipped, with "up-to-date cleaners, clippers and scales." The Rosenbaum company—a member of the "leading grain exchanges" in the United States—also brought Fort Worth into the mainstream of grain dealing.[83]

In 1916, the US Congress passed the US Warehouse Act, which established national standards for grain and cotton storage and, more importantly, created a mechanism through which farmers could receive loans, using their stored grain as collateral.[84] By 1921, 274 licensed grain warehouses and 259 cotton warehouses existed across the nation.[85] In 1925, a writer for the *Sherman Daily Democrat* explained that Elevator A of the Diamond Mills Company

> operated as a public storage elevator, being bonded under the federal warehouse act, and this service is appreciated by many Grayson county farmers who desire to hold their wheat for favorable market or for seed. . . . Mill men of Sherman pay the highest market price and frequently more for top notch wheat. If the market does not happen to be as good as the farmer thinks it should be, the mill man will store it in his elevator and take care of it until the farmer gets ready to sell it.[86]

With the new option of receiving as much as 80 percent of their crop value as a loan, farmers suddenly had new incentive to store their grain rather than sell it in a fluctuating market. Storage, not milling, would become the growth industry in North Texas.

Series of regional elevators developed across North Texas. The smallest elevators were the so-called country elevators, dispersed in small towns throughout the region. Larger elevator companies maintained a variety of lesser satellites, all with rail lines for easy transportation. For example, in 1905 the Burrus Mill had seven country elevators, and in 1913 Bewley had facilities at Keller and the Denton County towns of Krum and Roanoke, in addition to Fort Worth.[87] Also in Denton County, the town of Ponder supported elevators for the Alliance Mill, Whaley, and Kimbell, while tiny Myra, in Cooke County, hosted facilities for Alliance and Whaley.[88] Farmers sold their grain directly to the country elevator, which acted on behalf of the larger company, and local dealers strove to cultivate trust. William W. Collins managed the elevator in Howe for more than forty years, first for the Smith Company and then for Kimbell. His son recalled that Collins succeeded because of his "thorough knowledge of grain, his business acumen, his fairness and honesty, and his ability to gain the confidence and respect of all with whom he dealt."[89]

Small mills began shifting their operations from milling to storage. In 1909, for example, the mill building at Denison Mill and Elevator burned. The directors of the company elected not to replace the mill but rather to erect a $40,000 grain elevator on the old site.[90]

Like everything in the grain business, country elevators carried risks. In 1925, a group of men from Lindsay, Cooke County, organized an independent elevator company with a clear set of rules for capitalization and dividends. Most years they barely turned a profit, if at all, and by 1936 they were trying to sell the elevator. In 1938, the stockholders decided "to let the elevator set as is and operate as best we can," declaring, "If the elevator is to be padlocked, we'll take our medicine." A historian from Lindsay concluded, "With the arrival of the motor vehicles and the use of trucks for hauling, the elevator had outgrown its usefulness. Several years later the elevator was torn down for the lumber."[91] The investors, caught by shifting needs and transportation changes, did indeed have to "take their medicine."

The cities of North Texas, particularly Fort Worth and Sherman, rapidly developed their grain storage capacities, and they constantly toted up the volume of their elevators. In 1905, Fort Worth had a total elevator capacity of 1.31 million bushels.[92] In 1910, the local newspaper enumerated eleven elevators where grain could be held, cleaned, mixed, or milled. In 1917, the newspaper excitedly reported elevator storage capacity of 3.74 million bushels, divided among nine companies. Almost a third of the capacity belonged to the Fort Worth Elevator Company.[93] The company was chartered in 1908, with capital of $75,000. Four of the incorporators were brothers—Jule, Marcus, Bert, and Marshall Smith. Bert was married to Maizie Bewley, daughter of mill owner Murray Bewley. The Smiths also bought a mill and elevator in Justin, Denton County.[94] In 1932, capacity in

Sherman totaled 3.125 million bushels.[95] Boosters counted, recounted, and crowed over the amount of grain that they could store.

Technology made possible these huge caches. In the 1890s, grain silos and bins were constructed of steel and clad with iron. Sometimes the structures were "cribbed," or reinforced with an exterior structure of steel. Still, the danger of fire and explosion remained real.[96] Benton McMillin, a cotton buyer in Whitewright, had a grain elevator built in the 1890s. When it burned, he replaced it with another. That one burned too, and McMillin went back to handling only cotton. Apparently he had had enough of volatile stores of grain.[97] Between 1909 and 1921, at least four elevator fires occurred in North Texas. In an August 1909 fire at the Burrus Mill, firefighters struggled with sizzling summer temperatures, heavy smoke, and "the grain dust, which exploded from time to time in the heat."[98] A 1913 incident at the Bewley Mills in Fort Worth was particularly destructive. Spontaneous combustion ignited the wheat, and an explosion blew the roof off the elevator. City firefighters kept the blaze confined to the elevator, sparing the mill, but the company lost fifty thousand bushels of wheat and the building, with losses totaling $125,000.[99] In 1921, the Pearlstone Mill and Elevator Company in Dallas lost everything when its four-story mill and elevator, built of "wood and tin," spontaneously combusted.[100] And in 1922, Roach Grain and Elevator Company in Frisco, the largest elevator between Sherman and Dallas, was consumed by fire.[101]

The defense against such destruction came in the form of concrete silos.[102] Invented by a Belgian engineer, the first reinforced-concrete silo in the United States was built in Minneapolis in 1899, and the design spread quickly throughout the United States.[103] Concrete silos were completely fireproof, waterproof, rodent-proof, and nearly insect-proof, and they resisted the pressure of the grain on the side walls of the bin.[104]

Throughout the first quarter of the twentieth century, concrete grain elevators sprang from the North Texas prairies, commanding the visual landscape as nothing had before. Older mills added elevators and retrofitted their existing plants. In 1914, the Burrus Mill in Fort Worth, for example, constructed six concrete grain bins, each twenty-one feet in diameter and eighty-four feet—about nine stories—high.[105] The new facility of the Kimbell Milling Company, built in 1924, overshadowed south Fort Worth. The silos reached ninety feet, and the "head house," which housed the conveyor machinery, was a staggering 180 feet—eighteen stories. The company's addition of more silos in 1928, 1930, and 1931 gave it a storage capacity of two million bushels of grain. Company owner Kay Kimbell asserted that these were the largest elevators in the United States outside Chicago and Kansas City.[106] When Burrus built its new plant in Saginaw in 1936, its silos stored half a million bushels of grain.[107] Grain storage factored significantly in the economy and appearance of Tarrant County.

As businesses grew in size and complexity, the grain industry became more organized. Large-scale millers and grain dealers in Texas had communicated with one another since the 1870s. In 1898, the millers formed the Texas Millers' Association, and the Texas Grain Dealers' Association held its first convention in Fort Worth the following year.[108]

For the first few years of its existence, the Texas Millers' Association stuck to predictable matters that arose as the nation became increasingly concerned about the quality of its food supply: accurate weights, transportation rules, the requirements of new animal feed regulations, and so on.[109] By 1905, however, things were, or at least appeared to be, amiss. Investors, led by M. P. Bewley of Fort Worth, rechartered the Texas Grain and Flour Company of Fort Worth to "produce and sell grain and grain products." What they were actually doing was buying grain in the Midwest to be milled in Texas.[110] The State of Texas took a dim view of the association's actions, believing them to be in violation of the Texas anti-trust laws of 1889 and 1903, which forbade "conspiracy in restraint of trade."[111] In 1907, Texas Attorney General Robert Vance Davidson filed suit against the 120 members of the Texas Millers' Association, alleging that the association was formed for the purpose of fixing the price of grain and flour in restraint of trade. The state enumerated fifteen charges against the association, all dealing with aspects of price fixing and monopoly control of the grain supply.[112] Davidson further asserted that the association's executive committee organized the Texas Grain and Flour Company "'for the purpose of more efficaciously carrying out the aforesaid conspiracy,' and more particularly for the purpose of fixing the price of wheat and other grains and lessening competition in the purchase of wheat." The Texas Grain and Flour Company and the Texas Grain Dealers' Association were "alleged to be parts of the conspiracy" but were not named as defendants. About thirty of the companies named in the case were from North Texas, as were eleven of the individuals named in the complaint.[113]

The case *State of Texas v. the Wichita Mill and Elevator Company et al.* was litigated throughout 1908 in the Twenty-Sixth District Court under Judge Charles A. Wilcox.[114] The state asked that the defendants pay damages of $129,250 and stop violating the anti-trust laws of Texas.[115]

The case settled in January 1909. The mills agreed to pay a total fine of $35,000, divided between all of them, and to stop "conspiring to combine or otherwise violate the anti-trust laws of Texas." The charter of the Texas Grain and Flour Company was canceled, and the Millers' Association was "enjoined from doing business or maintaining its organization." Basically the association was out of business, even though it retained its charter.[116] Shortly after the case settled, J. N. Rayzor, president of the Alliance Mill in Denton, called the suit an "outrage" when he spoke with the local newspaper. He declared that the millers decided to settle with the state "on a compromise basis," but that the settlement was "no indication of guilt upon the part of the defendants."[117] The grain dealers had chosen the wrong time to try to control the market, and their formal efforts failed.

The Fort Worth Board of Trade began conducting grain inspections in 1907.[118] Businesspeople in Fort Worth believed that reliable grain inspection was critical to the reputation of the city as a solid trading partner, and they installed a well-equipped testing laboratory. Inspectors evaluated about 25 percent of the grain that came into the city of Fort Worth, looking for mold, pests, and damaged kernels.[119] The State of Texas, like other parts of the United States, had begun to be concerned about issues of food purity early in the twentieth century. In 1907, the state legislature passed the Pure Food Law, which covered many matters, particularly processed foods. The law created the new position of state dairy and food commissioner, a chemist and bacteriologist who was to begin work in January 1909, and the state took charge of grain inspections. Local millers complained loudly about the impure shipments of grain received from outside, and they stated their dependence on local inspectors to protect Texans' interests.[120] Surprisingly, they did not object to the state taking an active role in the process, given their later objections to government intervention.

Fort Worth businessmen also opened the Fort Worth Grain and Cotton Exchange in 1907. From the beginning, grain dominated over cotton in the work of the exchange, which dropped "Cotton" from its name in 1916. The exchange provided market news and grain inspection, and it operated a weighing department and protein laboratory with "the full equipment recommended by the Dep't of Agriculture for the inspection of grain, under the U.S. Grain Standards Act."[121] Their "registrar" had "direct control" over elevators and warehouses in Fort Worth.[122] The scientists would ensure that Fort Worth grain held to the highest quality standards.

Throughout the first third of the twentieth century, large mills in North Texas often employed fifty to a hundred men, sometimes working around the clock and every day of the week.[123] They labored in production, in the offices, and as maintenance staff and watchmen.[124] An undetermined number of African American men worked in the mills as laborers, doing the heaviest and dirtiest work.[125] The head miller oversaw every step of the operation of turning wheat into flour. Skilled millers made a crucial difference between success and failure, and they were in high demand. When D. R. Montgomery retired as the head miller at Morten in 1908, his son, W. T. Montgomery, moved from Cherokee, Oklahoma, to take his father's place.[126] L. W. Gruver left his post as general manager and head miller of a company in Peoria, Illinois, to become head miller for the Smith Mill in Sherman. A reporter commented, "He is a good man well versed in milling and will make good."[127] Under each miller, scores of men carried out the various stages of milling.

Working at a mill or elevator could be hazardous. David Tarbet, who labored in a mill as a teenager, observed, "Grain dust is everywhere in an elevator. It's a constant and unavoidable companion." Many workers developed skin rashes and respiratory problems.[128] As we have seen, workers received injuries when they got caught in machinery. And as silos increased in height, the danger of life-threatening falls grew as well.[129] Other types of accidents persisted. In March 1925, John T. Russell was crushed between two railroad cars at the Fort Worth Grain Elevator. His widow, Mary Russell, sued the company. Testimony in the trial spelled out the horrible details of John Russell being told to check the coupling and then a coworker turning on the power to the cars, with Russell caught in between. Mary Russell won the case. The company lost its appeal of the verdict: it was indeed guilty of negligence.[130]

Grain mills did not oversee the private lives of their employees, as textile and steel mills did elsewhere. Mill workers lived in their own housing and were dispersed throughout the towns and cities where they lived. In North Texas, mill owners did try to keep employees happy and loyal through sponsorship of baseball teams. Throughout the first quarter of the twentieth century, a baseball league thrived in Fort Worth, with players from among the workers at numerous large employers. A separate "millers' league" featured competitions between the Medlin, Bewley, Burrus, and Smith brothers' mills in 1910 and evolved over the decades with changing mill owners.[131]

The milling industry saw small bursts of labor activism before World War I. In June 1916, the Bewley Mills signed a contract with the "Mill Employes' [*sic*] Union, giving them the right to use the label of that organization." In September, in a Labor Day parade, "flour and cereal mill employees of local No. 14939, thirty-two strong, marched in attire of snow white from head to foot."[132] Nationally, men who worked with flour often appeared in white to evoke the purity of their product, but their appearance was also likely to remind viewers of the racial stigmas of the day. When the union voted to grant a benefit of $4 per week to members who were ill, E. E. Bewley announced that he would do the same for his non-union employees.[133] And in the fraught summer of 1919, when labor disputes broke out across the United States, fifty men at the Bewley Mills walked out rather than "handle 'scab' flour from an unfair mill." A grievance committee was to call on E. E. Bewley, the company president. The local newspaper, which favored the owners, made no further comment.[134] Overall, however, mills fostered little solidarity among workers before 1930.

The National Labor Relations Act, enacted in 1935, significantly strengthened unions in the United States and in North Texas. In 1938, officials at the Morten mill ordered "a general wage cut" for all employees. Twenty-one Morten employees organized as members of the Flour, Feed Mill and Cereal Workers' Union, affiliated with the American Federation of Labor. Responding unfavorably to the development, Morten bosses verbally harassed union members, threatened to shut down the plant, circulated an anti-union petition, and ultimately fired union members. Inside the fancy new Burrus Mill in Saginaw, Tex-O-Kan also ordered a "general wage cut," which they blamed on "the new Wage and Hour Law." Seventy-two Burrus employees also elected to join the Flour, Feed Mill and Cereal Workers' Union. They faced actions identical to those carried out against their comrades at Morten. When eighteen men lost their jobs in March 1939, thirteen of them sought redress from the National Labor Relations Board, the federal investigative body. The NLRB found clear patterns of discrimination in the layoffs and ordered that the employees be reinstated and reimbursed for back pay. Intimidation and unfair labor practices abounded in the North Texas mills and were perhaps one reason that union activity remained small.[135]

Although much of the grain milled in North Texas stayed in the area, after 1900 most North Texas mills marketed their products throughout Texas and Louisiana. Perhaps 20 percent of the output from Texas mills went to the Caribbean and Mexico and, to a much lesser extent, to the Netherlands, England, and Germany.[136] These markets were a fraction of the size of those supplied by midwestern US companies, such as Washburn/Pillsbury, in terms of both volume and geographic spread. But they were significant to North Texas companies nonetheless.

The competition among local flour brands and mills was stiff, even as North Texas millers had to contest the onslaught of imported flour. They advertised extensively in print media, mainly newspapers but also local venues such as high school and college yearbooks. In 1915, an ad for Denton Milling in *The Yucca*, the yearbook of the North Texas State Normal School, instructed the new graduate teachers: "When your school teaching days are over start housekeeping right by ordering a sack of Verabest the Flour that makes light flakey biscuits." The ad reflected the widespread belief that young women would teach for a while, then marry and become stay-at-home housewives—and consumers of flour products.[137] And as housewives, they would make biscuits, the universal bread of the South.

In addition to vigorous print marketing, mills turned to innovative means of getting their products before buyers. Like many businesses, flour mills gave away small items, from biscuit cutters to dolls, each bearing the mill's logo. In the twentieth century, the sacks in which flour was sold became marketing tools. Historically, most flour had been shipped in wooden barrels. In the 1850s, cotton sacks became the preferred packaging for small amounts, since it was more suitable than barrels for railroad transport. Housewives quickly recognized the value of repurposing the sacks as dishcloths and cup towels, and milling companies sold empty sacks by the dozen.[138] Early cotton sacks were plain white and printed with the manufacturer's logo. Women labored to remove all the ink but sometimes failed. Bettie Whitehead, from Grayson County, recalled that her Aunt Hazel made her clothing "on an old treadle Singer sewing machine. My undergarments were made from flour sacks, and I was slow to realize why one of our neighbors called me Bewley's Best. That was the brand name of the flour we bought, and all the dye didn't come out in the wash."[139] Oleta Maberry Derr remembered, "Mama made all of Lois Glenn's and my clothes. I've worn many a dress made out of flour and feed sacks. After she put rickrack, braid, and buttons on them, they were pretty. She starched them stiff and ironed them with black irons that she kept hot by setting them on the stove."[140] An unsigned article from the *Dallas Morning News* in 1908 urged readers to save flour sacks, dye them, and make them into "comforters"—bed coverings created from multiple layers of fabric that were tied together with knots. The writer observed that "one of the prettiest comfort[er]s I ever saw is made thus, dyed a dark blue and knotted with red yarn."[141]

By 1932, the US Department of Agriculture reported, almost three-quarters of the flour in the United States was packaged in cotton bags.[142] A one-hundred-pound bag measured forty-two by thirty-six inches, yielding more than a square yard of fabric, useful for all kinds of home sewing projects.[143] In McKinney, for example, American Beauty flour came in size ranges from six to forty-eight pounds, and advertisers carefully noted which products came in cloth bags and which in paper.[144] Manufacturers began printing their sacks with patterns, dolls, and other motifs that made the bags desirable.[145] They used two types of ink: one permanent and one that would wash out. Fant Milling in Sherman took a particular interest in decorated flour sacks and printed "a big green, red and orange elephant" called "Gladdy-Fant" on its sacks. Buyers could cut out two halves of a figure printed on a sack, sew the halves together, stuff it with cotton, and have a new toy.[146]

Fort Worth flour executive W. Lee O'Daniel used sacks to combine flour marketing with his campaign for Texas governor in 1938. In a *Dallas Morning News* column supposedly written by O'Daniel's sixteen-year-old daughter Molly, she described the pattern: "It's an all-over print with all the

Hillbilly Boys' pictures on it and the bus and the barrels we passed, and the dome of the Capitol and bluebonnets, and the Alamo and goodness knows what all. It's in real bright colors and fast print, so you can wash the printing off the sacks and then have this cute material for shirts and pajamas and whatever you want to make out of it."[147] (O'Daniel also played on his customers' piety by enclosing a "tithing certificate" in each sack of flour. The buyer filled it out with the name of her church and returned it to the company, which allegedly sent 10 percent—a tithe—of its profits to the churches of its customers.[148])

Mills often took part in public exhibitions such as parades and trade shows. In June 1907, the Grocers and Butchers' Association of Fort Worth sponsored a parade. The Medlin and Burrus Mills both had floats featuring sacks of flour. Women on the floats were dressed in white, and the male employees marching on foot behind the float were also wearing "snowy white garments"—again, probably to make viewers think of both snowy-white flour and snowy-white people.[149] In static exhibits, fresh, hot bread served on-site neatly tied together milling and baking and became a hallmark of flour marketing between 1900 and World War II. At the Fort Worth Retail Grocers and Butchers' Pure Food Show in 1906, the Bewley Mill exhibit featured "a pile of flour reaching almost to the ceiling" and a fancy new "string of incandescent lamps." Medlin exhibitors gave away fresh biscuits made in a kitchen at the rear of their space that was "elaborately decorated with electric lights." The Burrus Mill also served bread. Waples-Platter was a grocery company, not a mill, but it took a page from the Aunt Jemima craze in offering "cakes served by an old negro mammy."[150] Like the St. Louis mill whose marketers invented Aunt Jemima (who sold their pancake mix in North Texas as early as 1892), the Fort Worth grocers leaned into the racist stereotype for marketing. The next year the Burrus Mill gave away more than twenty-five thousand waffles in ten days; the Medlin Mill had "an inexhaustible supply of hot biscuits" made with its flour; and the Brown Cracker and Candy Company from Dallas offered "a couple of appetizing graham crackers in a small box."[151]

Mills also sponsored competitions at local fairs. At the Seventh Annual Cooke County Fair in Gainesville in 1913, the Whaley Mill and Elevator Company funded prizes of money and flour for the best baked goods made from its products: yeast-rising loaf bread, salt-rising bread, layer cakes, cookies, and doughnuts. The cash prizes were mostly $3.20, with cookies and doughnuts bringing $1.60, and they were accompanied by either fifty or one hundred pounds of Whaley's "Oriole" Flour. At the fair in Pilot Grove in 1928, the Taylor Milling Company of Van Alstyne made an award for the "best cake from Van Alstyne flour."[152] By contrast, Gainesville grocers—not millers—sponsored prizes made from imported flour. Grocer Owen Saunders honored the best loaf of bread made from Wolf's Premium flour from Ellinwood, Kansas, with a prize of $5.00 in store merchandise, and his competitor, Ben F. Witt, offered $3.20 and one hundred pounds of "Royal Seal" flour from Edmond, Oklahoma, for the best cake made with that product.[153] With differing priorities, the millers and the grocers failed to agree on the best sources of flour.

North Texas mills played a noteworthy role in the Texas Centennial observance in Dallas in 1936, seizing the opportunity to expose their wares to millions of fair attendees. Six mills—Burrus, Morten, Fant, Collin County, Texas Star Flour Mills of Galveston, and Liberty Mills of San Antonio—and three elevator companies—Perry Burrus Elevators of Dallas, Lone Star Elevators of Fort Worth, and Burrus Panhandle Elevators of Amarillo—joined to create a fine exhibit in its own building, which still stands in 2025. The building's exterior replicated the first Burrus Mill, built in 1875 near McKinney, complete with a millpond and a waterwheel, parts of it built from original materials salvaged from the site. On the inside, the building had a "modern experimental flour mill," three kitchens, and a tearoom. The mill ground wheat into flour, and bakers in the kitchens turned the flour into biscuits for fairgoers.[154] The millers hired Ida Keener Chitwood, who taught cooking shows across the Southwest as "director of home economics" for the mill; she was also "in charge of the tea room." They styled the kitchens as the "Southern Laboratory Kitchens" where they would conduct experiments on wheat and flour as well as develop recipes. Between August 7 and October 2, 1936, the *Dallas Morning News* ran occasional recipes given to it by Chitwood, "courtesy of Southern Laboratory Kitchens."[155] The mills promised that they would use the discoveries they made in the Southern Laboratory Kitchens through "experimental and laboratory methods" to improve their flours.[156] Chitwood, already well known in Texas, compiled a cookbook of "100 Famous Recipes" for standard baked goods.[157] She assured readers that the recipes for the "sacred art" of baking had been "both KITCHEN and DINING room tested in the beautiful SOUTHERN LABORATORY KITCHENS, in the Chitwood School of cookery[,] and in my own home."[158] With all that testing, presumably the recipes produced excellent quality and flavor.

Through the medium of radio, North Texas flour mills shaped the music of the region in the 1930s. WBAP, a powerful Fort Worth station, began producing musical shows very early with a "radio barn dance" in 1928, similar to the fantastically popular "National Barn Dance" begun in Chicago on radio station WLS in 1924.[159] Flour mills started getting involved in 1929, when the Burrus Mill sponsored a group of saxophonists, the "Burrus Octet," on WBAP.[160] In 1930, a performer named Culpepper, billed as a "nationally known vaudeville star of the Keith Orpheum Circuit," appeared on the "Burrus Mill Radio Program."[161]

The use of music to market North Texas flour took a substantial step in 1931, when the Burrus Mill began sponsoring a musical variety program on the small Fort Worth radio station KFJZ. After the program by fiddler Bob Wills and his band, with their pioneering blend of country, blues, and jazz, lost its sponsor, Fort Worth businessman Ed Kemble approached W. Lee O'Daniel, the sales manager for Burrus, about stepping in. O'Daniel agreed to do so, on the condition that each band member work a forty-hour week in the mill for a salary of $7.50 a week. Wills drove a truck, guitarist Herman Arnspiger sacked flour, and singer Milton Brown went into sales.[162]

The Burrus sponsorship of the Wills band began in January 1931 with a program that aired at seven in the morning. Wills and the band members began referring to themselves as the Light Crust Doughboys, after the mill's "Light Crust" flour brand. After five weeks, O'Daniel allowed the band members to stop working in flour production as long as they practiced their music for eight hours a day at the mill.[163]

In March 1931, O'Daniel chartered a bus and wired it with a loudspeaker to transport the band to a bakers' convention in Galveston. The stunt succeeded so well that O'Daniel then bought a seven-passenger Packard automobile and emblazoned it with Depression-era slogans such as "Patronize Texas Industry and Texas Agriculture and Prosperity Will Return."[164]

The marketing was a smashing success. O'Daniel wrote all the ad copy and composed short poems and songs. In November 1931, O'Daniel filled in when the usual emcee couldn't make a performance. He thereafter became the regular announcer, "delivering flour-inspired song introductions and sermonettes." O'Daniel's "blend of homey Christian philosophy, sentimental poetry, and rural music" struck a chord with North Texas audiences, and the show moved to radio station WBAP in a very favorable noon time slot. Stations in San Antonio and Houston picked up the show, spreading the word about Burrus flour throughout the state.[165]

The association of Bob Wills with Burrus lasted less than two years, as band members chafed under O'Daniel's rules. O'Daniel refused to let the band accept a recording contract with Victor Records, and he objected to them playing in dance halls, which he associated with alcohol consumption.[166] Most radio music became less innovative stylistically after Wills's departure, with stations playing gospel and hillbilly music for their mostly white audiences.

The Burrus show and the Light Crust Doughboys (with new performers) went on, however, and O'Daniel's "deep melodic voice" took on an ever more prominent role.[167] When Burrus dedicated its giant new mill and elevator in February 1936, WBAP broadcast the event for an hour and a half. The Doughboys provided the music, and band member Eddie Dunn "act[ed] as commentator on the series of remote control pickups" in the new mill, "including one from the scale room, located 160 feet in the air at the top of the huge grain elevators." The program promised a broadcast of "actual sounds of the machinery."[168]

The new mill had a first-rate recording studio on the second floor of the office building.[169] The Doughboys also continued performing on the road. In 1935, O'Daniel purchased a touring bus with its own generator and a public address system with built-in speakers. A sound engineer traveled with the band, which could then broadcast from the bus over a telephone line.[170] For example, the "Burrus Mills Doughboys" entertained at the rodeo in Stamford, 150 miles west of Fort Worth, in July 1939.[171]

The Doughboys' activity extended to Hollywood films and to other types of radio broadcasting. In 1936, the Light Crust Doughboys appeared in the movie *Oh Susanna* with Gene Autry. They filmed a second movie, *The Big Show,* with Autry at the 1936 Texas Centennial.[172] They even provided the music for a soap opera, *Your Home Town,* which aired on NBC Radio and starred Doughboy announcer Parker Willson.[173]

The dedication of the new Burrus Mill in 1936 happened without O'Daniel. Jack Burrus, the company's owner, took a dim view of his financial dealings and his use of company employees for personal tasks, and he fired O'Daniel in August 1935.[174] Undeterred, O'Daniel founded the W. Lee O'Daniel Flour Company, brokers and distributors of Hillbilly Flour, which was milled mostly in the Wichita Falls area. He formed a new band, the Hillbilly Boys, with his sons Pat and Mike playing guitar and fiddle and company employees as other band members.[175] The band would play an integral part in O'Daniel's political career.

To celebrate its fiftieth anniversary, Bewley Mills began sponsoring a musical program on WBAP in late December 1932. It announced that *Kernel Wheat and His Chuck Wagon Gang* would be on the air every weekday at 1:00 p.m. and also four evenings a week. The first programming included a "male quartet with the colonel as master of ceremonies," and they sang "familiar hymns and old favorite songs."[176] A 1935 photograph of the band shows them decked out in leopard-print shirts and ten-gallon hats. The instruments that the singers played included the fiddle, harmonica, jaw harp, and washboards.[177]

Not to be outdone by Burrus, the Chuck Wagon Gang appeared at events around North Texas. Beginning in March 1933, the band traveled in a "Chuck Wagon," a bus tricked out with advertising and musical facilities. A reporter commented on their first trip to Wills Point in Van Zandt County, about ninety miles east of Fort Worth, "The chuck wagon is completely equipped for traveling—it contains even a small piano so the boys can broadcast right from the wagon, so don't be surprised at the announcement of where the program is coming from when you tune in on the Chuck Wagon Gang's broadcasts from WBAP."[178] The motorized "chuck wagon" also carried two portable wood-burning stoves and a cook who cranked out hot biscuits on-site—made, of course, from "Bewley's Best" flour.[179] In December 1933, the *Timpson Times* in Shelby County, more than two hundred miles east of Fort Worth, reported that "several hundred people" turned out to hear the Chuck Wagon Gang in front of A. F. Burns's grocery store. Although the band arrived late, Burns, the local dealer for Bewley's flour, was "well pleased with the reception."[180]

Late in 1935, a singing family named Carter (no relation to the Grand Ole Opry's Carter family) moved from Lubbock to Fort Worth, hoping to make the big time. Bewley officials decided to create two units of the Chuck Wagon Gang: one to travel and one to perform on the radio. As the radio unit, the Carters sang "Western ballads, parlor songs, folk songs, some Stephen Foster tunes, and an occasional religious song."[181] Unlike the Burrus Mill show, with O'Daniel's constant patter, the Chuck Wagon Gang shows consisted simply of singing and commercials for Bewley.[182] Listeners loved the gospel singing, and the Wednesday program soon became devoted exclusively to hymns. By 1940, the Carters abandoned the rest of their repertoire and sang gospel music exclusively. In 1942, radio station KVOO in Tulsa lured them north with larger salaries, and the Chuck Wagon Gang left Bewley's sponsorship and Texas.[183]

Fant Mills tried its hand at radio advertising with music, sponsoring the Gladiola Gloom Chasers from 1933 to 1936 on Dallas radio station WFAA. The show began at 7:00 a.m. with an orchestral rendition of "Reveille" and included a whistler and a xylophonist, all meant to give listeners a "smile, good cheer, pep and enthusiasm to start the day."[184] The star of the show was a hillbilly performer named Peg Moreland, so called because he had a wooden peg to replace the part of his right leg lost in a railroad accident. Moreland's nonsensical song "Ain't We Crazy" became the theme for the show.[185] During its three-year run, the show included regionally themed programs such as "Texas Independence" on March 2.[186] The company also tried to have a "radio club for a cheer-up campaign." They announced that only people from Texas and Louisiana were eligible for membership, but the only other requirement was a promise "to do something to make somebody happy every day." Members would receive a certificate with a photograph of the Gladiola Gloom Chasers and a membership button. As new members were added, their names would be read during the morning programs.[187] The show disappeared in February 1936, its time slot taken by a new program, *Old Man Texas and His Boys,* also featuring Peg Moreland.[188]

Universal Mills, too, ventured briefly into musical radio advertising with the Universal Cowboys. The five members of the Cowboys played "cowboy ballads and popular string band music." They began broadcasting September 13, 1938, at first on WBAP and then on KGKO.[189] Charlie Willhoite, Universal's advertising manager, served as master of ceremonies. The band, billed as "riders of the range of rhythm," traveled to small West Texas towns with their "guitars, violins, [and] other musical instruments" to play "request numbers" at stores and rodeos.[190] While the showmanship of the Burrus Mill had the greatest impact, numerous mills affected the daily lives of Texans who enjoyed the mills' radio shows and the traveling musicians.

With the wealth that they accrued through their work, the millers of North Texas built fine homes that reflected the taste and refinement of the region. The architectural trends of the time often shaped the houses. Mill owners C. F. and Celestine Pillot Saigling began construction on their Plano home in 1906. Dallas architects Lang and Witchell designed the two-story Craftsman-style home. The 4,300-square-foot house was the first brick-veneer residence in the town, and most likely the first with a basement and central heating. A porch with a low-pitched roof and square brick columns ran the width of the house.[191] In McKinney, Perry Burrus built a fine Prairie School–style home in 1914, with details such as continuous window groupings, a broad porch with piers, and wide overhanging eaves that emphasized the horizontality of the house.[192] The Dallas home of E. W. Morten at 4015 Lemmon Avenue, erected in the early 1920s, was a three-story American Foursquare-style house with a green tile roof and dormer windows. The living room and dining room featured quarter-sawn oak beams, and the front stairwell was "finished in polished oak." A second structure at the back of the lot, measuring three thousand square feet, held a garage and servants' quarters.[193]

In Fort Worth, millers and grain merchants bought property and built houses in prestigious neighborhoods. The Smith brothers, co-owners of the Smith Brothers Grain Company, had homes in the same block of Elizabeth Boulevard in Fort Worth. In 1918, Bert K. Smith bought the Italian Renaissance Revival home that developer John C. Ryan had built in 1915. The same year, his brother, Jule G. Smith, built a 6,500-square-foot house. Prominent Fort Worth architect Wiley Clarkson designed the two-story structure of tile and stucco with a full terrace across the 90-foot front facade.[194]

As Fort Worth expanded to the west, the River Crest enclave included the large, painstakingly designed homes of milling magnates. In 1935, Universal

Mills's Gaylord and Harriet Stone built a 6,500-square-foot Mission-style home of buff-colored brick with a tile roof. But perhaps the most notable house was the one that Houston architect John F. Staub designed in 1926 for Martha Jennings and Edwin E. Bewley. Best known for his design of the Houston mansion Bayou Bend, Staub tailored the house to the site overlooking the West Fork of the Trinity River. Curving gently along the ridgeline and only one room deep, the house centers on a "steeply raked gabled entrance bay of orange, red, and black clinker brick." Staub tried to make it appear that the house "grows out of its site."[195] The Bewley house remains one of the premier architectural accomplishments in Fort Worth.

Gaylord Stone exhibited his taste in architecture and art in his business as well as his home. In 1940, his company, Universal Mills, built a two-story, air-conditioned office building, at a cost of $30,000. Civil engineer Charles Moss Davis designed the cement building measuring one hundred by thirty-eight feet with glass brick and fluorescent lighting to maximize interior brightness.[196] The building featured several elegant ornaments. Martha Zoe Davis, the builder's daughter, painted a brightly colored mural depicting Yum Kaax, the Mayan god of agriculture, in the stairwell. Fort Worth artist Dwight Clay Holmes sculpted a bas relief over the entry door showing a huge grain elevator and silos and a man holding a scythe. And one end of the building had "open grillwork, Spanish in design."[197]

People associated with grain became patrons of the visual arts. Perhaps the first person in Fort Worth to connect the world of wheat with the fine arts was Hallie Samuel Bewley, wife of Murray Percival Bewley. Hallie Samuel was born in Bowling Green, Kentucky, in 1852. She married Bewley in 1877, and the newlyweds moved to Fort Worth. Her husband's milling business thrived, and Hallie Bewley began collecting art.[198] She was the founding president of the Fort Worth Art Association (FWAA) in 1910 and remained so until her death in 1930. She donated many works to the permanent collection of the association, which became the foundation of the Modern Art Museum; she also donated works to the Fort Worth public schools and the local Carnegie Library. For many years she chaired the art committee of the Texas Federation of Women's Clubs.[199]

Hallie Bewley's son, Murray Percival Bewley Jr., born in 1884 in Fort Worth, became a noted portrait painter. He studied art in locations from Fort Worth to Florence. A 1910 exhibit by the FWAA, "Exhibition by Dallas and Fort Worth Artists," included his paintings.[200] Bewley worked in Paris between 1906 and 1913, then returned to Fort Worth and set up a studio. In 1916, he married Bernice Wren of Fort Worth and they moved to New York, where he specialized in portraits, particularly of children. In 1926, the women's clubs of Fort Worth presented his portrait of his mother to the FWAA.[201]

When the Bewleys built a handsome three-story brick building at the corner of Throckmorton and Seventh Streets in downtown Fort Worth, it included a fine art gallery. The gallery brought notable works to Fort Worth, including, most notoriously, a nude painting by the Russian artist Marceli Suchorowski entitled *Nana*. *Nana* toured Europe and the United States for decades, often provoking great controversy over its sensuality. In it, "a young woman [is] shown lying naked on a bed decked with furs, her left hand under her head, her right lifting a tress of her fair hair."[202] The Bewleys brought *Nana* to Fort Worth for ten days in May 1908.[203] Far from gasping in dismay, North Texas writers praised the painting as a "brilliant success" and noted its "startling life-like look."[204] "Thousands of people" paid to see the painting; for men, admission fees were 25 cents between 10:00 a.m. and 3:00 p.m. and 15 cents from 3:00 p.m. until 10:00 p.m., and "ladies" paid 15 cents all day.[205] The Bewleys had transported the world, scandalous and otherwise, to North Texas.

Edwin E. Bewley, son of Hallie Bewley and older brother of Murray Bewley, became president of the FWAA in 1938, eight years after his mother's death. Bewley's tenure launched the FWAA into a new era, with strong patronage of a group of local artists who came to be known as the Fort Worth Circle. Under his leadership, the FWAA inaugurated a new gallery with an exhibition featuring the work of young modernist painters, some trained at the Fort Worth School of Fine Arts and all living in Fort Worth. For the next fifteen years, the FWAA gallery, "through the worst and best of times . . . served as a prime mover in changing the art of the city." In 1946, the year of Edwin Bewley's death, the artists clustered around the FWAA staged an exhibition, "Six Texas Painters," at the Weyhe Gallery in New York City. The Bewleys' enthusiasm and encouragement had launched an artistic movement.[206]

The seeds of the Kimbell Art Museum in Fort Worth began in the 1930s. Kay Kimbell and his wife, Velma Fuller Kimbell, moved to Fort Worth from Sherman in 1924 and began collecting art in 1931. Their first purchase was *The Beechey Children*, a work by eighteenth-century British portrait painter Sir William Beechey, which was in a temporary exhibit at the public library sponsored by the FWAA.[207] By the mid-1930s, the Kimbells were giving tours of their collection in their home in Fort Worth, including works by European painters Sir Joshua Reynolds, Sir Thomas Lawrence, Francis Cotos, and Jean-Jacques Henner.[208] The couple established the Kay Kimbell Art Foundation in 1936 and continued collecting for the rest of their lives.[209]

Wealthy mill owners and bakers participated in other types of philanthropy as well. Some donated land or money. In Plano, Celestine Pillot Saigling gave five acres adjacent to her home for the creation of Haggard Park.[210] Gainesville mill owner James Oscar Andrew Whaley, the son of a Methodist minister, assisted the Gainesville Methodist community until his death in 1909. When the Broadway Methodist Church in downtown Gainesville burned in 1913, his widow, Mary Isabelle Keith Whaley, donated funds for a new building, including a stained-glass window in her husband's memory. The congregation renamed the church Whaley Memorial Methodist Episcopal Church at its dedication in 1916. The new building, with Doric columns on two sides and an impressive dome, served the church until 1971.[211]

Two notable women transformed the money that their husbands earned into help for unmarried pregnant women in Dallas and Fort Worth. Jennie Nathanson Schepps, born Zlotte Yuselovsky in Zabaline, Russia, in 1872, married Joseph Schepps in 1891. They immigrated to the United States in 1891, and to Dallas in 1901. Joseph, a baker by trade in Russia, tried his hand as an entrepreneur in St. Louis before they made their way to Dallas. He found employment at the Model Bakery, and he then set up a retail store that sold Model Bakery products. Jennie created routes where their three oldest children sold bread door to door from a horse-drawn wagon. Eventually the family bought the Kleber Bakery, which made and sold bread: rye, pumpernickel, "twisted egg bread, pan bread (which was a light bread that non-Jews liked)," as a family member wrote, and bagels. In 1915, the Schepps family became a part of the Butternut Bread franchise. By 1922, they were baking an estimated 80 percent of the bread sold in Dallas.[212]

Jennie Schepps, known in her family as "the Duchess," was active in a variety of charitable causes in Dallas, chief among them caring for unmarried pregnant women. Schepps began this work in the 1920s, when she bought a cottage and deeded it to United Charities, which evolved its use into the care of unmarried mothers.[213] In the late 1930s, the Family Consultation Bureau, as the organization came to be known, served about fifty unmarried mothers a year, giving them shelter and helping to place their babies with adoptive families.[214] Jennie Schepps also bought a building for the Dallas Community Chest organization in the 1940s.[215]

Much better known is the work of Edna Browning Kahly Gladney, whose husband, Sam Gladney, spent his boom-and-bust career in flour milling. Edna Gladney was born in Milwaukee in 1886 to a single mother and an unknown father. Beset with respiratory problems, she moved in 1904 to Fort Worth to live with an aunt and uncle. In 1905, Sam Gladney, a native of Comanche, Texas, came to Fort Worth to work at the Medlin Milling

Company. Edna and Sam married in 1906. In 1913, Sam Gladney and Perry Burrus bought Sherman Mill and Grain in Grayson County and renamed it Gladney Milling; there they would make a flour called "Gladiola."[216]

According to all reports, Edna Gladney burst with both energy and kindness. In Sherman, she became involved with local reform movements. Among them was the fight to clean up the Grayson County Poor Farm, which served destitute Texans, old and young. Attempting to alleviate the horrific conditions there, she took children from the poor farm and put them in the care of the Texas Children's Home and Aid Society. As she continued to work with single mothers, Gladney came into increasing contact with birth mothers, "mostly single women facing society's scorn." She became "mother confessor, legal counsel, nurse and temporary guardian of every girl within 40 miles of Sherman who needed confidential help." Gladney began placing infants with families across the United States whose households she termed "saddened homes without children."[217]

In 1921, Sam Gladney's web of investments crashed, and he was forced to sell his mill to Fant Milling. The Gladneys sold almost all of their possessions and moved to Fort Worth.[218] In 1923, Sam established the wholesale Gladney-Muchmore Grain Company.[219] Edna worked in the office, but she also went to work for the Texas Children's Home and Aid Society at no salary. In 1927, still unpaid, she became the superintendent.[220] A. J. Duncan, the head of Fort Worth Light and Power, bought and donated an empty mansion that became a "much-needed baby home and hospital."[221] By 1936, the home had accommodations for fifteen children and accepted children up to the age of fourteen—but only from their "mothers, doctors, guardians, or charitable organizations." It was not an orphanage but rather a "handling home" that accepted children for placement and cared for them until families could found.[222] Unlike other adoption authorities, Gladney believed in placing a baby as early as possible rather than following custom to wait and see how the child turned out.[223]

Edna Gladney worked hard for causes that she believed to be right. In 1933, she successfully lobbied the Texas legislature for two new laws regarding children and adoption. The first ended the use of the word "illegitimate" on birth certificates. The other gave adopted children the same inheritance rights as biological children.[224]

In 1941, a Hollywood film entitled *Blossoms in the Dust* fictionalized the work of Edna Gladney. Noted writer and actress Anita Loos authored the screenplay. Starring Greer Garson, the film was one of the most popular of the year and earned four Academy Award nominations. Back in Sherman, the Fant Milling Company proudly claimed Gladney's work, extolling her in a newspaper ad headlined as "Filmland's Tribute to a Great Work by a

Texas Woman!" Saluting "Mrs. Sam Gladney, played by Greer Garson in 'Blossoms in the Dust,'" the ad crowed, "Gladiola Mill . . . built in Sherman by the late Mr. Sam Gladney, is still milling flour of unusual quality and packing it in Gladiola sacks."[225]

In the years between 1900 and 1940, millers saw their livelihoods change as the old ways passed away and big business came to rule the industry. The fortunes rose of those able to adapt, and those people used their funds to further causes they cared about. Wheat and flour money built houses, churches, art museums, and charitable institutions.

North Texans bought the products of these millers for baking, both at home and commercially. In the early twentieth century, people brought innovation to all kinds of baked goods—bread, of course, but also lots of biscuits and a rising number of sweets. In the next chapter, we follow the aromas of yeast and spices into North Texas kitchens and bakeries.

8 / HOMEMADE SWEETS AND STANDARDIZED BREAD: BAKING, 1900–1940

CAKES, PIES, COOKIES, BREADS BOTH SWEET AND plain—North Texans ate all of these baked goods in the years before 1940. Abundant flour, both from the region and from distant markets, made baked goods an increasing part of the North Texas diet.

As North Texas mills became ever larger and the number of wheat farmers shrank, more people in the region bought their flour from grocers rather than at a mill. Still, some old ways persisted as North Texans used time-honored methods to get money for flour. Amos Dotson hunted opossums and skunks and sold their hides in Gainesville and Pilot Point. Receiving 10 to 15 cents per hide, Dotson went to the mill and bought fifty pounds of flour for 55 cents. He recalled, "So, if you could go out on a pretty good night of hunting you could buy a sack of flour. It wasn't easy but it was something to supplement the grocery."[1] More conventionally, Orbie Ingram sold corn to the mill and then took the money to the grocer for "eight sacks of flour, a hundred pounds of sugar, three boxes of dried fruit, a big can of baking powder, et cetera." He vividly recalled, "The flour was first grade flour at 75c a sack."[2]

Bessie Gooch Steele told the story of what her husband, Jim Tom Steele, and his brother, Arthur Steele, did during a particularly lean time: "Arthur Steele lived east of Burns City. He came to our house on a horse. He tied his horse, came in and talked for a while. Then he said, 'Jim, how much money have you got?' Jim went down in his pocket and pulled out some change. Arthur said, 'We're out of flour. Do you suppose between us we've got enough to buy a sack of flour?' Arthur went to the store. Jim Rainey ran it then. He came back to the house and they divided the sack of flour half and half. That was how hard times was."[3] With cooperation and determination, the Steele brothers got flour for their families. They would not go back to cornmeal alone.

Mills, always looking for a way to market to housewives, sought to instruct home cooks on how best to use their products. Cooking shows were one way to do that, often in combination with baking competitions. Cooking schools had existed in the northeastern United States for decades, but they did not reach Texas until the twentieth century. In Texas these shows often brought in experts from the Northeast, perhaps capitalizing on the reputation of entities such as Fannie Farmer's Boston Cooking School, established in 1879. In Dallas in 1901, for example, the New Century Mill put on a cooking school at the A. Harris Department Store, taught by Bertha Haffner, "an expert bread and cake baker" who came "recommended from many of the Northern cities."[4] Haffner, a widow with two children, was an "instructor" at the Detroit Cooking School, established in 1889 in Michigan, and she taught at various short-term schools across the United States, mostly in the Midwest. As North Texans had not hesitated to link wheat and flour with the North, they extolled Haffner's northern connections.

As elsewhere in the United States, local newspapers hosted many schools, with backing from resident businesses, including mills. The *Dallas Morning News* featured La France flour, from the New Century Mill, at its cooking school in 1913. Presumably the mill offered an incentive to the newspaper to make its flour the choice for the school.[5] The cooking demonstration culminated in a baking contest, with more than seven hundred entrants vying for prizes for layer cakes, loaf cakes, doughnuts, pies, and breads. Two chefs at Dallas hotels and the chief pastry cook at the opulent Adolphus Hotel served as judges. The first-place winners received large appliances such as ranges and refrigerators, with smaller rewards for six or seven other entrants in each category. When auctioned off for charity, the prize-winning creations raised more than $200.[6] In Fort Worth, Bewley's Best was the "official flour" of the 1916 cooking school staged by the *Fort Worth Star-Telegram*. Eliza Q. Fothergill, the "domestic economy expert" for the *Pittsburgh Post*, used only Bewley's flour in her demonstrations.[7] Bakers took home prizes for layer cakes, white loaf cakes, bread, pies, and doughnuts. The first prize in each category included a barrel of Bewley's Best flour.[8] In the 1930s, Bewley Mills tied the visit of Viola Decker, a home economist from the General Electric Company, and her "Free Electric Cooking School" to its radio program. In addition to making personal appearances, Decker also appeared "daily" on the Bewley Mills Golden Jubilee Program on radio station WBAP.[9] Each cooking demonstration and competition tried to yoke the idea of excellence with a certain brand of flour.

Another method of instruction from the mill to the home cook was the cookbook. Across the United States, many corporations published cookbooks to peddle their products, starting in the 1920s. Advertising disguised as cookbooks encouraged consumers to engage with the product and made the brand appear helpful.[10] North Texas mills, following the national trend, began creating cookbooks focused on their flour. Although there was nothing regionally distinctive in the recipes, advertisers tried to make consumers believe that buying a certain brand would ensure success in the kitchen—and thus in larger realms of life.

Perhaps the first cookbook praising Texas flour was published in 1909 in Bowie, Montague County (population 2,800), fifty miles northwest of Denton. For unknown reasons, the women of the Baptist Ladies' Aid and Missionary Society of the First Baptist Church of Bowie produced *The Peace Maker Cook Book: Named in Honor of the Celebrated Peace Maker Flour Made by Alliance Milling Co., Denton, Texas,* specifying Peace Maker flour in its recipes. It was not published by Alliance Milling, but it definitely showcased the company's products. The slender paperbound book, seventy-five pages in length, featured all types of recipes contributed by the women of Montague County, including au courant entrées made in chafing dishes and meals featuring oysters, canned or obtained from the Gulf of Mexico almost four hundred miles away. The book includes recipes for the standard fare of the time—breads, cakes, pies, and custards, including Baltimore Filling made from sugar, cornstarch, milk, salt, vanilla, raisins, currants, walnuts, and grated chocolate—one of the innumerable variations on the Lady Baltimore cakes that were all the rage at the time.[11] The book was evidently well received. Between 1909 and 1922, it went through four editions, all featuring the flour from Denton. The origins of the strong connection remain a mystery.

The mills themselves got into the game in the 1930s. Bewley Mills hired Irene Nevill Aby, who held a master's degree from Columbia University and had taught "Foods and Cookery" at the College of Industrial Arts in Denton, to compile its cookbook, *Bewley's Best Bakes Better Bread Pastry Cake,* published in 1935.[12] In thirty-two quick pages, Aby included recipes for yeast bread, quick bread, cakes, cream puffs and éclairs, cookies, fried breads, fillings, griddle cakes, muffins, and pies. The Bewley cookbook also highlighted the mill's connection with Lucille Bishop Smith, a noted Fort Worth caterer who was African American. Her recipe for "Lucille's Whole Wheat 'Two Hour Rolls'" used whole-wheat flour as well as white flour—both, of course, produced by Bewley.[13] In her capacity as "teacher trainer industrial education" at Prairie View A&M College, a historically black institution near Houston, Smith commented that a housewife hiring a cook always wanted her domestic worker to know "all kinds of baking." Smith observed, "I know from my long experience as a caterer and as a teacher of cooking, that successful home baked breads, biscuits, pastry and cake is the backlog of all meal preparation. With piping hot rolls or delicious hot biscuits, any meal can be 'lifted' out of the ordinary."[14] Smith spoke authoritatively even as she addressed the stereotypical—and declining—employment of African American women in white women's houses.

About 1935, Stanard-Tilton Milling published an eight-page pamphlet featuring "Recipes Used by First Prize Winners in the State Fair of Texas Baking Contest." Tellingly, the pamphlet did not include yeast bread, which was losing favor with home bakers, but it did have several cakes and both baking powder and buttermilk biscuits, as well as salt-rising bread.[15] Bread making was leaving the home, and the staff members at Stanard-Tilton knew it. Again, by featuring prize-winning recipes, marketers implied that ordinary housewives could produce extraordinary products with their flour.

Fant Milling combined its cookbook with radio programming and employed an unusual format for the book. In 1936 the company began sponsoring *Mary Lane's Kitchen Club,* which first aired on Dallas radio station WFAA on Thursday mornings at 10:30. The program featured home economist "Mary Lane," who introduced a new recipe each week, answered listeners' questions, and introduced the week's musical entertainer.[16] Fant was apparently hoping to have the same success General Mills found with "Betty Crocker," its fictional spokesperson who had been the first cooking expert on the airwaves, beginning in 1924.[17]

The character of Mary Lane described the program. She promised to answer every letter that listeners wrote to the show. She would present on the show at least one recipe "that I have adjusted in my laboratory kitchen." The laboratory to which she referred was the "Better Baking Institute" that Fant Milling created to use its Gladiola flour. The Fant writers explained that they had created "experimental kitchens" and placed "Mary Lane, home economist, food authority, and baking expert . . . at its head." Lane was there to develop "recipes that will turn out well in your oven, whether you burn gas, wood, coal, kerosene, or oil."[18]

Listeners could sign up for the Kitchen Club and receive a cookbook with recipes for quick breads, yeast breads, cakes, sponge cakes, cookies, and pies and pastry. Each section contained two printed recipes. Each month, the club "member" was mailed a new recipe; after filing it in the appropriate section of the book, she was to write the name of the recipe in the table of contents. Examination of one archived copy of the 1936 cookbook, for example, shows that it arrived already containing quick-bread recipes for baking powder biscuits and breakfast muffins. Over the months, the book's owner received recipes for other quick breads, including nut bread, shortcake, scones, Sally Lunn, and sweet rolls. She dutifully filed the recipes and wrote the recipe names on the section title card in a beautifully clear script. Dispersed across the categories, a total of fifty-four recipes were mailed to her. If the recipes arrived once a month, that means they were sent for four and a half years, through the middle of 1940.[19]

Fant Milling also produced more conventional editions of *Mary Lane's Book of Baking*, in 1938 and 1939. The 1938 edition had "a beautiful plastic binding" and contained eighty-two recipes "generously illustrated with photographs." A careful consumer could find a coupon in sacks of Gladiola flour that would reduce the cost of the cookbook from 25 cents to 10 cents. The company urged readers to "ask your grocer for the flour with the Mary Lane coupons."[20] The 1939 edition, also in book form and ring-bound with red plastic, had recipes for biscuits, waffles, hot cakes, muffins, shortcake, yeasted breads and rolls, cakes, frosting, cookies, and pies.

Fort Worth resident and home economist Lenore Miller Standifer conducted cooking schools for the Burrus, Morten, and Smith Mills throughout Texas and Louisiana in the late 1920s and early 1930s.[21] In 1940, she compiled *Practical Recipes for Using La France Flour* for Morten Mills. Her recipes included waffles, gingerbread, biscuits, muffins, puddings, pies, cakes, cookies—including "frozen cookies," an early version of icebox cookies that could be kept cold, sliced, and baked on demand—and fillings and icings. Her recipes for bread included two yeasted loaves and two recipes for rolls.[22]

No matter how clear the instructions, home bakers still had to be careful with the ingredients for their culinary creations. The editors of the *True and Tried Cook Book* from Fort Worth made much the same warning to readers as nineteenth-century cookbook writers had made to earlier users: "Some flours contain more moisture than others. That made from spring wheat is likely to be sticky and the same may be said of new flour generally. Any excess of moisture may be removed by drying before the fire."[23] Vegetable shortening, a new invention that quickly took the place of lard, had a bland taste that a skilled cook had to compensate for. In 1913, Mary Cushman of Fort Worth warned that a cook should add salt to a recipe if using shortening.[24]

Even as urban kitchens increasingly had ovens fueled with gas, kerosene, or even electricity, baking without a thermometer or thermostat remained a skill. Minnie Rider Rhome of Fort Worth in 1913 advised baking her white loaf cake (leavened with twelve egg whites as well as baking powder) for "1 ¼ hours in a moderate oven, having the oven just hot enough to bear the hand until the cake is risen about ½ hour, increase the heat and finish baking; should cook 1 ¼ hours."[25] Bakers like Rhome had to learn to gauge the heat in their ovens, just as their grandmothers had done.

For many North Texans in the early part of the twentieth century, home baking still centered on the daily rituals of cornbread and biscuits. Particularly in rural areas, Texans ate biscuits for breakfast and cornbread for their midday and evening meals. As in the past, cornbread was baked in many forms, from simple pones made only with cornmeal and milk to rich, eggy, soft spoonbread. Sometimes wheat flour was added to cut the grittiness of the cornmeal.[26] People still considered cornmeal decidedly inferior to wheat flour. Velma Lee Crutsinger Ingram recalled, "One time we had an April Fool party. I made a cornbread cake! I never will forget Lofton Ward. He was in the kitchen playing 42 and we were serving cake. I made the layers real thin and iced it with chocolate icing. Lofton thought that cornbread cake was delicious!" Ingram found Lofton's acceptance of cornmeal in place of flour, even with lots of chocolate icing, hilarious.[27]

For breakfast, and often for dinner and supper, biscuits took center stage. Thelma Harris, who grew up in Grayson County, recalled, "I can also remember when my mother made all our bread. With her wooden bread bowl in front of her, she mixed her biscuits and pastry doughs. We had biscuits for breakfast, biscuits for dinner, and biscuits again for supper. It was a long time before I had my first piece of toast for breakfast."[28] The descendants of Pearl Perry Gravley well remembered her biscuits. Her son Wilton Gravley commented that with ten children to feed, "Mama's cooking was aimed more at 'quantity' than 'quality.' Breakfast consisted of a platter of two or three dozen fried eggs piled on a platter, an equal number of home-made (from scratch) biscuits, a hot cereal, and molasses with butter." Granddaughter Martha Finch Lang remembered the quality as well: "big fluffy biscuits (and not the can type)."[29] Pearl Gravley fed a dozen people biscuits every day for decades.

Women still gauged their worth by the quality of their biscuits. A McKinney woman named Etha wrote to Mary Ann Moore in 1909 that her daughter Opal was now as tall as her mother, and "she learned to cook last summer. John says she can beat me making biscuit."[30] Thousands of North Texas women rose each morning to combine flour, salt, and lard or shortening, with either baking soda and sour milk or baking powder for leavening. Most rolled and cut their biscuits, although some dropped soft dough onto a pan.[31] To speed the baking process, Bewley Mills urged housewives to use the company's "biscuit base" recipe—flour, salt, baking powder, shortening. They could store the mix in their refrigerator or icebox and pull it out at a moment's notice for biscuits, "sweet bread, pie topping, shortcakes or waffles." Etta Pratt Mansfield of Fort Worth swore that "Bewley's Biscuit Base is more than a good start—it is half-way there."[32]

Mothers made school lunches with biscuits and ham or sausage, and they created treats from biscuit dough. Jewel Potts Cook remembered her mother, Mary Etta Rayzor Potts, crafting something that the family called a "stickish": "It was kind of a sugar pie. It was made out of some of the dough she had left from her biscuits. She put cinnamon, butter and sugar [on it] and it was kind of a half moon pie. She put it in the oven and baked it."[33] Similarly, Mary Jeanette Courts Daniel, the mother of Richard Daniel, made "butter rolls." Her son recalled, "We nearly always had a butter roll in our lunch pail. Mother would roll the dough out and she'd put butter, little hunks of butter all over that and nutmeg and sugar. Then she'd roll that up and bake it."[34] Fred Haynie put butter and sugar on biscuits, "rolled them up in a newspaper," and carried them to school in his pocket.[35] In Dallas County, immigrant mothers from Europe sent their children to school with homemade yeasted loaf bread. The children swapped their delectable light bread for their classmates' biscuits. Rosa Winder Lively, whose parents came from Switzerland, happily traded light bread for biscuits with butter and sugar. Bernice Ledbetter Graham remembered, "I always considered myself lucky if I could swap food with some of the German-descent children. They always brought such delicious light bread and pastries."[36]

Bread, whether leavened with yeast or baking powder, remained a central component of Texas diets. With reliable ingredients, housewives continued making homemade yeast bread, though the number of home bakers was declining. The list of prize breads from the 1917 Cooke County Free Fair included yeast-rising wheat bread, salt-rising wheat bread, brown bread, and rolls.[37]

Some women baked bread regularly. Estelle Haizlip Thompson remembered the loaf bread made by her mother, Essie Rankin Haizlip, on a farm northwest of Howe: "I can almost taste Mama's homemade lightbread now. For our large family [eight children] she made seven loaves at a time."[38] Women from Germany and Switzerland also continued the bread-baking traditions of their homelands.[39]

Sometimes bread nourished the family and then became a delight for others. Nick Ciaccio's parents, Guiseppe and Antonina Siragusa Ciaccio, immigrated from Italy and bought a farm east of Denison about 1920. He recalled, "Bread was baked in an outside 'furno' (oven) that Papa had built from stone gathered from the farm. She made from twenty to thirty loaves at least once a week. You could smell bread baking for blocks away, and we always had visitors about the time bread was ready. They knew there would be a loaf for them to take home."[40] Annabelle McGuire Sanguinet in the late 1930s still made bread once a week, as she had done for fifty-two years. The homemade bread was special enough, however, that she also gave loaves as Christmas gifts.[41]

Most home cooks used commercially made yeast, sometimes specifying Fleischmann's.[42] Some women, however, continued to make their own starters. Nick Ciaccio remembered, "Mama made her own yeast for the bread and pasta for cooking."[43] Salt-rising bread persisted, still an oddity. Fort Worth philanthropist Ida Van Zandt Jarvis submitted three recipes to a local cookbook, noting, "You cannot make this yeast with artesian water." Presumably the pure artesian water lacked necessary bacteria to activate the yeast.[44] Mary Taylor Field, the young wife of architect Stanley Field, advocated making the starter in a "fireless cooker," the heat from the stones helping to activate the enzymes. Field did not say whether the fireless cooker lessened the stink.[45]

As with biscuits, diners each had their own serving with individual rolls or buns, which also could be baked using less fuel than it took to bake loaves of bread.[46] Parker House rolls, slightly sweet and folded into half rounds before baking, were extremely popular. The Woman's Club of Fort Worth rechristened the recipe "Woman's Club Tea Room Rolls."[47]

North Texas women also championed brown or graham bread, widely touted for its health benefits. They steamed it or baked it as muffins, in baking powder cans, or in coffee cans.[48] Some recipes had raisins or nuts, and some specified locally made flour.[49]

Rural North Texans prepared flour dumplings to accompany wild game. Bernice Ledbetter Graham recalled the process of making squirrel dumplings. The cook cut up the squirrel and parboiled it, drained it, then boiled it again in "fresh salty water." The cook then added pepper, butter, and milk to the broth, dropped "small pieces" of dumplings into the broth, and boiled them for about ten minutes. North Texans also fried wild game. Rabbit and squirrel pieces received a good coating of flour before they were "fried in lard till brown."[50]

Sweet quick breads, leavened with baking powder or baking soda rather than yeast, became very popular after World War I.[51] Many women cooked nut bread, and date bread also proved to be a family favorite. Muffins of all kinds also appeared on North Texas tables, hot and fresh.[52]

As it had been for centuries, gingerbread was one of the simplest sweets in the home cook's collection. North Texas housewives used various combinations of flour, baking powder, baking soda, brown sugar, molasses, butter, buttermilk, eggs, and of course ginger to make their gingerbreads.[53]

Cookies, as always, were easy treats. Many North Texas cooks produced the same types of cookies as cooks elsewhere, such as oatmeal or sugar cookies. Tea cakes—slightly sweet cookies that were rolled and cut—were particular favorites.[54] Refrigerator cookies, also known as "icebox" or "Westinghouse" cookies, could be kept chilled as rolled raw dough, then sliced and baked as needed.[55] Some cookies, such as Post Toastie Macaroons, used boxed cereals as their base.[56] And bar cookies—for example, brownies and date bars (made with newly fashionable dried fruit)—were a snap to serve.[57]

While some home cooks raised doughnuts with yeast, most leavened their doughnuts with baking powder. And though many cooks continued to use lard for frying, a few specified new plant-based fats, such as Cottolene and Crisco, both made from cotton seed oil.[58]

Rural women continued baking cobblers with wild blackberries and dewberries. They grew peaches and blackberries in their yards. Oleta Maberry Derr recalled, "We had blackberries on one side of the fence around the garden. Mama would pick the berries and make berry cobblers that would melt in our mouths. All summer she canned the berries and vegetables out of the garden to last us all winter."[59] Maurine McDaniel Lewis remembered drying peaches about 1920—washing them, cutting them open, and removing the pit. Women placed the peach halves on boards covered with cloth and put them on the house roofs each morning to dry in the sun. Each night they brought down the fruit, then returned it to the roof the next morning until they were satisfied with its dryness. Lewis recalled, "These dried peaches were placed in jars and sealed for cooking fried pies, custard peach pies, or just stewed for eating with biscuits, fresh bread and butter."[60]

North Texas cooks made pies of all kinds from ingredients like fresh or dried peaches, lemon, molasses, pumpkin (from fresh or canned pumpkin), bananas, and apples, as well as chess pies and mincemeat pies. They continued to use the ancient form of mincemeat, usually made with meat and suet but sometimes leaving it out. One Dallas mincemeat recipe from the Prohibition period had no meat, but it did have whiskey.[61] But new trends showed up as well. The Osgood pie—the name possibly a corruption of "Oh! So Good" pie—made its rounds through North Texas kitchens in the 1920s. Its filling consisted mainly of raisins, spiced and mixed with egg yolks and butter.[62] Pecan pie began appearing in the sticky, gooey form that people loved. Before the twentieth century, pecans showed up only occasionally in recipes because they were hard to grow commercially. After 1900, when orchards became viable, the nuts were more often used and cherished in Texas cooking. The earliest pecan pies were custards, with the nuts in a base of milk, butter, and eggs. By the 1920s, however, the version made with corn syrup—specifically Karo, from Chicago—began taking over. A 1925 cookbook from the First Baptist Church of Dallas had both kinds, and a 1930 pie from Denton had both Karo syrup and cream in the filling.[63]

Even with increasingly reliable baking powder, cakes were still the acme of a fancy baker's repertoire. In 1917, despite wartime limits on flour and sugar, the Cooke County Free Fair offered prizes for five types of cakes: spice, caramel, angel food, white loaf, and the deep dark chocolate known as devil's food.[64] Seventeen years later, at the Pure Food Show in Celina, the prizes went for angel food, loaf, white layer, and devil's food cakes. Each first-prize winner received a twenty-four-pound sack of "White Billows" flour from the Collin County Mill.[65]

Two long-revered forms of cake, pound cake and fruitcake, were still baked in North Texas kitchens. Cooks flavored their pound cakes with vanilla, nutmeg, or citron.[66] Fruitcake remained the heavy, challenging holiday treat with a typically long list of ingredients.[67]

Layer cakes, baked in multiple shallow pans, were the showiest of all cakes—maybe of all baked goods, period. A towering construction with glossy frosting, a layer cake could command any table. A spice cake from "Mrs. A.C.B." in Dallas, for example, featured three layers, two simple and a third made with raisins and "ground spices to taste." The baker assembled the layers with the dark one in the middle and cemented them together with icing, the contrast ensuring a visually arresting sight when the cake was cut.[68] Spice cakes, silver cakes, and gold cakes also continued to find favor.[69]

Home bakers mixed jam into the batter of blackberry jam cake, and one recipe from Fort Worth topped out at four layers.[70] The gorgeous and extravagant Lady Baltimore cake, described earlier, came in many varieties, each claiming to be the original.[71] Katherine Thomas Good from Carrollton, born in 1900 and educated at Southwest Texas Normal College in San Marcos, specialized in Lady Baltimore cakes. Kent Adair remembered, "No one could make [Lady Baltimore cake] like Katherine. She literally had a cottage industry in the kitchen of her home. She would sell the cakes to the local grocery stores, because there were no bakeries in the area." Dorotha Good Russell concurred: "If you've never eaten one of Mrs. Rex (Kathryn [*sic*]) Good's Lady Baltimore cakes you've missed a treat. They are pretty to look at too! For special occasions my mother always liked to have one of Kathryn's cakes."[72]

Even the homeliest layer cakes could take a lot of labor. Sarah Jane Cornelius Gooch gathered wild plums "down on the creek" during the summer and made jelly, which she used between the layers of "plain cake" for her family's Christmas celebration.[73]

Skilled bakers turned out angel food cakes made with numerous egg whites as the only leavening. Stella Pratt Carrington of Fort Worth wrote of her "Perfect Angel Food" around 1912: "This is my original recipe and if all directions in regard to quantity, quality and combining of material,

FIGURE 9.1. *Rosamond Cayce Harvison of Fort Worth mixes a birthday cake for her daughter Rosalyn's Leap Year birthday, February 29, 1940.* (Fort Worth Star-Telegram *collection, University of Texas at Arlington Special Collections 20041179)*

as well as directions for baking are followed, success is assured." She used both granulated and powdered sugar, the "finest pastry flour" as well as egg whites, cream of tartar, vanilla extract, almond extract, and salt.[74] For her chocolate angel food cake, one Denton baker specified "Swans Down," a soft cake flour from Evansville, Indiana, that was available at grocers across North Texas by 1920.[75] Georgia McCluskey of Waco argued, however—in a Bewley-published cookbook—that Bewley's all-purpose flour was plenty good enough without resorting to imported cake flours: "I always use all-purpose flour in making my finest cakes. I reduce each cup of flour by three tablespoons, and sift it six to eight times. I also sift the sugar I use in my cakes. I find that all-purpose flour gives body, flavor, and the fine texture that I want in a cake."[76]

North Texas cooks also embraced new trends. The pineapple upside-down cake made its appearance in the United States shortly after World War I.[77] Cooks across the region were soon placing pineapple rings in syrup in their well-seasoned iron skillets and topping them with cake batter for a fashionable new dessert.[78] They also made cupcakes—small versions of larger cakes. Oleta Maberry Derr remembered that her neighbor Stella Tutt baked "cup cakes and covered them with the best caramel icing I ever ate."[79] Caramel icing could confound the most confident cook, so Tutt must have had a sure hand.

Some North Texas women mastered the art of choux pastry, which uses hot water as leavening. Mattie Gilmer, who probably was a highly skilled domestic worker in Fort Worth, submitted a recipe for cream puffs for the *True and Tried Cook Book* about 1912.[80] Louise Chapman Marshall, a wealthy housewife in Dallas, also knew the complexities of choux pastry, as shown in the recipe for cream puffs she contributed to the cookbook for the Episcopal Church of the Incarnation in 1929.[81]

Women used their baking skills to support charitable causes in a variety of ways, one of which was to contribute baking recipes to cookbooks that supported benevolent activities. More than a dozen cookbooks appeared in North Texas between 1900 and 1940, often compiled by churches but also by various women's clubs. Housewives also used their culinary skills to assist all kinds of worthy causes through bake sales. Church circles, school groups, and even reform organizations, such as the Woman's Christian Temperance Union, offered homemade bread and cakes to raise funds.[82] Women also donated pies and cakes for auction at community events known as pie suppers and for prizes at beauty contests. Maude Riley Davis recalled that during her girlhood around World War I, "at the pie suppers and box suppers they always had a pretty girl contest. Votes were usually a penny a vote and whoever won got a cake."[83] They also donated baked goods directly to charities. For example, the women of the Ladies Aid at the First Baptist Church of Carrollton made cookies for the children at Buckner Orphans Home in East Dallas.[84]

The women of St. Peter's Episcopal Church in McKinney began assisting the church in 1920 with their baking. Some accounts say that the altar guild needed money for new linens, while others aver that the women wanted to donate $100 to the organ fund. But sources agree that Nellie Daw Ritch suggested baking and selling fruitcakes, using "an old family recipe brought from England" to fund the project. The cake recipe included the usual array of ingredients plus wine and mincemeat. The first year they sold the cakes for 50 cents per pound. "Peddling door to door," they reached their financial goal. The women of St. Peter's took their calling so seriously that the church history refers to the activity as the "fruitcake ministry," and it continued for more than fifty years. In the 1960s, St. Peter's shipped out as many as eight thousand pounds of cake to destinations across the United States and around the globe. As late as 1979, the women of the small congregation were still at their work.[85]

Throughout the first third of the twentieth century, many housewives, particularly in the towns and cities, increasingly gave up bread baking at home and began buying their loaves. As yeast bread baking shifted from the home to commercial bakeries, observers expressed disapproval at the loss of the domestic skill. In 1922, the Fort Worth newspaper ran a nationally syndicated column by James J. Montague, blaming the "silliness" of young women on their inability to make bread:

> They talk most inanely and vapidly
> Their dress fills their mothers with shame.
> They're growing intractable rapidly,
> But the baking machine is to blame![86]

At the same time, Poindexter Furniture in Fort Worth covered all its bases as it deployed local products to lure buyers. When a customer bought a "Napanee Dutch" kitchen cabinet, they received twenty-five items, including a six-pound bag of flour from Bewley and six cakes of yeast from the Fleischmann Company with which to make their own bread, but they also got a loaf of bread from Mrs. Baird's Bakery and "Saltine Flakes" from the Brown Cracker and Candy Company.[87] Whatever observers thought, the trend was unmistakable: storebought yeast bread was replacing the home-baked variety.

Commercial bakeries played on women's sentiments in their advertising. If they bought their bread, they wouldn't have to worry about a baking failure and could always get the highest-quality product. In McKinney in 1922, Seeger's Bakery advertised its services to "do away with all fuming, worrying, vexations and trouble and insure the best light bread, cakes, cookies and rolls."[88] And should a Fort Worth housewife try and fail at making her "pastry," she could simply call Calhoun Catering for rescue.[89] Bakery bread, advertisers bragged, was uniform, dependable, and sanitary, and the home kitchen remained cooler without the oven being in use for hours.

In the large cities of Fort Worth and Dallas, the number of bakeries grew dramatically between 1900 and 1940. Fort Worth's retail bakeries increased in number from six to twenty-three, and twelve wholesale bakeries supplied retail outlets rather than sell directly to consumers. Dallas saw an increase from seventeen to fifty retail bakers, plus seventeen wholesale bakers. In Dallas and Oak Cliff, the Schepps family and their relatives built a web of bakeries between 1905 and 1926: Schepps, the Adolphus, Oak Cliff Baking, and Golman Baking. They boasted about their "Twist-Style loaf": "fine, rich bread made by twisting the dough before it is baked, thereby reducing to a minimum the air pockets found in ordinary bread, resulting in a velvetlike texture heretofore unknown to the housewife."[90] The big city bakeries created arrays of goods, from bread to éclairs, and as time passed some focused on one specialty—cakes, cookies, pies, or doughnuts. The number of bakeries in the smaller county seats varied widely over time. Denton, which had a population of more than seven thousand people and two universities in 1920, had only two commercial bakeries in 1924. By 1935, Sherman, with a population of fifteen thousand people, had seven bakeries—six retail and one wholesale.[91]

German and eastern European baking traditions continued to heavily influence North Texas commercial baking. In Denison, Swiss immigrant Jacob Kratiger and his son, John, worked at several bakeries in the little railroad town, and after 1900 they opened two establishments of their own: the Home Steam Bakery and the Denison Bakery.[92] Austrian immigrant Frank Schaefer proudly announced the opening of the Sanitary Bakery in Fort Worth in 1917; he explained that he was "a Baker and Confectioner of life experience, having traveled and worked in the most important cities."[93] The names of many proprietors—Reich, Stegman, Rubin, Krautter, Kronsberg—showed similar roots. The New York Bakery, first run by Polish immigrant Louis Gootgeld, advertised "baking with a Jewish flavor and taste" and offered hot rye bread every day at 5:00 p.m.[94] German immigrant Theodore Pauls specialized in a "health bread" made from whole-wheat flour imported from Germany. Pauls ran a union shop and "was a man with a lot of color and took a lot of interest in his employees and personally managed his bakery."[95]

The Berkowitz and Rubin family operated the Fort Worth German Bakery between about 1900 and 1924. Austrian immigrant David Berkowitz established the business and then died in 1906 when the horse pulling his bakery wagon was frightened by a train whistle. Berkowitz's Russian-born son-in-law, Oscar Rubin, took over the business. The family maintained the name German Bakery through World War I and then changed it to Fort Worth Bakery about 1921.[96]

Only one North Texas baker seems to have run into difficulty with anti-German prejudice during World War I. Fred Hamel of Dallas, born in Hanover, was arrested in May 1918 for making "many disloyal remarks." Although Hamel had dutifully registered for the draft, he was held in the Dallas County jail and faced internment in Fort Oglethorpe, Georgia. After the war ended, he returned to Dallas and resumed his occupation until his death in 1956.[97]

For some plucky bakers, World War I represented good fortune. Doherty Bakery in Fort Worth furnished "a good many thousand loaves of our bread" to the army troops at Camp Bowie.[98] For others, however, the need to conserve wheat posed interesting questions and some difficulties. In Fort Worth, local food administrators ordered bakeries to limit the amount of bread they sold to hotels and restaurants. When 30 percent of them did not comply, the food administrator halted all bakery sales to hotels and restaurants, forcing the eating establishments to offer cornbread to their patrons.[99] Other bakers used flours other than wheat. Frank Schaefer offered pumpernickel bread made of "pure rye," and the Kunze Bakery in Denton used 75 percent wheat flour and 25 percent "substitutes."[100] The Home Steam Bakery in Denison paid a significant $500 fine for "failure to observe regulations regarding the use of substitutes in making bread."[101] Many bakeries endured both the shortages and the punishments.

The number of Latin American immigrants to North Texas increased after 1910, although the overall population remained small. Nonetheless, cooking and baking quickly became a way for immigrants to excel in the cities. The 1905–1906 Fort Worth city directory listed about forty heads of households with Mexican names. Among them were two male tamale peddlers, two male proprietors of "chili stands," and two restaurateurs, one male and one female. We don't know what the restaurants served, but the menu almost certainly included the flatbreads *tortillas de harina*, made from wheat flour, and *tortillas de mais*, made of corn.[102] By the 1920s, Mexican grocery stores and bakeries were springing up on the north side of Fort Worth, near the stockyards and slaughterhouses. José Jesús Domínguez, a native of Guanajuato, founded a grocery store in 1926 that sold tortillas for 5 cents a dozen. In 1927, San Luis Potosí–born Gregorio Esparza opened Fort Worth's first full-scale Mexican bakery, which catered to the stockyard area while also supplying stores in other Latino neighborhoods. In the 1920s, Benito Cardona, from Torreón, launched bakeries in both Dallas and Fort Worth; besides offering many kinds of cookies and biscuits, both bakeries specialized in "a wide variety of quality *pan dulce*" (literally "sweet bread").[103] Entrepreneurs such as these spread Mexican cuisine throughout North Texas and changed regional tastes.

Over the decades, small-town bakeries struggled, particularly as transportation networks improved and consumers could shop in larger cities. The little town of Whitewright in Grayson County provides a good example of how the supply of baked goods ebbed and flowed in its market. The town's population hovered around 1,500 in the first third of the twentieth century, while bakeries came and went. Judson Badgett established the first bakery in Whitewright about 1887 and ran it until 1912.[104] That year, L. C. Long owned the Home Bakery, providing bread, pies, and cakes. But soon, imported goods began showing up on store shelves. By 1917, the Mangrum Bros. grocery store was bringing in "Stone's Loaf Cakes," which were sold in grocery stores across Texas and the South. The store's ads tempted customers with the ease and uniformity of its products, arguing, "'Why bake your own cakes?' Stone's is better than most people can bake: prepared by expert bakers in a model sanitary bakery." Dallas bread from the Kleber Bakery appeared in Whitewright by 1918, and competition from the Adolphus and Schepps bakeries showed up in 1919.[105]

William Norman McFatridge, a native of Whitewright, served in the US Army's 361st Quartermaster Baking Company in France during World War I. In early 1923, he returned home and opened the City Bakery, selling "Whitewright Bread" as well as cakes and pies. He tried gimmicks, such as including a movie ticket with each loaf of bread, and laborious practices such as selling fresh, hot rolls from 10:00 a.m. to noon and then from 4:00 to 7:00 p.m. "every day." But in November, the brick oven at the bakery caved in, and McFatridge gave up. He moved to Tyler to work as foreman of a large bakery there.[106] Less than a month later, McKinney residents J. T. Roberts and C. V. Magers had leased the bakery and were "putting in a new oven." In only two weeks, they were offering "fresh pastries and bread daily" as well as "a complete line of rolls." They commented that "a lady will have charge of the front," presumably meaning that a delicate shopper would not have to deal with a hot, flour-covered baker coming from the back of the store. In January 1924, the bakery was dazzling the people of Whitewright with rolls, cakes, macaroons, cream puffs, and "French Pastry." By May, however, Roberts and Magers had cut their ambitions to offering cakes and pastries only on Friday and Saturday, and hot rolls only on Monday, Wednesday, and Friday, in time for "the noonday meal." Alas, the bakery closed in August.[107] Roberts and Magers could not sustain their ideal for even a year.

In November 1924, L. C. Long returned to Whitewright and bought back his old bakery. He began offering whole-wheat bread and hot rolls "every day at 11:45." In August 1925, he bought a special mixing machine to enable him to offer cakes.[108]

But by 1928, Gordon's Cash Grocery was "receiv[ing] fresh daily cakes, doughnuts, cinnamon rolls, coffeecakes, pies, etc." from an unnamed source, but one most likely outside of Whitewright.[109] In early 1932, a bakery run by William Gates fought to reclaim the territory, declaring his bakery "a Whitewright Institution." He declared, "Most People Are Using Home Bread and they all like it!" Gates also offered rolls, buns, cinnamon rolls, and cakes, either at the bakery or through grocers. But the bakery was closed by October.[110] Gates shifted to importing "Burnett's bread" from Wichita Falls and selling it at "all the grocery stores in Whitewright."[111] By 1936, Knott's Bakery in McKinney was bringing in its franchised "Aunt Betty Bread."[112] The bakers of Whitewright tried valiantly to stay in business, but the small size of their market and the ease of imported big-city bread proved obstacles too difficult to overcome.

Even in the larger markets of county seats, bakers clearly understood the threat that outside competition posed to their businesses, and in their advertising they emphasized the importance of buying locally. About 1925, Grube Brothers Bakery in Denton bluntly stated: "Big Dandy Bread Made in Denton for Denton People. We Need Your Business." (Ironically, Big Dandy was a national franchise and thus not completely a Denton product, as we discuss later in the chapter.)[113] The Denton Retail Merchants' Association in 1929 pointed out that the three local bakeries employed twenty-five people who supported more than two hundred other people, with a yearly payroll of $25,900. They paid more than $500 in taxes annually, which went "for the support of our streets, schools, parks, and the upkeep of our city government." The boosters counseled: "The next time you order Bread—specify 'Denton Made Bread.'"[114] A few weeks later, the bakers sponsored an essay contest, "Why We Should Use Denton Made Bread." Mrs. Paul Simpson won the essay contest, receiving a prize of $12.50.[115]

North Texas bakers sometimes made a point of using locally sourced flour. In 1908, ads for the Medlin Milling Company showcased the Eagle Steam Bakery in Fort Worth, which consumed forty thousand pounds of Medlin flour each week. Bakery owner Walter J. Doherty had previously used "northern flour" but was "won over" by the "superiority of 'Medlin's Best' baker's flour."[116] The Duke Bakery in 1912 advertised itself as a "Home Industry Baker" that used flour "delivered to us fresh from the mill daily."[117] The Dutch Oven Bakery, however, hedged its bets in 1932, using not only flour from three Fort Worth mills for its bread and rolls but also Pillsbury flour.[118] Most likely, given their small profit margins, most bakeries used the cheapest flour that met their standards.

Some North Texas bakeries began affiliating with national franchises after 1910, as other bakeries were doing across the United States. The franchises provided uniform recipes and ingredients, noteworthy packaging, and vigorous marketing. Mother's Bread, Butternut Bread, Holsum, ButterKrust, Eatmore, Buster Brown, and Big Dandy, among other brands, all made their way into North Texas by 1925 through contracts with local bakeries.[119] In Fort Worth in 1918, for example, a large newspaper ad for the Doherty Bakery touted its affiliation with Holsum. In plugging the advantages of Holsum bread, the Doherty advertisers declared, "If this were not true we could never have standardized HOLSUM quality, flavor, and texture as we have. You will find every HOLSUM loaf firm, close-grained, yet light, and with the finest flavor you have ever known in bread." The alignment of a local bakery with a national franchise assured uniformity and sameness. Doherty most likely discontinued its use of local Medlin flour for another type supplied or suggested by the franchise.[120]

Owning a bakery, even a small one, became increasingly capital-intensive. The equipment of Louis Gootgeld in 1921 included two bread proofing boxes—one made of iron and one of wood—one thousand bread pans, three hundred cake and pie pans, and a "doughnut outfit." Furniture included two dough troughs, three "working tables," a "working counter," and a wrapping table. The bakery's sales area had two counters and five showcases. Fort Worth's Union Bakery, which failed in 1917, had five showcases, an iron safe, a desk, and a cash register. Both bakeries had refrigerators, and the Union Bakery also had an icebox and gas stoves. Tellingly, both bakeries advertised the presence of ceiling fans, designed to alleviate the oppressive heat.[121]

Like farmers and millers, bakers increasingly relied on machines to do critical tasks.[122] As early as 1907, the Eagle Steam Factory in Fort Worth had automatic weighing machines, dough mixers, cutting and molding machines, a conveyor belt, and a steam room for raising the dough. Its ovens could bake twenty-five thousand loaves of bread per day.[123] In 1921, the H. C. Walker Bakery built a fine new facility in Fort Worth, complete with six heavy tile ovens. Along with the machines, which made sixty thousand loaves of bread each day, the new factory also had an automatic wrapping machine. Literally no human hands touched the product before the consumer unwrapped it.[124] When Louis Gootgeld declared bankruptcy in 1921, his machines included a bread molding machine, a dough mixer, and a cake mixer.[125] The trend toward mechanization grew throughout the first decades of the century.

Some bakers owned their buildings, which had permanent brick ovens built into them. W. T. Fields in Denton in 1903 sought to sell his restaurant and bakery. The brick oven at the back of the building was eight by ten feet in area.[126] A baker who leased space might use one of the portable ovens that were growing in popularity during the early twentieth century, distributed by numerous, fiercely competitive companies, all in the North. Despite their so-called portability, the steel and tile ovens were substantial and could hold as many as 240 loaves of bread at a time.[127]

Although some small bakeries remained solvent for decades, bakery businesses generally held high risk and appeared for sale frequently in North Texas newspapers. The ads often extolled the equipment and the health of the business, citing the death of a family member or a desire to retire as the reason for selling a prosperous company.[128] In 1922, an unnamed baker was trying to sell his business for cash but said he would consider remaining in business with a partner in the business: a "good hustler . . . with some money and delivery car."[129] The baker needed energy and transportation.

Many bakeries simply failed. Of the fifty bakeries in Dallas in 1920, only four—a mere 8 percent of them—were still around by 1941. In June 1940, the Purity Bakery in Denton, which produced both bread and pastries, held a party to celebrate its tenth anniversary in business, featuring a movie and tours of the bakery plant, because ten years in business was a notable milestone for a bakery.[130]

Increasingly, large wholesale bakeries controlled the market, particularly in bread sales. The most notable in North Texas was Mrs. Baird's, for both its compelling story and its great success. The tale of the company's founding, often repeated, firmly rooted it in the pluck and courage of Fort Worth wife and mother Ninnie Baird. An orphan, Ninnie Harrison met William Allen Baird in their home state of Tennessee, and they married in 1886. In 1901, the couple, with four children, moved to Fort Worth. They opened a restaurant, and Ninnie gained a reputation for her "excellent bread, cakes and pies." William developed diabetes, which at the time was untreatable. The three oldest children, Bess, Dewey, and Hoyt, worked with their parents in learning the bakery trade. Dewey recalled baking "nickel pies" that the boys sold at the packinghouses in North Fort Worth. All the baking took place in a four-loaf wood-burning oven.

Ninnie realized that she could make a living by baking bread, and she and William sold the restaurant. She founded Mrs. Baird's Bread in 1908, and William died in 1911. The boys delivered bread after school. They also sold bread door to door, first with a small wagon, then on bicycles, and finally in the family buggy, pulled by a horse named Ned. Hoyt Baird remembered, "Mama put flour sacks in big baskets, hinged at the top like picnic baskets, and then set the bread in them, and covered them over with another sack." Ninnie converted the servants' quarters of their house to a bakery, buying a used forty-loaf commercial oven from the Metropolitan Hotel. She paid $70 for the oven: $25 in cash and the balance in bread and rolls. When the family moved to a different house, she repeated the conversion process and also "cajoled her landlord into building another structure on the property, the front of which became the first retail store." To her stock of bread, rolls, and cakes Baird added cream puffs, cinnamon rolls, and pies. The family got its first delivery truck in 1917 and also its first three wholesale accounts. When Hoyt Baird went into the army in 1918, the family decided to focus only on wholesale. The company had grown quickly and had big dreams.

To attain their vision of success in the wholesale business, the Bairds built a brick bakery at Sixth and Terrell Streets, investing $8,800 in the new facility. They installed a Peterson gas-fired peel oven that had a capacity of four hundred one-pound loaves. The bakery enlarged nine times between

1928 and 1938.[131] The company expanded to Dallas in 1928, with a two-story, $250,000 brick building, built in the Prairie Style with cast stone ornaments.[132] In 1938, the company built a state-of-the-art facility on Summit Avenue; designed by noted architect Wyatt C. Hedrick, it housed the Fort Worth part of the company until 1992. In the new facility, each loaf of bread went through a dozen automated steps before entering one of the "two 72-foot tunnel-type traveling ovens" that baked the bread in thirty-two minutes. The ovens, which had been displayed at the Bakery Machinery Show in New York, had shiny chrome-plated pipes. The new plant produced 75,000 loaves each day and had 175 employees.[133]

On a smaller but still significant scale, the Golman family opened a beautiful new bakery in the Dallas suburb of Oak Cliff in 1930. The Oak Cliff Baking Company was a one-story building of "light faced brick with stone trim." The bakery promised a capacity of 25,000 loaves daily and employment for "forty-five Oak Cliff people." Its "Cliff-Maid Bread," sold in more than 350 grocery and food stores in the Dallas area, was a "perfect loaf—smooth textured, richly flavored—honey-gold and pure as sunshine."[134]

Even in the best of circumstances, however, working in a bakery was never easy. Before air conditioning, the heat was a dangerous concern. In 1937, J. O. Rogers received a settlement of $6,500, or about two years' salary, from the New York Bakery in Fort Worth when heat stroke and a back injury "totally and permanently incapacitat[ed] him."[135] Even in a sophisticated plant like Mrs. Baird's, interior temperatures easily reached over 100 degrees in the summer. Near the ovens, "which ran constantly," the heat was even greater.[136] Hot weather made even icing a cake difficult. Bess Hornbeak, who began working at Mrs. Baird's in the early 1920s, described icing work as "very hot and sticky" and the conditions as "very rugged."[137]

Automation brought new dangers. In 1914, T. W. Follin sued bakery owner Walter J. Doherty for "injuries received while cleaning rollers."[138] Ben Golinski was hospitalized after his right arm became caught in a dough separator.[139] Fourteen-year-old Glen Cude Tate died at a bakery in Van Alstyne in 1914 when his right arm "became entangled in a mixing machine which he was operating" and "the knives" mangled the arm and his right side. The editors of the *Whitewright Sun* fretted that Tate's employment in the bakery had been illegal under the new child labor laws: "Young Tate was not only too young to be employed at the dangerous work of operating a mixing machine, but was too young to be employed in any occupation except farm work, and his employer is subject to prosecution, as are all other employers of children in violation of this law, which was enacted for the purpose of preventing just such tragedies as that at Van Alstyne."[140]

FIGURE 9.2. *Fort Worth baker Roy Lee Brown with his son, Daniel Melvin Brown, on Father's Day 1939.* (Fort Worth Star-Telegram *collection, University of Texas at Arlington Special Collections AR406-6-1111*)

Although safer than in the past, bakeries continued to be fire hazards. Fires that began in ovens damaged several North Texas businesses, though improved emergency responses limited the destruction and avoided the conflagrations of the past. In 1918, night watchman Edward Huggins died at the Els Bakery in Dallas in a fire started by an overheated oven. Seven members of the Els family narrowly escaped.[141] In 1937, Denison baker Kalitan Stewart received serious burns on his hands and body when he struck a match to light the oven and accumulated natural gas exploded.[142] Problems remained.

While automation removed the skill from an ancient art, workers still found ways to demonstrate expertise in their work. Allen Baird remembered watching the bakers unload fresh loaves of bread from their gigantic ovens:

> I used to marvel at watching those guys—how they could slide a pan into a particular spot in that oven. They would slide the pans over to one side of the oven as they were taking out baked bread at the other side of it. Those peels [a wide, flat wooden board attached to a handle] were probably 20 feet long and they would slide that pan back into the oven on one side and reach under and pull one out and they'd slide the peel back over their shoulder and then catch the pan as it was coming out and pitch the bread onto a tray. How they could keep up with it, I don't know. It was a constant thing.[143]

Despite the difficult circumstances, employers had high expectations for their bakers. They were expected to be "sober" (as stipulated in employment ads), healthy, and happy. The Eagle Bakery in Fort Worth hired only "men who have passed a medical examination, and are known to be healthy."[144] A writer in Fort Worth gushed about the mood of the bakers at Pangburn's chocolate shop: "Pangburn's Heart is in their work and they simply Love to make wedding cakes! So you see they are in the perfect mood to make THE cake!"[145] A bride, such bakery ads assumed, should expect the cake for her happy day to be made by happy people.

One way in which bakers, like millers, tried to keep their employees happy was by sponsoring baseball teams. Industrial leagues were popular across the United States before World War II, and numerous bakeries in Dallas and Fort Worth fielded teams. One of the oldest in Dallas was the Brown Cracker Company, which was formed as early as 1907.[146] The Sure-Best Bakery won the state amateur baseball championship in 1931, and the league continued until at least 1935.[147]

It took more than a baseball uniform, however, to keep a baker content. In the United States as well as in North Texas, bakers were much more likely to join labor unions than millers were. Many bakers were easier to organize than millers because they were clustered in the large cities of the Northeast, thus creating a strong union base.[148] Also, European immigrant bakers brought with them a history of activism and a willingness to protest that was lacking in millers, most of whom were American-born. With a national infrastructure in place for encouragement, union activity ebbed and flowed across North Texas for decades. Between 1900 and 1940, the issues remained the same: unions' right to bargain on behalf of their members; the desire for "closed shops," in which only union members could work; and wage, hours, and safety issues.

A strike in Fort Worth in 1900 illustrates the issues at stake. In November 1900, Fort Worth bakers went on strike, with demands for a closed shop, weekly wages of $16 per week for foremen, $14 per week for the "second hand," and $11 per week for the "third hand or rollerman." They requested a maximum schedule of sixty hours per week, four holidays with double pay if required to work, and one and a half times the hourly rate (known as "time and a half") for all overtime—in addition to the sixty hours they were already working. They also addressed the needs of their families: "All married men are to receive what bread is needed by their families," and "no baker is compelled to board with their boss."[149] It was time to stop trying to sleep in dismal rooms over the bakery. Some bakery owners signed the new agreement, while others hired scab (non-union) labor.[150] The union struck again in 1912 and nearly did so in 1916.[151] Dallas bakers began organizing in 1900, holding "secret meetings with picked men and eventually [getting] enough together to apply for a charter." Bakery Workers Union Local was formed in April 1904 and lasted for more than sixty years.[152]

In 1921, Fort Worth bakers struck as management announced their intent to cut wages by 10 to 20 percent while increasing the workday to nine hours.[153] The union members countered by demanding renewal of a previous agreement "calling for an eight-hour day, $36 a week for bench hands, $40 for doughmakers and $45 for foremen." The shop owners agreed to restore previous wages and working hours, and the journeyman (rank-and-file) bakers consented to a wage cut if the price of bread fell by 10 percent or more.[154]

Between 1923 and 1926, union activity remained at a relatively low level, although one strike occurred in Dallas and three in Fort Worth.[155] By 1930, Dallas bakers had eight-hour shifts during the week and worked ten hours on Friday, for a total of fifty hours spread over six days or nights. "Bench and machine hands" received 72 cents an hour, and all workers received time and a half for overtime. When they staged a strike that failed, the union almost failed too. Just enough workers remained in the union to "hold the charter," and they "kept Local No. 111 alive."[156] The master bakers cut wages in Fort Worth and Dallas once again in early 1931, taking them down to a fraction of their levels in the late 1920s. In 1932, Dallas master bakers punished union workers by locking out (forbidding employment to) thirty-two members in nine shops, and in Fort Worth, forty-four men in seven shops were locked out. The lockouts lasted ten weeks in both places.[157]

Shortly after Franklin Roosevelt assumed the US presidency in 1933, the federal government and union activists swung into action. In June, the National Industrial Recovery Act established the rights of unions to bargain collectively—that is, to act as a body on behalf of all employees in a given workplace. The act also fixed prices and wages in numerous industries, including baking. Almost 150 bakers joined the Bakers Union in Fort Worth, still angry about the actions of the large bakeries the year before. Union members who had been fired for their activities expected to get their old jobs back, but many continued to keep their membership secret for fear of retribution by their employers.[158]

By January 1934, restless workers threatened a strike over wages and hours. Across North Texas, bakeries fired workers for union membership, and their fellow workers struck in support of their brethren.[159] Still, labor leaders reported that "the bakeries in Fort Worth at this time were 95 per cent organized," and that they were making considerable progress in Dallas. They also noted that Mrs. Baird's had "absolutely refused to negotiate."[160] But by December 1934, five small bakeries in Dallas had union workers.[161]

In 1935, the US Congress passed the Wagner Act, which gave employees the right to form and join unions and obligated employers to bargain collectively with unions. North Texas bakery owners, however, failed to comply with the rules. George Kogan, the owner of Fort Worth's New York Bakery, proved particularly combative. In April, twelve bakers walked out after Kogan dismissed two union members. Workers began picketing, and Kogan pulled a pistol on them. After intervention by the National Labor Relations Board, Kogan's bakery became the first union shop in Fort Worth. The following week, the Sure-Best and B. C. Reich bakeries also unionized.[162] In Dallas, union representatives vigorously sought to organize, to no avail.

With or without unions, change was afoot. The minimum wage law established by the Fair Labor Standards Act in June 1938 covered wholesale bakeries such as Mrs. Baird's. The big firm sold cake outside Texas and therefore fell within the guidelines governing interstate commerce.[163] In Dallas, the bakers' union vigorously sought to organize wholesale bakeries. By the spring of 1940, eight large companies had closed union shops. The five hundred workers under the agreement received increased salaries, paid holidays and vacation, and time and a half for overtime.[164] Although relations calmed down, some tensions remained. For example, the owner of the Dallas Bakery fired shots at union members in 1940, accusing them of throwing bricks through a window.[165] Unions made significant strides, but opposition remained even in the face of federal intervention.

While many North Texas bakeries specialized in bread, they extended their repertoires well beyond plain white bread. Dark breads like rye and pumpernickel came from bakeries run by eastern Europeans. Graham, brown, and salt-rising breads kept abreast of health trends.[166] Soft-crusted Viennese-style bread had its fans, while stiff-crusted French bread challenged the teeth of its eaters.[167] As we have seen, some aspiring bakeries attempted to sell rolls hot from the oven at set times of the day, but others merely stocked room-temperature rolls along with other types of bread. Cinnamon rolls were popular as well.[168]

North Texas bakery ovens also produced all kinds of sweets—multitudes of pies and dozens of varieties of cookies.[169] Upscale offerings included "Fancy French Pastry," "all kinds of puff paste," and chocolate éclairs.[170] A few specialty bakeries sold doughnuts, though the true heyday of the doughnut was yet to come.[171] But no one bested McKinney baker Paul Lewis in his attempts to bring fine baked goods to North Texas. For a brief, sweet period in 1936, he offered daily specials, advertised in the local newspapers: nut bread, macaroons, cream puffs, Boston cream pie, mocha rolls, and ice cream cakes, along with other more pedestrian fare such as angel food cakes and fruit pies. Unfortunately, Paul Lewis's dreams were short-lived: his bakery was gone by 1937.[172]

Cakes, of course, topped the list of sweet bakery goods. Old standbys fruitcake and pound cake were still sold.[173] Angel food and jelly rolls were staples. Layer cakes, the most troublesome to produce, anchored many bakers' trades. Besides classics such as coconut and caramel, bakers also offered trendy cakes: devil's food; marshmallow, filled and frosted with a confection made from the candy; and Baby Ruth, which was pink-and-white-striped and predated the candy bar of the same name.[174] Creative bakers might have their own signature creations. The Turner and Dingee grocery store touted its Swiss layer cake, "a most delicious three-layer cake evolved by our English baker."[175] The Leonard Brothers Department Store extolled its "Betty Crocker Milk Chocolate Cake" both in print media and on radio in 1933: "You've seen it pictured on the back cover of this week's Saturday Evening Post! You've heard Betty Crocker herself tell about this cake over the radio. A Rich, Light, Milk Chocolate Layer Cake with chocolate icing and filling."[176] The Betty Crocker Milk Chocolate Cake appeared across the United States, baked by local businesses, and the Leonard Brothers were right there in the middle of the trend.

Decorated cakes, usually with ornaments such as swags and flowers made of frosting, were baked for special occasions. Lottie Thurman Raley and her husband, C.R., bought the Sanitary Bakery in Fort Worth in 1920. She learned to decorate cakes "from a Swiss-French decorator, Hans Herzog," combining her "artistic talents with her knowledge of baking." She taught her daughter, Mildred Raley Spratling, and her sister-in-law, Myrtle Baker Thurman, "the knack of making attractive cakes," and the bakery won awards for its decorated products. Raley had more angles to her business than beauty, however. In 1931 she began supplying Stripling's Department Store with baked goods, including layer cakes, raisin bread, and salt-rising bread, and in 1932 she extended her sales to the new Chicotsky's Quality Grocery and Market, which sold her angel food cakes, cherry pies, and fudge squares. The bakery also had a contract with the Fort Worth school district for more than two decades, presumably to supply sturdy, simple fare for the children of the city.[177] Raley's business continued until 1959.[178] Lottie Raley, who turned fanciful design and careful business sense into a forty-year career, and Rae Wright Morris (professionally known as Mrs. Emory Morris), who owned her own cake shop in the 1920s, demonstrated that women could succeed in the retail bakery business. Wholesale baking, however, despite the use of Ninnie Baird's name, remained the province of men. Ninnie Baird's sons ran the wholesale bakery after 1920.

As they produced a source of vital nutrition and pleasure, bakers supported local causes. Fort Worth bakers sent loaves of bread to families displaced by the flooding of the Trinity River in 1915.[179] When fire devastated much of the town of Paris, Texas, in 1916, Dallas bakeries sent their products to victims.[180] On a lighter note, Mrs. Baird's Bakery made and donated a cake nearly six feet tall, decorated with "small pink sugar rosebuds," to the Texas Children's Home and Aid Society.[181] Bakers also gave cash. In June 1921, every bakery in Fort Worth donated part of its proceeds collected in a two-hour period to the "Baby Hospital." Walker Bread Company donated half of its sales.[182] At the onset of the Great Depression, Dallas bakers responded to help the hungry. In November 1931, as the city received applications for unemployment relief from more than eighteen thousand people, the Community Chest organized a "temporary emergency bureau." Seven bakeries agreed to provide three thousand loaves of bread each week.[183] Generous baker Jake Golman also provided cash, giving $100 a month to the parent-teacher association fund to defray the cost of school lunches.[184]

Baked goods can be crushed easily, and they go stale quickly. Selling their goods safely and quickly remained a concern for bakers. Throughout the first quarter of the twentieth century, bakeries delivered their goods to customers at their homes. In 1901, the *Fort Worth Morning Register* measured companies' output by the number of delivery wagons they used: three bakeries each had one wagon, and the Eagle Bakery had two.[185] These delivery vehicles seemed exceptionally vulnerable to accidents: horses bolted, and cars and trucks collided with trains, streetcars, and each other. At least two North Texas people died as the result of such accidents in a short time span.[186] As late as the 1920s, bakeries supplemented their grocery store business with delivery service. Long's Bakery in Denton advertised, "If your groceryman doesn't have it phone and we will deliver it to you."[187]

Some bakeries continued retail sales from their front areas.[188] Fort Worth resident Marion Day Mullins recalled that before 1900, bakeries were separate from grocery stores: "The grocery clerk came to your kitchen door every morning and took your order for the day and then delivered your food soon after. Bakeries and meat markets were separate stores. The grocerymen handled neither bakery goods nor meats."[189] A consumer wanting baked goods had to go directly to the bakery. After the turn of the twentieth century, however, the lines between grocery stores and bakeries began to blur.

Grocery stores entered the baking business in several ways. Some sold the goods of specific bakers. Nolting's Bakery in Fort Worth was housed in Heldt's Grocery on Houston Street, where it provided cakes and pies. Rae Wright Morris sold through the Fort Worth grocer Turner and Dingee, which advertised her cakes, cookies, and rolls as being "well known as the best."[190]

Turner and Dingee installed its own bakery in 1899, complete with "one of the largest of the famous Middleby portable ovens made: the finest baking oven and the most expensive in the world." The store hired Englishman Charles West as head baker and added a second oven in 1901.[191] On the other hand, Lewis Duke left Turner and Dingee's employ in 1908 and opened his own bakery, selling his "Our Own" Bread at twelve Fort Worth competitors.[192] In Denton in 1930, the Helpy-Self Grocery established its bakery for doughnuts, rolls, pies, and whole-wheat bread, while the Wyatt Food Store, in an upscale Dallas neighborhood, secured its reputation as the "Department Store of Food" with its in-house bakery and delicatessen.[193]

In Fort Worth, department stores also housed bakeries (though Dallas department stores appear to have stuck to dry goods and housewares). Stripling's installed an "oven reel" bakery in 1920, telling customers it was "so handy to buy your bread and pastry when in shopping."[194] The oven produced ninety-four loaves every thirty-five minutes.[195] Leonard Brothers, which sold everything from automobile parts to a full line of groceries, all at low prices, added its bakery in the late 1920s. A new store built in 1932 doubled its bakery capacity. The owners sent Claud L. Gafford, the manager of the bakery, to Buffalo, New York, to take a "special course in baking" and announced that henceforth the bakery would use only Betty Crocker recipes. Leonard Brothers could keep bread prices low, the store said, because it did not have to store the bread or pay for distribution. Low-cost, delicious-smelling bread enticed shoppers throughout the store.[196]

As we have seen, larger bakeries supplied small towns with their products. The Edwards Bakery in Fort Worth shipped its goods five hundred miles.[197] And even some smaller bakeries sent their products to country stores. The owner of Star Bakery in McKinney went to Farmersville to procure business, and Long's Bakery in Denton supplied "hundreds of loaves daily to Krum, Sanger, Ponder, Garza and Bolivar."[198] Decent roads and fast trucks made it possible for small-town residents and even farm families to buy rather than bake their bread.

The early twentieth century was marked by new regulations on the baking industry, as well as on many types of manufacturing. Bakers had been the subject of laws for centuries—millennia, really—but North Texas cities began regulating the weight and price of bread only after 1900. In 1907, for example, Dallas and Denison passed new city charters that enacted the regulation of bakers and set the "weight, quality and price for bread manufactured or sold in the city of Dallas [or Denison], according to the price of the material or otherwise."[199] The following year, the City of Fort Worth set the price of a one-pound loaf of bread at 5 cents.[200] The city had difficulty, however, controlling all bakers. In 1919, one bakery that had been selling 14.5-ounce loaves as a full pound announced its contrition and promised customers true 16-ounce loaves.[201] Diligent bakers advertised their full-weight loaves, which by then had risen to 10 cents a pound.[202]

Although problems with sanitation in bakeries paled in comparison with such problems in slaughterhouses and dairies, they still attracted dirt, insects, rats, mice, and filthy humans.[203] In 1906, Turner and Dingee advertised that in both its grocery and bakery "we absolutely have no rodents, no mice, no roaches, and very, very few flies."[204] The Eagle Steam Bakery claimed that mechanization saved its dough from being "contaminated by absorption of the perspiration from the arm and face of the workmen."[205] Eventually the State of Texas got involved when it filed a complaint against a Fort Worth baker who failed to screen his products to keep away flies and dirt.[206] Officials also urged bakers to wrap their bread in waxed paper.[207] As we have seen, bakeries used their cleanliness as a selling point, and the baking process drew ever closer to a laboratory science.

In the first four decades of the twentieth century, the relationship of people to grain and flour shifted. Agriculture, milling, and baking all became more automated. Small communities lost their mills and their bakeries. Yet agricultural workers still had to pick straw from their hair, and some commercial bakers bore scars from injuries inflicted by ovens and equipment. As the price of flour dropped, more ordinary people ate biscuits and light bread than ever before. Texans loved the music that the mills sponsored, and lucky folks also goggled at the works of art that wheat money brought to North Texas. Young women could give birth, free from society's disapproving eyes, in the safe space of new hospitals because of the efforts of women whose husbands worked with wheat.

World War II brought changes to postwar America, including North Texas. One important change was visible by 1972, when the Kimbell Art Museum was dedicated: Texans were thinking less and less often of the importance of wheat in the region.

9 / FADING GLORY, WANING MEMORY: 1940–1972

BETWEEN 1940 AND 1972, THE RAW PRODUCTION OF wheat faded in importance to North Texas. Growing proceeded unevenly, and milling came to almost a complete halt. As the cities of the region continued to grow, baking remained important. People still wanted the wheat needed to produce bread, cakes, cookies, and pies. But the grain in the foods they ate was no longer a product of the Texas prairies, usually coming from distant places.

In the first three-quarters of the twentieth century, North Texas wheat production rose and fell unpredictably. In Collin, Dallas, Denton, and Tarrant Counties, production began declining shortly after 1900 and reached its low point in the 1950s. In Cooke and Grayson Counties, the dip began in the 1920s. By 1950, all six North Texas counties were producing only a fraction of what they had half a century earlier. The land in the east was planted in cotton, and cattle marked the landscape to the west. During the 1950s, however, wheat production rebounded. With timely rains, 1953 and 1954 saw "bumper crops" in the region, but severe drought in the ensuing years lowered annual production.[1] By 1970, wheat farming ranged unevenly across the counties.

Rather than keeping their wheat at home, Texas farmers found an international export market. They shipped wheat to India, Pakistan, Europe, and the Soviet Union, according to trade agreements set up by the federal government. In 1954, the United States created a program, later named Food for Peace, that shipped surplus commodities to hungry nations. Other government trade programs profoundly affected the demand for wheat in the world, and North Texas farmers responded to those requirements. Little of the wheat grown in North Texas remained in the area.

Even as production rose and fell, Texas farmers continued to evolve their crops. Wheat scientists kept an eye on the flour market, observing that milling companies surveyed crops for variety and quality "just before harvest time each year."[2] Agronomists at the Denton agricultural experiment station developed new strains of wheat, often with North Texas names, and farmers adopted them. Comanche, a variety with "good baking quality," was introduced in the early 1940s and thrived in North Texas. Quanah was a disease-resistant and productive hybrid of Comanche and several other varieties. Strong in gluten and high in protein, Quanah was specially designed for commercial bakers.[3] The strain known as Frisco appeared on the market in 1954.[4] It was a hybrid of the old standby May, developed by the "Texas station for growing in the Dallas–Sherman area to supply an improved variety for family flour production." The hybridizers made Frisco earlier maturing, resistant to rust, and short in stature. Soft and low in protein, it was better suited to the varied needs of the home baker than its tougher companions.[5] Blending the interests of farmers with those of ranchers, researchers recommended that North Texans continue the old practice of grazing cattle on the growing wheat, observing that "wheat provides a source of succulent, high protein feed during the winter when such feed are at a premium." A wheat grower could lease his field to a cattle grower for increased income. The grazing could start as soon as the plants were well established and went on as late as March 1.[6]

Mechanization, too, continued to evolve, becoming ever more sophisticated and expensive. Frances Muller remembered that in Denton County on her grandmother's farm in the 1940s, "all the farmers had wheat ready for harvesting and there was a storm coming. The co-op had brought in three huge combines to help harvest all the wheat. They were much faster than the smaller combines that the local farmers had. Mack and my grandmother were very excited about the larger combines because without them, the wheat would rot in the field."[7] The agricultural cooperative—an association of farmers who pooled expenses—had resources that exceeded those of individual farmers and could rent or even purchase huge equipment. In the late 1960s, the Copp family of Krum owned five air-conditioned combines. Jerry and Gerald Copp took the combines out for ninety days a year, starting in Tarrant County and ending in Canada. Their father, B. F. Copp, said that farmers found it cheaper to hire his family than to invest in their own combines and find labor.[8]

By 1970, the population of the six North Texas counties had reached 2.3 million people. Of that number, almost 54 percent lived in the cities of Dallas and Fort Worth. The suburbs of the two cities spread in all directions, and the open area between the cities would be filled in with the international airport next to Grapevine. The US Department of Agriculture closed and sold the Denton agricultural experiment station in 1972.[9]

During World War II, the challenges of milling continued. Some trials were familiar, like the fire that struck the Burrus Mill in February 1943. An elevator with almost four million bushels of wheat and corn exploded, injuring five employees and causing more than $5 million damage to the elevator. Two of the men, trapped in the headhouse of the elevator, were "badly burned" and had to be lowered with ropes. The fire also destroyed the mill's precious sound truck, valued at $7,000.[10]

A more widespread crisis stemmed from war-related worker shortages. Mill maintenance became an issue because parts were "scarce or not to be had."[11] Storage companies were overwhelmed because of wartime labor scarcities. The Burrus Mill in Fort Worth boasted "five parallel tracks, with combined length of almost three miles . . . loading facilities for 32 cars under sheds, unloading facilities for 48 cars, also under cover."[12] But with worker shortages and a huge wheat harvest in 1944, even those facilities were insufficient. Grain storage facilities across Texas, including Fort Worth and Dallas facilities, became swamped in June 1944. The American Association of Railroads' institution of an embargo on the overwhelmed yards embarrassed and infuriated North Texas "grain men." The AAR limited shipments to the amount that a yard could unload in three days. With the help of the US Employment Service, the elevator companies aggressively recruited workers and also used German prisoners of war from Camp Wolters in Mineral Wells, fifty miles away.[13] Even with labor scarcities, grain facilities worked diligently to keep their products moving. Flour was not rationed, but producers remained conscious of the wartime conditions.

Universal Mills kept up the practice of sponsoring musical radio shows. In 1941, it hired Ernest Tubb, spurring his rise to fame. He became the mill's "Gold Chain Troubadour," named for their best flour, on Fort Worth radio station KGKO, between 10:45 and 11:00 a.m. on weekdays. Tubb remained with the mill for about a year and a half, touring grocery stores and singing on town squares. He recorded his smash hit "Walking the Floor over You" in Fort Worth in 1941 with fellow KGKO employee Fay "Smitty" Smith playing electric guitar—a first in country music. That success took Tubb to Nashville to join the Grand Ole Opry and eventually to the Country Music Hall of Fame.[14] The name of his band, the Texas Troubadours, harks back to the days of the Universal Mills. The Light Crust Doughboys continued their radio performances into the 1950s and kept making public appearances into the 1970s.[15]

Like much of America, the milling industry sprang into new life at the end of World War II; old mills were repaired, new ones were added, and, especially, storage capacity was increased. To avoid a repetition of the wartime gridlock, the Burrus Mill began making improvements in November 1945 "designed to maintain Fort Worth's position as hub of the wheat market in Texas." It built a soaring new steel-and-concrete headhouse, seventeen stories high, and installed a new car unloader and conveyor system. The car unloader, a reporter explained, "lifts a grain car, rocks it from end to end and from side to side and unloads it in 4.5 minutes." Burrus officials anticipated being able to unload three hundred cars of grain each day.[16]

The global food shortage after World War II affected North Texas millers—and indeed, all American residents—in 1946 and 1947, although not to the extent that millers had gloomily forecast. On February 7, 1946, US President Harry S. Truman called on American millers to extract up to 80 percent of the wheat kernel in order to make wheat supplies go further and free up more grain for hunger relief abroad.[17] Rather than eagerly stepping up to combat world hunger, North Texas millers met the new regulations with hesitance and anxiety about the quality of their products. While they freely admitted that flour with more bran in it would be "just as healthful and nutritious" as pure-white flour, they feared "public acceptance" of the coarser flour. Americans, Fort Worth miller William P. Bomar declared, had failed to accept whole-wheat flour during wartime and would be unlikely to do so in peace. The flour would be darker in color and require more liquid and a little more salt, but it would actually be just fine for everything except fancy cakes. Still, millers reacted unfavorably, dubbing the new product "Truman flour" and unhappily telling consumers that it was not their choice but rather "government regulation."[18] A month after the order, North Texas mills began to plan shutdowns of three days to a week to convert to the coarser grade of flour. They predicted that "considerable experimentation" would be required to develop a flour of uniform quality.[19] In less than six months, however, the crisis had passed. Wholesalers began delivering white flour in early September, "with an ample supply expected early next week."[20] The United States shipped 500 million bushels of wheat abroad in 1947—about one-third of its harvest.[21] The effect of the presidential appeal was short-lived, and North Texas millers continued to resist any involvement by the federal government unless it benefited their bottom lines.

Between 1940 and the early 1970s, milling almost disappeared from North Texas. The largest mills continued for the longest time, with several waves of consolidation as national corporations took over regional ones. Part of the contraction was due to Americans eating less wheat. As American diets diversified, people preferred other types of food—more meat and dairy, for example.[22] But much of the reduction was attributable to mergers in the milling industry, with most of the resulting companies owned by large midwestern entities.

At first, the number of Texas-based corporations shrank because regional companies were buying competitors. By the early 1940s, Fort Worth–based Kimbell Milling operated six mills across Texas, including the Sanger Mill and Elevator Company in Denton County and the Whaley Mill and Elevator Company in Gainesville.[23] The Fant Milling Company in Sherman bought the Whaley Mill from Kimbell in 1947. It increased its flour production and began manufacturing "flour mix" in 1949. In 1954, Fant expanded into refrigerated dough with its Gladiola Biscuit Company, which had plants in Dallas and Greensboro, North Carolina.[24] The Tex-O-Kan holding company changed its name back to Burrus in 1951.

National companies continued making inroads into North Texas in the 1940s. Two substantial purchases, both by companies from the Upper Midwest, came in 1941. Minneapolis-based Russell-Miller Milling Company bought all the Stanard-Tilton holdings, including its mill in Dallas.[25] It made large additions to the facility in 1947, and for a time Russell-Miller was the only unionized flour mill in North Texas, with labor contracts negotiated in Minnesota.[26] Quaker Oats, from Chicago, purchased the Kimbell–Diamond Mill in Sherman. Although Quaker promised to continue producing flour as well as breakfast cereals and animal feeds, one of its first actions was to remove the "800-barrel flour mill unit of the Kimbell–Diamond mill, in the frame building facing Houston [Street]" and replace it with a unit to process cornmeal.[27] In 1944, Quaker bought the G. B. R. Smith Milling Company, also in Sherman, and began milling flour. Flour was never a priority, however. Quaker shut down 75 percent of its flouring operations in Sherman and by 1946 operated only one unit with a capacity of 1,200 barrels of flour a day and twelve employees. The flour sold under the national trade name "Aunt Jemima" and the local name Smith's Best.[28] Aunt Jemima pancake mix had been sold in Texas since 1892, only three years after its creation, and now the highly racialized mix was made in North Texas.

Contraction continued into the 1950s. The Universal Mills, which had begun as a feed mill, in 1952 dropped flour milling to concentrate again on feed.[29] In August 1955, five North Texans—J. M. Ferguson Jr., Kay Kimbell, Phillip Norris, and William P. Bomar of Fort Worth, and Charles A. Sammons of Dallas—as well as Al Liebscher of New Braunfels, bought a controlling interest in the Kansas City–based Flour Mills of America (FMA), the seventh-largest milling firm in the United States, with plants in Missouri, Oklahoma, and Kansas. The company bought Bewley Mills in 1956, thus gaining properties in six Texas cities and New Orleans. In

October 1957, FMA closed the Bewley flour mill in Fort Worth, planning to use only the elevators and warehouses. More than a hundred people lost their jobs in the change.[30] Sentiment for an old local institution and local employment counted little.

Quaker, on the other hand, continued to improve its facilities in Sherman. Its $250,000 upgrades in 1955 included new flour packing and mixing equipment and an expansion of its "tortilla plant."[31] In 1963, the company headquartered its flour sales department in Sherman.[32]

In 1960, a writer for the *Fort Worth Press* observed, "Just a few years ago, Fort Worth had three flour mills turning out flour under various brands, milling some 8000 barrels daily. Now there is one, Burrus Mill and Elevator Co., left in business here, with a daily volume of about 5000 barrels." In the state of Texas, the number of mills was down to fifteen.[33] Burrus fought to stay relevant. In 1950, the company bought land and built a mill in Cuba, which the new Communist government nationalized in 1960. The American company estimated its losses at almost $10 million.[34] In the 1960s, the company contracted with the US government to produce rolled wheat and bulgur wheat for export through the Food for Peace program and US Aid for International Development.[35] Rolled wheat had a texture similar to oatmeal and could be used for cereal or baking, while the wheat for bulgur, a cereal with Middle Eastern origins, was boiled and cracked before packaging. Through the federal government, Burrus extended its international market. By 1965, Kimbell–Diamond in Denton had ceased retail sales, concentrating on "bulk flour to area bakeries, biscuit companies and macaroni companies," commercial animal feed, and grain storage.[36]

The trend toward consolidation continued into the 1960s. In 1963 Peavey Grain of Minneapolis bought Russell-Miller in Dallas, and in 1965, Nebraska Consolidated Mills (later ConAgra) purchased Fant Milling in Sherman. Fant Milling's 230 full-time employees in its Sherman and Gainesville plants made cornmeal, baking powder, and "various prepared mixes" in addition to flour.[37] Peavey closed its Dallas plant in 1973, "due to escalating costs and the burden of obsolescent equipment."[38] In 1971, multinational corporation Cargill, also based in Minneapolis, bought Burrus Tex-O-Kan and Morten Milling in Dallas. Burrus remained open, but Cargill closed Morten and its building was razed in 1974.[39]

A few mills soldiered on into the 1970s. In 1976, ConAgra (formerly Fant) continued to make "bulk baker flour" in its Sherman plant, with 126 employees and an annual payroll of more than $1 million.[40] In Denton, the Morrison Mill (formerly Whaley) doubled its flour and bread mill output in 1982. Still owned by the Morrison family, the company made "flour, flour and cornmeal convenience foods, and institutional bread mixes." Burrus/

Cargill still sold Light Crust flour throughout North Texas as well as biscuit and pancake mixes.[41]

Although grain millers in North Texas never unionized to the extent that bakers did, organized labor had some impact on mills in the region. In 1949, more than three hundred members of the American Federation of Grain Millers struck Quaker Oats in Sherman over wages.[42] In the late 1950s, several facilities voted to become union: Bewley and a small General Mills facility in Fort Worth; Fant in Sherman; and the branch of Pillsbury in Denison.[43] Quaker Oats employees struck again in 1962, holding out thirty-seven days for improvements in wages, holidays, and insurance.[44] After Nebraska Consolidated Mills bought Fant Milling in Sherman and Gainesville, its union covered the Texas facilities. A 1967 contract offered improvements in wages, holiday pay, jury pay, health insurance, and the retirement program, as well as a stronger grievance policy.[45] North Texas mills still had a role in the larger panorama of American milling.

Even as the grain industry modernized, with power shovels and more powerful equipment, some of the old woes continued. In 1967, Jessie Turner Garrett died at the Burrus Mill when he dislodged wheat in the bottom of a silo and suffocated under the falling grain.[46] Despite technological changes, human lungs still proved helpless under a stream of flowing grain.

Grain storage far surpassed milling as an economic factor in North Texas in the second half of the twentieth century. North Texas businessmen eagerly became part of a national trend, working with the federal government. The Commodity Credit Corporation, created by the national government in 1933, loaned farmers money on wheat they harvested and stored rather than releasing it on the market all at once. If the farmer did not repay the loan, the government retained the grain.[47] With its excellent rail connections, Fort Worth became the center of grain storage in the southwestern United States, and the amount of stored grain in the region rose steadily. By 1947, Tarrant County had a storage capacity of twenty-seven million bushels; that was a much smaller capacity than Minneapolis, Kansas City, Duluth, and Chicago had, but it was by far the largest in the southern United States.[48] On the western fringe of the South, North Texas remained distinctive.

The Fort Worth Grain Exchange played an integral role in the storage empire. W. L. Newsom, president of the grain exchange in 1961, outlined its responsibilities. When a "carlot" of grain reached Fort Worth, Exchange inspectors, licensed by the US government, sampled the grain and weighed and graded the lot. The farmer consigning the grain received a warehouse receipt negotiable at a bank or through the government agency known as the Commodity Stabilization Service. The grain then went into storage until market conditions became favorable.[49] By 1961, the grain exchange represented thirty-four members, including the giant American companies Francis I. duPont and Company, General Mills, Merrill Lynch, and Ralston Purina, as well as the French mammoth Louis Dreyfus Company. Fort Worth, they declared, was the second-largest grain market in the United States.[50]

Like milling operations, grain storage companies in North Texas gradually became part of multinational corporations. The Lathrop Grain Corporation, headquartered in Kansas City, opened in Fort Worth in 1948 and soon became affiliated with Interstate Grain Corp., also from Kansas City. In 1950, the company built a two-million-bushel elevator "north of the city," with a fine office building and lunch and locker rooms for the employees. Smaller Lathrop elevators operated across West Texas and shipped their grain to the terminal in Fort Worth.[51]

Country elevators continued to have a role in grain storage, but they were now components of larger corporations. Dorchester, in Grayson County, had had an elevator since about 1900, when the St. Louis–San Francisco Railway arrived there. In the 1950s, Kimbell Milling built a "tall metal grain elevator" that would become a landmark; it could be seen from quite a distance away because "Dorchester is near the highest point in the county."[52] From Dorchester, Kimbell took Grayson County grain into the international market.

Through the 1950s, the inventory of grain obligated to the US government rose to 4.2 billion bushels nationwide. The government "encouraged building of storage structures," and businesspeople seized the opportunity.[53] In 1957, the Topeka-based C-G-F Grain Company built "Texas' largest" elevator in Fort Worth in only four months—considered "record time"—at a cost of $2.5 million. The massive silo stored eight million bushels of grain. The manager, W. E. Armstrong, said that C-G-F had come into North Texas because of the nine railroads and strategic location for exporting. At that time, most of the grain stored in North Texas belonged to the Commodity Credit Corporation, which was paying the storage companies 1.41 cents per bushel per month of storage. C-G-F had eighteen employees most of the year and forty-six at peak season.[54]

By 1960, six elevator companies were operating in Tarrant County. At least four—C-G-F, Interstate Grain Corp., Uhlmann Grain, and the Katy and Rock Island Railroads—were national companies, while Kimbell remained locally owned. A writer for the *Fort Worth Press* observed, "The business of storing grain for the federal government is as important these days as the growing of the grain and its harvesting and transport."[55]

In the early 1960s, grain storage in Fort Worth reached almost sixty million bushels, of which the US government owned more than 95 percent through the Commodity Credit Corporation. Fort Worth grain elevators raked in almost $14 million a year.[56] Despite that income, a majority of the eleven grain dealers in the area voiced disapproval of the government program, saying that they wanted the government out of the grain business and to return to free trade. (Notably, the companies earning the largest sums of money preferred to make no comment.) Garvey Elevators in Saginaw (formerly C-G-F) was "the largest storage facility for grain in the nation."[57] Milling had dwindled, but storage remained a significant part of the North Texas economy.

And what of the products made of flour? The people of North Texas continued to eat wheat, though more often as sweet treats than as bread. After World War II, home baking in North Texas came to resemble home baking in the rest of the United States, and baking technology continued to evolve. In the 1940s, a few people still baked with wood-burning stoves, but gas and electricity eventually became the sole sources of heat for ovens. Some ovens still lacked thermostats. Thus, some recipes still called for "moderate" ovens, while others specified definite temperatures.

During World War II, flour was not rationed, but the government encouraged the use of whole-wheat flour, leaving more refined white flour for the troops. As early as January 1942, advertisers began pushing whole-wheat flour as part of a healthy diet. Burrus Mills juxtaposed whole-wheat flour between pancake flour and cake flour in a newspaper ad.[58] Home demonstration agents, part of the US Department of Agriculture extension service, taught cooks how to use whole-wheat flour.[59] We don't know how home cooks perceived the change to whole-wheat flour, but newspapers carried recipes and instructions for the duration of the war. Baked goods, even those made with white flour, became more nutritious in the 1940s. In response to dietary studies and the concern of the US government, mills began adding thiamine to white flour in 1938, and then riboflavin, niacin, and iron in 1940. By 1942, 80 percent of all household flour was being enriched. Adding vitamins to white bread almost eliminated the "deficiency diseases," such as pellagra, that had plagued poor Americans—including a large number of Texans—since the late nineteenth century.[60]

Sugar was among the first items rationed after the United States entered World War II. Corn syrup, usually called by the trade name Karo, was not rationed, however, and North Texas cooks adapted baking recipes to use either Karo syrup or honey. In 1942, the Highland Park Parent–Teacher Association published a cookbook with several recipes that showcased these changes. The Ration Devil Cake was a chocolate cake made with Nestle's "nugget chocolate," buttermilk, and light Karo syrup and frosted with an icing of egg whites, light Karo, and marshmallows. Frances Ostott Strong, a

Highland Park housewife, submitted recipes for Sugarless Layer Cake, Easy Fluffy Frosting, Sugarless Apple Pie, and Sugarless Custard Pie, all sweetened with corn syrup. Her Sugarless Chocolate Cream Pie and Sugarless Rhubarb Pie were enhanced with honey, which also remained unrationed. Katherine Schieffelin Pryor contributed a recipe for the soon-to-be-classic pecan pie made with Karo syrup, but that was hardly wartime exigency. As we have seen, Americans had already fallen in love with that pie.[61]

After rationing ended in 1947, Americans rejoiced in the return of abundant sugar, and their baking reflected both old ways and new. The American Association of University Women in Dallas published a cookbook in 1947. Besides traditional recipes for biscuits, cornbread, and fruitcake, the book included seven recipes for yeast rolls and two full pages of icebox cookies. One throwback was a recipe for a bland pie made of eggs, sugar, butter, cream, and flour and given the name Jeff Davis Pie, after the president of the Confederacy.[62] Even educated women remained under the sway of Old South sentiment.

In the late 1940s, the Russell-Miller Milling Company, based in Minneapolis with a facility in Dallas, introduced "Virginia Roberts," a fictional character who spoke as though she were a personal friend of home bakers. Newspaper ads called Virginia Roberts the "director of the American Beauty Home Baking Institute," which most likely was similarly fictitious. At any rate, home economists in the employ of Russell-Miller came up with five booklets showcasing photographs that illustrated step-by-step baking instructions—perhaps a precursor to Betty Crocker's smash hit *Picture Cookbook*, published in 1950. Writers referred to this technique as "this New Photo-Method tested and perfected in the American Beauty Home Baking Institute[,] Dallas, Texas." (The pamphlets with the Dallas publication information were identical to those published in Minneapolis, where Russell-Miller was headquartered, so Minnesotan information was probably being passed off as Texan.) A cook could receive one of the booklets at no cost by mailing in a coupon from a newspaper ad. Four booklets covered specific types of baked goods: "quick light bread," biscuits, cake, and rolls. Two booklets, one for "home baking" and another for "party baking," had recipes for multiple types of baked goods. The party baking booklet pulled out all the stops for experienced, adventurous cooks, with recipes for cream puffs, éclairs, puff pastry, and popovers.[63] Russell-Miller had joined the parade of flour companies marketing their flour by using made-up women teaching baking skills from basic to advanced. One wonders how many women attempted the sophisticated choux pastry required for cream puffs—and how many succeeded.

Even as they stuck with familiar favorites, North Texas home bakers continued to adopt fresh recipes. In 1958, members of the Oak Cliff Methodist Church offered German Sweet Chocolate Cake, which had been introduced only two years previously, and Icebox Cheese Cake. Cheesecake, a cross between a cake and a pie made of sweetened cream cheese and baked in a crust, grew dramatically in popularity after World War II, and by 1958 an iconic version had made it into Dallas County.[64] In the early 1960s, cheesecake enjoyed an exalted status in North Dallas; the Preston Hollow Presbyterian Church cookbook, for instance, included three cheesecake recipes. Up-to-date Presbyterian cooks made good use of mixes too, employing Bisquick for a crumb cake and yellow cake mix and lemon Jell-O for a "dump cake" made in one bowl. Like their counterparts elsewhere, the Preston Hollow women adopted nationally popular recipes, including the Waldorf-Astoria Cake, a chocolate cake made with red food coloring and also known as Red Velvet Cake, and the lemon icebox pie introduced by Borden using its Eagle Brand condensed milk. Next to the pie recipe, contributor Maxine Barsh noted, "Men Love This."[65]

The Woman's Society of Christian Service at Southwood Methodist Church in Dallas published its cookbook in 1966, also blending the old and new. Like cooks across Texas, they continued to make yeasted icebox rolls, pinching off just the amount of dough they needed and returning the rest to the refrigerator "for future use," as Ruby Neal Kerr wrote.[66] The Southwood cooks dressed up mixes for biscuits and hot rolls to create several types of quick breads, such as Apricot Tea Ring with a filling of dried apricots and lemon juice. The cookbook borrowed freely from recipes from the national competition known as the Pillsbury Bake-Off, including the Tunnel of Fudge Cake, invented by Houston cook Ella Rita Helfrich. Another Texas creation that appeared in the book was Chocolate Sheath/Sheet Cake, a delectable chocolate cake made with buttermilk and cinnamon and topped with pecan fudge icing while it was still hot. Other trend-setting recipes in the Woman's Society cookbook were Mexican Cornbread, which specified cream corn and generic green peppers, and Milky Way Cakes, which began with a base of Milky Way candy bars melted with margarine.[67]

The doyenne of North Texas cooks in the 1950s and 1960s was Helen Corbitt, who oversaw the Zodiac Room Restaurant at Neiman Marcus in Dallas. Corbitt, a native of New York, circulated through the Driskill Hotel in Austin, the Houston Country Club, and Joske's Department Store in Houston and Austin before coming to Dallas in 1955. After Stanley Marcus lured her to the Zodiac Room, she established herself firmly in the North Texas food scene. Corbitt lectured widely, always extolling excellent food that women could prepare themselves at home, and she taught cooking demonstrations as fundraisers for nonprofit groups.

In 1957, Corbitt published *Helen Corbitt's Cookbook*, which went through multiple printings and included numerous baking recipes. About bread, Corbitt wrote, "Homemade breads have gone with the wind in the majority of homes. With all the mixes, frozen foods, and what not flirting with the housewife, it is a small wonder she cannot resist." But, Corbitt advised, a home cook should produce a surprise occasionally. And the product of home bread baking need not disappear quickly, she counseled: "You can bake and freeze your own, too!" Her cookbook included a variety of quick breads, such as lemon muffins and nut breads, but she also included some recipes for bread made with yeast. Her Plain Roll Dough could be transformed into Sticky Rolls, with the addition of dark Karo syrup, or Orange Rolls, made with orange rind and orange juice. A devoted Roman Catholic, Corbitt included a recipe for Hot Cross Buns (for Good Friday and Ash Wednesday). Corbitt's cookie recipes covered many fronts, and she used them for diplomacy: "A box of homemade cookies makes your most difficult neighbor a slave forever." She borrowed recipes from other Texas women and declared that her personal favorite was Lemon Crumb Squares: a bar cookie with a dough of oatmeal and brown sugar and a topping of lemon juice and rind and condensed milk. She gave short shrift, however, to cakes, declaring that one should just take recipes from other sources: "Surely everyone has a Betty Crocker Picture Cookbook." The secret, Corbitt said, was the icing. She particularly loved Colonnade Icing, an endlessly adaptable cooked icing made of sugar, water, light Karo syrup, egg whites, and confectioners' sugar. She advised making a simple butter cake, dividing it into seven layers, and frosting it with chocolate icing; this cake, she declared, was "*the* cake men most loved to eat." No holiday or debutante reception, Corbitt asserted, was complete without Snowballs: the same butter cake cut into small squares, covered with Colonnade Icing and rolled in freshly grated coconut. The most popular cake at Neiman Marcus was the Coffee Angel Food Cake, an angel food cake flavored with powdered coffee and frosted with icing similarly enhanced. Corbitt learned from her Texas friends about pie as well. Her recipe for pecan pie came from a friend in Austin, although she called it Dixie Pecan Pie. Corbitt, and presumably her followers, embraced new and old alike.[68]

Like Corbitt, many North Texas women knew how to use their domestic skills to raise money for causes that they cared about. Across the region, women of all races and ages held bake sales to make money for clubs, churches both Catholic and Protestant and synagogues, scout troops, and numerous other organizations. There are few accounts of the goods they sold, but one can imagine the variety. One rare photograph of a bake sale in the African American community of Mosier Valley, Tarrant County, shows three long tables laden with almost forty different cakes. Each cake took time, skill, and ingredients, and its sale would have supported something the baker cared about.[69] Consumers got both something yummy to eat and the knowledge that they were spending money on a good cause. Women carefully assayed their profits. The Denton newspaper in 1955 reported sales of $27 for the Sanger–Union Home Demonstration Club, $52 for the Soroptimists, and $50 for the Order of the Eastern Star. Baked goods became good works in the hands of compassionate cooks.

Families in North Texas bought other kinds of baked goods, particularly those made by large bakeries. After 1940, commercial baking, like milling, began to consolidate into major corporations, particularly those that made bread. The percentage of bread baked outside the home continued to rise, and commercial bakeries grew ever larger.

World War II affected North Texas commercial bakers in a variety of ways. Although flour was never rationed, sugar rationing began in May 1942, and shortening and lard followed.[70] The War Food Administration (WFA) aimed to stabilize bread prices and obtain greater numbers of products for military use and shipment to the allies. In January 1943, the WFA issued War Food Order No. 1, limiting to sixteen the varieties of loaf bread that bakeries could make, along with three varieties of rolls. It also eliminated excess wrapping.[71] In Fort Worth, for example, Mrs. Baird's Bread cut the number of its products and decreased its sales of sweets to focus on white bread, wheat bread, and hamburger and hot dog buns.[72]

For some small bakeries, World War II proved a boon. Joseph and Emilie Duderstadt Hirscy opened their bakery in Muenster, Cooke County, in 1939. They worked hard to provide baked goods, especially pies and sweet rolls, for the soldiers and prisoners of war at nearby Camp Howze.[73] After the war, businesses took advantage of the growing urban population by expanding into the small towns that were rapidly becoming suburbs, particularly those ringing Dallas. In 1955, for example, Cartwright's Bakery opened a second location in an Irving shopping center with a "big, gas-fired oven."[74]

Some small bakeries thrived in the decades after World War II. William B. Finney bought Knott's Bakery in McKinney in 1938. By 1951, the bakery employed sixty people who made "assorted pastries and 'Finney's Fresh Bread'" for grocers in Collin and nearby counties. In 1955, they operated bakeries in McKinney and Gainesville and the Dixie Pastry Shop in

McKinney. The bakery had forty-seven employees, with fourteen "baker and machine operators" and seventeen salesmen. The rest were office and transportation workers. All but two were male. The pastry shop had two bakers, two decorators (both female), a wrapper-icer (female), a baker's helper, and a janitor. Their shop in Gainesville had a manager, two male bakers, and two female salespeople.[75]

Bakery ads praised the experience of their bakers. Buddies Supermarket in Denton brought in Harry Furst, who, as Hans Furst, had fled Nazi Germany in 1937 at the age of thirteen. He became a baker in New York and then in the US Army. His family recalled him as a "pastry chef extraordinaire and a marvelous Challah baker."[76] When Cartwright's Bakery moved from Main Street in Irving to a shopping mall in 1955, the *Irving News* reported that, between them, owner William Cartwright and his assistants Harold Schaefer and Dewitt Smith had racked up eighty-five years' experience as bakers.[77]

Although these bakeries were small independent businesses, they produced wide arrays of traditional fare, from simple brownies and pound cakes to cream puffs and éclairs. They also kept up with trends in baking. German chocolate cake and carrot cake, both new in the 1950s, appeared in North Texas bakeries by the 1960s. The carrot cake sold in Texas at that time probably didn't have cream cheese icing, which was developed after the original cake.[78] North Texas bakers also were not above playing on sentiment. At the Shamrock Cake Shop in Grand Prairie, Mrs. Vic Ballowe offered bread made from a ninety-year-old family recipe. Customers were to place their orders by five p.m. on Thursday and pick up their "hot loaves fresh from the oven after 3 p.m. each Friday."[79]

Custom cakes, made bespoke for special occasions, were an arena where small bakeries dominated the baking industry. Baker William Finney noted that "the dainty doll cake or cowboys cakes are especially popular with the youngsters for their birthday celebrations."[80] In 1965, the Wilson Bakery in Denton carefully laid out the prices for its custom cakes. An eight-inch two-layer cake would serve fourteen people at a cost of $2.50, while a mammoth five-tier wedding cake, nineteen inches across at the bottom, would serve three hundred people and cost $45.[81] Rick's Bakery in Denton praised the skill of its cake decorator, who was a rare male in the role: "Special occasion cakes decorated by Jim Loyd. Rick's cakes are extra light, moist and tender. The icing is not gummy and sticky . . . and the smallest details get the personal attention of Jim Loyd." The allure was amplified by a photograph of Loyd.[82]

Another area of growth for small bakeries was the sale of doughnuts. Fried doughnuts, not baked, still came from bakeries. Although commercially made doughnuts had been around for decades, they were a perfect treat for the emerging American car culture. As North Texans bought cars in unprecedented numbers, they wanted foods they could eat with one hand while holding the steering wheel with the other. By 1955, one-quarter of the bakeries in Dallas sold only doughnuts—in other words, they had only fryers, not ovens. In 1965, Rick's Bakery in Denton, which was locally owned, offered thirty varieties of doughnuts to its customers at its drive-up window.[83] A customer could have their treat without leaving the driver's seat.

Small bakeries often strived to be good community members by sponsoring local efforts with their money and products. The Shamrock Cake Shop, which operated in Grand Prairie from 1950 to at least 1974, sent thousands of doughnuts to Waco, ninety miles south, in the wake of a devastating 1953 tornado. The company cooperated with a women's group, the Soroptimist Club, to share the profits of fruitcake sales.[84] In Richardson, the Richardson Heights Bakery, owned by Scottish-born Edith Moore Fitchett, emphasized its role in a "Shop Richardson" campaign by offering a 10 percent discount coupon for all purchases.[85]

Two women turned their small-scale baking into entrepreneurial ventures. In Sherman, home demonstration agent Eunice King developed cake into a big business. In the 1930s, she began serving pecan cake in a tearoom in Sherman. Educated in food preservation, she learned to vacuum-pack the cakes so that they could be shipped, and relatives of servicemen began sending the cakes overseas to their loved ones during World War II. In 1944, she bought "the home bakery business of the late Miss Maybelle Hope" and opened at her residence in Sherman "the Pecan Home Food shop, specializing in baked and canned foods for service men, particularly for overseas shipment." In 1955, King built a commercial kitchen to produce cakes. The company contracted with the US military to provide cakes into the 1990s, employing up to seventy-five people.[86]

We met Lucille Bishop Smith in the previous chapter as an expert for the Bewley Mills. Born in 1892, Smith began cooking at a girls' camp in the 1920s and worked as a caterer in Fort Worth. She also taught at Prairie View Normal and Industrial College near Houston. She developed a highly regarded recipe for hot rolls. Smith also published a recipe collection in a file box rather than in book form.[87] In 1947, she decided to package her hot roll mix, sell it, and donate the profits to her church, St. Andrew's Methodist. Within a month she had raised $800. By April 1948, Fort Worth grocery stores were buying more than two hundred cases of the mix every week.[88]

Grocery stores provided keen competition for local bakeries. In 1955, McKinney bakers had to go against the in-house bakeries of the national grocery chains A&P and Safeway, as well as the giant Nabisco, with its packaged cookies and crackers. The grocers sold everything from multiple types of bread to "Snails," puff pastry rolled into spirals. A&P announced that its angel food cake was "made from 13 egg whites," while Safeway sold its "Skylark"-brand white bread, cracked wheat bread, and raisin bread.[89] Grocery stores, like other chains, brought the uniformity to their products that many consumers wanted.

By 1950, commercial bakeries were producing 85 to 90 percent of all bread and probably 50 percent of sweet goods in the United States.[90] The march of consolidation and franchising continued. In 1955, the Golman Baking Company from Oak Cliff became a Holsum–Sunbeam franchise and was supplying grocers in Denton, forty miles north. The affiliation by the Golmans with the franchise was marked by multiple public appearances in Dallas by corporate mascot "Miss Sunbeam," a blue-eyed nine-year-old girl with blond curls; these events also included a motorcade and a children's party at the State Fair of Texas.[91] New products included partially baked goods that cooks could finish at home. Brown-and-serve rolls, invented in Florida in 1949, spread very quickly into North Texas, appearing in Denton as "the newest thing out" later that year. In 1955, Safeway offered four varieties, including cloverleaf rolls, starting at 17 cents a dozen.[92]

Sweets still required more handwork and preparation than mechanized bread, but bakeries continued to increase their production nonetheless.[93] While men still did all the commercial baking, women were hired to do fine work such as frosting cakes. One bakery union official referred to the women working at the Continental Bakery as "cup cake girls."[94] Men might heave heavy loaves of bread, but women handled delicate, small treats.

Large commercial bakeries continued to expand. In 1953, Mrs. Baird's opened an up-to-date, air-conditioned factory on Mockingbird Lane in Dallas that produced two million pounds of bread a week.[95] By 1960, the Mrs. Baird's empire included bread bakeries in eight Texas cities as well as a cake plant in Fort Worth. When Ninnie Baird died in 1961, the company employed more than 2,500 people. Mrs. Baird's Bakeries had become the largest independent family-owned bakery in the country.[96] The bakery in Fort Worth on Summit Avenue remained a local landmark until 1992, perfuming the surrounding area with the smell of yeast and hosting thousands of schoolchildren on field trips.[97] In 1965, the Denton newspaper reported that thirty-two third- and fourth-graders from Krum toured the Mrs. Baird's plant along with six preschool children, eight mothers, the teacher, and the bus driver.[98] Like visitors before and after them, each Krum schoolchild returned home with a fresh loaf of Mrs. Baird's bread.

By 1949, wholesale bakeries produced a wide variety of baked goods: at least six varieties of loaf bread, including rye and French bread, cookies, an assortment of cakes, including fruitcake and confections for weddings and birthdays, and crackers. The Golman Baking Company specialized in hamburger and hot dog buns, supplying the State Fair of Texas and "the ball park."[99] The Manor Baking Company continued home delivery, but three of the largest bakeries were housed in national chain grocery stores, where shoppers could pick up fresh baked goods along with the rest of the food for their household.[100]

New technologies made possible new products. Home consumers loved buying canned biscuits and partially baked products, such as rolls, and finishing the process at home. By the middle of the 1950s, three Dallas plants made canned biscuits and partially baked rolls. The Ready-to-Bake Foods Company, for example, built a new plant in Dallas "with refrigeration rooms instead of the ovens." They employed seventy-five people.[101] In Denison, the Ballard & Ballard Company from Louisville, Kentucky, opened a biscuit plant in 1945, making "oven-ready" biscuits. National giant Pillsbury came to North Texas in 1951 by acquiring the Ballard & Ballard plant.[102] About 1948, the Frozen-Rite Company in Fort Worth began making Parker House and cloverleaf rolls as well as waffles; coffee cakes; apple, cherry, and blueberry pies; and gold, white, and fudge cakes, ready for the home cook to finish the baking.[103]

After World War II, all the large wholesale bakeries in Dallas, as well as a few small shops, were unionized, their employees members of the Bakery and Confectionery Workers affiliated with the American Federation of Labor. In Dallas, union contracts covered about five hundred workers. The contracts included forty-hour workweeks spread over six days; time and a half pay for overtime; paid vacation prorated by a worker's length of employment; and five paid holidays. Workers were to submit their grievances to arbitration rather than striking. In 1947, workers were divided into nineteen categories. The most highly paid was the foreman, at $1.34 per hour, followed by "mixers" at $1.24. Women working as cake icers and wrappers received the lowest wages, between 63 and 86 cents per hour. Workers on the night shift got an additional 5 cents per hour.[104] After years of inactivity, Fort Worth bakers chartered a new union, Local No. 376, in August 1949.[105] Over the years, union contracts expanded benefits to include funeral leave, pension plans, time off with pay to procure required health cards, and company-furnished and -laundered uniforms.[106]

Even with unionization and automation, bakeries still proved challenging places to work. In 1949, Bakers' Union secretary William A. Nitsche began writing a weekly column in the union newspaper, the *Dallas Craftsman*. In friendly, homey language, Nitsche advocated tirelessly for bakery workers. He reminded readers of the toll that working at night took on bakery workers: "These people cannot attend church or visit friends as they would like. They miss the ball games and places of amusement where folks meet because they have to be on a job where each worker is part of a fast stream-lined production and it is important that he be there every work day."[107]

Familiar difficulties remained in the baking industry. Nitsche reported often on injuries to workers. Crushed fingers, the most common type of injury, took workers off the job for several months. Some wounds proved even more grave. Nitsche commented that Richard Reynolds, "injured on the job . . . is totally disabled."[108] Into the 1960s, most bakeries remained un-air-conditioned, and the heat, as always, presented problems. Occasionally a manager tried to cut staff when summer business was slow and get the remaining workers to "speed up," despite the sweltering conditions. William Nitsche observed, "It never works. Some of the workers have to go home and it is over."[109] Some small bakeries also tried to evade federal wage laws.[110]

Into the early 1960s, the bakers continued to organize unions in new plants and faced familiar opposition from management. The employees of the Gladiola Biscuit Company rejected unionization in 1954, then reversed themselves in 1961, accepting Local 111 as their bargaining unit.[111] The Lone Star Donut Company in Dallas faced a National Labor Relations Board investigation in 1964 for allegedly firing three members of the committee that was attempting to organize the bakery.[112]

After decades of relative harmony, one of the frozen food companies provoked direct action. In March 1962, fifty-six union members went on strike against the Frozen-Rite Company, which, in addition to providing a variety of products for home cooks, also supplied baked goods to the Dallas public schools. The workers had had no raise in more than two years and were being paid at least 25 percent less than their peers in other North Texas "frozen roll" plants. The strike continued for six weeks, when negotiators came to an agreement.[113] Workers at the American Bakery began a brief work stoppage in April 1965, but the union steward quickly intervened, as the workers risked losing their jobs for stopping work without following a formal grievance procedure.[114] The grievance procedure could work to the employees' benefit by reinstating them, after being fired or laid off, with back pay.[115]

By the time the Kimbell Art Museum was dedicated in 1972, the role of wheat in the lives of North Texans had shifted significantly. It was still grown on large farms, though the yield was only a fraction of that from the Upper Midwest. A few mills owned by holding companies still turned out flour, but their products joined the national supply chain, and North Texans couldn't buy specifically Texas-grown or Texas-ground flour. Home baking yielded mostly treats, not sustenance, and large bakeries produced almost all the bread that people ate.

Wheat slipped into the back of the minds of almost all North Texans. For well over a century, it had occupied an important place in the culture and the economy. But late in the twentieth century, few people knew about its former glory.

EPILOGUE

IF YOU KNOW WHERE TO LOOK, THE STORY OF WHEAT can still be found in North Texas in 2025.

The Kimbell Art Museum celebrated its fiftieth anniversary in 2022. The weeklong party included a special exhibition on the history of the museum and the acquisition of three new masterworks. The artwork—a bronze vessel from China's Shang dynasty; a sculpture, *The Mountain (La Montagne)*, by Aristide Maillol; and a sixteenth-century French alabaster statue, *Virgin and Child*—exemplified the Kimbell commitment to acquiring only the finest.[1] The sculptor Maillol was, of course, also the creator of *L'Air*, which so charmed visitors at the museum opening in 1972. The latest acquisition provided a beautiful bookend to a half-century of excellence.

In Tarrant County, motorists on Interstate 30 speed past the exit for Randol Mill Road, most likely seldom wondering where the name came from. The curious can still see remnants of the mill where Precinct Line Road crosses the Trinity River. In Dallas County, riders can board a Green Line train at the Trinity Mills Station and reach professional basketball games, the Deep Ellum entertainment district, and even the State Fair of Texas. Trinity Mills Road carries commuters to the North Central Expressway.

Concrete silos and fireproof mill buildings still punctuate the landscape of the region, long after the appearance of even taller buildings on the horizon. In Dallas, the Russell-Miller American Beauty Mill has been turned into condominiums, its silos abutting the residences. The silos of the Collin County Mill in McKinney now feature the artwork of the "photorealist" muralist Guido van Helten, part of his series *Monuments*, which also cover silos in the Midwest. The mill building is now a wedding venue, with two large rooms for ceremonies and receptions (featuring "custom grain shoot chandeliers") and a garden for outdoor events. In other towns, large and small, the silos stand as reminders, some marked and others unremarked.

FIGURE 10.1. *The silos of the Collin County Mill in McKinney with a mural by Guido van Helten. (Courtesy of City of McKinney)*

A handful of mills, all units of international conglomerates, remain active. In Denton, the Morrison Mill—now owned by the C. H. Guenther Company of San Antonio, which is in turn the property of Pritzker Private Capital—cranks out its popular cornbread, muffin, and tortilla mixes. In Saginaw, the old Burrus Mill houses a facility of Denver-based Ardent Mill. Eighty-five employees make flour from wheat grown between North Dakota and Texas. The silos still read "Home of Light Crust Flour and Texo Feeds."[2] Miller Milling, owned by the Nisshin Seifun Group from Japan, declares that its Saginaw mill has "excellent sourcing capabilities thanks to its location in a hard red wheat belt" and produces three types of flour.[3]

Mrs. Baird's advertises its wares as "Texas born and Texas bread," although the Mexican firm Grupo Industrial Bimbo has owned the company since 1998. Artisan bakeries thrive, producing fancy specialties such as macarons and croissants. In brightly lit *panaderias*, customers pile trays high with a stunning variety of sweet Latin American baked goods. Restaurants turn out baskets of piping hot naan and bánh mì for hungry diners.

Almost ninety years after its founding, the Gladney Center for Adoption, formerly the Edna Gladney Center, now shelters preteen and teen girls in the foster care system. Its mission has shifted over the years, but its compassion remains strong. As its website says, "Today we still believe every child deserves a loving and caring family, and every means every."[4]

Plants, native and imported, continue to sink roots into the deep soils of North Texas. In the cities and countryside alike, pockets of prairie remnants, never felled by the plow, flourish in out-of-the-way places. Even as more farmland yields to housing developers every day, both Collin County and Grayson County farmers grew more than a million bushels of wheat in 2021.[5]

If you listen carefully, you might hear, beyond the roaring freeways and the fighter jets and airliners overhead, the North Texas wind continuing to ruffle the prairie grasses and fields of wheat turned golden in the late spring.

In the past, wheat mattered to the people who grew it to make flour for their families and for the market. Flour mattered to the people who worked to mill it and those who bought it to make it edible. And baked goods mattered to the people who made them and those who ate them for nutrition and for pleasure. Wheat, flour, and baked goods still matter to the people of North Texas, not only in their own right but in the institutions and landmarks they created. Whether they know it or not, millions of Texans remain people of the wheat.

ACKNOWLEDGMENTS

MOST ACKNOWLEDGMENTS HOLD FAMILY TILL THE END, but this project is so intertwined with my beloved husband, Tom Charlton, that I put him first. This work began shortly after we moved to Fort Worth in 2010. Exploring our new home, we came upon the blocks of concrete silos north of the city, known locally as "the Saginaw Mountains." Fascinated, I set out to learn the story of those silos, and from that beginning came this book. Tom, twenty-two years older than I, was trained as a "consensus school" business historian in the early 1960s. I heard cosmic laughter from him and his major professor, Joe Frantz, as this postmodern feminist pored over credit reports and learned about grain futures. Although he died in 2019, Tom runs as a bright thread throughout the book.

Historians' work is only as good as their sources, and so I thank the authors of local histories, who literally know where the bodies are buried, and the host of folks who made materials available on the internet, especially the Portal to Texas History. I owe special gratitude to the keepers of the flame at the Sherman Public Library; the Sherman Museum; the Tarrant County Archives; the Gainesville Public Library; the Haggard Library, Plano; the Fort Worth History Center, Fort Worth Public Library; the Dallas Historical Society; the Dallas History and Archives Division, Dallas Public Library; the Briscoe Center for American History, University of Texas at Austin; the Texas Collection, Baylor University; the DeGolyer Library, Southern Methodist University; Special Collections, University of Texas at Dallas; the Woman's Collection, Texas Woman's University; Special Collections, Texas Christian University; Special Collections, University of Texas at Arlington; and the Baker Library, Harvard University.

For illustrations, I thank the McKinney Arts Commission, the Dallas Historical Society, the Dallas Museum of Art, Steve Irick, Jennifer Rogers at the Collin County Farm Museum, Shelly Threadgill at the Kimbell Art Museum, and Matt White.

And as always, I owe literally everything to the home folks at the Mary Couts Burnett Library at Texas Christian University: every single person, but especially Robyn Reid, Beth Callahan, and the interlibrary loan staff. I couldn't do my work without you. Also at TCU, I thank my deans, Andy Schoolmaster and Sonja Watson, for time to research and a collegial intellectual home in AddRan College.

At the University of Texas Press, Casey Kittrell has been encouraging from the start. Sarah McGavick has been an author's dream editor, and Mia Uribe Kozlovsky has been patient and kind. Outside readers made valuable critiques, for which I am most grateful.

Smart, generous people have shared their expertise to make the manuscript stronger. I gladly acknowledge the help of Matthew Abel, Linda Barrett, Patricia Benoit, Sam Haynes, Ruth Hosey Karbach, the late Deborah Kilgore, Debby Lowery, Meredith May, Amanda Milian Hill, Jackson Pearson, Gary Pinkerton, Claire Strom, Kimball Tolar, and Keith Volanto.

I am particularly thankful for the manuscript workshop that the TCU Department of History sponsored in October 2023. Todd Kerstetter proposed it, and chair William Meier made it happen, with the usual excellent logistical support from Lesley Mackinson and Stacey Theisen. Pamela Riney-Kehrberg read the manuscript with care and had invaluable insights as she led the session with grace and good humor. Thank you to Jodi Campbell, Gregg Cantrell, Light Cummins, Victoria Cummins, Sam Haynes, Zsofia Hutvagner, Debbie Linsley Liles, Sofía Gómez Pichardo, Jennifer Jensen Wallach, and Kyle Wilkison for your thoughtful participation.

Attendees at the Dallas Area Society of Historians, the Texas State Historical Association, Foodways Texas, and especially the Agricultural History Society also made astute and helpful comments.

Melissa Walker read the entire manuscript, as she has done for everything I have written in the past quarter-century. Here's to another twenty-five years of amazing simpatico.

I can hardly begin to describe what Debbie Linsley Liles has brought to the project, from generously shared primary sources to discussions of life and Texas history (and historians), often over cups of proper English tea. I am grateful.

My friends continue to hold me close: Candy Boxwell, Jodi Campbell, Ann Short Chirhart, Theresa Strouth Gaul, Sharon Grigsby, Tracy Hull, Brady King, Mary Larson, Theresa Furgeson McClellan, Cathy Gawloski Montgomery, Carolyn Coke Reed, Linda Shopes, Sharlande Sledge, Kara Dixon Vuic, and Melissa Walker. And then there are the unequaled Wild

Women: Anji Boswell, Jensen Branscombe, Stephanie Cole, Nancy Baker Jones, and Debbie Liles. I love you all.

My family anchors my life: my brother, Lester Sharpless; my nieces and nephews, Nathan Sharpless, Amanda Sharpless, Joshua and Jennifer Ables, Kayley and Ryan Leckich, and Trey, Alex, and Amaya Ables; my "Plano Charltons," Hannah, Sarah, Jan, and Richard; Elizabeth and Bryce Watt; and my goddaughter Bonnie Devany.

The book is dedicated to the memories of Robert A. Calvert, professor of history at Texas A&M University, and Jack Temple Kirby, professor of history at Miami University of Ohio, both early mentors in my work in rural history. Bob could not have been kinder to me had I been one of his own students, and Jack, as editor of the series in which my first book was published, provided model guidance through that intimidating process. I hope I am making them proud.

NOTES

PROLOGUE

1. McConal, "Critics Unanimous in Praising Kimbell."
2. Kimbell Art Museum, "Kahn Building in Detail"; Butterfield, "Kimbell Building among Kahn Best."
3. Kimbell Art Museum, "History: The Vision of the Founders."
4. "Party in Park Opens Preview by Kimbell," *Fort Worth Star-Telegram*, September 29, 1972.
5. Cronon, *Nature's Metropolis*.
6. Fitzgerald, "Fort Worth," 112; Rich, "Beyond Outpost," 30, 244, 246.
7. Rhode, "Do Crops Shape Culture?," 416.

INTRODUCTION

1. Bennett et al., *Soil Survey of Grayson County*, 5–6; Carter and Beck, *Soil Survey of Denton County*, 1; Carter et al., *Soil Survey of Dallas County*, 1213; Beck, Fitzpatrick, and Ragsdale, *Soil Survey of Collin County*, 1.
2. Bennett et al., *Soil Survey of Grayson County*, 6; Carter and Beck, *Soil Survey of Denton County*, 2; Hawker, Gearreald, and Beck, *Soil Survey of Tarrant County, Texas*, 860; Carter et al., *Soil Survey of Dallas County*, 1214; Beck, Fitzpatrick, and Ragsdale, *Soil Survey of Collin County*, 1.
3. Bomar, *Weather in Texas*, 64; Mock, "Drought and Precipitation Fluctuations," 40, 41, 44; Woodhouse and Overpeck, "Two Thousand Years," 2694, 2702; Stahle and Cleaveland, "Texas Drought History," 64, 67.
4. Starling, *Land Is the Cry!*, 100; email to author from Sam W. Haynes, October 28, 2023.
5. Connor, *Peters Colony of Texas*, 14–15.
6. Connor, *Peters Colony of Texas*, 16.

CHAPTER 1: "OUR PRAIRIE FLOUR"

1. Horn, *Annals of Elder Horn*, 10.
2. Horn, *Annals of Elder Horn*, 11–12.
3. Hill, *Dallas*, xviii.
4. Cowling, *Geography of Denton County*, 13–14.
5. Connor, *Peters Colony of Texas*, 104, 108, 119.
6. Connor, *Peters Colony of Texas*, 105; US Department of Commerce, US Census of Agriculture, 1860; Jordan, "Imprint of the Upper and Lower South," 689.
7. Enstam, *Women and the Creation of Urban Life*, 5.
8. Perkins, *The Fort in Fort Worth*, 31, 47, 91; Selcer, "The Widow vs. the Bureaucrats," 363–364.
9. Selzer and Pécontal, *Adolphe Gouhenant*, 136, 139–140, 145, 182, 204.
10. Campbell, *Empire for Slavery*, 264–266; US Department of Commerce, Eighth Census of the United States, 1850, and Ninth Census of the United States, 1860.
11. Lowe and Campbell, *Planters and Plain Folk*, 12.
12. Cochran, *Dallas County*, 15.
13. Gray, *History of Agriculture*, 876; Bogue, "Farming in the Prairie Peninsula," 6.
14. Cochran, *Dallas County*, 15, 16.
15. Perkins, *The Fort in Fort Worth*, 204, 208.
16. Campbell et al., *Plano: The Early Years*, [87?]; Cochran, *Dallas County*, 14; Krohe, "The Breaking of the Prairie."
17. *Dallas Daily Herald*, November 21, 1860.
18. Horn, *Annals of Elder Horn*, 9.
19. Irwin, "Exploring the Affinity of Wheat," 295, 297; Gray, *Agriculture in the Southern United States*, 816, 817; Rood, "An International Harvest," 91–94.
20. US Department of Commerce, Census of Agriculture, 1860: Collin, Cooke, Dallas, Denton, and Grayson Counties.
21. I have identified twenty-seven people in North Texas who enslaved more than twenty people. Of that group, five raised more than a thousand bushels of wheat. The other twenty-two focused on cotton and cattle. For comments on Virginia, see Koons and Hofstra, "Preface," xiii.
22. Richardson, *Frontier of Northwest Texas*, 147.
23. Atkins et al., "Wheat Production in Texas," 7, 10.
24. Shields, "On the History of Southern Winter Wheats."
25. Adair, "Dallas Was an Island."
26. *Dallas Herald*, August 17, 1859; *Dallas Herald*, December 19, 1860; Campbell et al., *Plano: The Early Years*, 92; Santerre, *White Cliffs of Dallas*, 53.
27. Campbell et al., *Plano: The Early Years*, 92; Santerre, *White Cliffs of Dallas*, 53.
28. Latimer, "The Wheat Region and Wheat Culture," 66.
29. *Dallas Daily Herald*, November 21, 1860.

30. Winters, *Tennessee Farming*, 157. It is likely that enslaved women also cradled wheat, as they engaged in many other field labors.
31. *The Texian Advocate* [Victoria, Texas], March 30, 1848; *History and Reminiscences of Denton County*, 300–301.
32. Santerre, *White Cliffs of Dallas*, 61; Cochran, *Dallas County*, 14.
33. Santerre, *White Cliffs of Dallas*, 61; Cochran, *Dallas County*, 14.
34. B. D. Burch letter, November 16, 1913, *Mt. Springs Oral History*, 42.
35. B. D. Burch, letter, November 16, 1913, *Mt. Springs Oral History*, 42; Bates, *History and Reminiscences of Denton County*, 300–301; Cochran, *Dallas County*, 14; Campbell et al., *Plano: The Early Years*, 92.
36. Charlie Davis, *Mt. Springs Oral History*, 21.
37. Cochran, *Dallas County*, 14; Hurt, *American Agriculture*, 143–144.
38. Hansen, "How a Threshing Machine Works."
39. Peterson, "Flour and Grist Milling," 103.
40. Latimer, "The Wheat Region and Wheat Culture," 67.
41. *Dallas Herald*, March 23, 1859; Latimer, "The Wheat Region and Wheat Culture," 67.
42. *Dallas Daily Herald*, May 10, 1856.
43. *Dallas Daily Herald*, October 12, 1859.
44. *Dallas Daily Herald*, November 10, 1858.
45. Cochran, *Dallas County*, 14.
46. *Dallas Daily Herald*, February 16, 1859.
47. *Dallas Daily Herald*, November 9, 1859.
48. *Dallas Herald*, December 12, 1860.
49. Gage, "Wheat into Flour," 84, 87; David, *English Bread*, 17–18.
50. Campbell et al., *Plano: The Early Years*, 37.
51. Jackson, *Sixty Years in Texas*, 31.
52. Bates, *History and Reminiscences of Denton County*, 301.
53. Bates, *History and Reminiscences of Denton County*, 301. A peck is two dry gallons. I have been unable to find anything on the man named Al.
54. US Department of Commerce, Eighth Census of the United States, 1850.
55. Collin County Deed Records, Book M, 296–297, notes in possession of Deborah Linsley Liles.
56. Francaviglia, *Cast Iron Forest*, 7.
57. Butler, "Pioneer Personified," 12; Price, "Vanished Glory of Trinity Mills."
58. Danvers, "Charles B. Moore Collection," 107; Bryan, "Henry S. Moore," 165.
59. Henry Moore to Charles Moore, March 5, 1860, Charles B. Moore Family Papers, 1832–1917, University of North Texas Archives, Portal to Texas History [hereafter Moore Family Papers].
60. Henry Moore to Charles Moore, July 12, 1860, Moore Family Papers.
61. Melugin, *Pilot Point*, 26.
62. *Dallas Herald*, August 17, 1859; *Dallas Daily Herald*, October 12, 1859.
63. *Dallas Herald*, August 2, 1856.
64. *Dallas Herald*, August 2, 1856; Buecker, *Water Powered Flour Mills*, 12.

65. Butler, "Pioneer Personified," 12.
66. Price, "Vanished Glory of Trinity Mills"; Flatt, "Trinity Mills' Company 'B,'" 12.
67. Foote, "Millwood 72 Years Ago"; Pettit, "Spring Was Important Feature at Fitzhugh Mill," August 11, 1991, in *Between the Creeks*, 357.
68. Henry Moore to Charles Moore, March 5, 1860, Henry Moore to Charles Moore, March 18, 1860, and Henry Moore to Charles Moore, July 12, 1860, Moore Family Papers.
69. *Dallas Herald*, September 8, 1858.
70. Hunter, "Rage for Grain," 23–24; Bates, *History and Reminiscences of Denton County*, 76–77.
71. *Dallas Daily Herald*, February 2, 1859.
72. *Dallas Daily Herald*, October 5, 1859.
73. Charles Moore to Henry Moore, November 18, 1857, Moore Family Papers.
74. "Lanson Cullum Clark," FindaGrave.com; Campbell et al., *Plano: The Early Years*, 12.
75. Jones, *Early Days in Cooke County*, 14.
76. Foote, "Millwood 72 Years Ago"; "The Wetsel Re-union," *McKinney Courier and Democrat*, August 18, 1904.
77. Beam, "History of Collin County," 87; Cochran, *Dallas County*, 116.
78. Leighton, *Southern Harvest*, 15.
79. Henry Moore to Charles Moore, March 5, 1860, Moore Family Papers.
80. *Dallas Herald*, August 7, 1858; Stambaugh and Stambaugh, *A History of Collin County*, 33; Campbell et al., *Plano: The Early Years*, 12, 19.
81. Campbell et al., *Plano: The Early Years*, 19; *Dallas Herald*, August 2, 1856; "George Washington Baird."
82. Latimer, "The Wheat Region and Wheat Culture," 69.
83. Davis, *WPA Guide to Texas*, 51.
84. Henry Moore to Charles Moore, July 12, 1860, Moore Family Papers.
85. Buecker, *Water Powered Flour Mills*, 10.
86. "Dick," "Letter on the Overland Mail Route."
87. Acheson and O'Connell, "George Washington Diamond's Account," 398.
88. "The Wetsel Re-union," *McKinney Daily Courier*, August 11, 1904.
89. Pointer, *Carrollton*, 11; Butler, "Pioneer Personified," 12; Cochran, *Dallas County*, 116.
90. Fulkerson, *Wylie Area Heritage*, 141; *Dallas Herald*, September 8, 1858.
91. Latimer, "The Wheat Region and Wheat Culture," 69.
92. Latimer, "The Wheat Region and Wheat Culture," 69.
93. Leighton, *Southern Harvest*, 20.
94. US Department of Commerce, Census of Manufactures, 1860, 582, 584.
95. *Dallas Herald*, September 8, 1858; *Dallas Herald*, November 16, 1859; US Department of Commerce, Ninth Census of the United States, 1860.
96. Castleberry, *Daughters of Dallas*, 72–73.
97. Henry Moore to Charles Moore, March 18, 1860, Moore Family Papers.

98. Adair, "Dallas Was an Island."
99. Castleberry, *Daughters of Dallas,* 42, 44; "$100,000 Worth of Dry Goods," *Dallas Daily Herald,* May 30, 1860.
100. Charles Moore to Elizabeth Moore, Matilda Dodd, and Josephus Moore, August [day torn from manuscript] 1858, Moore Family Papers.
101. Price, "Vanished Glory of Trinity Mills."
102. Ogle, "1860–61 Trinity Mills," 5–6; Butler, "Pioneer Personified," 12.
103. Lake, "A. F. Leonard"; Garrett, *Fort Worth,* 103.
104. McCaslin, *Tainted Breeze,* 197–198.
105. *Dallas Herald,* November 16, 1859, May 18, 1859, August 3, 1859, and November 7, 1860.
106. *Dallas Herald,* February 22, 1860.
107. Collin County probate minutes, reprinted in *Collin Chronicles* 21, no. 1 (2000/2001): 12, 13; *Collin Chronicles* 23, no. 2 (2002/2003): 48.
108. Lindsley, *History of Greater Dallas,* 42; Bates, *History and Reminiscences of Denton County,* 333.
109. B. D. Burch, *Mt. Springs Oral History,* 42.
110. Paddock, *History of Texas,* 2:859.
111. Lindsley, *History of Greater Dallas,* 42; Bates, *History and Reminiscences of Denton County,* 333; Richardson, *Frontier of Northwest Texas,* 146.
112. Bates, *History and Reminiscences of Denton County,* 351.
113. Bates, *History and Reminiscences of Denton County,* 300.
114. Campbell et al., *Plano: The Early Years,* 12; *Dallas Herald,* August 2, 1856, and August 7, 1858; *Dallas Weekly Herald,* January 21, 1863.
115. Terrell, *Reminiscences of the Early Days of Fort Worth,* 67–68.
116. Hunter, "Rage for Grain," 16.
117. *Dallas Herald,* February 8, 1860.
118. *Dallas Daily Herald,* February 29, 1860.
119. Latimer, "The Wheat Region and Wheat Culture," 69.
120. *Dallas Herald,* August 2, 1856, February 8, 1860, and April 25, 1860; Cochran, *Dallas County,* 116.
121. *Dallas Herald,* December 8, 1855.
122. Knight, *Fort Worth,* 32; Garrett, *Fort Worth,* 136; Austin, "Feild, Julian."
123. *Dallas Herald,* May 18, 1859.
124. R. G. Dun & Company credit reports, vol. 28, 206 [water-stained; unclear], Baker Library Special Collections and Archives.
125. Casstevens, "Neighbors We Know"; Texas Historical Commission, "Details for Mansfield Mill."
126. Stark, "History of Dallas County," 56; Lindsley, *History of Greater Dallas,* 62.
127. *Dallas Daily Herald,* August 24, 1859.
128. "Receipts of Produce," *New Orleans Times-Picayune,* June 15, 1850; "Manufacture of Flour at St. Louis [1848]," 54; "Commercial Statistics of New Orleans" [1848], 575; "Western Staples [1848]," 26.
129. *Texas Republican,* March 10, 1855.

130. McElhaney, "From Oxen to Rails," 12.
131. "Dick," "Letter on the Overland Mail Route."
132. "A Source of Wealth," *Dallas Daily Herald*, December 21, 1859 [reprinted from the *Houston Telegraph*].
133. *Dallas Daily Herald*, September 29, 1858.
134. *Dallas Herald*, July 10, 1858.
135. *Dallas Daily Herald*, September 6, 1856.
136. Carpenter, "William Creager," 210.
137. Cox, *Historical and Biographical Record*, 331.
138. Hamilton, "City's 99 Tomorrow."
139. Hamilton, "City's 99 Tomorrow"; Fulkerson, *Wylie Area Heritage*, 116; Beam, "History of Collin County," 106; Cochran, *Dallas County*, 60–61.
140. Stark, "History of Dallas County," 66.
141. *Dallas Herald*, December 21, 1859.
142. "A Source of Wealth," *Dallas Daily Herald*, December 21, 1859 [reprinted from the *Houston Telegraph*].
143. *Texas Almanac for 1860*, 218. Presumably the "Central Railroad" was the Houston and Texas Central, which ran northwest from Houston. By 1860 the railhead was somewhere between Hempstead and Millican.
144. Smith, *US Army and the Texas Economy*, 8–9, 106–107; *Dallas Herald*, June 21, 1856, October 19, 1859, November 16, 1859, and February 29, 1860; Neighbours, *Robert Simpson Neighbors*, 175, 179, 182; Wooster, *Soldiers, Sutlers, and Settlers*, 107, 110, 111; Jordan, "Imprint of the Upper and Lower South," 685.
145. *Dallas Daily Herald*, October 4, 1856.
146. Green, "Beginnings of Wheat Culture," 62.
147. *Dallas Daily Herald*, February 16, 1859.
148. *Dallas Daily Herald*, October 5, 1859; "Flour and Beef!," *Dallas Daily Herald*, November 16, 1859; "Texas Flour Wanted," *Dallas Daily Herald*, February 29, 1860.
149. Floyd, "Early Days in Dallas County," 26.
150. *Dallas Herald*, May 10, 1856, April 13, 1859, and September 7, 1859.
151. Jones, *Early Days in Cooke County*, 13; Latimer, "The Wheat Region and Wheat Culture," 64–65, 68.
152. "Dick," "Letter on the Overland Mail Route."
153. "A Source of Wealth," *Dallas Daily Herald*, December 21, 1859 [reprinted from the *Houston Telegraph*]. "Extra double" was a term for very fine flour used in the second half of the nineteenth century.
154. *Dallas Daily Herald*, September 29, 1858.
155. "County Mechanical and Agricultural Association," *Dallas Daily Herald*, November 2, 1859; "The Fair," *Dallas Daily Herald*, November 14, 1860. I have been unable to identify Mr. Spencer.
156. Storck and Teague, *Flour for Man's Bread*, 223.
157. "George Washington Baird"; US Department of Commerce, Ninth Census of the United States, 1860.

158. Floyd, "Early Days in Dallas County," 27. I have been able to find nothing else on "Aunt Jane."
159. "Everard Sharrock Jr. Farmstead," US Department of the Interior, 8, 9–10, 14, 19–23, 27.
160. Pettit, "Dugger Tells Stories of Life in Pioneer Community," July 8, 1990, in *Between the Creeks*, 335.
161. Pettit, "Pioneer Homes, Part II," June 15, 1986, in *Between the Creeks*, 172.
162. *Dallas Daily Herald*, February 9, 1856.
163. Horn, *Annals of Elder Horn*, 29.
164. *Dallas Herald*, October 24, 1860.
165. *Dallas Weekly Herald*, November 2, 1859.
166. Beecher, *Miss Beecher's Domestic Receipt-Book*, 208.
167. *Dallas Herald*, May 18, 1859.
168. "Archibald T. Buchanan," 53.
169. Floyd, "Early Days in Dallas County," 24.
170. Floyd, "Early Days in Dallas County," 24.
171. Floyd, "Early Days in Dallas County," 26.
172. *Dallas Weekly Herald*, November 17, 1858, May 2, 1860, and November 7, 1860.
173. *Dallas Weekly Herald*, August 24, 1859.
174. Hammond and Hammond, *La Réunion*, 88.
175. Davis, *WPA Guide to Texas*, 273.
176. Campbell et al., *Plano: The Early Years*, 37.
177. Bates, *History and Reminiscences of Denton County*, 300–301.
178. *Dallas Herald*, October 31, 1860.
179. *Dallas Herald*, November 14, 1860.
180. "Mr. and Mrs. Wm. H. Beeman," *Dallas Morning News*, January 26, 1902. I have been unable to identify greedy Mr. Wilburn.
181. *Dallas Weekly Herald*, November 17, 1860.

CHAPTER 2: "THE GRANARY OF THE CONFEDERATE STATES"

1. Buenger, *Secession and the Union*, 67.
2. Campbell, *Empire for Slavery*, 264–266.
3. Baum, *Shattering of Texas Unionism*, 53, 73.
4. *Memorial and Biographical History of Dallas County*, 177.
5. Lake, "A. F. Leonard"; Garrett, *Fort Worth*, 103; Nichols, *Lost Fort Worth*, 131.
6. *San Antonio Ledger and Texan*, July 28, 1860.
7. Foote, "Millwood 72 Years Ago"; Pettit, "Spring Was Important Feature at Fitzhugh Mill," August 11, 1991, in *Between the Creeks*, 357.
8. I have been unable to identify Lattimer or Richie.
9. Acheson and O'Connell, "George Washington Diamond," 398, 400.
10. *Dallas Herald*, May 29, 1861.

11. *Dallas Herald,* November 14, 1860; "Trip to Pleasant Run," March 13, 1861.
12. "J. E. Wheeler Built First Two-Story House in County," *Gainesville Daily Register,* August 19, 1950; "Judge John E. Wheeler," FindaGrave.com.
13. *Dallas Herald,* May 8, 1861.
14. *Dallas Herald,* May 29, 1861.
15. *Dallas Daily Herald,* July 17, 1861; "Flour for Southern Texas," *Dallas Daily Herald,* July 24, 1861.
16. *Dallas Herald,* October 2, 1861.
17. Wikipedia, "31st Texas Cavalry Regiment."
18. Stark, "History of Dallas County," 153–154.
19. Halbach, "Domesticity," 36.
20. Campbell, *Empire for Slavery,* table 2.
21. *Dallas Daily Herald,* March 25, 1863.
22. Cochran, *Dallas County,* 88.
23. Sharpless, *Grain and Fire,* 88.
24. Stambaugh and Stambaugh, *Collin County,* 223.
25. "Yeary, Walter R.," Ancestry.com.
26. "Mauck, Eliza Smith," Ancestry.com.
27. *Dallas Herald,* April 8, 1863.
28. *Dallas Herald,* November 19, 1864.
29. *Dallas Herald,* November 6, 1861.
30. "Military Depot at Dallas," *Dallas Herald,* October 30, 1861.
31. Cochran, *Dallas County,* 87.
32. Garrett, *Fort Worth,* 199.
33. Enstam, *Women and the Creation of Urban Life,* 30–31.
34. "Military Depot at Dallas," *Dallas Herald,* October 30, 1861.
35. Beam, "History of Collin County," 83; "Yeary, John Benedict," Ancestry.com.
36. *Dallas Herald,* March 18, 1863.
37. *Dallas Herald,* July 22, 1863.
38. Lake, "A. F. Leonard"; Garrett, *Fort Worth,* 103; Nichols, *Lost Fort Worth,* 131.
39. Cochran, *Dallas County,* 116; *Dallas Morning News,* June 14, 1909.
40. *Dallas Weekly Herald,* April 29, 1863.
41. *Dallas Herald,* April 8, 1863.
42. Halbach, "Domesticity," 35.
43. Abshire, *Garland,* 4.
44. *Dallas Herald,* September 16, 1863.
45. *Dallas Herald,* August 13, 1864.
46. *Dallas Herald,* August 12, 1863.
47. *Dallas Herald,* November 2, 1861.
48. "Anniversary Timeline for Dallas County,"4.
49. Davis, *WPA Guide to Texas,* 57; *Dallas Herald,* August 2, 1862.
50. *Dallas Herald,* September 30, 1863. Unfortunately, the prices, printed on the edge of the page, are illegible.
51. Campbell et al., *Plano: The Early Years,* 201.

52. "A Confederate's Experience," 3; Gates, *Agriculture and the Civil War,* 40.
53. *Dallas Herald,* April 13, 1865.
54. Clampitt, *Lost Causes,* 142.
55. Campbell et al., *Plano: The Early Years,* 201.
56. Thrall, *Pictorial History of Texas,* 392; Cochran, *Dallas County,* 88, 117.
57. Casstevens, "Neighbors We Know."
58. Campbell et al., *Plano: The Early Years,* 201.

CHAPTER 3: FROM PRAIRIE TO PRODUCTION

1. Horn, *Annals of Elder Horn,* 154.
2. Horn, *Annals of Elder Horn,* 187.
3. Texas Bureau of Immigration, *Texas, the Home for the Emigrant,* 13.
4. Morgan, *Field Crops for the Cotton-Belt,* 326.
5. Thrall, *Pictorial History of Texas,* 26–27.
6. *Texas Almanac,* "Population History of Counties"; email to author from Keith Volanto, March 2, 2024.
7. "State News," *Brenham Daily Banner,* June 24, 1898.
8. *Bryan–College Station Eagle,* June 16, 1898.
9. "State News," *Brenham Daily Banner,* August 25, 1898.
10. Kerr, "Migration into Texas," 104; Jordan, "Imprint of the Upper and Lower South," 671, 673, 674.
11. Worrall, "Northern Texas," 156.
12. Cline, *Historic Downtown Plano,* 20.
13. *Dallas Weekly Herald,* December 15, 1866.
14. Horn, *Annals of Elder Horn,* 62.
15. Cochran, "Blue Mound Community."
16. Kimmey, "Short History"; Cooper, "Flusche Brothers."
17. Robert Jamison, *Mt. Springs Oral History,* 34–35.
18. "Hermann Christian Barthold Sr.," Findagrave.com; Gose, "Stories of Some of the Older Families of Krum," 36.
19. Maxwell, "Wheatland, TX (Dallas County)."
20. *Texas Almanac for 1867,* 225.
21. Powell, *Cooke County History,* 600.
22. *Dallas Herald,* June 30, 1866.
23. The Brothers Flusche, "Pilot Point."
24. Fulkerson, "Ben Bowman," 31.
25. Charles Moore to Will Boyd, November 3, 1873, Moore Family Papers.
26. Danvers, "Charles B. Moore Collection," 396.
27. Horn, *Annals of Elder Horn,* 201.
28. *Texas Almanac for 1867,* 221–222.
29. Atkins et al., "Wheat Production in Texas," 7.
30. *Dallas Herald,* May 23, 1868, October 17, 1896, and October 22, 1899.

31. *Dallas Herald*, October 15, 1899; Morgan, *Field Crops for the Cotton-Belt*, 321.
32. *Premium List . . . Second Annual Industrial Exposition and Agricultural Fair*, Briscoe Center for American History, 18.
33. "Trying Out New Wheat," *Dallas Herald*, October 22, 1899; *Dallas Herald*, December 5, 1897.
34. Hill, "Texas Agricultural Experiment Station."
35. Connell and Clayton, *Field Experiments at McKinney*, 252, 531, 532.
36. *Dallas Weekly Herald*, September 5, 1868; Danvers, "Charles B. Moore Collection," 396.
37. Horn, *Annals of Elder Horn*, 225–226.
38. Danvers, "Charles B. Moore Collection," 397; Evans, "Texas Agriculture," 121–122; Jordan, "Imprint of the Upper and Lower South," 681; *Texas Almanac for 1867*, 222.
39. *Dallas Herald*, April 28, 1866.
40. *Dallas Herald*, December 4, 1869.
41. *Dallas Herald*, October 27, 1877.
42. Evans, "Texas Agriculture," 122.
43. Danvers, "Charles B. Moore Collection," 396; Horn, *Annals of Elder Horn*, 153.
44. Danvers, "Charles B. Moore Collection," 377.
45. Danvers, "Charles B. Moore Collection," 417.
46. Land and Thompson, *Historical and Descriptive Review of the Industries of Dallas*, 63, 66–67, 80–81, 108.
47. *Texas Almanac for 1867*, 222.
48. Danvers, "Charles B. Moore Collection," 350; Campbell et al., *Plano: The Early Years*, 92.
49. Jordan, "Imprint of the Upper and Lower South," 681; *Texas Almanac for 1867*, 222.
50. McCoy, *Historic Sketches of the Cattle Trade*, 130.
51. Evans, "Texas Agriculture," 123.
52. Clark, *Lebanon on the Preston*, 51; *Dallas Weekly Herald*, October 26, 1867, November 2, 1867, and November 23, 1867.
53. *McKinney Democrat*, July 9, 1885.
54. *Denton County News*, October 13, 1898.
55. Danvers, "Charles B. Moore Collection," 336, 337.
56. Liza Moore and Charles Moore to Elvira Moore, March 15, 1872, Moore Family Papers; Grayson County, Texas Genealogical Society, "Agriculture," 19.
57. Woodhouse and Overpeck, "Two Thousand Years," 2702; Mock, "Drought and Precipitation," 44.
58. Charles Moore to unknown recipient, July 2, 1872, Moore Family Papers; Danvers, "Charles B. Moore Collection," 69, 332; *McKinney Democrat*, August 21, 1884; "Some Facts for the Home-Seeker," *Gainesville Daily Register*, 18, 19; *Fort Worth Gazette*, July 6, 1887; Spaight, *Resources, Soil, and Climate*, 63, 73, 76, 81, 123, 295; Denton Board of Trade, "The Best County in North Texas," 3.

59. *Texas Almanac for 1867*, 222; Jordan, "Imprint of the Upper and Lower South," 681.
60. Horn, *Annals of Elder Horn*, 205.
61. *Texas Almanac for 1867*, 222.
62. Collin County Historical Society, *Collin County in Pioneer Times*, 109.
63. *Dallas Daily Herald*, June 19, 1875, quoting the *Enquirer*. I have been unable to identify Mrs. Tucker.
64. Campbell et al., *Plano: The Early Years*, 251.
65. *Texas Almanac for 1867*, 222.
66. Collin County Historical Society, *Collin County in Pioneer Times*, 109, 111.
67. Danvers, "Charles B. Moore Collection," 337.
68. Myers, "Farming-Grain-Harvest," 23.
69. *McKinney Democrat*, July 9, 1885.
70. Hurt, *American Agriculture*, 196–197; Campbell et al., *Plano: The Early Years*, 92; *William Deering, Born in Maine*, 11–12.
71. Myers, "Farming-Grain-Harvest," 23.
72. *Texas Almanac for 1867*, 222.
73. Bridges, *History of Denton*, 163.
74. Campbell et al., *Plano: The Early Years*, 89; Danvers, "Charles B. Moore Collection," 264, 265, 324–325, 349–350, 363.
75. Texas Genealogical Society, *Ancestors and Descendants*, 196.
76. Wells, "Farmer's Song," 93.
77. Danvers, "Charles B. Moore Collection," 428, 429; Stambaugh and Stambaugh, *Collin County*, 118.
78. Wells, "Farmer's Song," 94.
79. Danvers, "Charles B. Moore Collection," 429–430, 435.
80. *Texas Almanac 1867*, 97.
81. "Queen City," *Dallas Weekly Herald*, October 14, 1876; *Dallas Weekly Herald*, January 20, 1877.
82. R. G. Dun & Company credit reports, vol. 8, 233 and 97; vol. 14, 183, Baker Library Special Collections and Archives.
83. *Dallas Morning News*, November 23, 1889.
84. *Dallas Morning News*, August 24, 1892.
85. *McKinney Democrat*, June 23, 1898.
86. "Some Facts for the Home-Seeker," *Gainesville Daily Register*, 26.
87. R. G. Dun & Company credit reports, vol. 28, 287.
88. Land and Thompson, *Historical and Descriptive Review of the Industries of Dallas*, unpaginated.
89. Carlson, *Monetary and Banking History of Texas*, 32.
90. *Texas Almanac for 1867*, 222.
91. *Texas Almanac for 1867*, 97; Thrall, *Pictorial History of Texas*, 657.
92. *Dallas Herald*, April 28, 1866.
93. Land and Thompson, *Historical and Descriptive Review of the Industries of Dallas*, 63.
94. "Some Facts for the Home-Seeker," *Gainesville Daily Register*, 26.

95. Hurt, *American Agriculture*, 200–201.
96. *Texas Almanac for 1867*, 222.
97. Danvers, "Charles B. Moore Collection," 280.
98. "Saved by His Little Daughter," *Dallas Herald*, September 8, 1892.
99. Danvers, "Charles B. Moore Collection," 325.
100. *Dallas Herald*, March 10, 1866.
101. Enstam, "When the Homefront Was the Frontier," 7; *Dallas Herald*, November 4, 1865.
102. *Dallas Herald*, September 1, 1866; *Dallas Herald*, October 14, 1865, November 5, 1865, and April 28, 1866.
103. Paddock, *History of Texas*, 2:615.
104. Land and Thompson, *Historical and Descriptive Review of the Industries of Dallas*, 74.
105. Danvers, "Charles B. Moore Collection," 347, 362.
106. "Farmer's General Store Ledger," 53.
107. Charles Moore to Elvira Moore, October 21, 1871, Moore Family Papers; Danvers, "Charles B. Moore Collection," 347.
108. *Texas Almanac for 1867*, 92, 95, 99, 112, 160.
109. *Dallas Herald*, September 30, 1865, October 21, 1865, June 30, 1866, and July 14, 1866.
110. *Dallas Herald*, July 14, 1866; Spaight, *Resources, Soil, and Climate*, 123; *Texas Almanac for 1867*, 223.
111. Lindsley, *History of Greater Dallas*, 106.
112. *Denison Daily News*, March 15, 1878.
113. "Some Facts for the Home-Seeker," *Gainesville Daily Register*, 18.
114. Denton Board of Trade, "The Best County in North Texas," 6.
115. *Dallas Weekly Herald*, March 30, 1882.
116. *Dallas Weekly Herald*, September 1, 1882.
117. Land and Thompson, *Historical and Descriptive Review of the Industries of Dallas*, 87.
118. Land and Thompson, *Historical and Descriptive Review of the Industries of Dallas*, 96.
119. Markham, *History of Commodity Futures*, 3–4, 7.
120. *Dallas Herald*, April 14, 1882, and August 2, 1882.
121. *Dallas Weekly Herald*, April 20, 1882, May 4, 1882, and June 8, 1882.
122. *Morrison & Fourmy's General Directory of the City of Dallas, 1883–84*, 1883, 26–27.
123. *Dallas Morning News*, June 16, 1887, and June 29, 1887.
124. *Dallas Morning News*, January 14, 1893.
125. "Trying Out New Wheat," *Dallas Herald*, October 22, 1899.
126. *Fort Worth Daily Gazette*, February 3, 1889; Simpson, *Corn Palaces and Butter Queens*, xv.
127. "Texas Spring Palace," *Fort Worth Daily Gazette*, January 15, 1889.
128. Simpson, *Corn Palaces and Butter Queens*, 127.

129. Simpson, *Corn Palaces and Butter Queens*, 21.
130. Simpson, *Corn Palaces and Butter Queens*, 30; "The Spring Palace," *Sioux City Journal*, June 18, 1889.
131. "Where They Came From," *Fort Worth Gazette*, July 4, 1889.
132. "New Texas Spring Palace," *Fort Worth Daily Gazette*, May 11, 1890.

CHAPTER 4: OXEN TO ELECTRICITY

1. *Dallas Herald*, September 2, 1865.
2. *Dallas Herald*, March 17, 1866.
3. *Dallas Herald*, July 28, 1866.
4. *Dallas Herald*, April 14, 1866.
5. *Dallas Herald*, September 1, 1866.
6. R. G. Dun & Company credit reports, vol. 8, 98; US Department of Commerce, Tenth Census of the United States, 1870; "Rev. James E. Scott," Findagrave.com.
7. R. G. Dun & Company credit reports, vol. 8, 99.
8. R. G. Dun & Company credit reports, vol. 28, 202B.
9. *Dallas Herald*, July 13, 1876.
10. *Dallas Herald*, December 14, 1876.
11. "The Queen City," *Dallas Herald*, October 14, 1876.
12. R. G. Dun & Company credit reports, vol. 7, 171. I have been unable to discover what became of the mill after its sale.
13. R. G. Dun & Company credit reports, vol. 8, 20, 53, 189, 256.
14. Enstam, "Opportunity versus Propriety," 106, 111.
15. *Dallas Daily Herald*, April 19, 1874, and July 1, 1874.
16. *Dallas Daily Herald*, October 2, 1875.
17. *Dallas Morning News*, June 14, 1888, June 12, 1889, April 16, 1891, May 5, 1891, May 26, 1891, and June 12, 1892.
18. *Dallas Weekly Herald*, March 21, 1874.
19. Marion Day Mullins, interviewed by Ruby Schmidt, April 25, 1977, Tarrant County Archives.
20. Mansfield Historical Services, "Mansfield Cemetery"; Mansfield Historical Services, "Story of the Man Family."
21. Hulse, "History of the Man House."
22. Gray, *Story of Sanger*, 4, 25, 36–38.
23. Powell, *Cooke County History*, 7; Miller and Scoggin, "Collinsville," 52.
24. Henry Moore to Charles Moore, February 5–6, 1870, Moore Family Papers.
25. Henry Moore to Charles Moore, February 21, 1870, Moore Family Papers.
26. Charles Moore to Henry Moore, March 8, 1870, Moore Family Papers. Henry was at Gray Rock in Titus County.
27. Charles Moore to Henry and Elvira Moore, October 29, 1870, Moore Family Papers.

28. Laura Jernigan to Charles, Mary, and Linnet Moore, March 11, 1898; Belle Jernigan to Linnet Moore, March 12, 1898, Moore Family Papers.
29. "School to Honor Frank W. Jackson," *Plano Star Courier*, October 3, 1975 [reprinted in *Collin Chronicles*].
30. *McKinney Advocate*, April 3, 1880.
31. Clark, *Lebanon on the Preston*, 29, quoting *Plano Review*, October 18, 1884.
32. "Digital Sanborn Fire Maps" (Gainesville, 1885; McKinney, 1885; Plano, 1885; Whitesboro, 1885), ProQuest.
33. Collin County Historical Society, *Collin County in Pioneer Times*, 109.
34. Lucas and Hall, *A History of Grayson County*, 85.
35. Jones, *Early Days in Cooke County*, 76, 90.
36. Bridges, *History of Denton*, 87, 162; Abelson and Marshall, "History of Bolivar."
37. Harris, *112 Years in Little Elm*, 81.
38. Steen, *Flour Milling in America*, 53.
39. Steen, *Flour Milling in America*, 47, 48; Storck and Teague, *Flour for Man's Bread*, 226–229.
40. Gray, *Business without Boundary*, 21; Gage, "Wheat into Flour," 90.
41. Smalley, "Flour Mills," 38, 39, 40, 42, 43, 44, 46.
42. *Dallas Weekly Herald*, September 20, 1883.
43. "Another Industry," *Fort Worth Daily Gazette*, July 12, 1883.
44. Clark, *Lebanon on the Preston*, 29, quoting *Plano Review*, October 18, 1884.
45. "A New Era: What Is to Be Seen at the Mammoth Mill and Elevator of Cameron & Tatum," *Fort Worth Gazette*, December 6, 1888; Steen, *Flour Milling in America*, 403.
46. "A New Era," *Fort Worth Gazette*, December 6, 1888.
47. Gray, *Business without Boundary*, 19.
48. Washburn-Crosby Co., *Wheat and Flour Primer*, 4–5.
49. Land and Thompson, *Historical and Descriptive Review of the Industries of Dallas*, 126.
50. *Morrison & Fourmy's General Directory of the City of Dallas, 1886–87.*
51. US Census of Manufacturing, 1870 and 1880.
52. Campbell et al., *Plano: The Early Years*, 256.
53. R. G. Dun & Company credit reports, vol. 7, 209.
54. R. G. Dun & Company credit reports, vol. 7, 193.
55. R. G. Dun & Company credit reports, vol. 8, 89.
56. Platt, *The Law as to the Property Rights of Married Women*, 5.
57. R. G. Dun & Company credit reports, vol. 8, 73; R. G. Dun & Company credit reports, vol. 8, 120. I have been unable to identify Miller or Ewing.
58. R. G. Dun & Company credit reports, vol. 8, 120.
59. Barnhart and Estes, *McKinney*, 34; "Digital Sanborn Fire Maps" (Dallas, 1888), ProQuest.
60. "Fire Bells," *Gainesville Daily Hesperian*, January 5, 1888; *Gainesville Daily Hesperian*, January 7, 1888, and January 12, 1888. Although the newspaper says "Allen," it almost surely meant Edward P. Allis.

61. Powell, *Cooke County History*, 596.
62. *Fort Worth Gazette*, February 19, 1889; *Dallas Morning News*, August 11, 1894; *Weekly Northwestern Miller* 38 (August 17, 1894): 271.
63. Texas Historical Commission, details for Harrison Cemetery.
64. Bridges, *History of Denton*, 180.
65. R. G. Dun & Company credit reports, vol. 8, 171; Andrews, "Agricultural Cooperation," 59.
66. Raven and Howard, "The Salt Creek Massacre"; Wooster, *Soldiers, Sutlers, and Settlers*, 107, 110, 111, 116, 118.
67. *Dallas Morning News*, April 16, 1891, and February 4, 1892; Frank M. Cockrell, letter to Mr. J. Perry Burrus, February 25–27 [1927?], Folder: 1880s, 1900s, Sarah Horton Cockrell Collection, Dallas Historical Society; *Dallas Herald*, March 26, 1885.
68. *Dallas Morning News*, June 14, 1888, June 12, 1889, May 5, 1891, May 26, 1891, and June 12, 1892.
69. Cantrell, *People's Revolt*, 446–465; "The Record," *American Miller*, 728; Barnes, *Farmers in Rebellion*, 89.
70. "The Record," *American Miller*, 147; *Hand-Book of Northern Texas*, 33.
71. Bridges, *History of Denton*, 181.
72. "The Record," *American Miller*, 147.
73. Steen, *Flour Milling in America*, 407.
74. *McKinney Democrat*, October 5, 1893.
75. "The Chapman Milling Company's New Mill at Sherman, Texas," *The Roller Mill*, 26; Steen, *Flour Milling in America*, 411.
76. Banham, *Concrete Atlantis*, 109–110; Tarbet, *Grain Dust Dreams*, 6; Brown, *American Colossus*, 14, 64.
77. Brown, *American Colossus*, 36.
78. Tarbet, *Grain Dust Dreams*, xiii, 19, 20, 56; Banham, *Concrete Atlantis*, 113, 115.
79. *Dallas Herald*, September 11, 1875.
80. Land and Thompson, *Historical and Descriptive Review of the Industries of Dallas*, 84.
81. *Fort Worth Gazette*, December 6, 1888; "Digital Sanborn Fire Maps" (Fort Worth, 1898), ProQuest.
82. "Digital Sanborn Fire Maps" (Dallas, 1892 and 1899), ProQuest.
83. Land and Thompson, *Historical and Descriptive Review of the Industries of Dallas*, 88.
84. "Some Facts for the Home-Seeker," *Gainesville Daily Register*, 21; Gray, *Story of Sanger*, 42, 45–46; Texas Genealogical Society, *Ancestors and Descendants*, 53.
85. Andrews, "Agricultural Cooperation," 65–66.
86. Frank M. Cockrell, letter to Mr. J. Perry Burrus, February 25–27 [1927?], Folder: 1880s, 1900s, Sarah Horton Cockrell Collection, Dallas Historical Society.
87. "Some Facts for the Home-Seeker," *Gainesville Daily Register*, 9.

88. *McKinney Democrat*, July 23, 1896.
89. R. G. Dun & Company credit reports, vol. 7, 171.
90. *Denton County News*, June 24, 1897.
91. *Denton County News*, October 17, 1895.
92. *Denton County News*, October 13, 1898.
93. Texas Real Estate & Collection Bureau, *Immigrants Guide to Texas*, 158.
94. *Denton Business Review and Directory*, [20].
95. "Convention of Texas Mill Proprietors," *Dallas Weekly Herald*, June 12, 1875.
96. "Grinders of Grit. A Select Coterie of Capitalist Millers Convene in the Fort in Marked Exclusion and Grandeur," *Fort Worth Daily Gazette*, June 16, 1886.
97. "Grain Dealers," *Fort Worth Gazette*, October 29, 1891.

CHAPTER 5: FROM BISCUITS TO ANGEL FOOD CAKE

1. *Dallas Daily Herald*, June 19, 1873.
2. Land and Thompson, *Historical and Descriptive Review of the Industries of Dallas*, 123.
3. *McKinney Democrat*, February 16, 1899.
4. Fulkerson, *Wylie Area Heritage*, 159; Mary and Charles Moore to Linnet Moore, November 9, 1898, Moore Family Papers.
5. Collin County Historical Society, *Collin County in Pioneer Times*, 60.
6. Horn, *Annals of Elder Horn*, 83.
7. "Queen City," *Dallas Herald*, October 14, 1876; Land and Thompson, *Historical and Descriptive Review of the Industries of Dallas*, 60.
8. Halbach, "Domesticity," 45.
9. [Farmer's Wife], "Salt Rising for Bread"; "Ladies Column," *Fort Worth Daily Gazette*, July 10, 1887.
10. *Dallas Morning News*, October 15, 1896; *Dallas Morning News*, November 4, 1894, October 26, 1896, September 17, 1897, October 21, 1897, October 8, 1898, October 25, 1899, and October 15, 1900.
11. "Texas State Fair," *Dallas Morning News*, October 12, 1894.
12. "Queen City," *Dallas Herald*, October 14, 1876; Land and Thompson, *Historical and Descriptive Review of the Industries of Dallas*, 69–70, 72, 105, 796–797.
13. *Dallas Morning News*, November 20, 1894, November 28, 1897, and December 19, 1897.
14. Mary Moore to Linnet Moore, January 4, 1899, Moore Family Papers.
15. *Dallas Morning News*, November 28, 1897; *Dallas Morning News*, November 20, 1894, and November 26, 1894.
16. *Premium List . . . Second Annual Industrial Exposition and Agricultural Fair*, Briscoe Center for American History, 16, 17; "North Texas Fair," *Dallas Daily Herald*, October 28, 1877.

17. *Dallas Morning News,* January 19, 1891, November 4, 1894, October 15, 1896, October 26, 1896, September 17, 1897, October 21, 1897, October 8, 1898, and October 25, 1899.
18. *Dallas Morning News,* January 19, 1891, November 4, 1894, October 15, 1896, October 26, 1896, September 17, 1897, October 21, 1897, October 8, 1898, and October 25, 1899.
19. Mary and Charles Moore to Linnet Moore, November 9, 1898, Moore Family Papers.
20. *Dallas Morning News,* September 6, 1892.
21. *Fort Worth Star-Telegram,* November 18, 1921, and November 22, 1921.
22. US Department of Commerce, Eleventh Census of the United States, 1880.
23. *Gainesville Daily Hesperian,* May 19, 1889.
24. *Fort Worth Daily Gazette,* September 12, 1886.
25. *McKinney Democrat,* October 3, 1895.
26. *Fort Worth Morning Register,* July 7, 1900.
27. *Fort Worth Daily Gazette,* May 17, 1885, October 12, 1895; *Dallas Morning News,* July 2, 1887, May 11, 1888, February 5, 1889, and February 18, 1900; *Gainesville Daily Hesperian,* November 28, 1889.
28. R. G. Dun & Company credit reports, vol. 28, 266.
29. *Directory of the City of Fort Worth for the Year 1877,* 62; *Fort Worth Daily Gazette,* March 8, 1885.
30. *Fort Worth Daily Democrat,* March 1, 1883, and July 30, 1883; *Fort Worth Daily Gazette,* March 1, 1883, and July 15, 1885.
31. *Fort Worth Daily Gazette,* December 30, 1887.
32. *Fort Worth Daily Gazette,* April 19, 1890, and April 23, 1890.
33. *Fort Worth Daily Gazette,* October 31, 1890; *Dallas Morning News,* January 5, 1886.
34. *Dallas Morning News,* June 26, 1887.
35. *Fort Worth Gazette,* December 13, 1894; *Dallas Morning News,* April 16, 1886, and July 21, 1887.
36. *Fort Worth Gazette,* December 13, 1894; *Dallas Morning News,* February 10, 1886, July 21, 1886, July 21, 1887, and June 13, 1899.
37. *Dallas Morning News,* March 14, 1897.
38. *Fort Worth Morning Register,* September 3, 1899.
39. *Fort Worth Daily Gazette,* December 31, 1888.
40. *Dallas Morning News,* July 2, 1899.
41. *Dallas Morning News,* August 29, 1900.
42. *Fort Worth Gazette,* January 11, 1896.
43. *Fort Worth Register,* June 16, 1897.
44. *Denison Daily News,* March 14, 1878.
45. *Fort Worth Daily Gazette,* May 17, 1884, May 20, 1884, and May 25, 1884.
46. *Fort Worth Daily Gazette,* March 29, 1886.
47. *Fort Worth Daily Gazette,* October 15, 1887, and October 16, 1887.
48. *Fort Worth Daily Gazette,* September 20, 1890.

49. *Dallas Morning News*, September 8, 1891.
50. *Fort Worth Morning Register*, July 15, 1899, and August 5, 1899; *Dallas Morning News*, March 19, 1899.
51. *Dallas Weekly Herald*, December 20, 1873.
52. *Dallas Daily Herald*, February 4, 1875.
53. Speed, *History of Industry*, 12.
54. Charles Moore to Mary Ann Moore, October 26–27, 1897, Moore Family Papers.
55. *Fort Worth Business Directory, 1884*, n.p.
56. *Fort Worth Daily Gazette*, December 21, 1886; *Fort Worth Gazette*, March 26, 1892.
57. "Some Facts for the Home-Seeker," *Gainesville Daily Register*, 22; *Fort Worth Business Directory, 1884*, n.p.; *Fort Worth Daily Gazette*, May 20, 1884; *Dallas Morning News*, December 20, 1889.
58. *Dallas Morning News*, March 19, 1899.
59. *Dallas Morning News*, December 14, 1894, and December 12, 1897.
60. *Dallas Morning News*, March 10, 1886.
61. *Fort Worth Gazette*, April 30, 1893.
62. *Torchlight Appeal* [Fort Worth], February 22, 1890.
63. *Denison Daily News*, August 8, 1879.
64. *Dallas Morning News*, April 24, 1888.
65. *Dallas Morning News*, November 12, 1899.
66. *Denison Sunday Gazetteer*, June 17, 1883.
67. *Dallas Morning News*, November 11, 1888.
68. *Fort Worth Gazette*, April 16, 1896.
69. *Fort Worth Daily Gazette*, January 30, 1885.
70. "Report of the Re-Union Finance Committee," *McKinney Enquirer*, August 18, 1883.
71. *Dallas Morning News*, August 6, 1886.
72. *Fort Worth Daily Gazette*, February 1, 1892, and November 26, 1892.

CHAPTER 6: WHEAT IN THE SPRING AND COTTON IN THE FALL

1. *Texas Almanac*, "City Population History."
2. US Department of Commerce, Census of Agriculture, 1900; "Collin County Farm Museum Digital Collection," 5.
3. Brown, *Tenant Farming*, n.p.; Davis, *WPA Guide to Texas*, 403, 404, 405; Davis, *Encyclopedia of Texas*, 812.
4. White, "Robert Alexander Davis," [219?]; Litchford, "Thomas Ables Jackson," 310; Hanning, "Presley, James Royal (Jim)," 537.
5. "J. Perry Burrus Offers Farmers $1 for All No. 2 Wheat Raised in Collin during Year 1915," *McKinney Weekly Democrat-Gazette*, September 10, 1914.

6. *McKinney Democrat,* April 9, 1903.
7. *McKinney Weekly Democrat-Gazette,* June 13, 1918.
8. Cooke County Public Library, *Premium List,* Cooke County Free Fair, 169, 170.
9. Speed, *History of Industry,* 31; A. M. Ferguson and Company, *Field Seeds as Good as We Can Make Them,* 22–23.
10. Leidigh, Mangelsdorf, and Dunkle, "Denton Wheat," 5; Cowling, *Geography of Denton County,* 63.
11. Leidigh, Mangelsdorf, and Dunkle, "Denton Wheat," 8–9, 16.
12. Leidigh, Mangelsdorf, and Dunkle, "Denton Wheat," 17.
13. *McKinney Democrat,* June 7, 1900.
14. Evans, "Texas Agriculture," 123; Morgan, *Field Crops for the Cotton-Belt,* 337; Leidigh, Mangelsdorf, and Dunkle, "Denton Wheat," 15; Bilsing, "Green Bug."
15. A. M. Ferguson and Company, *Field Seeds as Good as We Can Make Them,* 23.
16. Holsen, *Economic Survey,* 147.
17. *Texas Almanac and State Industrial Guide for 1904,* 85.
18. *Texas Almanac and State Industrial Guide for 1904,* 8.
19. Bizzell, *Rural Texas,* 177.
20. Speed, *History of Industry,* 31.
21. Morgan, *Field Crops for the Cotton-Belt,* 329–330.
22. Morgan, *Field Crops for the Cotton-Belt,* 331; Fort Worth Chamber of Commerce, "Livestock and Agriculture in the Fort Worth Area," pamphlet in "Agriculture" vertical file, Fort Worth History Center.
23. *Texas Almanac and State Industrial Guide for 1904,* 85; *McKinney Weekly Democrat-Gazette,* June 13, 1918.
24. *Lindsay, Texas,* 104; Zimmerer, "Life of the Early Settlers," 30; White, "Robert Alexander Davis," 219.
25. Morgan, *Field Crops for the Cotton-Belt,* 332.
26. Campbell et al., *Plano: The Early Years,* 93.
27. Scoggin, "Sanders, Roy Clyde and Edith Annie," 567.
28. *Lindsay, Texas,* 104; Bezner, "Bezner Bros. Threshers," 113.
29. Hartman, "Agriculture," 38; Frisco Bicentennial Society, *History of Frisco, 1902–1976,* 188.
30. Litchford, "Thomas Ables Jackson," 311.
31. Litchford, "Thomas Ables Jackson," 310.
32. Jenkins, *Murphy,* 29.
33. Myers, "Farming-Grain-Harvest," 23.
34. Hartman, "Agriculture," 36; Jenkins, *Murphy,* 29.
35. Bezner, "Bezner Bros. Threshers," 113.
36. Richard Daniel, *Mt. Springs Oral History,* 18.
37. McCullum, "Robert Thomas Stark Family," 188.
38. Grayson County Frontier Village, *History of Grayson County,* vol. 1, 64.
39. Myers, "Farming-Grain-Harvest," 24.

40. Myers, "Farming-Grain-Harvest," 23.
41. Bezner, "Bezner Bros. Threshers," 113.
42. Wilde, "Wilde Bros. Threshing Co.," 66.
43. Bezner, "Bezner Bros. Threshers," 113.
44. Myers, "Farming-Grain-Harvest," 23–24.
45. Myers, "Farming-Grain-Harvest," 24.
46. Hartman, "Agriculture," 37–38.
47. Zimmerer, "Life of the Early Settlers," 30.
48. Scoggin, "Sanders, Roy Clyde and Edith Annie," 567.
49. Myers, "Farming-Grain-Harvest," 24.
50. Wilde, "Wilde Bros. Threshing Co.," 66.
51. Frisco Bicentennial Society, *History of Frisco, 1902–1976*, 188.
52. Scoggin, "Sanders, Roy Clyde and Edith Annie," 567.
53. Brinkley, "Cunningham, Howard Houston," 97.
54. Lucas, "Graham," 262.
55. Patterson, "Lillie, Our Little Lady," 44.
56. Frisco Bicentennial Society, *History of Frisco, 1902–1976*, 188; Bezner, "Bezner Bros. Threshers," 113.
57. Hartman, "Agriculture," 39.
58. Hartman, "Agriculture," 39; Wilde, "Wilde Bros. Threshing Co.," 66; McMahan and Banfield, "McMahan, Eli Franklin," 462.
59. Wilde, "Wilde Bros. Threshing Co.," 66.
60. Chambers, "Aubrey Nesbit Chambers," 195.
61. *Lindsay, Texas*, 126.
62. Hartman, "Agriculture," 38; Evans, "Texas Agriculture," 127.
63. Douglas, "County's 'No. 1 Tenant Farmer.'"
64. Bezner, "Bezner Bros. Threshers," 113; Hartman, "Agriculture," 38.
65. Parsons and Bush, *Fair Park Deco*, 73.
66. Adams, *State of Texas Building*, 33.
67. Parsons and Bush, *Fair Park Deco*, 94, 97, 100, 103, 104; Stewart, *Lone Star Regionalism*, 57–60; Carraro, *Jerry Bywaters*, 102–103.

CHAPTER 7: MECHANIZATION, MARKETING, AND MUSIC

1. Barry, "History of Krum," 34.
2. Victor Tinsley, interviewed by Ruby Schmidt, March 4, 1975, Tarrant County Archives.
3. Barry, "History of Krum," 34.
4. Katherine O'Riley Hester, interviewed by Ruby Schmidt, April 16, 1975, Tarrant County Archives.
5. Charles Moore to Mary Ann Moore, January 13, 1900, Moore Family Papers; Hawks, "Rural Life in the Twenties and Thirties," 124.

6. Barry, "History of Krum," 34.
7. Hestand, "Country Boy's Dream," 30.
8. Tarrant County, Fort Worth, Texas, *Farmers, Stockmen*, 7.
9. Phillips, "Krum Main Street Once Was Lined with Wheat Wagons"; "Wheat Brought Fame to Krum," *Denton Record-Chronicle*, February 3, 1956.
10. Davis and Hubbard, *Krum*, 17.
11. Owens, "Chester A. Good," 6.
12. Davis and Hubbard, *Krum*.
13. Litchford, "Thomas Ables Jackson," 311; Stambaugh and Stambaugh, *Collin County*, 49.
14. *McKinney Democrat*, April 9, 1903.
15. Cooke County Public Library, "Complete History of Myra, Texas."
16. *Federal Reporter* 279 (May–July 1922): 579, 580, 583.
17. *Fort Worth Star-Telegram*, September 14, 1922.
18. Smith, "The Grapevine Mill."
19. Campbell et al., *Plano: The Early Years*, 256–257; "Commercial Feeding Stuffs, 1916–17," 18–20; Barry, "History of Krum," 37.
20. *Fort Worth Star-Telegram*, October 30, 1918.
21. "Commercial Feeding Stuffs, 1916–17," 24.
22. "Sherman Leading Milling Center of the Southwest," *Sherman Daily Democrat*, May 12, 1925.
23. "New Mill to Work 30 Men Starts July 1," *Fort Worth Star-Telegram*, May 19, 1922; "Pioneer Firms Made City Regional Milling Center," *Fort Worth Star-Telegram*, October 30, 1949; Steen, *Flour Milling*, 405; "New Universal Plant Running," *Fort Worth Star-Telegram*, November 27, 1932.
24. "Feed Mill for Sherman," *Fort Worth Star-Telegram*, August 17, 1931.
25. "Burrus Texo Feeds Have Given Proof of Their Merit," *Fort Worth Star-Telegram*, January 8, 1940.
26. "Stock Food Mill Burns; Loss $75,000," *Fort Worth Star-Telegram*, May 10, 1910.
27. "Collin County Farm Museum Digital Collection," 5.
28. "Digital Sanborn Fire Maps" (McKinney, 1902), ProQuest.
29. "Stanard-Tilton Flour Mill," US Department of the Interior.
30. *McKinney Daily Courier Gazette*, May 14, 1914; "Digital Sanborn Fire Maps" (McKinney, 1914, 1927), ProQuest.
31. "Testing Out of McKinney's Greatest Industry," *McKinney Weekly Democrat-Gazette*, January 28, 1915.
32. Steen, *Flour Milling*, 405; *Operative Miller* 23 (1918): 337; "Digital Sanborn Fire Maps" (Gainesville, 1902, 1913, 1922), ProQuest; "Whaley Mill Established 71 Years Ago, Is Gainesville's Oldest Business Institution," *Gainesville Daily Register*, September 23, 1940.
33. Davis, *Encyclopedia of Texas*, 862.
34. "Pride of the Southwest," 131.
35. "Digital Sanborn Fire Maps" (Sherman, 1914, 1922), ProQuest.

36. "Milling Company Sued for $51,000 Damages," *Fort Worth Star-Telegram*, October 7, 1931.
37. Mouzon, "Musings."
38. *Operative Miller* 13 (1908): 471.
39. "Pride of the Southwest," 131.
40. "Burrus Company Dedicates Texas' Largest Flour Mill," *Fort Worth Star-Telegram*, February 16, 1936.
41. "Two Nordberg Diesels Serve the Burrus Mill," *Fort Worth Star-Telegram*, February 16, 1936.
42. "Two Nordberg Diesels Serve the Burrus Mill," *Fort Worth Star-Telegram*, February 16, 1936.
43. "Bewley Mills Open," *Fort Worth Star-Telegram*, June 23, 1907.
44. *Fort Worth Star-Telegram*, July 7, 1913.
45. "Bewley Plans Big Increase in Mill Here," *Fort Worth Star-Telegram*, September 20, 1916.
46. Gordon, "Bewley Mills Ship Flour."
47. *Texas Almanac and State Industrial Guide for 1904*, 85.
48. Cowling, *Geography of Denton County*, 64.
49. "J. Perry Burrus Offers Farmers $1 for All No. 2 Wheat Raised in Collin during Year 1915," *McKinney Weekly Democrat-Gazette*, September 10, 1914.
50. *Fort Worth Star-Telegram*, June 23, 1934; "100-Car Shipment of Wheat Is Sold," *Fort Worth Star-Telegram*, July 4, 1934; "First Texas Wheat Arrives," *Fort Worth Star-Telegram*, June 1, 1939.
51. "Grinding Floor Gossip," 354; "Year's First Carload of Grain Arrives," *Fort Worth Star-Telegram*, May 29, 1939; "1939 Wheat Crop Now Moving in Direction of Fort Worth," *Fort Worth Star-Telegram*, May 29, 1939.
52. "6 Cars of Wheat, Valued at $10,000, Confiscated Here," *Fort Worth Star-Telegram*, May 11, 1909.
53. "First Wheat Brought from Argentine since 1916 Is Due in Week," *Fort Worth Star-Telegram*, March 23, 1920.
54. "Sherman Leading Milling Center of the Southwest," *Sherman Daily Democrat*, May 12, 1925.
55. *Fort Worth Star-Telegram*, January 2, 1920, January 13, 1920, December 4, 1920, January 27, 1922, and April 17, 1925; *McKinney Courier-Gazette*, January 7, 1924.
56. "O'Daniel Tells of Inducing Bakers to Use Texas Flour: 'State's Product Proved Superior to Competitors,'" *Dallas Morning News*, August 31, 1938.
57. *Fort Worth Star-Telegram*, February 12, 1933.
58. Aby, *Bewley's Best Bakes Better*, 1.
59. Storck and Teague, *Flour for Man's Bread*, 315.
60. "Whaley Mill Established 71 Years Ago, Is Gainesville's Oldest Business Institution," *Gainesville Daily Register*, September 23, 1940.
61. "Largest Month's Business," *McKinney Democrat*, September 10, 1903.

62. "Sherman Leading Milling Center of the Southwest," *Sherman Daily Democrat*, May 12, 1925.
63. *I'll Tell You about Sherman*.
64. "Dallas Factory to Sell Mixed Biscuit Flour," *Dallas Morning News*, May 8, 1932.
65. *Dallas Morning News*, May 14, 1932; *Dallas Morning News*, September 10, 1932.
66. *Dallas Morning News*, October 29, 1932.
67. *Celina Record*, December 22, 1932.
68. "Sherman Leading Milling Center of the Southwest," *Sherman Daily Democrat*, May 12, 1925; Steen, *Flour Milling*, 413.
69. *Operative Miller* 15 (1910): 425.
70. Steen, *Flour Milling*, 413.
71. Davis, *Encyclopedia of Texas*, 107.
72. Kimbell, "Kimbell, Kay," 253.
73. Steen, *Flour Milling*, 404; "Digital Sanborn Fire Maps" (Whitewright, 1905), ProQuest.
74. *Operative Miller* 26 (1921): 279.
75. Steen, *Flour Milling*, 404, 411.
76. Steen, *Flour Milling*, 411; "Digital Sanborn Fire Maps" (Sherman, 1902, 1914), ProQuest.
77. "Kimbell Buys Grain Elevator at Melissa," *Fort Worth Star-Telegram*, September 14, 1937.
78. "9 Flour Mills Will Merge," *Fort Worth Star-Telegram*, June 19, 1929.
79. Stambaugh and Stambaugh, *Collin County*, 152–153, 202; Beam, "History of Collin County," 81.
80. "Fant Milling Company," *Fort Worth Star-Telegram*, May 27, 1938.
81. "Fort Worth Grain Center of South," *Fort Worth Star-Telegram*, October 23, 1910.
82. "Fort Worth a Growing Grain Market," 224; *Morrison & Fourmy's General Directory of the City of Fort Worth 1899–1900*, 235.
83. "Fort Worth a Growing Grain Market," 222.
84. *Warehousing Farm Products*, 1, 3, 7, 10, 11.
85. "Federal Storage Space," *New York Times*, October 27, 1921.
86. "Sherman Leading Milling Center of the Southwest," *Sherman Daily Democrat*, May 12, 1925.
87. "Fort Worth Mills Grind for Europe," *Fort Worth Star-Telegram*, June 25, 1905; *Fort Worth Star-Telegram*, July 7, 1913.
88. Seals, *Ponder*, 41; "Complete History of Myra," Cooke County Public Library, 33.
89. Collins, "William Wheat Collins," 204.
90. *Operative Miller* 15 (1910): 205.
91. *Lindsay, Texas*, 22–23.
92. "Fort Worth Mills Grind for Europe," *Fort Worth Star-Telegram*, June 25, 1905.

93. "Improvements Will Raise City's Grain Storage Capacity," *Fort Worth Star-Telegram*, January 8, 1917.
94. *Fort Worth Star-Telegram*, June 12, 1908.
95. "Sherman to Increase Grain Storage Room," *Fort Worth Star-Telegram*, April 23, 1932.
96. Banham, *Concrete Atlantis*, 113.
97. "E. C. Gibson Tells about Birth of Whitewright," *Whitewright Sun*, October 7, 1948.
98. "Shafting Causes Elevator Fire," *Fort Worth Star-Telegram*, August 19, 1909.
99. "Grain Elevator Explodes; Loss Reaches $125,000," *Fort Worth Star-Telegram*, June 7, 1913; "Bewley Elevator at Krum to Be Rebuilt," *Fort Worth Star-Telegram*, January 11, 1915.
100. "Elevator Fire Causes Loss of $75,000," *Dallas Daily Times Herald*, October 25, 1921.
101. Frisco Bicentennial Society, *History of Frisco, 1902–1976*, 166.
102. Banham, *Concrete Atlantis*, 111, 115.
103. Kowsky, "Monuments of a Vanished Prosperity," 39.
104. Tarbet, *Grain Dust Dreams*, 19–20; Banham, *Concrete Atlantis*, 115.
105. "Flour Mill Enlarges," *Fort Worth Star-Telegram*, February 17, 1914; "Testing Out of McKinney's Greatest Industry," *McKinney Weekly Democrat-Gazette*, January 28, 1915.
106. "Grain Elevator under Construction," *Fort Worth Star-Telegram*, June 22, 1924; "Contract Is Let for Ten New Tanks," *Fort Worth Star-Telegram*, October 19, 1924; "$80,000 Elevator Permit Is Granted," *Fort Worth Star-Telegram*, December 16, 1928; "New Addition to Elevator Planned," *Fort Worth Star-Telegram*, January 9, 1930.
107. "Burrus Company Dedicates Texas' Largest Flour Mill," *Fort Worth Star-Telegram*, February 16, 1936.
108. "Welcome Visitors to the Twenty-Fifth Annual Convention Texas Grain Dealers Association," *Fort Worth Star-Telegram*, May 26, 1922.
109. "Watch for Swindling," *Southern Mercury*, July 27, 1899; "Texas Millers," *Sherman Daily Register*, July 5, 1900; "Grain and Mill Men Meeting," *Weekly Democrat-Gazette* (McKinney), May 30, 1907.
110. "Charters Filed," *Dallas Morning News*, June 8, 1901, and August 17, 1905; "Millers Form a Buying Company," *Fort Worth Record and Register*, August 9, 1905.
111. Gardner, "Texas Antitrust Law," 16.
112. "Sues Texas Flour Trust," *New York Times*, November 10, 1907; "Sues the Miller: Attorney General Asks over Fifteen Million Dollars in Penalties," *Dallas Morning News*, November 10, 1907.
113. "Sues the Miller: Attorney General Asks over Fifteen Million Dollars in Penalties," *Dallas Morning News*, November 10, 1907.
114. "Millers' Case in Fall," *Denison Daily Herald*, February 12, 1908.
115. "Sues the Miller: Attorney General Asks over Fifteen Million Dollars in Penalties," *Dallas Morning News*, November 10, 1907.

116. "Agreed Judgment in Millers' Suits," *Dallas Morning News*, January 6, 1909; "The State of Texas vs. Wichita Mill & Elevator Company et al."
117. "Alliance Mill Officer Talks," *Denton Record and Chronicle*, January 8, 1909.
118. "An Inspector of Grain at This Market," *Fort Worth Star-Telegram*, November 17, 1904.
119. *Book of Fort Worth*, 107.
120. Letters from A. Grant and Farmersville Mill and Light Co., *Operative Miller* 15 (1910): 325; *Operative Miller* 16 (1911): 165.
121. Barr, "Flour Mills of Fort Worth"; "Fort Worth a Growing Grain Market," 222.
122. "Custodian for Elevators New Exchange Plan," *Fort Worth Star-Telegram*, May 20, 1917.
123. "Burrus Mill and Elevator," *Fort Worth Star-Telegram*, August 30, 1907; *Fort Worth Star-Telegram*, August 7, 1913; Davis, *Encyclopedia of Texas*, 862; "Sherman Leading Milling Center of the Southwest," *Sherman Daily Democrat*, May 12, 1925; "New Universal Plant Running," *Fort Worth Star-Telegram*, November 27, 1932.
124. *Retail Merchants' Association's Denton City Directory*, 24, 31, 40, 47, 54, 63, 68, 82, 83, 84.
125. See, for example, the entry for John H. Hopkins, a laborer at the Burrus Mill, *Fort Worth City Directory 1920*.
126. "Grinding Floor Gossip," 354.
127. "Pride of the Southwest, 131.
128. Tarbet, *Grain Dust Dreams*, xiii.
129. "Mill Employee Will Recover from Fall," *Fort Worth Star-Telegram*, March 6, 1922; "Cleburne Family Immune from Accidental Death, Friends Believe," *Fort Worth Star-Telegram*, July 13, 1924; "Cot Is Used to Rescue Worker," *Fort Worth Star-Telegram*, July 21, 1931; "Injured in Fall," *Fort Worth Star-Telegram*, October 22, 1939.
130. *Fort Worth Elevator Co. v. Russell*, April 12, 1930, https://www.courtlistener.com/opinion/4152912/fort-worth-elevator-v-russell/.
131. "Miller's [*sic*] Teams Play Fast Sunday Game," *Fort Worth Star-Telegram*, June 13, 1910; *Fort Worth Star-Telegram*, April 10, 1922.
132. "Labor Notes," *Fort Worth Star-Telegram*, June 18, 1916; "1,600 in Labor Day Parade," *Fort Worth Star-Telegram*, September 4, 1916.
133. "Union Votes Sick Fund; Mill Owner Adds to Benefit," *Fort Worth Star-Telegram*, August 16, 1917.
134. "50 Quit Work at Flour Mill Here," *Fort Worth Star-Telegram*, August 29, 1919.
135. National Labor Relations Board, "In the Matter of Tex-O-Kan Flour Mills Company"; National Labor Relations Board, "Decisions and Orders."
136. "Flour for the Family," *Fort Worth Star-Telegram*, May 17, 1903; "Fort Worth Mills Grind for Europe," *Fort Worth Star-Telegram*, June 25, 1905; "Group of Employees of Burrus Mills," *Fort Worth Star-Telegram*, May 23, 1910; *Fort*

Worth Star-Telegram, July 7, 1913; "'Light Crust' Flour Invades Foreign Field," *Fort Worth Star-Telegram*, November 25, 1913; Jack Gordon, "Bewley Mills Ship Flour to All Parts of Globe," *Fort Worth Press*, January 20, 1923; "Sherman Leading Milling Center of the Southwest," *Sherman Daily Democrat*, May 12, 1925; Davis, *Encyclopedia of Texas*, 862; Cowling, *Geography of Denton County*, 62.

137. *The Yucca 1915*, 220.
138. *Dallas Morning News*, October 20, 1891, and August 31, 1913.
139. Whitehead, "Life Used to Be Different," 113; Hawks, "Rural Life in the Twenties and Thirties," 124; Hestand, "Country Boy's Dream," 30; Amos and J. D. Dotson, *Mt. Springs Oral History*, 23; Jones and Park, "From Feed Bags to Fashion," 97; Montgomery, *Cotton and Thrift*, 5.
140. Derr, "Memories of Living on 'Crow's Nest,'" 32; McVay, "Colwell Family," 14.
141. "Points for the Family," *Dallas Morning News*, October 25, 1908.
142. Montgomery, *Cotton and Thrift*, 6.
143. Montgomery, *Cotton and Thrift*, 19.
144. *McKinney Examiner*, March 12, 1936.
145. Montgomery, *Cotton and Thrift*, 5.
146. "Sherman Milling Firm Merchandises Flour in Cut-Out Package," *Dallas Morning News*, September 1, 1935.
147. O'Daniel, "Molly O's Pen Pals."
148. Gouldy, "25 Years Later."
149. "Rain of Course: G & B Picnic Day," *Fort Worth Star-Telegram*, June 5, 1907.
150. "Plenty to Eat at Pure Food Display," *Fort Worth Star-Telegram*, March 20, 1906.
151. "40 Gay Booths and Pretty Girls in Big Food Show," *Fort Worth Star-Telegram*, March 8, 1908; "Wins Bride at Food Show," *Fort Worth Star-Telegram*, March 18, 1908; *Fort Worth Daily Gazette*, February 2, 1892.
152. "Pilot Grove Fair Was Big Success," *Whitewright Sun*, September 27, 1928.
153. Cooke County Public Library, *Premium List*, Cooke County Free Fair.
154. *Dallas Morning News*, April 6, 1936, May 10, 1936, and June 7, 1936.
155. *Dallas Morning News*, June 7, 1936.
156. Southern Laboratory Kitchens, *100 Centennial Recipes*, 6.
157. Southern Laboratory Kitchens, *100 Centennial Recipes*, contents; Nichols, "The History of Dallas Food."
158. Southern Laboratory Kitchens, *100 Centennial Recipes*, [3].
159. Boyd, *Western Swing*, 9.
160. "Burrus Mills Entertainers to Be Heard," *Fort Worth Star-Telegram*, June 21, 1929.
161. "'Cully' Culpepper Appears on Burrus Mill Radio Program Tonight," *Fort Worth Star-Telegram*, February 8, 1930.
162. Stricklin, "Development of the Musical Career of Bob Wills," 26–27, 28–30; Dempsey, *Light Crust Doughboys*, 24–25, 27, 29.

163. Stricklin, "Development of the Musical Career of Bob Wills," 27; Dempsey, *Light Crust Doughboys*, 28.
164. Stricklin, "Development of the Musical Career of Bob Wills," 30; Dempsey, *Light Crust Doughboys*, 31.
165. O'Daniel, "O'Daniel Subs for Regular Announcer," *Dallas Morning News*, September 2, 1938; Stricklin, "Development of the Musical Career of Bob Wills," 30–31; Dempsey, *Light Crust Doughboys*, 33–34.
166. Stricklin, "Development of the Musical Career of Bob Wills," 34–35, 38; Dempsey, *Light Crust Doughboys*, 28–29, 33–34, 45, 51–53.
167. Fowler and Crawford, *Border Radio*, 163–165; Dempsey, *Light Crust Doughboys*, 39–42.
168. "Burrus Mills Dedication to Be Broadcast," *Fort Worth Star-Telegram*, February 15, 1936.
169. Dempsey, *Light Crust Doughboys*, 98.
170. Dempsey, *Light Crust Doughboys*, 82, 83, 85, 91.
171. "Calf Roping Is Hit at Rodeo," *Fort Worth Star-Telegram*, July 5, 1939.
172. Dempsey, *Light Crust Doughboys*, 92, 104, 106, 107, 108.
173. Dempsey, *Light Crust Doughboys*, 116; "Radio Artists Here to Make Records," *Fort Worth Star-Telegram*, August 21, 1937.
174. Dempsey, *Light Crust Doughboys*, 58.
175. Fowler and Crawford, *Border Radio*, 166.
176. *Fort Worth Star-Telegram*, December 25, 1932, December 26, 1932, and January 22, 1933.
177. "Have Sung over 5,000 Numbers," *Fort Worth Star-Telegram*, October 20, 1935.
178. *Fort Worth Star-Telegram*, March 12, 1933.
179. Terrell, *Chuck Wagon Gang*, 28.
180. *Timpson Weekly Times*, December 15, 1933.
181. Terrell, *Chuck Wagon Gang*, 27–28. The family was apparently no relation to the Carter family of Virginia and Tennessee, who made their first recordings in 1927.
182. Terrell, *Chuck Wagon Gang*, 31.
183. Terrell, *Chuck Wagon Gang*, 32, 48.
184. *Dallas Morning News*, January 9, 1933, and January 10, 1933.
185. "Peg Moreland," Hillbilly-Music.com.
186. *Dallas Morning News*, March 2, 1933, and August 31, 1934.
187. *Dallas Morning News*, March 4, 1933.
188. *Dallas Morning News*, February 18, 1936.
189. *Fort Worth Star-Telegram*, April 30, 1939; *Dallas Morning News*, October 2, 1938, and June 16, 1939; *Grand Saline Sun*, September 22, 1938.
190. *Comanche Chief*, March 31, 1939; *Stamford Leader*, June 30, 1939; *Goldthwaite Eagle*, July 14, 1939.
191. Saigling, "The Saigling House"; "Saigling House," US Department of the Interior.

192. "Burrus-Finch House," US Department of the Interior.
193. Reily, *Georgia O'Keeffe*, 43.
194. Roark, *Fort Worth and Tarrant County*, 74–75.
195. Fox, *Country Houses of John F. Staub*, 136–144.
196. "Universal Mills Occupies New Office Building," *West Texas Today* (November 1940).
197. Nichols, "Mix One Part Cement with Two Parts Family"; "Fort Worth Mill Sets Celebration," *Dallas Morning News*, September 27, 1953; Parsons and Bush, *DFW Deco*, 64–65.
198. Karbach, "Modern Woman," 76.
199. "Mrs. M. P. Bewley," *Fort Worth Star-Telegram*, July 28, 1930; Barker, "Samuel Moore Gaines," 445; Oglesby, "History of the Fort Worth Art Association," 20.
200. Oglesby, "History of the Fort Worth Art Association," 25.
201. Oglesby, "History of the Fort Worth Art Association," 70.
202. Suchurowsky, *Nana*.
203. "'Nana' Returns," *Fort Worth Star-Telegram*, May 10, 1908.
204. "First Appearance Here since 1894. Nana, the World's Greatest Painting," *Fort Worth Star-Telegram*, May 10, 1908.
205. "Nana Must Soon Leave Ft. Worth," *Fort Worth Star-Telegram*, May 19, 1908.
206. Barker and Myers, *Intimate Modernism*, 11–12, 14–15, 21.
207. Curlee, "Kimbell, Velma Fuller."
208. *Fort Worth Star-Telegram*, June 30, 1935.
209. Loud, "History of the Kimbell Art Museum," 3.
210. Saigling, "The Saigling House."
211. "Digital Sanborn Fire Maps (Gainesville, 1922), ProQuest; Whaley Church, [home page]; "A Flour Mill and a Church," Ancestry.com; "History of Whaley United Methodist Church in Cooke County, Texas," Ancestry.com.
212. Durham, "Uncle George"; Biderman, *They Came to Stay*, 234.
213. "Schepps Cottage History Related to Family Bureau," *Dallas Morning News*, April 25, 1941.
214. "Many Despondent Humans Saved by Family Consultation Bureau," *Dallas Morning News*, September 13, 1940.
215. Biderman, *They Came to Stay*, 234.
216. McLeRoy, *Adoption Activist Edna Gladney*, 21, 23, 26, 29.
217. McLeRoy, *Adoption Activist Edna Gladney*, 33.
218. McLeRoy, *Adoption Activist Edna Gladney*, 36.
219. McLeRoy, *Adoption Activist Edna Gladney*, 39, 41.
220. Piester, *For the Love of a Child*, 11.
221. Piester, *For the Love of a Child*, 11.
222. Piester, *For the Love of a Child*, 13–14.
223. McLeRoy, *Adoption Activist Edna Gladney*, 46.

224. Piester, *For the Love of a Child*, 13.
225. Undated clipping in "Gladney, Edna W. Mrs. Sam" vertical file, Sherman Public Library.

CHAPTER 8: HOMEMADE SWEETS AND STANDARDIZED BREAD

1. Amos and J. D. Dotson, *Mt. Springs Oral History*, 23.
2. Orbie and Velma Ingram, *Mt. Springs Oral History*, 32.
3. Bessie Gooch Steele, *Mt. Springs Oral History*, 65.
4. *Dallas Morning News*, October 17, 1901.
5. *Dallas Morning News*, February 20, 1913.
6. "Winners Announced in Cooking Contests," *Dallas Morning News*, February 23, 1913.
7. "Exhibits for Free Cooking School Put In," *Fort Worth Star-Telegram*, April 8, 1916.
8. "Baking Contest Prize Winners," *Fort Worth Star-Telegram*, April 16, 1916.
9. *Fort Worth Star-Telegram*, February 5, 1933; *Fort Worth Star-Telegram*, February 12, 1933.
10. Neuhaus, *Housework*, 110–111, 115.
11. Baptist Ladies' Aid and Missionary Society, *Peace Maker Cook Book*, 43.
12. Aby, *Bewley's Best Bakes Better*, inside front cover.
13. Aby, *Bewley's Best Bakes Better*, 8.
14. *Better Bread Foods*, 37.
15. "Recipes Used by First Prize Winners," 1–8.
16. "A New Morning Program," *Dallas Morning News*, November 12, 1936; "Kitchen Club," *Dallas Morning News*, January 7, 1937. I have found no evidence that Mary Lane was a real person.
17. "How Betty Crocker Got Its Start," General Mills.
18. *Mary Lane's Book of Baking* [1936]. This copy of the cookbook is in the Texas Collection at Baylor University in Waco.
19. *Mary Lane's Book of Baking* [1936].
20. *Bryan Eagle*, March 4, 1938.
21. *Abilene Reporter-News*, June 12, 1928; *Bryan Eagle*, November 9, 1931; *Waco Tribune-Herald*, December 11, 1932.
22. Standifer, *Practical Recipes for Using La France Flour*.
23. Fort Worth Charity Club, *True and Tried Cook Book*, 22.
24. *Lone Star Cookbook by the Ladies of the First Christian Church*, 83–84.
25. *Lone Star Cookbook by the Ladies of the First Christian Church*, 83–84.
26. Broadway Baptist Church, *Broadway Baptist Cook Book*, 31–32; Ladies' of the Dallas Free Kindergarten, *Lone Star Cookbook*, 69; Woman's Shakespeare Club, *Woman's Shakespeare Club Cook Book*, 63.

27. Orbie and Velma Ingram, *Mt. Springs Oral History*, 33.
28. Harris, "How Times Have Changed," 159; "Life Sketches," 105.
29. "Memories of 'Ga Ga,'" 41, 46.
30. Etha [probably Etha Ann Chandler Drury] to Mary Ann Moore, February 12, 1909, Moore Family Papers.
31. *Lone Star Fort Worth*, 15; Aby, *Bewley's Best Bakes Better*, 12.
32. Aby, *Bewley's Best Bakes Better*, 17.
33. Jewel Potts Cook, *Mt. Springs Oral History*, 15.
34. Richard Daniel, *Mt. Springs Oral History*, 18.
35. Fred and Edna Jones Haynie, *Mt. Springs Oral History*, 30.
36. Baker, "Rosa Winder Lively," 27; Ledbetter and Graham, "Bethel Community," 8.
37. Cooke County Public Library, *Premium List*, Cooke County Free Fair, 65.
38. Thompson, "Vincent Haywood Haizlip," 267.
39. Baker, "Rosa Winder Lively," 27; Ledbetter and Graham, "Bethel Community," 8.
40. Ciaccio, "From Sicily, Italy, to Texas," 105–106.
41. Aby, *Bewley's Best Bakes Better*, 3.
42. Thompson, "Vincent Haywood Haizlip," 267; *Lone Star Fort Worth*, 3.
43. Ciaccio, "From Sicily, Italy, to Texas," 105–106.
44. *Lone Star Fort Worth*, 3, 5.
45. *Lone Star Fort Worth*, 5.
46. *Lone Star Fort Worth*, 11; Three Married Men of the Central Presbyterian Church, *50 Selected Recipes by 50 Denton Women*, 44.
47. Woman's Club of Fort Worth, *Woman's Club of Fort Worth Cook Book*, 135.
48. Broadway Baptist Church, *Broadway Baptist Cook Book*, 31; St. Paul's Episcopal Church, *Delicious Tidbits*, 33; *Lone Star Fort Worth*, 7.
49. *Lone Star Fort Worth*, 9; Three Married Men of the Central Presbyterian Church, *50 Selected Recipes by 50 Denton Women*, 14, 20; Woman's Shakespeare Club, *Woman's Shakespeare Club Cook Book*, 63.
50. Graham, "Churning for Butter," 45.
51. St. Peter's Guild, *St. Peter's Guild Cook Book*, 14; Woman's Club of Fort Worth, *Woman's Club of Fort Worth Cook Book*, 138; Episcopal Church of the Incarnation, *Culinary Crinkles*, 6.
52. *Lone Star Fort Worth*, 19.
53. *Lone Star Fort Worth*, 78–79; Three Married Men of the Central Presbyterian Church, *50 Selected Recipes by 50 Denton Women*, 60.
54. *Lone Star Fort Worth*, 76.
55. Junior League of Dallas, *Junior League of Dallas (Incorporated) Cook Book*, 120.
56. Episcopal Church of the Incarnation, *Culinary Crinkles*, 24.
57. First Baptist Church of Dallas Sodalitan Bible Class, *Cook Book*, 70; Three Married Men of the Central Presbyterian Church, *50 Selected Recipes by 50 Denton Women*, 28.

58. Broadway Baptist Church, *Broadway Baptist Cook Book,* 37; *Lone Star Fort Worth,* 80.
59. Derr, "Memories of Living on 'Crow's Nest,'" 31.
60. Lewis, untitled, 25.
61. St. Paul's Episcopal Church, *Delicious Tidbits,* 43; Woman's Shakespeare Club, *Woman's Shakespeare Club Cook Book,* 46; Junior League of Dallas, *Junior League of Dallas (Incorporated) Cook Book,* 169.
62. First Baptist Church of Dallas Sodalitan Bible Class, *Cook Book,* 52, 53; Junior League of Dallas, *Junior League of Dallas (Incorporated) Cook Book,* 168.
63. First Baptist Church of Dallas Sodalitan Bible Class, *Cook Book,* 54; *Favorite Recipes of Ex-Students,* 35.
64. Cooke County Public Library, *Premium List,* Cooke County Free Fair, 65.
65. "Presbyterian Ladies Stage Successful Show," *Celina Record,* October 18, 1934.
66. *Lone Star Fort Worth,* 84; Three Married Men of the Central Presbyterian Church, *50 Selected Recipes by 50 Denton Women,* 44, 46.
67. Broadway Baptist Church, *Broadway Baptist Cook Book,* 39; *Lone Star Fort Worth,* 86–87; Three Married Men of the Central Presbyterian Church, *50 Selected Recipes by 50 Denton Women,* 16.
68. Broadway Baptist Church, *Broadway Baptist Cook Book,* 35.
69. Broadway Baptist Church, *Broadway Baptist Cook Book,* 41; Three Married Men of the Central Presbyterian Church, *50 Selected Recipes by 50 Denton Women,* 40; *Lone Star Fort Worth,* 83.
70. *Lone Star Fort Worth,* 85.
71. *Lone Star Fort Worth,* 84.
72. Adair, "Katherine Thomas Good," 8; Russell, "I'm Reminded," 32.
73. Bessie Gooch Steele, *Mt. Springs Oral History,* 65.
74. Fort Worth Charity Club, *True and Tried Cook Book,* 26.
75. Three Married Men of the Central Presbyterian Church, *50 Selected Recipes by 50 Denton Women,* 60; *McKinney Weekly Democrat-Gazette,* July 14, 1921.
76. Aby, *Bewley's Best Bakes Better,* 28.
77. "Queries and Answers," *American Cookery.*
78. First Baptist Church of Dallas Sodalitan Bible Class, *Cook Book,* 64; Woman's Club of Fort Worth, *Woman's Club of Fort Worth Cook Book,* 153, 167.
79. Derr, "Memories of Living on 'Crow's Nest,'" 29.
80. Fort Worth Charity Club, *True and Tried Cook Book,* 19.
81. Episcopal Church of the Incarnation, *Culinary Crinkles,* 15.
82. *Fort Worth Morning Register,* February 12, 1916; *Gainesville Daily Register and Messenger,* April 6, 1917; *Whitewright Sun,* June 8, 1939; *Denison Press,* December 2, 1939.
83. Maude Riley Davis, *Mt. Springs Oral History,* 22; Gilmore, *Ozark Baptizings,* 103–110.
84. Patterson, "Lillie, Our Little Lady," 46.

85. Hall, *The Way It All Began*; St. Peter's Episcopal Church, "Fruitcake Ministry"; "Yearly Fruitcake Project Begins at Episcopal Church," *McKinney Courier-Gazette*, September 25, 1951; Baskin, "McKinney Fruitcake."
86. Montague, "More Truth than Poetry."
87. *Fort Worth Star-Telegram*, April 2, 1922.
88. St. Peter's Guild, *St. Peter's Guild Cook Book*, frontispiece.
89. *Lone Star Fort Worth*, 40.
90. Biderman, *They Came to Stay*, 238; *Dallas Morning News*, May 12, 1930; "Three Brothers Opening Up Own Bakery in City," *Dallas Morning News*, June 8, 1930; "Ad-Right Contest," *Dallas Morning News*, November 8, 1930.
91. *Retail Merchants' Association's Denton City Directory*, 90.
92. Hunt and Bryant, *Denison*, 76.
93. *Fort Worth Star-Telegram*, October 29, 1917.
94. *The Jewish Monitor*, January 16, 1920.
95. Nitsche, "Bakery Workers"; "Rites Today for 65-Year Resident," *Dallas Morning News*, October 25, 1949.
96. Rubin, "The Rubin and Steinberg Families Get to Texas," 10.
97. *Fort Worth Star-Telegram*, May 12, 1918.
98. *Fort Worth Star-Telegram*, September 9, 1917.
99. *Fort Worth Star-Telegram*, June 10, 1918.
100. *Fort Worth Star-Telegram*, March 9, 1918; *Denton Record-Chronicle*, November 11, 1918.
101. *Whitewright Sun*, August 23, 1918.
102. *Directory of the City of Fort Worth, 1905–06*; Cuellar, "Stories," 77–78.
103. Cuellar, "Stories," 177, 186, 188, 192–193, 205. Maria Luna opened her Dallas factory in 1924, but she made only corn tortillas.
104. *Whitewright Sun*, January 21, 1937.
105. *Whitewright Sun*, July 19, 1912, May 11, 1917, August 9, 1918, April 25, 1919, and August 29, 1919.
106. *Whitewright Sun*, March 8, 1923, June 21, 1923, and November 15, 1923.
107. *Whitewright Sun*, December 13, 1923, December 29, 1923, January 10, 1924, May 1, 1924, and August 21, 1924.
108. *Whitewright Sun*, October 9, 1924, November 13, 1924, April 2, 1925, and August 27, 1925.
109. *Whitewright Sun*, March 15, 1928.
110. *Whitewright Sun*, January 28, 1932.
111. *Whitewright Sun*, October 13, 1932, and May 25, 1933.
112. *Whitewright Sun*, October 15, 1936.
113. Three Married Men of the Central Presbyterian Church, *50 Selected Recipes by 50 Denton Women*, 53.
114. *Denton Record-Chronicle*, June 28, 1929.
115. *Denton Record-Chronicle* July 12, 1929. Unfortunately, the newspaper did not publish Simpson's essay.
116. *Fort Worth Star-Telegram*, October 22, 1908.

117. *Fort Worth Star-Telegram*, April 6, 1912.
118. *Fort Worth Star-Telegram*, February 1, 1932.
119. *Fort Worth Star-Telegram*, June 25, 1904, June 18, 1907, January 18, 1908, June 23, 1910, July 5, 1920, August 2, 1921, October 24, 1922, and December 5, 1922; Three Married Men of the Central Presbyterian Church, *50 Selected Recipes by 50 Denton Women*, 27.
120. *Fort Worth Star-Telegram*, December 5, 1918.
121. *Fort Worth Star-Telegram*, December 25, 1921; September 6, 1917.
122. Panschar, *Baking in America*, 59–62.
123. *Fort Worth Star-Telegram*, March 31, 1907.
124. *Fort Worth Star-Telegram*, May 29, 1921.
125. *Fort Worth Star-Telegram*, December 25, 1921.
126. *McKinney Democrat*, August 27, 1903.
127. *Fort Worth Morning Register*, August 24, 1901; *Fort Worth Star-Telegram*, August 12, 1920; April 11, 1916, and June 1, 1919.
128. *Fort Worth Star-Telegram*, April 16, 1922, and December 10, 1939.
129. *Fort Worth Star-Telegram*, August 1, 1922.
130. "Purity Bakery Invites You to Their 10th Anniversary Party Saturday," *Denton Record-Chronicle*, June 5, 1940.
131. "Mrs. Ninnie L. Baird Foundation History," in "Baird Family" vertical file, Fort Worth Public Library; "Mother's Legacy Lives On," *Fort Worth Star-Telegram*, May 8, 1977; "Mrs. Baird First Baked Bread in Kitchen Stove," *Fort Worth Press*, January 24, 1960; "Mrs. Baird's Bread: Over 90 Years of Baking," pamphlet in "Baird Family" vertical file, Fort Worth History Center.
132. "Mrs. Baird's Bread Company," US Department of the Interior.
133. "Rolling Pin Has Come and Gone for Mrs. Baird," *Fort Worth Star-Telegram*, July 19, 1938; "Mrs. Baird's Bread: Over 90 Years of Baking," pamphlet in "Baird Family" vertical file, Fort Worth History Center.
134. "Opening New Bakery May 1 in Oak Cliff," *Dallas Morning News*, February 16, 1930; *Dallas Morning News*, May 12, 1930.
135. "Ex-Bakery Employe [*sic*] Wins Damage Suit," *Fort Worth Star-Telegram*, April 15, 1937.
136. "Mrs. Baird's Bread: Over 90 Years of Baking," pamphlet in "Baird Family" vertical file, Fort Worth History Center.
137. "Mrs. Baird's Bread: Over 90 Years of Baking," pamphlet in "Baird Family" vertical file, Fort Worth History Center.
138. *Fort Worth Star-Telegram*, September 19, 1914.
139. "Bakery Employe [*sic*] Hurt," *Fort Worth Star-Telegram*, October 9, 1934.
140. *Whitewright Sun*, July 30, 1925.
141. "Man Burns to Death in Els' Bakery Fire," *Dallas Morning News*, March 5, 1918; June 15, 1906, July 3, 1922, and September 15, 1922.
142. "Whole Block Shaken When Blast Occurs," *Denison Press*, January 18, 1937.
143. "Mrs. Baird's Bread: Over 90 Years of Baking," pamphlet in "Baird Family" vertical file, Fort Worth History Center.

144. *Fort Worth Star-Telegram*, April 14, 1916.
145. *Fort Worth Star-Telegram*, September 27, 1931.
146. *Dallas Morning News*, April 29, 1907.
147. *Fort Worth Star-Telegram*, September 13, 1931; July 22, 1935.
148. See Kaufman, *A Vision of Unity*, for a general history of bakers' unions in the United States before World War II.
149. "The Bakers' Strike: Little New Developments Yesterday—Meeting of the Union to Be Held Sunday," *Fort Worth Morning Register*, November 24, 1900.
150. "Causes Little Surprise. The Telegraphers' Strike Was Considered Hopeless," *Fort Worth Morning Register*, December 22, 1900.
151. "Fort Worth Bakers Threaten to Strike over Wage Scale," *Fort Worth Star-Telegram*, April 17, 1912; "Pickets Out in Bakery Strike; No Disorders. Both Sides Claim to Be in Control of Situation—No Concessions," *Fort Worth Star-Telegram*, April 20, 1912; *Fort Worth Star-Telegram*, May 12, 1912, and May 13, 1912; "Union Bakers Hold Joint Picnic Today. 'Get Acquainted' Gathering Is Announced for Hermann Park," *Fort Worth Star-Telegram*, June 23, 1912; *Fort Worth Star-Telegram*, August 3, 1913, and May 31, 1916.
152. Nitsche, "The Bakery Workers."
153. "Bakers' Union Has Enrolled 106 Members," *Fort Worth Star-Telegram*, July 6, 1919; "Bakers on Strike as Result of Wage Cut," *Fort Worth Star-Telegram*, May 3, 1921.
154. "Bakers Resume Work under Former Scale," *Fort Worth Star-Telegram*, May 4, 1921.
155. Bakery and Confectionery Workers' International Union, *Official Report 1926*, 40.
156. Nitsche, "The Bakery Workers."
157. Bakery and Confectionery Workers' International Union, *Joint Report 1936*, 43.
158. "Packing Firms Will Conform," *Fort Worth Star-Telegram*, August 6, 1933; "Union Baker Use Expected," *Fort Worth Star-Telegram*, September 17, 1933.
159. "Order Further Bakery Complaint Hearing," *Fort Worth Star-Telegram*, August 10, 1934; "Labor Investigator Due in Bakery Case," *Fort Worth Star-Telegram*, August 16, 1934; "Leonard Labor Row Hearing Is Resumed," *Fort Worth Star-Telegram*, August 19, 1934.
160. "Proceedings, Dallas Central Labor Body, Friday, January 19." *Dallas Craftsman*, January 26, 1934.
161. "Wheat Shortage Affects Bakers," *Dallas Craftsman*, August 17, 1934; "Another Dallas Bakery Signs Up with Bakers Union," *Dallas Craftsman*, November 23, 1934; *Dallas Craftsman*, December 21, 1934.
162. "Baking Plant's Growth Steady since 1912," *Fort Worth Star-Telegram*, March 5, 1937; "12 Bakers in Walkout Here," *Fort Worth Star-Telegram*, April 12, 1937; "12 Bakers Still Out," *Fort Worth Star-Telegram*, April 13, 1937; "Arbitration Agreed Upon," *Fort Worth Star-Telegram*, April 14, 1937; "See Amicable End

of Bakers' Strike," *Fort Worth Star-Telegram*, April 16, 1937; "Bakers Fail to Settle Strike," *Fort Worth Star-Telegram*, April 17, 1937; "Fort Worth Strikes End," *Fort Worth Star-Telegram*, April 18, 1937; "Bakery Talks May Reopen," *Fort Worth Star-Telegram*, April 19, 1937; "Settlement in Bakery Strike," *Fort Worth Star-Telegram*, April 19, 1937; "Bakery, Union Reach Accord," *Fort Worth Star-Telegram*, April 22, 1937; "Union Plans Drive among Bakeries," *Fort Worth Star-Telegram*, May 1, 1937; "Bakery Workers Will Meet to Form Union," *Fort Worth Star Telegram*, May 21, 1937.

163. "New Wage-Hour Law Hits 1,000 in Ft. Worth," *Fort Worth Star-Telegram*, October 22, 1938.
164. "A. & P. Employs Only Skilled Union Bakers," *Dallas Craftsman*, May 19, 1939; "Purity Baking Company Unfair to Bakers Union," *Dallas Craftsman*, September 29, 1939; "Dallas Central Labor Council Happenings," *Dallas Craftsman*, December 8, 1939; "Grennan Bakeries Sign Agreement with Local 111," *Dallas Craftsman*, April 19, 1940.
165. "Bricks and Shots Fly; 9 Held in Dallas Strike," *Fort Worth Star-Telegram*, May 7, 1940; "Bakers Enjoined to Halt Violence," *Dallas Morning News*, May 28, 1940; "Union Denies Part in Rock Throwing," *Dallas Morning News*, May 8, 1940.
166. *Fort Worth Star-Telegram*, April 13, 1915, May 20, 1921, August 21, 1921, and June 13, 1922; *The Jewish Monitor*, February 18, 1921.
167. *Fort Worth-Mail Telegram*, July 2, 1902; *Fort Worth Star-Telegram*, September 25, 1902, November 26, 1920, May 20, 1921, and August 21, 1921.
168. *Fort Worth Star-Telegram*, June 23, 1910, and August 21, 1921.
169. *Fort Worth Star-Telegram*, November 26, 1920, August 21, 1921, November 20, 1921, and February 8, 1930.
170. *Fort Worth Star-Telegram*, April 2, 1909, November 26, 1918, and August 21, 1921.
171. *Dallas Morning News*, November 30, 1919, and December 14, 1919; *Fort Worth Star-Telegram*, November 16, 1921.
172. *McKinney Democrat*, March 7, 1936, March 9, 1936, March 12, 1936, March 14, 1936, March 16, 1936, June 15, 1936, and June 20, 1936.
173. *Fort Worth Record and Register*, December 2, 1904; *Fort Worth Star-Telegram*, December 18, 1904.
174. *Fort Worth Star-Telegram*, April 8, 1910, August 11, 1910, November 26, 1920, August 21, 1921, and November 28, 1922.
175. *Fort Worth Star-Telegram*, February 1, 1906.
176. *Fort Worth Star-Telegram*, March 19, 1933.
177. Sloan, "Family Affair Business"; *Fort Worth Star-Telegram*, June 19, 1931, and December 2, 1932; "School Food Supplies Are Contracted," *Fort Worth Star-Telegram*, August 31, 1933.
178. "$4,000 Estimated Fire Damage to Bakery," *Fort Worth Star-Telegram*, June 18, 1934, September 7, 1934, and June 14, 1959.
179. "Second Flood Imperils Levees," *Fort Worth Star-Telegram*, April 28, 1915.
180. "Dallas Responds to Call for Help," *Dallas Morning News*, March 23, 1916.

181. "Monster Cake Brings Joy to Poor Children," *Fort Worth Star-Telegram,* May 6, 1921.
182. "Bakers to Give Parts of Sales to Baby Fund," *Fort Worth Star-Telegram,* June 3, 1921.
183. "Bakers See Needs, Give Daily Bread," *Dallas Morning News,* November 25, 1931.
184. Simpson, "Builders of Dallas."
185. "Fort Worth Industries. Manufacturing. What We Do to Give Employment to Our Home Workers. Big Tin-Bucket Brigade," *Fort Worth Morning Register,* August 4, 1901; *Fort Worth Morning Register,* August 7, 1901.
186. *Fort Worth Star-Telegram,* January 22, 1908, July 26, 1921, and November 21, 1921; Rubin, "The Rubin and Steinberg Families Get to Texas," 10.
187. *Denton Record-Chronicle,* May 6, 1919; *Fort Worth Star-Telegram,* February 1, 1922, and February 12, 1922.
188. *Fort Worth Star-Telegram,* November 1, 1905, and April 14, 1920.
189. Marion Day Mullins, interviewed by Ruby Schmidt, April 25, 1977, Tarrant County Archives.
190. *Fort Worth Star-Telegram,* November 20, 1921, and January 9, 1932.
191. *Fort Worth Morning Register,* August 24, 1901.
192. *Fort Worth Star-Telegram,* August 30, 1908.
193. *Denton Record-Chronicle,* May 30, 1930; *Dallas Morning News,* August 19, 1931.
194. *Fort Worth Star-Telegram,* April 21, 1920.
195. *Fort Worth Star-Telegram,* May 7, 1920.
196. "Leonard Bakes Bread, Cakes," *Fort Worth Star-Telegram,* December 4, 1932; "Food First of Many Branches," *Fort Worth Star-Telegram,* December 4, 1932; Buenger and Buenger, *Texas Merchant,* 68, 75.
197. "Fort Worth Industries. Manufacturing. What We Do to Give Employment to Our Home Workers," *Fort Worth Morning Register,* August 4, 1901.
198. *McKinney Democrat,* February 20, 1902; *Denton Record-Chronicle,* July 31, 1919.
199. *Local and Special Laws of the State of Texas,* 340, 577.
200. *Fort Worth Star-Telegram,* January 14, 1908.
201. *Fort Worth Star-Telegram,* September 9, 1919.
202. *Fort Worth Star-Telegram,* September 15, 1920.
203. Panschar, *Baking in America,* 96.
204. *Fort Worth Star-Telegram,* June 24, 1906.
205. *Fort Worth Star-Telegram,* July 2, 1911.
206. *Fort Worth Star-Telegram,* June 6, 1913.
207. *Fort Worth Star-Telegram,* August 6, 1913.

CHAPTER 9: FADING GLORY, WANING MEMORY

1. Robinson, "Dallas Area Crop Yield Outstanding."
2. Dines, Atkins, and Porter, *Wheat,* 16.

3. Atkins, *Quanah Wheat*, 3, 9.
4. "Alamo Is Good for Spring Oats," *Denton Record-Chronicle*, January 29, 1954; Bogan, "New Variety of Soft Wheat."
5. Atkins et al., "Wheat Production in Texas," 10.
6. Dines, Atkins, and Porter, *Wheat*, 12.
7. Muller, "Missed Opportunities," 39.
8. Vance, "Low Wheat Prices."
9. Denton County Texas, "Texas Agricultural Experiment Station No. 6."
10. "Blast Loss over 5 Million," *Fort Worth Star-Telegram*, February 25, 1943.
11. Steen, *Flour Milling*, 92.
12. Barr, "Flour Mills of Fort Worth."
13. "Grain Prices Rise Sharply," *Fort Worth Star-Telegram*, June 30, 1944; "Embargo on 2 Mills Spurs Hunt for Help," *Fort Worth Star-Telegram*, July 15, 1944; "Burrus Wheat Embargo Lifted," *Fort Worth Star-Telegram*, July 21, 1944.
14. *Fort Worth Star-Telegram*, June 18, 1941; Pugh, *Ernest Tubb*, 61–71.
15. Brooks, "'Lightcrust Doughboys' Ride Again."
16. "Mill Equips to Speed Unloading of Grain Cars," *Fort Worth Star-Telegram*, November 4, 1945.
17. Belair, "Asks We Eat Less."
18. Redus, "Familiar Brands Will Be Missing."
19. "Mills to Shut Down for Conversion," *Fort Worth Star-Telegram*, February 25, 1946.
20. "White Flour Returns to Counters Here," *Fort Worth Star-Telegram*, September 7, 1946.
21. Steen, *Flour Milling*, 95.
22. Steen, *Flour Milling*, 121.
23. Barr, "Flour Mills of Fort Worth"; Bounds, Payne, and Smith, *Around Sanger*, 43; *Fort Worth Star-Telegram*, June 20, 1942.
24. Steen, *Flour Milling*, 412.
25. *St. Louis Post-Dispatch*, May 21, 1941.
26. "Dallas Sets New Record in Building," *Dallas Morning News*, October 2, 1947; "Union Shopper Can Get Union-Made Goods Now," *Dallas Craftsman*, April 15, 1955.
27. "Quaker Takes over Mills Here for Operation in Southwest," unsourced newspaper clipping, June 1, 1941, vertical file, The Sherman Museum; undated partial clipping, May 21, 1941, vertical file, The Sherman Museum.
28. "Quaker: Biggest Industry Represented Here," *Sherman Democrat*, September 19, 1946.
29. "Fort Worth Mill Sets Celebration," *Dallas Morning News*, September 27, 1953.
30. "Old Milling Firm Closed after Sale," *Fort Worth Star-Telegram*, October 28, 1957.
31. "Quaker Adds Equipment; Makes Repairs," *Sherman Democrat*, undated, c. 1956.

32. "Quaker Co. Reports Good Third Quarter," *Sherman Democrat,* April 9, 1963.
33. "Fort Worth Exchange Checked 82,000 Carloads in Big Year," *Fort Worth Press,* January 24, 1960.
34. "In the Matter of the Claim of Burris Mills, Incorporated," Foreign Claims Settlement Commission of the United States.
35. Milligan, "Pioneer Texas Grain Firm Makes New Wheat Products."
36. "Parade of Progress, 1856–1965," *Denton Record-Chronicle,* November 28, 1965.
37. "Small Fant Bags Hold Good Things," *Sherman Democrat,* April 11, 1965.
38. "Stanard-Tilton Flour Mill," US Department of the Interior.
39. "Man Killed in Accident," *Dallas Morning News,* October 31, 1974.
40. "ConAgra Mills Produce 25 Tons of Flour Daily," *Sherman Democrat,* July 4, 1976.
41. Wren, "Milling Plant to Be Expanded."
42. "Quaker Oats Workers at Sherman to Strike," *Fort Worth Star-Telegram,* February 20, 1949; "300 Workers Strike at Sherman Plant," *Fort Worth Star-Telegram,* February 22, 1949.
43. "Bewley Mills Vote in Favor of Union," *Fort Worth Star-Telegram,* August 19, 1956; "General Mills Vote OK's Representation," *Fort Worth Star-Telegram,* November 5, 1958; "NLRB Powers in Inquiries Upheld," *Fort Worth Star-Telegram,* June 16, 1959; "Employes [*sic*] OK Union," *Fort Worth Star-Telegram,* July 19, 1960.
44. "165 Millers Strike Plant at Sherman," *Fort Worth Star-Telegram,* June 2, 1962; "Company, Millers Reach Agreement," *Fort Worth Star-Telegram,* July 8, 1962; "Strike at Sherman Plant Ends," *Fort Worth Star-Telegram,* July 9, 1962.
45. "Millers Ink Labor Pact at Sherman," *Fort Worth Star-Telegram,* January 31, 1967.
46. Blalock, "Worker Killed."
47. Danbom, *Born in the Country,* 211.
48. "City Ranks 6th in Grain Storage Centers of Nation," *Fort Worth Star-Telegram,* July 30, 1946.
49. Newsom, "City among Top Centers."
50. *Fort Worth Star-Telegram,* February 12, 1961.
51. "Interstate Has Finished Big Grain Elevator Here," *Fort Worth Star-Telegram,* May 21, 1950. I have been unable to determine the nature of the affiliation.
52. Lucas, "Dorchester," 75.
53. Tackett, "Almost $14 Million Paid."
54. Slaughter, "Elevator Here Texas' Largest."
55. "Fort Worth Exchange Checked 82,000 Carloads in Big Year," *Fort Worth Press,* January 24, 1960.
56. Tackett, "Almost $14 Million Paid."
57. McConal, "Grain Big Business in Fort Worth."

58. *Brownsville Herald*, January 8, 1942.
59. *Corsicana Daily Sun*, January 23, 1942.
60. Steen, *Flour Milling*, 119–120.
61. Highland Park Parent–Teacher Association, *Hi Park Cook Book*, 23, 64, 65, 68.
62. American Association of University Women, *Dallas College Club Cook Book*, 102–103, 119.
63. Roberts, *Photo-Method for Party Baking*, 4–5, 6–7, 8–9, 16–17.
64. Sharpless, *Grain and Fire*, 197; Friendship Class of Oak Cliff Methodist Church, *Favorite Recipes*, 35, 49.
65. Preston Hollow Presbyterian Church, *Food for Thee*, 120, 121, 122, 125, 141, 182, 187.
66. Woman's Society of Christian Service, *Kitchen Happiness*, 5.
67. Woman's Society of Christian Service, *Kitchen Happiness*, 2, 3, 5, 6, 7, 9, 71, 72, 74, 77, 81. The debate over whether the term is "sheath cake" or "sheet cake" continues into the twenty-first century. See Sharpless, *Grain and Fire*, 197–198.
68. Corbitt, *Helen Corbitt's Cookbook*, 221, 235, 252, 257, 259, 276, 300, 305.
69. "Women gathered at a bake sale in Mosier Valley," photograph caption, Portal to Texas History.
70. Panschar, *Baking in America*, 228.
71. Panschar, *Baking in America*, 224.
72. "Mrs. Baird's Bread: Over 90 Years of Baking," pamphlet in "Baird Family" vertical file, Fort Worth History Center.
73. "Hirscy Bakery," 100.
74. "Let's Bake a Cake," *Irving News*, February 24, 1955.
75. Beam, "History of Collin County," 116.
76. "Buddies Supermarket's New Store Opens Today," *Denton Record-Chronicle*, June 23, 1965; "Harry Furst Obituary," *Dallas Morning News*, September 30, 2007.
77. "Bakers Have 85 Years of Experience," *Irving News*, February 24, 1955.
78. *Denton Record-Chronicle*, June 23, 1965.
79. "Bread Enterprise Here Made from Age Old Recipe," *Grand Prairie Daily News*, February 24, 1955. Mrs. Ballowe's first name is unclear.
80. "Finney's Goes to King Sized Loaf," *McKinney Courier-Gazette*, October 6, 1955.
81. *Denton Record-Chronicle*, April 18, 1965.
82. *Denton Record-Chronicle*, November 3, 1965.
83. *Denton Record-Chronicle*, May 30, 1965.
84. *Grand Prairie Daily News*, May 17, 1953, July 9, 1953, May 5, 1960, and November 18, 1965.
85. *Grand Prairie Daily News*, January 14, 1965; *Plano Daily Star-Courier*, July 28, 1965.

86. "Miss King's Kitchens Plays Role in Operation Desert Storm," *Denison Herald*, March 31, 1991; Lyde, "Remembering Sherman's Miss King"; "Miss Zelma Moore Is Grayson Home Agent," *Whitewright Sun*, November 30, 1944.
87. Mims, "Little Red Box."
88. Duncan, "Smith, Lucille Elizabeth Bishop."
89. *McKinney Courier-Gazette*, August 11, 1955, and October 27, 1955.
90. Panschar, *Baking in America*, 237.
91. *Dallas Morning News*, May 9, 1955; *Denton Record-Chronicle*, May 19, 1955.
92. *Denton Record-Chronicle*, November 17, 1949, and July 14, 1955.
93. Panschar, *Baking in America*, 239.
94. Nitsche, "Bakers' Union No. 111."
95. Holmes, "Mrs. Baird's to Open Nation's Largest Plant."
96. "Good Bread Baking Is Baird's Job," *Austin American*, June 8, 1960.
97. "Breaking Bread: Landmark Fort Worth Baird's Plant Bakes Its Last Loaf," *Fort Worth Star-Telegram*, April 30, 1992; "History," US Department of the Interior; "Even Though We're Moving, We'll Still Be Right under Your Nose," pamphlet in "Baird Family" vertical file, Fort Worth History Center.
98. "Krum Personals," *Denton Record-Chronicle*, June 6, 1965.
99. Nitsche, "Bakers' Union No. 111."
100. Nitsche, "The Bakery Workers."
101. Nitsche, "Bakers' Union No. 111."
102. "Denison Get[s] Another Big M'f'g Plant," *Denison Press*, December 7, 1945; "Local Business Makes Change in Name," *Denison Press*, June 29, 1951.
103. *Fort Worth Star-Telegram*, July 11, 1949.
104. "Bakers Union Number 111 Signs Closed Shop Contract with Dallas Baking Concerns," *Dallas Craftsman*, April 11, 1947.
105. Nitsche, "The Bakery Workers."
106. "Bakery and Confectionary Workers," *Dallas Craftsman*, May 7, 1954; "Bakers Sign Three Year Agreement," *Dallas Craftsman*, June 13, 1958; "Bakery and Confectionary Workers," *Dallas Craftsman*, October 2, 1959.
107. Nitsche, "The Bakery Workers."
108. Nitsche, "Bakers' Union No. 111"; *Dallas Craftsman*, May 2, 1952, June 20, 1952, and August 28, 1959.
109. Nitsche, "Bakers' Union No. 111."
110. "Dallas Bakery Charged in Suit," *Dallas Craftsman*, November 18, 1966.
111. "Bakery and Confectionary Workers," *Dallas Craftsman*, July 23, 1954; *Dallas Craftsman*, May 1, 1959, and August 4, 1961.
112. "Bakery and Confectionary Workers," *Dallas Craftsman*, May 15, 1964; *Dallas Craftsman*, May 22, 1964.
113. "Bakery and Confectionary Workers," *Dallas Craftsman*, March 23, 1962; *Dallas Craftsman*, May 4, 1962.
114. "Bakery and Confectionary Workers," *Dallas Craftsman*, April 23, 1965.
115. "Bakery and Confectionary Workers," *Dallas Craftsman*, March 25, 1965.

EPILOGUE

1. Kimbell Art Museum, "Three New Masterpieces."
2. Ardent Mills, "Saginaw Mill."
3. Miller Milling, "Our Mills."
4. Gladney Center for Adoption, "Gladney Home."
5. US Department of Agriculture, *Texas Agricultural Statistics 2022*, 48.

BIBLIOGRAPHY

ARCHIVAL SOURCES: HARD COPY

Baker Library Special Collections and Archives, Harvard Business School, Cambridge, Massachusetts

R. G. Dun & Company credit report volumes. Series: Texas.

Collin County, Texas, 1851–1873. Texas, vol. 7, Mss:791 1840–1895 D987. Cooke County is in volume 7 as well.

Dallas County, Texas, 1851–1877. Texas, vol. 8, Mss:791 1840–1895 D987.

Denton County, Texas, 1850–1876. Texas, vol. 9, Mss:791 1840–1895 D987.

Grayson County, Texas, 1849–1879. Texas, vol. 14, Mss:791 1840–1895 D987.

Tarrant County, Texas, 1849–1878. Texas, vol. 28, Mss:791 1840–1895 D987.

Briscoe Center for American History, University of Texas at Austin

Premium List and Rules and Regulations of the Second Annual Industrial Exposition and Agricultural Fair of the North Texas Fair Association: To Be Held at Dallas, Texas, October 22 to 27, Inclusive, 1877. Dallas: Dallas Commercial Steam Printing House, 1877.

Cooke County Public Library, Gainesville, Texas

Premium List, Cooke County Free Fair, Gainesville, TX, 169, 170. Cooke County history files: Fair. September 19, 20, 21, and 22, 1917.

"A Complete History of Myra, Texas (Cooke County) by the Pupils of the Myra Highschool [*sic*] 1923–24" (typescript).

Dallas Historical Society, Dallas, Texas

Sarah Horton Cockrell Collection

Fort Worth History Center, Fort Worth, Texas

Vertical file: Agriculture: Fort Worth Chamber of Commerce "Livestock and Agriculture in the Fort Worth Area," pamphlet, c. 1940

Vertical file: Baird Family

Fort Worth Public Library

Vertical file: Baird Family, "Mrs. Ninnie L. Baird Foundation History"

Vertical file: Mills. Willard Barr, "Flour Mills of Fort Worth," *Fort Worth Press*, undated (c. 1940) clipping

Sherman Museum, Sherman, Texas

Vertical file: Sherman Business: Quaker Oats, Kimbell-Diamond Milling, BGR Smith Milling, "Quaker Takes over Mills Here for Operation in Southwest," unsourced newspaper clipping, June 1, 1941

Vertical file: Sherman Business: Quaker Oats, Kimbell-Diamond Milling, BGR Smith Milling, undated partial clipping, May 21, 1941

Sherman Public Library, Sherman, Texas

Vertical file: "Gladney, Edna W. Mrs. Sam," undated clipping

PRIMARY SOURCES: DIGITAL

Ancestry.com

"A Flour Mill and a Church." https://www.ancestry.com/mediaui-viewer?_phcmd=u(%27https://www.ancestry.com/search/?name=James+Oscar+Andrew_Whaley&birth=1845_rhea-tennessee-usa_2505&death=1909_gainesville-cooke-texas-usa_76706&child=Fannie_Whaley&child2=Robert+Marvin_Whaley&child3=Emonez+Tennessee+%E2%80%9CEmma%E2%80%9D_Whaley&child4=James+Neely_Whaley&child5=Amy+Gertrude_Whaley+Stapleton&child6=Nicholas+M._Whaley&child7=Summerfield_Whaley&father=John_Whaley&gender=m&marriage=1865_rhea-tennessee-usa_2505&mother=Mary+%E2%80%9CPolly%E2%80%9D_Airheart&priority=usa&residence=1870_gainesville-cooke-texas-usa_76706&residence2=1850_rhea-tennessee-usa_2505&residence3=1905_cooke-texas-usa_732&residence4=1900_justice-brazoria-texas-usa_76406&residence5=1880_cooke-texas-usa_732&searchMode=advanced&searchType=t&sibling=Missouri+Henneger_Whaley&sibling2=Tennessee+Catherine_Whaley&sibling3=Henry+A_Whaley&sibling4=Thomas+F_Whaley&spouse=Mary+Isabelle_Keith&treePerson=101604694_222379579644&successSource=Search&queryId=45657e05-b090-4a8f-b7a4-aaf764505957%27,%27success-Source%27. Accessed May 11, 2025.

"History of Whaley United Methodist Church in Cooke County, Texas." https://www.ancestry.com/mediaui-viewer/collection/1030/tree/12583157/person/12502290974/media/cce3e1a9-cd59-4887-a33f-9d02ae489b7c?queryId=35aceb79-e9fc-4ed0-a09d-5fc29b9ed7c8&searchContextTreeId=101604694&searchContextPersonId=222379579644&_phsrc=OKJ3338&_phstart=successSource. Accessed May 11, 2025.

Mauck, Eliza Smith. Pension application, September 14, 1914, "Alabama, Texas, and Virginia, US, Confederate Pensions, 1884–1958." https://www.ancestry.com/discoveryui-content/view/316011:1677?tid=&pid=&queryId=637d5cf9af9bc871d86a6f103b9f62da&_phsrc=ANT1755&_phstart=successSource. Accessed December 22, 2022.

Yeary, John Benedict. Soldier's application for Confederate pension, "Alabama, Texas and Virginia, US, Confederate Pensions, 1884–1958." https://www.ancestry.com/search/collections/1677/records/272068?tid=72498374&pid=142072383235&queryId=4107d994-6d9d-41a6-934b-1de199609131&_phsrc=OKJ2809&_phstart=successSource. Accessed January 25, 2025.

Yeary, Walter R. "US, Civil War Soldier Records and Profiles, 1861–1865." https://www.ancestry.com/search/collections/1555/records/2999860?tid=182223878&pid=382368216643&queryId=e09aca2f-fe77-4fbf-b587-0a3fa1008319&_phsrc=OKJ2803&_phstart=successSource. Accessed January 25, 2025.

Findagrave.com

"Hermann Christian Barthold Sr." Created March 28, 2008. https://www.findagrave.com/memorial/25573886/hermann-christian-barthold. Accessed January 25, 2024.

"Lanson Cullum Clark." Created January 19, 2008. https://www.findagrave.com/memorial/24055125/lanson-cullum-clark. Accessed January 25, 2025.

"Catherine Malloy 'Cattie' Bunting Coit." Created March 21, 2009. https://www.findagrave.com/memorial/35048438/catherine-malloy-coit. Accessed May 11, 2025.

"Rev. James E. Scott." Created March 14, 2011. https://www.findagrave.com/memorial/66895709/james-edward-scott. Accessed January 25, 2025.

"Judge John E. Wheeler." Created August 27, 2012. https://www.findagrave.com/memorial/96075711/john-e-wheeler. Accessed January 25, 2025.

Mt. Springs Community Club and the North Texas State University Oral History Project

Mt. Springs Oral History: A Community Project for the 1986 Texas Sesquicentennial. https://www.txgenwebcounties.org/cooke/mt_springs_pages-1-46.pdf and http://sites.rootsweb.com/~txcooke/pt2_mt_springs_pages-1-37.pdf. Both accessed December 16, 2022.

ProQuest.

"Digital Sanborn Fire Maps, 1967–1870: Texas." https://about.proquest.com/en/products-services/sanborn/.

US Department of the Interior, National Park Service

"National Register of Historic Places Continuation Sheet: Burrus-Finch House." October 8, 1987. https://atlas.thc.texas.gov/NR/pdfs/87001671/87001671.pdf. Accessed August 7, 2022.

"National Register of Historic Places Registration Form: Everard Sharrock Jr. Farmstead." October 19, 2015. https://npgallery.nps.gov/GetAsset/6cdbecd1-f2f3-4eb2-a49d-92c3a8fcfaca. Accessed December 11, 2023.

"National Register of Historic Places Nomination Form: Mrs. Baird's Bread Company." https://dallascityhall.com/departments/sustainabledevelopment/historicpreservation/HP%20Documents/Resources%20Page/Mrs.%20Bairds%20Bread%20NRHD%20Form.pdf. Accessed January 17, 2025.

"National Register of Historic Places Registration Form: Saigling House." March 27, 2018. https://atlas.thc.state.tx.us/NR/pdfs/100002434/100002434.pdf. Accessed August 8, 2022.

"National Register of Historic Place Registration Form: Stanard-Tilton Flour Mill," August 21, 1997. https://dallascityhall.com/departments/sustainabledevelopment/historicpreservation/HP%20Documents/Landmark%20Structures/American%20Beauty%20Stanard-Tilton%20Mill%20National%20Register%20Nomination%20Form.pdf. Accessed June 27, 2024.

Tarrant County Archives, Fort Worth, Texas

Katherine O'Riley Hester, interviewed by Mrs. W. A. Schmidt, Fort Worth, Texas, April 16, 1975. Ruby Schmidt Collection or Bicentennial Interviews, Oral Histories of Fort Worth, Inc. https://access.tarrantcounty.com/content/dam/main/archives/OHFWHesterKatherineO.pdf.

Victor Tinsley, interviewed by Mrs. W. A. Schmidt, Fort Worth, Texas, March 4, 1975. Ruby Schmidt Collection or Bicentennial Interviews, Oral Histories of Fort Worth, Inc. https://access.tarrantcounty.com/content/dam/main/archives/OHFWTinsleyVictor.pdf.

Portal to Texas History. https://texashistory.unt.edu/

Charles B. Moore Family Papers, 1832–1917.

"Women gathered at a bake sale in Mosier Valley," caption on photograph in Tarrant County College, Northeast Heritage Room. Accessed September 23, 2023.

PRINT SOURCES

A. M. Ferguson and Company. *Field Seeds as Good as We Can Make Them*. Sherman, TX: Ferguson Seed Farms, 1912.

Abshire, Richard. *Garland: A Contemporary History*. San Antonio: Historical Publishing Network, 2009.

Acheson, Sam, and Julie Ann Hudson O'Connell, eds. "George Washington Diamond's Account of the Great Hanging at Gainesville, 1862." *Southwestern Historical Quarterly* 66 (January 1963): 331–414.

Adair, Kent. "Katherine Thomas Good." *Elm Fork Echoes* 19, no. 1 (May 1991): 8–9.

Adair, W. W. "Dallas Was an Island in 1866." *Dallas Morning News*, September 3, 1922.

Adams, Frank Carter. *State of Texas Building: Central Exposition, Texas Centennial Celebrations, Dallas, 1836–1936*. Austin: Steck Co., 1937.

Andrews, John N. "Agricultural Cooperation in Collin County, Texas from 1870–1936." Master's thesis, University of Texas, 1926.

"An Anniversary Timeline for Dallas County." *Legacies: A History Journal for Dallas and North Central Texas* 25, no. 2 (Fall 2013): 4–7.

"Archibald T. Buchanan." *Elm Fork Echoes* 20 (May 1992): 53–54.

Atkins, I. M., K. B. Porter, Keith Lahr, Owen G. Merkle, and M. C. Futrell. "Wheat Production in Texas." *Texas Agricultural Experiment Station Bulletin* 948 (1969). https://hdl.handle.net/1969.1/87869.

Atkins, Irvin Milburn. *Quanah Wheat*. College Station: Texas Agricultural Experiment Station, Bulletin 734, May 1951.

Austin, Kenneth E. "Feild, Julian." Texas State Historical Association, January 1, 1995. https://www.tshaonline.org/handbook/entries/feild-julian.

Baker, Anna Brown. "Rosa Winder Lively Takes a Few Steps Down Memory Lane." *Elm Fork Echoes* 2, no. 1 (April 1974): 27–29.

Bakery and Confectionery Workers' International Union of America. *Official Report and Proceedings of the Convention, 1926*. Bakery and Confectionery Workers' International Union of America, 1926.

Bakery and Confectionery Workers' International Union of America. *Joint Report of the International Officers and the General Executive Board to the Twentieth Convention*. Bakery and Confectionery Workers' International Union of America, 1929.

Bakery and Confectionery Workers' International Union of America. *Joint Report of the International Officers and the General Executive Board to the Twenty-First and Golden Anniversary Convention*. Bakery and Confectionery Workers' International Union of America, 1936.

Banham, Reyner. *A Concrete Atlantis: US Industrial Building and European Modern Architecture*. Cambridge, MA: MIT Press, 1986.

Barker, Scott Grant. "Samuel Moore Gaines: A Pioneering Art Collector in Early Fort Worth." *Southwestern Historical Quarterly* 107, no. 3 (January 2004): 434–456.

Barnes, Donna A. *Farmers in Rebellion: The Rise and Fall of the Southern Farmers Alliance and People's Party in Texas*. Austin: University of Texas Press, 1984.

Barnhart, Ryan, and Ryan Estes. *McKinney*. Charleston, SC: Arcadia, 2011.

Barry, Billie. "History of Krum." In *Towns and Communities of Denton County, Texas*, edited by Emily Fowler and Alma Lain Chambers, 34–35. Denton County History Page, 2013. https://www.dentonhistory.net/page52/page88/krum.html. Accessed December 18, 2024.

Baskin, Robert E. "McKinney Fruitcake Wins World Fame." *McKinney Courier-Gazette*, November 19, 1954.

Bates, F., ed. *History and Reminiscences of Denton County*. Denton: McNitzsky Print Company, 1918.

Baum, Dale. *The Shattering of Texas Unionism: Politics in the Lone Star State during the Civil War Era*. Baton Rouge: Louisiana State University Press, 1998.

Beam, Harold. "A History of Collin County, Texas." Master's thesis, University of Texas, 1951.

Belair, Felix, Jr. "Asks We Eat Less: President Calls People to Help as Generously as They Did in War." *New York Times*, February 8, 1946.

Bezner, Hugo. "Bezner Bros. Threshers." In *Lindsay, Texas: First One Hundred Years—1882–1982*, 113. Muenster, TX: Muenster Enterprise, 1992.

Biderman, Rose G. *They Came to Stay: The Story of the Jews in Dallas*. Austin: Eakin Press, 2002.

Bilsing, S. W. "The Green Bug: Or Spring Grain Aphis." Texas Agricultural Experiment Station Circular 13 (March 1916).

Bizzell, William B. *Rural Texas*. New York: Macmillan Company, 1924.

Blalock, Fred. "Worker Killed as Grain Collapses in Bin Mishap." *Fort Worth Star-Telegram*, October 1, 1967.

Bogan, Allen. "New Variety of Soft Wheat, Frisco Showing Up Well Here." *Denton Record-Chronicle*, May 16, 1954.

Bogue, Allan G. "Farming in the Prairie Peninsula, 1830–1890." *Journal of Economic History* 23, no. 1 (March 1963): 3–29.

Bomar, George W. *Weather in Texas: The Essential Handbook*, 3rd ed. Austin: University of Texas Press, 2017.

The Book of Fort Worth. Fort Worth: Fort Worth Record, 1913.

Bounds, Helen Seely, Tona Batis Payne, and Nancy Campbell Smith. *Around Sanger*. Charleston, SC: Arcadia Publishing, 2011.

Bridges, Clarence A. *History of Denton, Texas: From Its Beginning to 1960*. Waco, TX: Texian Press, 1978.

Brinkley, Leola. "Cunningham, Howard Houston." In Grayson County Frontier Village, *The History of Grayson County Texas*, vol. 1, 97–98. Winston-Salem, NC: Hunter Publishing Co., 1979.

Brooks, Elston. "'Lightcrust Doughboys' Ride Again, via New LP Album." *Fort Worth Star-Telegram*, October 5, 1970.

Brown, Heather. *Tenant Farming in Collin County, 1890–1920*. Plano, TX: Heritage Farmstead Association, 1997.

Brown, William J. *American Colossus: The Grain Elevator, 1843 to 1942*, rev. ed. Brooklyn, NY: Colossal Books, 2015. (Originally published in 2009.)

Bryan, James. "Henry S. Moore: An Early Astronomer in Texas." *Southwestern Historical Quarterly* 107, no. 2 (October 2003): 163–199.

Buecker, Thomas R. *Water Powered Flour Mills in Nebraska*. Lincoln: Nebraska State Historical Society, 1983.

Buenger, Victoria L., and Walter L. Buenger. *Texas Merchant: Marvin Leonard and Fort Worth*. College Station: Texas A&M University Press, 1998.

Buenger, Walter. *Secession and the Union in Texas*. Austin: University of Texas Press, 1984.

Butler, Steven R. "Pioneer Personified: The Life and Times of Capt. Preston Witt." *Legacies: A History Journal for Dallas and North Central Texas* 11, no. 2 (Fall 1999): 4–16.

Butterfield, Jan. "Kimbell Building among Kahn Best." *Fort Worth Star-Telegram*, October 1, 1972.

Campbell, Mozelle Jones, Maribelle McLaurine Davids, Betty Harrington Stranz, Frances Bates Wells, and Shirley Carter Schell, eds. *Plano, Texas: The Early Years*. Friends of the Plano Public Library. Wolfe City, TX: Henington Publishing Company, 1985.

Campbell, Randolph B. *Empire for Slavery: The Peculiar Institution in Texas, 1821–1865*. Baton Rouge: Louisiana State University, 1989.

Cantrell, Gregg. *The People's Revolt: Texas Populists and the Roots of American Liberalism*. New Haven, CT: Yale University Press, 2020.

Carlson, Avery Luvere. *A Monetary and Banking History of Texas from the Mexican Regime to the Present Day, 1821–1929*. Fort Worth: Fort Worth National Bank, 1930.

Carpenter, Carrie Cooper. "William Creager." In *Ancestors and Descendants: Grayson County, Texas*, compiled and edited by Grayson County, Texas Genealogical Society, 210. Dallas: Taylor Publishing Co., 1980.

Carraro, Francine. *Jerry Bywaters: A Life in Art*. Austin: University of Texas Press, 1994.

Casstevens, Katie. "Neighbors We Know." *Mansfield News*, January 10, 1946.

Castleberry, Vivian Anderson. *Daughters of Dallas: A History of Greater Dallas through the Voices and Deeds of Its Women*. Dallas: Odenwald Press, 1994.

Chambers, Aubrey Nesbit. "Aubrey Nesbit Chambers." In *Ancestors and Descendants: Grayson County, Texas*, compiled and edited by Grayson County, Texas Genealogical Society, 194–195. Dallas: Taylor Publishing Co., 1980.

"The Chapman Milling Company's New Mill at Sherman, Texas." *The Roller Mill* (November 1898).

Ciaccio, Nick. "From Sicily, Italy, to Texas." In *Telling Our Stories: Grayson County Reminisces: The First 150 Years, 1846–1996*, edited by Jerry Bryan Lincecum, 104–109. Sherman: Big Barn Press, 1996.

Clampitt, Bradley R. *Lost Causes: Confederate Demobilization and the Making of Veteran Identity*. Baton Rouge: Louisiana State University Press, 2022.

Clark, Adelle Rogers. *Lebanon on the Preston: A Casual Biography of a Blackland Village*. Wolfe City, TX: Henington Publishing Company, 1959.

Cline, Janice Craze. *Historic Downtown Plano*. Charleston, SC: Arcadia Publishing, 2012.

Cochran, John H. *Dallas County: A Record of Its Pioneers and Progress*. Dallas: Arthur S. Mathis, 1928.

Cochran, Mike. "Blue Mound Community: A German Methodist Community in Denton County." Denton County History Page, n.d. https://www.dentonhistory.net/page65/page22/. Accessed June 27, 2024.

"Collin County Farm Museum Digital Collection." PDF document in author's possession.

Collin County Historical Society. *Collin County in Pioneer Times: Selections from the George Pearis Brown Papers*. McKinney, TX: Collin County Historical Society, 1985.

Collins, William W., Jr. "William Wheat Collins." In *Ancestors and Descendants: Grayson County, Texas*, compiled and edited by Grayson County, Texas Genealogical Society, 204. Dallas: Taylor Publishing Co., 1980.

"Commercial Feeding Stuffs, 1916–17. Texas Feed Law." *Texas Agricultural Experiment Station Bulletin* 216 (September 1917).

"Commercial Statistics of New Orleans." *Western Journal of Agriculture, Manufactures, Mechanic Arts, Internal Improvement, Commerce, and General Literature* 1, no. 10 (October 1848): 574–576.

"A Confederate's Experience," attributed to *Dallas Semi-Weekly*, October 18, 1904. *Elm Fork Echoes* 21 (May 1993): 3.

Connell, J. H., and James Clayton. *Field Experiments at McKinney, Wichita Falls, and College Station, with Wheat, Corn, Cotton, Grasses and Manures. Texas Agricultural Experiment Station Bulletin* 34 (February 1895).

Connor, Seymour V. *The Peters Colony of Texas: A History and Biographical Sketches of the Early Settlers*. Austin: Texas State Historical Association, 1959.

Cooper, Abby. "Flusche Brothers Founded Seven Catholic Colonies." *Wichita Falls Times*, May 26, 1957.

Cowling, Mary Jo. *Geography of Denton County*. Dallas: Banks Upshaw and Company, 1936.

Cox, James. *Historical and Biographical Record of the Cattle Industry and the Cattlemen of Texas and Adjacent Territory*. St. Louis: Woodward & Tiernan Printing Co., 1895.

Cronon, William. *Nature's Metropolis: Chicago and the Great West*. New York: W. W. Norton, 1991.

Cuellar, Carlos Eliseo. "Stories from the Barrios: A History of Mexican Fort Worth." PhD diss., Texas Christian University, 1998.

Curlee, Kendall. "Kimbell, Velma Fuller." Handbook of Texas Online, February 1, 1995. https://www.tshaonline.org/handbook/entries/kimbell-velma-fuller. Accessed August 31, 2022.

Danbom, David. *Born in the Country: A History of Rural America*. Baltimore: Johns Hopkins University Press, 1995.

Danvers, Rebecca. "The Charles B. Moore Collection: Interpretation and Annotation." PhD diss., University of Dallas, 1985.

David, Elizabeth. *English Bread and Yeast Cookery*. London: Grub Street, 2010. (Originally published in 1977.)

Davis, Della Isbell, and George U. Hubbard. *Krum*. Charleston, SC: Arcadia Publishing, 2011.

Davis, Ellis Arthur. *The Encyclopedia of Texas*. Dallas: Texas Development Bureau, 1922.

Davis, J. Frank. *The WPA Guide to Texas: The Federal Writers' Project Guide to Texas*. Austin: Texas Monthly Press, 1986.

Dempsey, John Mark. *The Light Crust Doughboys Are on the Air: Celebrating Seventy Years of Texas Music*. Denton: University of North Texas Press, 2002.

Denton Board of Trade. "The Best County in North Texas Is Denton: An Epitome of Her Matchless Resources, Artificial and Natural, Including Her Lands, Cheap in Price, but of Vast Possibilities When It Comes to the Cultivation of the Four Great Staple Crops of Texas." Denton: Chronicle Book and Job Printing House, 1890. Denton County History Page, https://www.dentonhistory.net/page63/. Accessed July 11, 2014.

Denton Business Review and Directory. Denton, TX: Blaine and Forshey, 1890.

Derr, Oleta Maberry. "Memories of Living on 'Crow's Nest.'" *Elm Fork Echoes* 5, no. 1 (April 1977): 29–34.

"Dick." "Letter on the Overland Mail Route." *Dallas Daily Herald*, September 15, 1858.

Dines, Fred T., I. M. Atkins, and K. B. Porter. *Wheat: A Major Cash Crop in Texas*. College Station: Texas Agricultural Extension Service, 1954.

Directory of the City of Fort Worth for the Year 1877. Fort Worth: Printed at the *Daily Democrat* office, 1877.

Directory of the City of Fort Worth, 1905–06. Galveston: Morrison & Fourmy Directory Company, 1905.

Douglas, C. L. "County's 'No. 1 Tenant Farmer' Began Career with One Asset—Determination." *Fort Worth Star-Telegram*, June 2, 1940.

Duncan, Robert J. "Smith, Lucille Elizabeth Bishop." Handbook of Texas Online, February 21, 2013. https://www.tshaonline.org/handbook/entries/smith-lucille-elizabeth-bishop. Accessed February 11, 2023.

Durham, Connie. "Uncle George." *D Magazine*, September 1, 1981. https://www.dmagazine.com/publications/d-magazine/1981/september/uncle-george/. Accessed August 25, 2022.

Enstam, Elizabeth York. "Opportunity versus Propriety: The Life and Career of Frontier Matriarch Sarah Horton Cockrell." *Frontiers* 6, no. 3 (1981): 106–114.

Enstam, Elizabeth York. *Women and the Creation of Urban Life: Dallas, Texas, 1843–1920*. College Station: Texas A&M University Press, 1998.

Enstam, Elizabeth York. "When the Homefront Was the Frontier." *Legacies: A History Journal for Dallas and North Central Texas* 20, no. 1 (Spring 2008): 4–11.

Evans, Samuel Lee. "Texas Agriculture, 1880–1930." PhD diss., University of Texas, 1960.

"Farmer's General Store Ledger." *Collin Chronicles* 20, no. 2 (1999/2000): 52–56.

Farmer's Wife. "Salt Rising for Bread." *Dallas Weekly Herald*, December 9, 1876.

Fitzgerald, Hugh Nugent. "Fort Worth." In *Texans and Their State: A Newspaper Reference Work*, edited by H. T. Warner, Hugh Nugent Fitzgerald, T. C. Gooch, J. S. Bonner, J. L. Mapes, and Edmunds Travis, 112–240. Houston: Texas Biographical Association, 1918.

Flatt, Curtis. "Trinity Mills' Company 'B,' 18th Texas." *Elm Fork Echoes* 31 (May 2003): 11–14.

Floyd, Alice West. "Early Days in Dallas County." *Elm Fork Echoes* 2, no. 2 (November 1974): 24–29.

The Brothers Flusche (Emil, Anton, and August). "Pilot Point: The Center of the Great German Catholic Settlement in Northern Texas." Denton County History Page, 1891. https://www.dentonhistory.net/page65/page23/. Accessed April 9, 2023.

Foote, M. L. "Millwood 72 Years Ago." *McKinney Weekly Democrat Gazette*, August 15, 1929.

Fort Worth Business Directory, 1884: Containing a History of the City and County, with the Business Cards of the Most Prominent and Reliable Business Firms of the City. Fort Worth: Fort Worth Printing House and Book Bindery, 1884.

Fort Worth City Directory 1920. Dallas: Morrison & Fourmy Directory Co., 1920.

"Fort Worth a Growing Grain Market." *Grain Dealers Journal* 41 (1918): 222–225.
Fowler, Gene, and Bill Crawford. *Border Radio: Quacks, Yodelers, Pitchmen, Psychics, and Other Amazing Broadcasters of the American Airwaves*. Austin: University of Texas Press, 2002.
Fox, Stephen. *The Country Houses of John F. Staub*. College Station: Texas A&M University Press, 2007.
Francaviglia, Richard V. *The Cast Iron Forest: A Natural and Cultural History of the North American Cross Timbers*. Austin: University of Texas Press, 2000.
Frisco Bicentennial Society. *The History of Frisco, 1902–1976*. Frisco, TX: Frisco Bicentennial Society, 1976.
Fulkerson, Beb. *Wylie Area Heritage*. Wylie, TX: Self-published, 1990.
Fulkerson, Beb. "Ben Bowman." *Collin Chronicles* 13, no. 2 (Winter 1993): 30–32.
Gage, Fran. "Wheat into Flour: A Story of Milling." *Gastronomica: The Journal of Food and Culture* 6, no. 1 (Winter 2006): 84–92.
Gainesville Daily Register. "Some Facts for the Home-Seeker about Gainesville and Cooke County, Texas," compiled and published by *Gainesville Daily Register*, July 1899.
Gardner, Brennan. "Texas Antitrust Law: Formulation and Enforcement, 1889–1903." Master's thesis, Texas Christian University, 2013.
Garrett, Julia Kathryn. *Fort Worth: A Frontier Triumph*. Austin: Encino Press, 1972.
Gates, Paul W. *Agriculture and the Civil War*. New York: Alfred A. Knopf, 1964.
Gilmore, Robert K. *Ozark Baptizings, Hangings, and Other Diversions: Theatrical Folkways of Rural Missouri, 1885–1910*. Norman: University of Oklahoma Press, 1984.
Gordon, Jack. "Bewley Mills Ship Flour to All Parts of Globe." *Fort Worth Press*, January 20, 1923.
Gose, J. C. "Stories of Some of the Older Families of Krum." In *Towns and Communities of Denton County, Texas*, edited by Emily Fowler and Alma Lain Chambers, 35–38. Denton County History Page, 2013. https://www.dentonpl.com/public/catalog/localhistory/townscommunitiesindentonco.pdf. Accessed December 20, 2023.
Gouldy, Mabel. "25 Years Later, Pappy Points to Old Prophecy." *Fort Worth Star-Telegram*, June 30, 1963.
Graham, Berneice L. "Churning for Butter." *Elm Fork Echoes* 7, no. 1 (April 1979): 45.
Gray, Eunice Sullivan. *The Story of Sanger*. Serialized in the *Sanger Courier*, 1982–1984. Sanger, TX: Self-published, 1986.
Gray, James. *Business without Boundary: The Story of General Mills*. Minneapolis: University of Minnesota Press, 1954.
Gray, Lewis Cecil. *History of Agriculture in the Southern United States to 1860*, 2 vols. Washington, DC: Carnegie Institution of Washington, 1933; reprint, Clifton, NJ: Augustus M. Kelley Publishers, 1973.
Grayson County Frontier Village. *The History of Grayson County Texas*, vol. 1. Winston-Salem, NC: Hunter Publishing Co., 1979.

Grayson County Frontier Village. *The History of Grayson County*, vol. 2. Denison, TX: Grayson County Frontier Village, Inc., 1981.

Grayson County, Texas Genealogical Society, comp. and ed. "Agriculture." In *Ancestors and Descendants: Grayson County, Texas*, 19–21. Dallas: Taylor Publishing Co., 1980.

Grayson County, Texas Genealogical Society, comp. and ed. *Ancestors and Descendants: Grayson County, Texas*. Dallas: Taylor Publishing Co., 1980.

Green, Donald E. "Beginnings of Wheat Culture in Oklahoma." In *Rural Oklahoma*, edited by Donald E. Green, 56–73. Oklahoma City: Oklahoma Historical Society, 1977.

"Grinding Floor Gossip." *Operative Miller* 13 (1908): 354.

Halbach, Mary Louise. "Domesticity in the American South: Catherine Bunting Coit, 1837–1883." Master's thesis, University of Texas at Dallas, 1982.

Hall, Helen Gibbard. *The Way It All Began: McKinney, Texas: A History*. McKinney: Collin County Historical Society, 2006.

Hamilton, Caroline. "City's 99 Tomorrow, but This Family Paved Way for Founding." *Fort Worth Star-Telegram*, June 5, 1948.

Hammond, William J., and Margaret F. Hammond. *La Réunion: A French Settlement in Texas*. Dallas: Royal Publishing Co., 1958.

Hand-Book of Northern Texas. Chicago: Burgh Publishing Company, 1886.

Hanning, Ethel. "Presley, James Royal (Jim)." In Grayson County Frontier Village, *The History of Grayson County Texas*, vol. 1, 537–538. Winston-Salem, NC: Hunter Publishing Co., 1979.

Harris, Mrs. J. M. [Mattie Ruth Witt], ed. *112 Years in Little Elm Community*. Dallas: Banks Upshaw and Company, 1957.

Harris, Thelma. "How Times Have Changed." In *Telling Our Stories: Grayson County Reminisces: The First 150 Years, 1846–1996*, edited by Jerry Bryan Lincecum, 158–163. Sherman, TX: Big Barn Press, 1996.

Hartman, Janie. "Agriculture." In Muenster Centennial Committee, *Muenster, Texas, a Centennial History, 1889–1989*, 36–40. Muenster: Centennial Committee, 1989.

Hawks, Lucille. "Rural Life in the Twenties and Thirties." In *Texas Millennium Book: The Way Things Used to Be*, edited by Jerry Lincecum, 123–126. Sherman: Big Barn Press, 1999.

Hestand, Glyn David. "A Country Boy's Dream." In *Texas Millennium Book: The Way Things Used to Be*, edited by Jerry Lincecum, 29–36. Sherman: Big Barn Press, 1999.

Hill, Patricia Evridge. *Dallas: The Making of a Modern City*. Austin: University of Texas Press, 1996.

Hill, Steve. "Texas Agricultural Experiment Station." Texas State Historical Association, 1976; updated August 13, 2020. https://www.tshaonline.org/handbook/entries/texas-agricultural-experiment-station. Accessed December 3, 2022.

"Hirscy Bakery." In Muenster Centennial Committee, *Muenster, Texas, a Centennial History, 1889–1989*, 100–101. Muenster: Centennial Committee, 1989.

Holmes, Sam F., Jr. "Mrs. Baird's to Open Nation's Largest Plant." *Dallas Morning News*, August 23, 1953.

Holsen, James N. *Economic Survey of Texas*. St. Louis, MO: Southwestern Bell Telephone Company, General Commercial Engineering Department, 1928.

Horn, Robert Cannon. *The Annals of Elder Horn: Early Life in the Southwest*, edited by Claude Harrison Thurman and John Wilson Bowyer. New York: R. R. Smith, 1920.

Hunt, Donna Hord, and Mavis Anne Bryant. *Denison*. Charleston, SC: Arcadia Publishers, 2011.

Hunter, Brooke. "Rage for Grain: Flour Milling in the Mid-Atlantic, 1750–1815." PhD diss., University of Delaware, 2002.

Hurt, R. Douglas. *American Agriculture: A Brief History*. Ames: Iowa State University Press, 1994.

Irwin, James R. "Exploring the Affinity of Wheat and Slavery in the Virginia Piedmont." *Explorations in Economic History* 25, no. 3 (July 1988): 295–322.

Jackson, George. *Sixty Years in Texas*, 2nd ed. Dallas: Wilkinson Print. Co., 1908.

Jenkins, Donna Brumit. *Murphy*. Charleston, SC: Arcadia Publishing, 2012.

Jones, C. N. *Early Days in Cooke County, 1848–1873*. Gainesville, TX: Cooke County Heritage Society, 1977. (Originally published in 1936.)

Jones, Lu Ann, and Sunae Park. "From Feed Bags to Fashion." *Textile History* 24, no. 1 (1993): 91–103.

Jordan, Terry G. "The Imprint of the Upper and Lower South on Mid-Nineteenth Century Texas." *Annals of the Association of American Geographers* 57 (December 1967): 667–690.

Karbach, Ruth. "The Modern Woman." In *Grace and Gumption: Stories of Fort Worth Women*, edited by Katie Sherrod, 63–86. Fort Worth: Texas Christian University Press, 2007.

Kaufman, Stuart Bruce. *A Vision of Unity: The History of the Bakers and Confectioners Workers International Union*. Bakery, Confectionery and Tobacco Workers International Union, 1987.

Kerr, Homer Lee. "Migration into Texas, 1865–1880." PhD diss., University of Texas at Austin, 1953.

Kimbell, [Velma] Mrs. Kay. "Kimbell, Kay (1886–1964)." In Grayson County Frontier Village, *The History of Grayson County*, vol. 2, 253. Tulsa, OK: Heritage Publishing Company, 1981.

Kimmey, John A., Jr. "A Short History of the Round Grove United Church." Denton County History Page, 1975. https://www.dentonhistory.net/page65/page17/. Accessed June 27, 2024.

Knight, Oliver. *Fort Worth: Outpost on the Trinity*. Fort Worth: Texas Christian University Press, 1990.

Koons, Kenneth E., and Warren R. Hofstra. "Preface." In *After the Backcountry: Rural Life in the Great Valley of Virginia, 1800–1900*, edited by Kenneth E. Koons and Warren R. Hofstra, vi–xxix. Knoxville: University of Tennessee Press, 2000.

Kowsky, Francis R. "Monuments of a Vanished Prosperity: Buffalo's Grain Elevators and the Rise and Fall of the Great Transnational System of Grain Transportation." In *Reconsidering Concrete Atlantis: Buffalo Grain Elevators,* edited by Lynda H. Schneekloth, 17–42. Buffalo, NY: Urban Design Project and Landmark Society of the Niagara Frontier, 2007.

Krohe, James, Jr. "The Breaking of the Prairie." *Illinois Issues* (October 1981): 18–24. https://www.lib.niu.edu/1981/ii811019.html. Accessed October 9, 2020.

Lake, Mary Daggett. "A. F. Leonard, Pioneer, Arrived in County 81 Years Ago Today." *Fort Worth Star-Telegram,* December 26, 1926.

Land and Thompson. *Historical and Descriptive Review of the Industries of Dallas, 1884–5.* Dallas: The authors (Land and Thompson), 1885.

Latimer, J. W. "The Wheat Region and Wheat Culture in Texas." In *Texas Almanac 1859,* 64–71. N.p., 1859.

Ledbetter, Buren, and Bernice Ledbetter Graham. "Bethel Community." *Elm Fork Echoes* 2, no. 2 (November 1974): 4–13.

Leidigh, A. H., P. C. Mangelsdorf, and P. B. Dunkle. "Denton Wheat, a New Variety for North Texas." *Texas Agricultural Experiment Station Bulletin* 388 (October 1928).

Leighton, Clare. *Southern Harvest.* New York: Macmillan, 1942.

Lewis, Maurine McDaniel. Untitled. *Elm Fork Echoes* 7, no. 1 (April 1979): 25.

"Life Sketches." *Collin Chronicles* 32, no. 2 (2011–2012): 104–108. Excerpted from *Plano Star Courier,* October 20, 1904.

Lindsay, Texas: First One Hundred Years—1882–1982. Muenster, TX: Muenster Enterprise, 1992.

Lindsley, Philip. *A History of Greater Dallas and Vicinity,* vol. 1. Chicago: Lewis Publishing Co., 1909.

Litchford, Juanita. "Thomas Ables Jackson." In *Ancestors and Descendants: Grayson County, Texas,* compiled and edited by Grayson County, Texas Genealogical Society, 310–311. Dallas: Taylor Publishing Co., 1980.

Loud, Patricia Cummings. "History of the Kimbell Art Museum." In Kimbell Art Museum, *In Pursuit of Quality: The Kimbell Art Museum: An Illustrated History of the Art and Architecture,* 1–95. New York: Harry N. Abrams, 1987.

Lowe, Richard G., and Randolph B. Campbell. *Planters and Plain Folk: Agriculture in Antebellum Texas.* Dallas: Southern Methodist University Press, 1987.

Lucas, Jane Davis. "Dorchester." In Grayson County Frontier Village, *The History of Grayson County Texas,* vol. 1, 63–65. Winston-Salem, NC: Hunter Publishing Co., 1979.

Lucas, Jane Davis. "Graham, William Valentine." In Grayson County Frontier Village, *The History of Grayson County Texas,* vol. 1, 562. Winston-Salem, NC: Hunter Publishing Co., 1979.

Lucas, Mattie Davis, and Mita Holsapple Hall. *A History of Grayson County, Texas.* Sherman: Scruggs Printing Company, 1936.

Lyde, Betsy Rice. "Remembering Sherman's Miss King, Her Contribution to History of City." *Sherman Herald Democrat,* December 24, 2003.

"The Manufacture of Flour at St. Louis." *Western Journal of Agriculture, Manufactures, Mechanic Arts, Internal Improvement, Commerce, and General Literature* 1, no. 1 (January 1848): 53–55.

Markham, Jerry W. *The History of Commodity Futures Trading and Its Regulation.* New York: Praeger Publishing, 1987.

Maxwell, Lisa C. "Wheatland, TX (Dallas County)." Texas State Historical Association, 1952; updated September 1, 1995. https://www.tshaonline.org/handbook/entries/wheatland-tx-dallas-county. Accessed July 14, 2021.

McCaslin, Richard B. *Tainted Breeze: The Great Hanging at Gainesville, Texas, 1862.* Baton Rouge: Louisiana State University Press, 1994.

McConal, Jon. "Grain Big Business in Fort Worth." *Fort Worth Star-Telegram,* July 15, 1962.

McConal, Jon. "Critics Unanimous in Praising Kimbell." *Fort Worth Star-Telegram,* October 3, 1972.

McCoy, Joseph G. *Historic Sketches of the Cattle Trade.* Kansas City, MO: Ramsey, Millett and Hudson, 1874.

McCullum, Vivian Stark. "Robert Thomas Stark Family." In Frisco Bicentennial Society, *History of Frisco, 1902–1976,* 187–190. Frisco, TX: Frisco Bicentennial Society, 1976.

McElhaney, Jackie. "From Oxen to Rails: The Development of Dallas as a Transportation Center." *Legacies: A History Journal for Dallas and North Central Texas* 7, no. 1 (Spring 1995): 8–14.

McLeRoy, Sherrie S. *Texas Adoption Activist Edna Gladney: A Life and Legacy of Love.* Charleston, SC: History Press, 2014.

McMahan, Marie, and Dorothy McMahan Banfield. "McMahan, Eli Franklin." In Grayson County Frontier Village, *The History of Grayson County Texas,* vol. 1, 462–463. Winston-Salem, NC: Hunter Publishing Co., 1979.

McVay, Mabel Colwell. "Colwell Family of Hackberry." *Elm Fork Echoes* 18, no. 1 (April 1990): 12–14.

Melugin, Jay. *Pilot Point.* Charleston, SC: Arcadia Publishers, 2009.

Memorial and Biographical History of Dallas County, Texas . . . : Containing a History of This Important Section of the Great State of Texas, from the Earliest Period of Its Occupancy to the Present Time . . . and Biographical Mention of Many of Its Pioneers, and Also of Prominent Citizens of To-day. Chicago: Lewis Publishing Company, 1892.

"Memories of 'Ga Ga' Pearl Gravley [Pearl Perry Gravley] Written by Her Descendants at Their Annual Pearl Gravley Reunion in 1993." *Elm Fork Echoes* 22 (May 1994): 40–51.

Miller, Ivah Brock, and Oma Lee Scoggin. "Collinsville." In Grayson County Frontier Village, *The History of Grayson County Texas,* vol. 1, 52–53. Winston-Salem, NC: Hunter Publishing Co., 1979.

Milligan, Tom. "Pioneer Texas Grain Firm Makes New Wheat Products." *Dallas Morning News,* August 9, 1964.

Mims, Mollie. "The Little Red Box." *Cleburne Times-Review,* October 12, 2004.

Mock, Cary J. "Drought and Precipitation Fluctuations in the Great Plains during the Late Nineteenth Century." *Great Plains Research* 1 (1991): 26–56.

Montague, James J. "More Truth than Poetry." *Fort Worth Star-Telegram,* April 15, 1922.

Montgomery, Marian Ann J. *Cotton and Thrift: Feed Sacks and the Fabric of American Households.* Lubbock: Texas Tech University Press, 2019.

Morgan, James Oscar. *Field Crops for the Cotton-Belt.* New York: Macmillan Company, 1917.

Morrison & Fourmy's General Directory of the City of Dallas, 1886–87. Dallas: Morrison & Fourmy, 1886.

Morrison & Fourmy's General Directory of the City of Fort Worth 1899–1900. Galveston, TX: Morrison and Fourmy, 1899.

Mouzon, H. D. "Musings." *McKinney Examiner,* March 15, 1962.

Muller, Frances Miers. "Missed Opportunities." *Collin Chronicles* 25, no. 2 (2004/2005): 39.

Myers, Darrell. "Farming-Grain-Harvest." *Elm Fork Echoes* 26 (May 1998): 23–24.

Myers, Jane, and Scott Grant Barker. *Intimate Modernism: Fort Worth Circle Artists in the 1940s.* College Station: Texas A&M University Press, 2008.

Neighbours, Kenneth Franklin. *Robert Simpson Neighbors and the Texas Frontier, 1836–1859.* Waco: Texian Press, 1975.

Neuhaus, Jessamyn. *Housework and Housewives in American Advertising.* New York: Palgrave Macmillan, 2011.

Newsom, W. L. "City among Top Centers for Grain Marketing." *Fort Worth Star-Telegram,* February 12, 1961.

Nichols, Mike. "Mix One Part Cement with Two Parts Family." Hometown by Handlebar (blog post), April 20, 2012. http://www.hometownbyhandlebar/?p=1239 (site discontinued).

Nichols, Mike. *Lost Fort Worth.* Charleston, SC: History Press, 2014.

Nichols, Nancy. "The History of Dallas Food: The Amazing Ida Chitwood." *D Magazine,* July 12, 2011. https://www.dmagazine.com/food-drink/2011/07/the-history-of-dallas-food-the-amazing-mrs-ida-chitwood/. Accessed August 6, 2022.

Nitsche, William. "The Bakery Workers: Do You Know Them." *Dallas Craftsman,* October 28, 1949.

Nitsche, William. "Bakers' Union No. 111." *Dallas Craftsman,* July 6, 1951.

O'Daniel, Molly. "Molly O's Pen Pals." *Dallas Morning News,* October 28, 1938.

O'Daniel, W. Lee. "O'Daniel Subs for Regular Announcer and Makes a Hit." *Dallas Morning News,* September 2, 1938.

Ogle, Georgia. "1860–61 Trinity Mills." *Elm Fork Echoes* 14, no. 1 (April 1986): 5–6.

Oglesby, Resa C. "History of the Fort Worth Art Association." Master's thesis, Texas State College for Women, 1950.

Owens, Virginia Bramblitt. "Chester A. Good." *Elm Fork Echoes* 11, no. 1 (April 1983): 5–7.

Paddock, B. B. *History of Texas: Fort Worth and the Texas Northwest Edition*, 4 vols. Chicago: Lewis Publishing Co., 1922.

Panschar, William G. *Baking in America*, vol. 1, *Economic Development*. Evanston, IL: Northwestern University Press, 1956.

Parsons, Jim, and David Bush. *Fair Park Deco: Art and Architecture of the Texas Centennial*. Fort Worth: TCU Press, 2012.

Patterson, Ollivene. "Lillie, Our Little Lady." *Elm Fork Echoes* 2, no. 1 (April 1974): 43–47.

Perkins, Clay. *The Fort in Fort Worth*. Keller, TX: Cross-Timbers Heritage Publishing Company, 2001.

Peterson, Arthur G. "Flour and Grist Milling in Virginia: A Brief History." *Virginia Magazine of History and Biography* 63 (1935): 97–108.

Pettit, Gwen. *Between the Creeks*. Collection of 1986–1992 columns written for the *Allen Leader* and the *Allen American*, compiled by Melinda Fisher. https://texashistory.unt.edu/ark:/67531/metapth752794/m2/1/high_res_d/Between%20_the_Creeks_by_Gwen_Pettit_compiled_by_Melinda_Fisher.pdf. Accessed June 27, 2024.

Phillips, Omalie. "Krum Main Street Once Was Lined with Wheat Wagons." *Denton Record-Chronicle*, October 24, 1954.

Piester, Ruby Lee. *For the Love of a Child: The Gladney Story*. Austin: Eakin Press, 1987.

Platt, Horace G. *The Law as to the Property Rights of Married Women, as Contained in the Statutes and Decisions of California, Texas, and Nevada*. San Francisco: Sumner Whitney and Co., 1885.

Pointer, Toyia. *Carrollton*. Charleston, SC: Arcadia Publishing, 2008.

Powell, William F. *Cooke County History: Past and Present*. Dallas: Curtis Media Corporation, 1992.

Price, T. A. "Vanished Glory of Trinity Mills Recalled as Town Century Old." *Dallas Morning News*, March 15, 1942.

"Pride of the Southwest." *Operative Miller* 23 (1918).

Pugh, Ronnie. *Ernest Tubb: The Texas Troubadour*. Durham, NC: Duke University Press, 1998.

"Queries and Answers." *American Cookery* 30 (June–July 1925): 24–25.

"The Record." *American Miller* 22 (1894).

Redus, W. L. "Familiar Brands Will Be Missing from New Beige-Colored Flour." *Fort Worth Star-Telegram*, February 25, 1946.

Reily, Nancy Hopkins. *Georgia O'Keeffe: A Private Friendship*, vol. 2, *Walking the Abiquiu and Ghost Ranch Lane*. Santa Fe, NM: Sunstone Press, 2009.

Retail Merchants' Association's Denton City Directory. Denton, TX: Lusk Printing Company, 1924.

Rhode, Paul W. "Do Crops Shape Culture? Contrasting Cotton and Wheat in Nineteenth-Century North America." *Agricultural History* 88, no. 3 (Summer 2014): 416–421.

Rich, Harold W. "Beyond Outpost: Fort Worth, 1880–1918." PhD diss., Texas Christian University, 2006.

Richardson, Rupert. *The Frontier of Northwest Texas, 1846–1976.* Glendale, CA: A. H. Clark Co., 1963.

Roark, Carol, ed. *Fort Worth and Tarrant County: An Historical Guide.* Fort Worth: Texas Christian University Press, 2003.

Robinson, Walter S. "Dallas Area Crop Yield Outstanding." *Dallas Morning News,* June 20, 1954.

Rood, Daniel. "An International Harvest: The Second Slavery, the Virginia-Brazil Connection, and the Development of the McCormick Reaper." In *Slavery's Capitalism: A New History of American Economic Development,* edited by Sven Beckert and Seth Rockman, 87–104. Philadelphia: University of Pennsylvania Press, 2016.

Rubin, Sherwin. "The Rubin and Steinberg Families Get to Texas." *Texas Jewish Historical Society* (Fall 2001, 9/11 Edition): 10–11.

Russell, Dorotha Good. "I'm Reminded." *Elm Fork Echoes* 7, no. 1 (April 1979): 31–33.

Saigling, Rick. "The Saigling House." *Plano Magazine,* January 17, 2017. https://planomagazine.com/saigling-house/. Accessed June 27, 2023.

Santerre, George H. *White Cliffs of Dallas: The Story of La Reunion, the Old French Colony.* Dallas: The Book Craft, 1955.

Scoggin, Oma Lee. "Sanders, Roy Clyde and Edith Annie." In Grayson County Frontier Village, *The History of Grayson County Texas,* vol. 1, 566–567. Winston-Salem, NC: Hunter Publishing Co., 1979.

Seals, Nita. *Ponder: The Little Town with the Big Rodeo.* Gainesville, TX: Gainesville Printing Company, 1985.

Selcer, Richard. "The Widow vs. the Bureaucrats: The Strange Case of Mrs. Captain Ripley Arnold." *Southwestern Historical Quarterly* 107, no. 3 (January 2004): 361–387.

Selzer, Paula, and Emmanuel Pécontal. *Adolphe Gouhenant: French Revolutionary, Utopian Leader, and Teas Frontier Photographer.* Denton: University of North Texas Press, 2019.

Sharpless, Rebecca. *Grain and Fire: A History of Baking in the American South.* Chapel Hill: University of North Carolina Press, 2022.

Sherman Chamber of Commerce. *I'll Tell You about Sherman, Texas.* Sherman, TX, c. 1937.

Simpson, Pamela H. *Corn Palaces and Butter Queens: A History of Crop Art and Dairy Sculpture.* Minneapolis: University of Minnesota Press, 2012.

Simpson, Wallace. "Builders of Dallas—Their Careers: Jake Golman." *Dallas Morning News,* March 26, 1933.

Slaughter, Tony. "Elevator Here Texas' Largest." *Fort Worth Star-Telegram,* August 4, 1957.

Sloan, Marjorie. "Family Affair Business Has Grown into 30-Year-Old Well-Known Bakery." *Fort Worth Press,* October 12, 1950.

Smalley, Eugene V. "The Flour Mills of Minneapolis." *Century Illustrated Magazine* 32 (May 1887): 37–47.

Smith, Thomas T. *The US Army and the Texas Economy, 1845–1900*. College Station: Texas A&M University Press, 1999.

Spaight, A. W. *Resources, Soil, and Climate of Texas by Counties*. Dallas: A. H. Belo, 1882.

Speed, Ronald C. *History of Industry, Sherman, Texas, 1846–2008*. Sherman: Speed 260 Corporation for the Sherman Economic Development Corporation, 2008.

Stahle, D. W., and M. K. Cleaveland. "Texas Drought History Reconstructed and Analyzed from 1698 to 1980." *Journal of Climate* 1 (1988): 59–74.

Stambaugh, J. Lee, and Lillian J. Stambaugh. *A History of Collin County, Texas*. Austin: Texas State Historical Association, 1958.

Stark, Anne. "A History of Dallas County." Master's thesis, University of Texas, 1935.

Starling, Susanne. *Land Is the Cry! Warren Angus Ferris, Pioneer Texas Surveyor and Founder of Dallas County*. Austin: Texas State Historical Association, 1988.

"The State of Texas vs. Wichita Mill & Elevator Company et al.," in *Report and Opinions of the Attorney General of the State of Texas for the Years 1906–1908*, 25–27. Austin: Von Boeckmann-Jones Co., 1909.

Steen, Herman. *Flour Milling in America*. Minneapolis: T. S. Denison and Company, 1963; reprint, Westport, CT: Greenwood Press, 1973.

Stewart, Rick. *Lone Star Regionalism: The Dallas Nine and Their Circle, 1928–1945*. Austin: Texas Monthly Press, 1985.

Storck, John, and Walter Dorwin Teague. *Flour for Man's Bread: A History of Milling*. Minneapolis: University of Minnesota Press, 1952.

Stricklin, David B. "The Development of the Musical Career of Bob Wills, 1929–1938: Folk Forces and Commercialization." Master's thesis, Baylor University, 1978.

Tackett, Johnny. "Almost $14 Million Paid for Grain Storage Here by US." *Fort Worth Press*, October 28, 1962.

Tarbet, David W. *Grain Dust Dreams*. Albany: State University of New York Press, 2015.

Tarrant County, Fort Worth, Texas, Farmers, Stockmen and Dairymen's Directory. Fort Worth: Taliaferro Publishing Co., 1917.

Terrell, Bob. *The Chuck Wagon Gang: A Legend Lives On*. Goodlettsville, TN: Bob Terrell, 1990.

Terrell, J. C. *Reminiscences of the Early Days of Fort Worth*. Fort Worth: Texas Printing Company, 1906.

Texas Almanac and State Industrial Guide for 1904. Dallas: Belo and Co., 1904.

Texas Almanac for 1860. Galveston: Galveston News, 1860.

Texas Almanac for 1867 with Statistics, Descriptive and Biographical Sketches, etc., Relating to Texas. Galveston: W. Richardson and Co., 1866.

Texas Bureau of Immigration. *Texas, the Home for the Emigrant, from Everywhere*. Houston: A. C. Gray, State Printer, 1875.

Texas Real Estate & Collection Bureau. *Immigrants Guide to Texas, 1889*. Dallas: L. A. Wilson, 1889.

Thompson, Estelle Haizlip. "Vincent Haywood Haizlip." In *Ancestors and Descendants: Grayson County, Texas,* compiled and edited by Grayson County, Texas Genealogical Society, 266–267. Dallas: Taylor Publishing Co., 1980.

Thrall, Homer S. *A Pictorial History of Texas, from the Earliest Visits of European Adventurers, to A.D. 1879*. St. Louis: N. D. Thompson, 1879.

"Trip to Pleasant Run." *Dallas Herald,* March 13, 1861.

Vance, James E. "Low Wheat Prices Dog Harvest Paths." *Fort Worth Star-Telegram,* June 1, 1969.

Washburn-Crosby Co. *Wheat and Flour Primer.* Minneapolis: Washburn-Crosby Co., 1915.

Wells, Frances. "Farmer's Song." In *Plano, Texas: The Early Years,* edited by Mozelle Jones Campbell et al., 61–113. Plano: Friends of the Plano Public Library, 1985.

"Western Staples: Wheat and Flour, Indian Corn, Barley, Oats and Rye, Hem, Tobacco, Lead, &c." *Western Journal of Agriculture, Manufactures, Mechanic Arts, Internal Improvement, Commerce, and General Literature* 1, no. 1 (1848): 25–29.

White, Zelda Davis. "Robert Alexander Davis." In *Ancestors and Descendants: Grayson County, Texas,* compiled and edited by Grayson County, Texas Genealogical Society, (219?). Dallas: Taylor Publishing Co., 1980.

Whitehead, Bettie. "Life Used to Be Different." In *Texas Millennium Book: The Way Things Used to Be,* edited by Jerry Lincecum, 111–117. Sherman, TX: Big Barn Press, 1999.

Wilde, Ray J. "Wilde Bros. Threshing Co." In Muenster Centennial Committee, Muenster Centennial Committee, *Muenster, Texas, a Centennial History, 1889–1989,* 66. Muenster: Centennial Committee, 1989.

William Deering, Born in Maine, 1826, Died in Florida, 1913. Chicago: Privately published, 1914.

Winters, Donald L. *Tennessee Farming, Tennessee Farmers: Antebellum Agriculture in the Upper South.* Knoxville: University of Tennessee Press, 1995.

Woodhouse, Connie A., and Jonathan T. Overpeck. "Two Thousand Years of Drought Variability in the Central United States." *Bulletin of the American Meteorological Society* 9 (1998): 2692–2714.

Wooster, Robert. *Soldiers, Sutlers, and Settlers: Garrison Life on the Texas Frontier.* College Station: Texas A&M University Press, 1987.

Worrall, I. R. "Northern Texas." In *Texas Almanac for 1868,* 147–156. Galveston: Galveston News, 1868.

Wren, Worth, Jr. "Milling Plant to Be Expanded." *Fort Worth Star-Telegram,* November 24, 1982.

The Yucca 1915. Denton: North Texas State Normal School, 1915.

Zimmerer, Magdalene Flusche. "Life of the Early Settlers in Muenster, Texas." In Muenster Centennial Committee, *Muenster, Texas, a Centennial History, 1889–1989,* 30–31. Muenster: Centennial Committee, 1989.

COOKBOOKS

Aby, Irene Nevill. *Bewley's Best Bakes Better Bread Pastry Cake*. Fort Worth: Bewley Mills, 1935.

American Association of University Women. *Dallas College Club Cook Book of Texas Recipes*. Dallas: American Association of University Women, 1946.

Baptist Ladies' Aid and Missionary Society. *The Peace Maker Cook Book: Named in Honor of the Celebrated Peace Maker Flour Made by Alliance Milling Co., Denton, Texas*. Bowie, TX: Baptist Ladies' Aid and Missionary Society of the First Baptist Church, 1909.

Beecher, Catharine. *Miss Beecher's Domestic Receipt-Book: Designed as a Supplement to Her Treatise on Domestic Economy*. New York: Harper, 1856.

Better Bread Foods with Bewley's Best Flour. NP, 1940.

Broadway Baptist Church. *Broadway Baptist Cook Book*. Fort Worth: Broadway Baptist Church, 1901.

Church of the Incarnation, Dallas, TX, Primary Mother's Guild. *Culinary Crinkles: Tested Recipes*. N.p., 1929.

Corbitt, Helen. *Helen Corbitt's Cookbook*. Boston: Houghton Mifflin Company, 1957.

Favorite Recipes of Ex-Students of C.I.A., Texas State College for Women. Denton: Texas State College for Women, 1930.

50 Selected Recipes by 50 Denton Women: Young People's Organization of the Central Presbyterian Church Cook Book, compiled and edited by Three Married Men of the Central Presbyterian Church. Denton, TX: Central Presbyterian Church, [c. 1925].

First Baptist Church of Dallas Sodalitan Bible Class. *Constitution and Directory, Cook Book*. Dallas: First Baptist Church of Dallas Sodalitan Bible Class, 1925.

Fort Worth Charity Club. *True and Tried Cook Book*. Fort Worth: Fort Worth Charity Club, 191–?.

Friendship Class of Oak Cliff Methodist Church. *Favorite Recipes*. Dallas: Oak Cliff Methodist Church, 1958.

Highland Park Parent–Teacher Association. *Hi Park Cook Book*. Dallas: Highland Park Parent–Teacher Association, 1942.

Junior League of Dallas. *The Junior League of Dallas (Incorporated) Cook Book*, rev. ed. Dallas: Junior League of Dallas, 1930.

Ladies' [*sic*] of the Dallas Free Kindergarten and Training School, Dallas, Texas. *The Lone Star Cookbook*. Dallas: Samuel Jones Co., 1901.

Ladies of the First Christian Church, Fort Worth, Texas. *Lone Star Cook Book*. Fort Worth: n.p., 1913.

Mary Lane's Book of Baking. Sherman: Better Baking Institute of Sherman, Texas, 1936.

Mary Lane's Book of Baking, rev. ed. Sherman: Better Baking Institute of Sherman, Texas, 1938.

Mary Lane's Book of Baking, rev. ed. Sherman: Scruggs Printing Company, 1939.

Preston Hollow Presbyterian Church. *Food for Thee.* Dallas: Preston Hollow Presbyterian Church, 1961.

"Recipes Used by First Prize Winners in State Fair of Texas Baking Contest with American Beauty Flour." Stanard-Tilton Milling Co., 1935.

Roberts, Virginia. *The Photo-Method for Party Baking.* Dallas: Russell-Miller Milling Co., 1947.

Southern Laboratory Kitchens. *100 Centennial Recipes Celebrating 100 Years of Progressive Flour Milling in Texas.* Dallas: Southern Laboratory Kitchens, 1936.

Standifer, Lenore Miller. *Practical Recipes for Using La France Flour, Tested and Approved by Mrs. Lenore Standifer.* Dallas: Morten Milling Co., [1940].

St. Paul's Episcopal Church. *Delicious Tidbits and Practical Receipts.* Gainesville, TX: St. Paul's Guild, 1904.

St. Peter's Guild, McKinney [Texas] Episcopal Church. *St. Peter's Guild Cook Book.* McKinney: n.p., 1922.

Woman's Club of Fort Worth. *The Woman's Club of Fort Worth Cook Book.* Fort Worth: Woman's Club of Fort Worth, 1928.

Woman's Shakespeare Club. *Woman's Shakespeare Club Cook Book,* compiled by the Woman's Shakespeare Club for the benefit of the Public School Fountain Fund. Denton, TX: "News" Job Office, [1910?].

Woman's Society of Christian Service, Southwood Methodist Church. *Kitchen Happiness Is . . . Granny's Cook Book.* Dallas: Southwood Methodist Church, 1966.

WEBSITES

Abelson, Frances Simpson, and Rheba Rippey Marshall. "History of Bolivar." http://files.usgwarchives.net/tx/denton/history/history.txt. Accessed July 26, 2014.

Ardent Mills. "Saginaw Mill." https://www.ardentmills.com/our-facilities/texas/saginaw-mill/. Accessed September 27, 2023.

Denton County, Texas. "Texas Agricultural Experiment Station No. 6." https://apps.dentoncounty.gov/website/HistoricalMarkers/PDFs/Texas-Agricultural-Experiment-Station.pdf. Accessed April 14, 2024.

"George Washington Baird." https://www.genfiles.com/baird-files/George_Washington_Baird.pdf. Accessed April 9, 2021.

Gladney Center for Adoption. "Gladney Home: A New Beginning." https://adoptionsbygladney.com/i-want-to-adopt/foster-adoption/gladney-home. Accessed September 21, 2023.

Hansen, M. V. "How a Threshing Machine Works." Farm Collector, February 9, 2011. https://www.farmcollector.com/equipment/how-a-threshing-machine-works. Accessed November 10, 2024.

"How Betty Crocker Got Its Start." General Mills, October 21, 2024. https://www.generalmills.com/news/stories/how-betty-crocker-got-its-start. Accessed December 25, 2023.

Hulse, James. "History of the Man House." Historical Marker Database, page last revised April 5, 2022. https://www.hmdb.org/m.asp?m=194867. Accessed April 26, 2023.

Kimbell Art Museum. "History: The Vision of the Founders." https://kimbellart.org/about/history. Accessed March 14, 2023.

Kimbell Art Museum. "Kahn Building in Detail." https://kimbellart.org/content/kahn-building-detail. Accessed March 14, 2023.

Kimbell Art Museum. "Three New Masterpieces Enter the Permanent Collection." October 4, 2022. https://kimbellart.org/news-and-stories/three-new-masterpieces-enter-permanent-collection. Accessed September 21, 2023.

"Mansfield Cemetery." Mansfield Historical Services. https://www.mansfieldtexas.gov/1389/Mansfield-Cemetery. Accessed April 26, 2023.

Miller Milling. "Our Mills." https://millermilling.com/mills/. Accessed September 27, 2023.

"Peg Moreland." Hillbilly-Music.com, n.d. http://www.hillbilly-music.com/artists/story/index.php?id=10453.

Raven, Vern, and Kathryn Howard. "The Salt Creek Massacre." Mansfield Historical Services, n.d. https://www.mansfieldtexas.gov/1370/The-Salt-Creek-Massacre. Accessed April 23, 2023.

Shields, David S. "On the History of Southern Winter Wheats—White May, Purple Straw, and Red May Wheats." Carolina Gold Rice Foundation, May 18, 2019. http://www.thecarolinagoldricefoundation.org/news/2019/5/18/on-the-history-of-southern-winter-wheats-white-may-purple-straw-and-red-may-wheats. Accessed November 8, 2024.

Smith, Thomas. "The Grapevine Mill." Historical Marker Database, last revised May 1, 2024. https://www.hmdb.org/m.asp?m=194690. Accessed June 19, 2023.

"Story of the Man Family." Mansfield Historical Services. https://www.mansfieldtexas.gov/1780/Story-of-the-Man-Family. Accessed April 26, 2023.

St. Peter's Episcopal Church. "Fruitcake Ministry." http://www.stpetersmckinney.com/about-st-peters/history-of-st-peters/fruitcake-ministry.html (site discontinued).

Suchorowski, Marcel. *Nana*, print by Richard Josey, Museum 2010,7081.6119. London: Henry Graves & Co., 1885. https://www.britishmuseum.org/collection/object/P_2010-7081-6119. Accessed August 29, 2022.

Texas Almanac. "City Population History from 1850–2000." https://www.texasalmanac.com/drupal-backup/images/CityPopHist%20web.pdf. Accessed December 18, 2024.

Texas Almanac. "Population History of Counties from 1850–2010." https://texasalmanac.com/sites/default/files/images/topics/ctypophistweb2010.pdf. Accessed January 17, 2025.

Texas Historical Commission. "Texas Historic Sites Atlas: Details for Mansfield Mill," Historical Marker, atlas no. 5439003198; and "Texas Historic Sites Atlas: Harrison Cemetery, atlas no. 5439002394. https://atlas.thc.texas.gov/. Accessed January 26, 2025.

Texas Historical Commission. "Texas Historic Sites Atlas: Details for Harrison Cemetery," Historical Marker, atlas no. 5439002394. https://atlas.thc.texas.gov/. Accessed January 26, 2025.

"31st Texas Cavalry Regiment." Wikipedia, last revised January 27, 2025. https://en.wikipedia.org/wiki/31st_Texas_Cavalry_Regiment. Accessed January 18, 2025.

Whaley Church. [home page]. http://www.whaleychurch.com/#!who-we-are/c55t. Accessed March 27, 2014.

GOVERNMENT DOCUMENTS

Beck, M. W., E. G. Fitzpatrick, and L. G. Ragsdale. *Soil Survey of Collin County, Texas.* US Department of Agriculture, Bureau of Soils. Washington, DC: Government Printing Office, 1935.

Bennett, Frank, Clarence Lounsbury, R. T. Avon Burke, A. T. Sweet, and Percy O. Wood. *Soil Survey of Grayson County, Texas.* US Department of Agriculture, Bureau of Soils. Washington, DC: Government Printing Office, 1910.

Carter, William T., A. H. Bauer, J. F. Stroud, W. B. Francis, and T. M. Bushnell. *Soil Survey of Dallas County, Texas.* US Department of Agriculture, Bureau of Soils. Washington, DC: Government Printing Office, 1924.

Carter, William T., Jr., and M. W. Beck. *Soil Survey of Denton County, Texas.* US Department of Agriculture, Bureau of Soils. Washington, DC: Government Printing Office, 1922.

Federal Reporter 279 (May–July 1922). St. Paul, MN: West Publishing Co., 1922.

Hawker, H. W., Neal Gearreald, and M. W. Beck. *Soil Survey of Tarrant County, Texas.* US Department of Agriculture, Bureau of Soils. Washington, DC: Government Printing Office, 1924.

"In the Matter of the Claim of Burris Mills, Incorporated." Foreign Claims Settlement Commission of the United States, Claim CU-0548, Decision CU 4234. https://www.justice.gov/fcsc/cuba/documents/1-1500/0548.pdf. Accessed January 17, 2025.

Local and Special Laws of the State of Texas Passed at the Regular Session of the Thirtieth Legislature. Austin: Van Boeckmann-Jones, 1907.

National Labor Relations Board. "In the Matter of Tex-O-Kan Flour Mills Company (Morten Milling Company Branch) and National Council of Grain Processors," and "In the Matter of Tex-O-Kan Flour Mills Company (Burrus Mill and Elevator Company Branch) and National Council of Grain Processors." Case nos. C-1483 and C-1484. Decided August 19, 1940.

National Labor Relations Board. "Decisions and Orders of the National Labor Relations Board," vol. 26 (August 1–26, 1940): 765–822. Washington, DC: Government Printing Office, 1942.

Texas Agricultural Statistics 2022. Austin, TX: National Agricultural Statistics Service, United States Department of Agriculture, 2022.

US Department of Agriculture, National Agricultural Statistics Service, Southern Plains Regional Field Office. *2022 Texas Agricultural Statistics*. Issued October 2022 in cooperation with Texas Department of Agriculture. https://www.nass.usda.gov/Statistics_by_State/Texas/Publications/Annual_Statistical_Bulletin/tx-bulletin-2022-web-updatedlinks.pdf.

US Department of Commerce, Bureau of the Census. Eighth Census of the United States, 1850. Manuscript census.

US Department of Commerce, Bureau of the Census. Ninth Census of the United States, 1860. Manuscript census.

US Department of Commerce, Bureau of the Census. Tenth Census of the United States, 1870. Manuscript census.

US Department of Commerce, Bureau of the Census. Eleventh Census of the United States, 1880. Manuscript census.

US Department of Commerce, Bureau of the Census. Thirteenth Census of the United States, 1900. Manuscript census.

US Department of Commerce, Bureau of the Census. Fourteenth Census of the United States, 1910. Manuscript census.

US Department of Commerce, Bureau of the Census. Fifteenth Census of the United States, 1920. Manuscript census.

US Department of Commerce, Bureau of the Census. Sixteenth Census of the United States, 1930. Manuscript census.

US Department of Commerce, Bureau of the Census. Seventeenth Census of the United States, 1940. Manuscript census.

US Department of Commerce, Bureau of the Census. Census of Manufactures, 1860.

US Department of Commerce, Bureau of the Census. Census of Industry, 1870.

US Department of Commerce, Bureau of the Census. Census of Industry, 1880.

US Department of Commerce, Bureau of the Census. Census of Manufactures, 1860.

US Department of Commerce, Bureau of the Census. Census of Manufactures, 1900.

US Department of Commerce, Bureau of the Census. Census of Agriculture, 1850.

US Department of Commerce, Bureau of the Census. Census of Agriculture, 1860.

US Department of Commerce, Bureau of the Census. Census of Agriculture, 1870.

US Department of Commerce, Bureau of the Census. Census of Agriculture, 1880.

US Department of Commerce, Bureau of the Census. Census of Agriculture, 1890.

Warehousing Farm Products under the US Warehouse Act. Washington, DC: Government Printing Office, 1924.

INDEX

Note: Page numbers in *italics* indicate figures. Page numbers in **bold** indicate tables.